# Empty Mills

# Empty Mills

## *The Fight Against Imports and the Decline of the U.S. Textile Industry*

Timothy J. Minchin

ROWMAN & LITTLEFIELD PUBLISHERS, INC.
Lanham • Boulder • New York • Toronto • Plymouth, UK

Published by Rowman & Littlefield Publishers, Inc.
A wholly owned subsidiary of The Rowman & Littlefield Publishing Group, Inc.
4501 Forbes Boulevard, Suite 200, Lanham, Maryland 20706
www.rowman.com

10 Thornbury Road, Plymouth PL6 7PP, United Kingdom



British Library Cataloguing in Publication Information Available

**Library of Congress Cataloging-in-Publication Data**

Minchin, Timothy J.
Empty mills : the fight against imports and the decline of the U.S. textile industry / Timothy Minchin.
p. cm.
Includes bibliographical references and index.
ISBN 978-1-4422-2082-9 (cloth : alk. paper) -- ISBN 978-1-4422-2083-6 (electronic)
1. Textile industry--United States. 2. Textile industry--Government policy--United States. 3. Clothing trade--United States. 4. Deindustrialization--United States. 5. Imports--United States. 6. Free trade--United States. I. Title.
HD9855.M53 2013
338.4'767700973--dc23

2012045157

The paper used in this publication meets the minimum requirements of American National Standard for Information Sciences Permanence of Paper for Printed Library Materials, ANSI/NISO Z39.48-1992.

Printed in the United States of America

This book is for John Salmond, friend, mentor, and scholar.

# Contents

# Acknowledgments

Any scholar who specializes in American history while living and working in Australia will incur many debts, and this book could not have happened without the generous support I received from many people on both sides of the Pacific. First up, I would like to thank the Australian Research Council, as *Empty Mills* is the main outcome of a three-year discovery grant that the Council awarded me for this project. This book could not have been undertaken, let alone completed, without the generous support of the ARC. I would also like to thank the U.S. Studies Centre at the University of Sydney, as one of the Centre's "external researcher" grants helped me to complete the writing of this book.

Many librarians and archivists in Australia and the United States provided me with invaluable help. They cannot all be named but are sincerely thanked. I would especially like to acknowledge Sheryl Vogt and Jill Severn at the Richard B. Russell Library for Political Research and Studies at the University of Georgia, who ably supported my research and assisted me in setting up several interviews. I would also like to thank Clare Sheridan at the American Textile History Museum in Lowell, Mass., and Martha Mayo at the Center for Lowell History at the University of Massachusetts Lowell. Both helped to make my trips to the "Spindle City" productive and enjoyable. Elsewhere, Desiree Butterfield at the University of Maine and Patrizia Sione at the Kheel Center for Labor-Management Documentation and Archives at Cornell University were particularly generous and helpful.

I would also like to acknowledge those who agreed to be interviewed for this project, many of whom were very gracious with their time and advice. They helped to enrich my research trips to the United States. I owe a special debt to former congressmen Ed Jenkins and Butler Derrick, who agreed to be interviewed and let me use their papers before they were fully processed. In addition, I am grateful to the staff of UNITE HERE, who gave me permission to use the restricted papers of their predecessor textile and apparel unions. Drawing on some of these papers, earlier versions of chapters 6 and 10 previously appeared as Timothy J. Minchin, " 'Us is Spelled U.S.': The Crafted With Pride Campaign and the Fight Against Deindustrialization in the Textile and Apparel Industry," *Labor History* 53:1 (February 2012), pp. 1-23, and Timothy J. Minchin, " 'It Knocked This City to Its Knees': The Closure of Pillowtex Mills in Kannapolis, North Carolina and the Decline of the U.S. Textile Industry," *Labor History* 50:3 (August 2009), pp. 287-311. Both are used by permission.

My research assistant, Bronwyn Naismith, deserves a special mention. Bronwyn worked on this project from start to finish, proving highly skilled at finding important material in a field far removed from her own. Her precision and efficiency were invaluable. I would also like to acknowledge the important preliminary research work undertaken by Bill Breen. At Rowman and Littlefield, Carrie Broadwell-Tkach and Jon Sisk have been encouraging and efficient editors. I thank them both, as well as other Press staff that worked on this manuscript.

Finally, I would like to thank my colleagues, friends, and family. Special mention goes to my wife Olya and our three children, Alex, Natasha, and Anton, as well as to my parents, Tony and Christine Minchin. I would also like to thank old friends in the U.S. who helped break my travels and provided enjoyable company, especially Richard and Bob Zieger, Rick and Hatsy Nittoli, Chris and Abbie VerPlanck, and Lee and Leeann Anderson. For the last nine years, many colleagues at La Trobe University have helped to provide me with a supportive research environment. In particular, I would like to mention those who have supported and guided my research since I moved to Australia, especially Professors Marilyn Lake and Tim Murray and emeritus Professor John Salmond. Special thanks are due to John, who has been a close friend and mentor since we first met in Chapel Hill, North Carolina, twenty years ago. My predecessor as Professor of North American history at La Trobe, John has spent his life eloquently capturing the humanity of everyday Americans who fought for economic and racial justice. His scholarship and sage advice motivated me to undertake and complete this book. It is dedicated to him.

# Abbreviations

AAM Alliance for American Manufacturing
AAMA American Apparel Manufacturers Association
ACTWU Amalgamated Clothing and Textile Workers Union
ACWA Amalgamated Clothing Workers of America
AFL–CIO American Federation of Labor–Congress of Industrial Organizations
AFTAC American Fiber, Textile, and Apparel Coalition
AMTAC American Manufacturing Trade Action Coalition
ATC Agreement on Textiles and Clothing (WTO)
ATMI American Textile Manufacturers Institute
ATTAC American Textile Trade Action Caucus
BLS Bureau of Labor Statistics (U.S. Department of Labor)
CAFTA Central America Free Trade Agreement
CITA Committee for the Implementation of Textile Agreements
CTC Congressional Textile Caucus
EEC European Economic Community
FFACT Fiber, Fabric, and Apparel Coalition for Trade
GAFTT Global Alliance for Fair Textile Trade
GATT General Agreement on Tariffs and Trade
ILGWU International Ladies' Garment Workers' Union
ILO International Labour Organization
ITC International Trade Commission
LTA Long-Term Agreement Regarding International Trade in Cotton Textiles (1962)
MFA Multi-Fiber Arrangement
NACM National Association of Cotton Manufacturers
NAFTA North American Free Trade Agreement
NCTO National Council of Textile Organizations
NLRB National Labor Relations Board
NTA Northern Textile Association
OECD Organisation for Economic Co-operation and Development
OTA Office of Technology Assessment (U.S. Congress)
RITAC Retail Industry Trade Action Coalition
TAA Trade Adjustment Assistance
TPA Trade Promotion Authority
TWUA Textile Workers Union of America
UNITE Union of Needletrades, Industrial, and Textile Employees

UNITE HERE Union of Needletrades, Industrial, and Textile Employees/Hotel Employees and Restaurant Employees Union
USTR United States Trade Representative
UTW United Textile Workers
WTO World Trade Organization

# Introduction

In August 2005, an old stone mill on the banks of the Tallapoosa River in Alabama shut down after 161 years in operation. Believed to be the oldest cloth factory in the country, Tallassee Mills had once made fabric for both slave clothes and Confederate uniforms. Workers, many of them the third or fourth generation of their families to labor at the mill, mourned the demise of a company that had, as Tallassee mayor Bobby Payne put it, "actually built the town." A mill that had survived the devastation of the Civil War, as well as subsequent natural disasters and economic depressions, had now been put out of business by foreign competition. By 2005 workers made $12.50 an hour, plus benefits, and the company simply could not compete with low-priced imports from China and other cheap labor markets. "The plant," declared journalist Jay Reeves, "is the latest U.S. mill to lose the fight to foreign imports."[1]

The Tallassee closure was indeed part of the broader demise of the American textile and apparel industry, which has gradually been decimated by import competition. According to the Bureau of Labor Statistics (BLS), in 1973 there were more than 2.4 million textile and apparel workers in the United States, but by 1987 the figure had dipped under two million.[2] Over the next two decades, the number fell rapidly, dropping to 1.5 million in 1996 and to just 383,600 in early 2012. Within less than four decades, therefore, over two million jobs have been lost in this industry, a devastating development.[3] "This is something historical," asserted textile union leader Harris Raynor in 1999, as he reflected on the industry's downfall. "The whole country is losing something here."[4]

Despite the textile industry's size, its decline has not received much attention from scholars.[5] Sparked by Barry Bluestone and Bennett Harrison's influential *The Deindustrialization of America* (1982), which introduced the term *deindustrialization* to a wide audience, in the last twenty-five years or so many scholars have explored the decline of manufacturing industries and how it has affected workers. They have thrown much light on a major shift in the U.S. economy: in 1950, half of the American workforce was employed in the manufacturing sector, but by 2006, just 10.4 percent were.[6] With the advent of the global financial crisis, moreover, job losses in manufacturing accelerated, and they were a major cause of the burgeoning trade deficit. Because of its sensitivity to import competition, the textile and apparel industry has been at the center of this story, regularly constituting 30 percent or more of America's trade deficit. As one labor leader has put it, textile workers "have been on the firing line of international trade for decades."[7]

Existing scholarship has concentrated almost entirely on heavy manufacturing industries in the "Rust Belt," the band of states in the Northeast and Midwest that have been hit hard by job losses, especially in the steel and automobile industries. In the late 1990s, works by Ruth Milkman and Thomas Dublin explored the fate of auto-manufacturing and coal-mining communities in New Jersey and Pennsylvania respectively, adding to earlier studies of classic postindustrial communities such as Flint, Michigan; Homestead, Pennsylvania; and Youngstown, Ohio.[8] In 2003, two scholars even dubbed the former steel-making center of Youngstown "a national 'poster child' for deindustrialization."[9] Taken as a whole, this literature has established that most workers identified closely with their jobs and were usually deeply affected by plant closures, with many left feeling devastated and bitter.[10]

There are several reasons why textiles and apparel has been largely omitted from the deindustrialization literature. A lot of the industry's production was concentrated in the South, a region more associated with economic growth rather than decline. In 1984, textiles and apparel was the major employer in terms of payroll in Alabama, Georgia, Mississippi, North Carolina, South Carolina, and Virginia. These six states were home to almost 75 percent of all textile and apparel jobs in the country. A decade later, the region still contained the top five states for textile and apparel employment, and in the leading textile state of North Carolina the industry provided over 273,000 jobs. Despite the textile industry's problems, scholars of deindustrialization have focused on classic Rust Belt communities rather than the southern textile belt. As one influential volume on deindustrialization has concluded, "The large northern cities capture the lion's share of scholarly attention."[11]

Because textile production was decentralized, the industry also lacked the huge, defining plants that have generally attracted scholarly attention. Like Tallassee Mills, most textile factories were relatively small, and it was easy to overlook their closure. In 1981, for example, there were over six thousand separate textile manufacturers in the United States, and even Burlington Industries, the industry's largest firm, controlled only 6 percent of the overall business. Unlike the steel or automobile industries, which were indelibly associated with particular cities, there were no major metropolises devoted to textile production, and there was certainly no "Big Three" to capture headlines. As one textile consultant fighting for import controls privately admitted in 1985, "Because of the nature of our industry, unlike steel or auto, there are no massive centers of production where mass lay-offs generate national attention. Our manufacturing base is spread out and located in towns often little known to the public. We have no Detroits or Pittsburghs. This makes our job harder."[12]

The textile industry was also a large employer of women, and most accounts of deindustrialization have focused on male workers. As historian Jefferson Cowie has written, it is important to "adjust the popular image of the unemployed male steel or auto worker as the quintessential victim of deindustrialization."[13] Finally, the decline of the textile and apparel industry has also been overlooked because the industry consistently suffered from an image problem, associated as it was with low wages and poor labor practices. In 1986, apparel workers earned an average of $5.84 an hour, while textile workers made $6.93; both amounts were much less than the average for manufacturing workers, which stood at $9.73 an hour. Despite constant efforts by unions to close this gap, it stubbornly persisted, partly because unions never became as strong as they were in heavy manufacturing industries. These relatively low wages led to a widespread perception that this was an undesirable industry that was not worth saving. They have also led scholars to be preoccupied with the interrelated questions of whether textile workers—especially those in the South—were distinctive and why they were unlikely to join unions that could have raised their wages. While some fine work has been produced on textile workers, especially in detailing how they used close community bonds to resist management domination, the industry's dramatic collapse has been overlooked. This is also due, of course, to the fact that the industry's demise is a relatively recent phenomenon.[14]

This work provides the first book-length account of the industry's decline, and it examines both textiles and apparel.[15] While the terms *textile industry* and *apparel industry* are often used interchangeably, the industries are distinct. They are inextricably linked, however, especially as most textile workers are involved in the manufacture of products that are used to make apparel. As a result, any discussion of deindustrialization has to consider both sectors together.[16] As the General Executive Board of the Amalgamated Clothing and Textile Workers Union (ACTWU) explained in 1978, "If imports of apparel increase this will adversely affect textiles as well." The fight against imports also brought unions in textiles and apparel together. ACTWU itself was created in 1976 partly to strengthen labor's battle for import controls, as the Amalgamated Clothing Workers of America joined forces with the Textile Workers Union of America to create a bigger union. Later, the International Ladies' Garment Workers' Union merged with ACTWU after years of cooperating with it to try to pass import quota legislation.[17] In 1997, a BLS economist also remarked on the links between the sectors, writing that "textile employment has been somewhat dependent on the health of the U.S. apparel industry." In the last four decades, textiles and apparel have certainly declined simultaneously, and the legislative effort to save jobs mobilized both sectors together.[18]

In this book, I argue that the textile and apparel industry has a strong claim to be at the heart of the literature on deindustrialization. In particular, the industry had size and considerable economic significance. In 1985, the textile and apparel industry employed well over two million people—more than steel or autos—as well as supporting at least two million other citizens in related industries. The industry was the principal customer for America's raw cotton and wool, as well as for man-made fibers, and it was also an important purchaser of chemicals, machinery, energy, transportation, and other services. Overall, in 1985 one out of every eight manufacturing jobs was in textiles and apparel, and the industry was America's largest single industrial sector. The textile complex generated $45 billion of the gross national product (GNP), compared to $43 billion for the automotive industry and $37 billion for aerospace and railroad equipment manufacturing. As late as 1996, textiles and apparel still employed 1.6 million U.S. workers; this was one in ten manufacturing workers and represented more than the auto and aircraft industries put together.[19] In addition, the industry was a key supplier to the U.S. military and was vital to national defense. Textile products had twenty-five thousand military applications, and the Pentagon ranked the industry as the second most important for national security needs, bettered only by steel.[20]

As these figures suggest, the textile and apparel industry was truly a national industry. Long after World War II, for example, the industry remained a major employer in both New England and the mid-Atlantic region.[21] Testifying before Congress in 1978, the Northern Textile Association stressed the industry's broad importance. "The fiber-textile-apparel complex is not only a big segment of the national economy and a major segment of the Southern economy, but it is also a major segment of the Northeast economy," declared director Kenneth V. Chace. As Chace pointed out, New England and the mid-Atlantic states were home to 633,000 textile and apparel jobs. In New England as a whole the industry still provided one in every ten manufacturing jobs, while in Maine, Massachusetts, and Rhode Island the figure was even higher. Moreover, every state in the Union had at least one textile or apparel plant.[22] A decade later, the Department of Commerce's Office of Textiles and Apparel found that the industry had twenty-eight thousand plants, and they were still distributed across all fifty states. Although the vast majority of these mills were situated east of the Mississippi River, there was also a sizeable cluster of apparel shops in California.[23]

The industry also has broad historical significance. As economic historians have shown, the mechanization of the cotton industry, which was first achieved in England in the late eighteenth century, was the "starting point of the modern technique of production that we call the factory system."[24] The industry played a central role in the development of the Republic, with one trade association calling it "America's First Great Industry." Even the *New York Times*, a regular critic of the industry, called textiles "America's oldest manufacturing industry."[25] As Congresswoman Marilyn Lloyd asserted on the industry's bicentennial, textiles was "an industry that helped launch the American industrial revolution and forever altered our national heritage."[26]

A few examples illustrate the point. In April 1789, when George Washington was inaugurated as president, he proudly announced that he was wearing a suit made in the United States, supplied by the country's fledgling wool industry. In the same year, Englishman Samuel Slater arrived in the New World and started building a small, water-powered spinning mill on the banks of the Blackstone River in Pawtucket, Rhode Island. Opening in 1790, the mill was the first permanent spinning mill in North America, and it came to hold a central place in the story of the American Industrial Revolution. Indeed, Slater mill was later listed on the National Register of Historic Places and designated as a National Historic Landmark. New England's early cotton industry also gave birth to the country's first trade association, the New England Cotton Manufacturers Association. Established in 1854, the NECMA later became the National Association of Cotton Manufacturers and then the Northern Textile Association, both of which played key roles in trying to stem the industry's demise.[27]

Another key development occurred in 1813, when Francis Cabot Lowell started the first textile mill to use a practical power loom and to perform all functions from opening to finishing under one roof. Before steel or automobiles existed as mass production industries, textile mills flourished. In New England, many small towns soon contained what William S. Cohen called "the familiar sight of an old mill perched above a mighty river." As the Maine senator explained in 1991: "Textiles not only represent an industry vital to the nation's economic well-being, but textiles also offer a window to our economic and historic heritage." A few years earlier, the U.S. Commissioner of Customs, William von Raab, had also stressed the industry's centrality to national identity. "The American textile industry is a critical part of the American economy," he declared. "It is steeped in American history, and it is an indelible part of our nation's heritage."[28]

The textile and apparel industry has certainly suffered greatly from deindustrialization. Between 1973 and 1996, the industry lost 39 percent of its workforce, while manufacturing employment as a whole fell by only 8 percent in the same period. As a result, the industry has more right to be at the center of the deindustrialization story than almost any other, especially as its demise actually accelerated after 1996. Of course, the service sector grew rapidly, and avid free-traders asserted that textile and apparel workers could simply switch to jobs in growing industries. Between 1973 and 1996, employment in the United States as a whole rose by 56 percent, while productivity in manufacturing (rather than employment) also rose.[29] It is important to take note of this increase in productivity and to understand what was happening to U.S. manufacturing as a whole. Writing at a time of widespread factory closures and an economic recession, as well as declining productivity growth, Barry Bluestone had in 1982 defined deindustrialization as "a widespread, systematic disinvestment in the nation's basic productive capacity." Twenty years later, however, he refined his position in light of an "economic renaissance" that was linked to sharp rises in manufacturing productivity. Indeed, between 1989 and 2000 increasing productivity allowed manufacturing to slightly increase its share of total real gross domestic product (GDP), from 16.9 percent to 17.3 percent. While traditional manufacturing industries, such as textiles and apparel, continued to decline, high-technology manufacturing of electronic equipment, industrial machinery, and chemical and pharmaceutical products did well. Between 1989 and 2000, the real dollar value of the apparel industry dropped by almost 20 percent, but U.S. production of electronic equipment rose by almost 400 percent. By its very nature, however, high-tech manufacturing needed fewer workers than its traditional counterpart, ensuring that manufacturing employment declined even during the economic recovery of the 1990s. Millions of workers lost their jobs in industries where productivity growth exceeded that of sales. In textiles and apparel, workers were laid off as jobs were automated and companies invested in high-tech equipment, a move that was itself partly a response to increasing imports. "This cannot be termed 'deindustrialization,'" acknowledged Bluestone in 2003, "but for the workers affected it feels the same."[30]

Despite the improvements in productivity, many Americans argued that it was manufacturing employment levels that were the key indicator of their country's economic strength. In 1984, a study by the U.S. Chamber of Commerce confirmed the value of manufacturing jobs, showing that for every one hundred jobs added to the manufacturing sector, another sixty-four were created in other industries. The study also found that counties with a strong manufacturing base were more prosperous than their counterparts without one. In a similar vein, this book shows that most displaced textile and apparel workers struggled to find comparable jobs in the service sector. It also highlights that the industry's decline had significant economic and social consequences. After 2000, moreover, and especially in the second half of the "noughties," a sustained downturn unleashed a fresh wave of job losses that affected the entire economy, with traditional manufacturing hit hard. In this period of accelerated decline, textiles and apparel was devastated, and imports again played the primary role.[31]

The decline of the textile and apparel industry certainly had broad ramifications. In the mid-1980s, only about one-quarter of the value added by the production and sales of textile goods went to textile and apparel companies, while for apparel the figure was around 40 percent. The rest of the value was distributed throughout the economy, especially to service industries, ensuring that the mills created many other jobs. The industry's tendency to locate in small towns also increased the economic and cultural impact of shutdowns. As a 1987 study by the Congressional Office of Technology Assessment concluded, "Failure on the part of textile and apparel companies can have dramatic effects on the local communities where they operate, especially in the many small towns of the southeastern United States where a textile plant represents the main source of industrial employment."[32] In 1988, federal data showed that about two-thirds of all textile mills were situated in nonmetropolitan areas. Although they are easily overlooked, mill closures had a devastating impact on small towns right across the country.[33]

There were other reasons why deindustrialization in textiles and apparel was especially devastating. As the authors of the landmark *Like a Family* have demonstrated, southern textile communities were distinguished by "a distinctive mill village culture" that "provided comfort and reassurance in an often hostile world." Building on this work, I argue that it was the strong attachment that mill workers had to their jobs and communities that made the closures so painful. This bond was linked to the industry's tendency to locate in small communities, as well as the fact that unskilled workers who landed mill jobs tended to stay put for life. These trends were not exclusively southern, it should be noted, but were also evident in northern textile communities.[34]

The industry also employed a disproportionate number of racial minorities and women, and they were particularly reliant on their mill jobs. Once the factories went, these workers struggled to secure comparable work. By the 1980s, as the Fiber, Fabric, and Apparel Coalition for Trade (FFACT) pointed out, the textile and apparel industries were "the nation's greatest manufacturing employers of women and minorities." More than half of all workers were female, compared to less than a third of employees in manufacturing as a whole. Helped by the passage of the landmark Civil Rights Act of 1964, which prohibited employment discrimination on the grounds of race and gender, both women and racial minorities had made important gains into these industries just as they were starting to contract. Between 1970 and 1980, for example, the percentage of minorities in the apparel industry jumped from 21 percent to 33 percent.[35]

The textile industry can also claim to be the first victim of deindustrialization in the country. In New England, for example, the industry began to shed jobs well before World War II, as production shifted to the low-wage South. Although the wartime boom temporarily helped the northern industry, it was soon declining again. At a time when most of the economy was booming, textile leaders were already worrying about imports. With some justification, the Textile Workers Union of America claimed that it was "the earliest proponent" of textile import quotas. In 1945, the union was already arguing that a quota system offered the "best approach" to the import problem, a point it repeated in the years that followed.[36]

The industry's role as a pioneer of deindustrialization is clear. According to the Department of Commerce, between 1950 and 1960 around 440,000 textile workers lost their jobs. In the fifteen years after World War II, meanwhile, some 670 U.S. mills shut down. "Since World War II, the textile industry in the United States has enjoyed only a few prosperous years," concluded a 1963 department study. A few years earlier, NTA secretary William F. Sullivan had summed up the industry's role as an initiator of industrial decline. "One of the country's principal industries," he told the group's 1956 annual meeting, "is drifting and loitering on a down grade, while the economy of this country as a whole, and other major individual industries, are climbing to pinnacles of prosperity never before achieved." As Sullivan admitted, the industry's problems were particularly acute in New England, where mills were old and wages were higher than they were in the South.[37]

Even in the South, executives and politicians worried about the industry's future. As early as 1959, Georgia senator Herman E. Talmadge expressed serious concerns about the industry, which he claimed was being sacrificed by U.S. policy makers. "It is no exaggeration," he wrote, "to conclude that it is the actual, if not officially-expressed, policy of the Government of the United States that the American textile industry is expendable and should be forced to help finance its own liquidation." Over the succeeding decades, industry supporters repeatedly insisted that trade policy was being driven by farm groups and other export-oriented lobbies, who were willing to give textiles away in return for greater market access for their goods.[38]

The industry's size gave it considerable lobbying power, and in the 1950s it started a major campaign to protect itself against increasing imports. While the industry won some protection through the Long-Term Cotton Agreement of 1961, it was the Multi-Fiber Arrangement of 1974—which was subsequently renewed on several occasions—that was particularly important. The agreements were apt illustrations of the industry's political muscle. In 1991, for example, the *Washington Post* called the textile-apparel coalition "one of the most potent economic lobbying forces in the nation." Going back to the 1960s, it had "strong-armed the White House and Congress into providing the greatest trade protection of any industry in the country."[39] The combination of the industry's size and its exposure to import competition ensured that it was at the heart of the wider battle between free-traders and protectionists, a key fault line of the postwar period. As the *New York Times* explained in 1979, "The American textile industry is among the most pained by imports, and its lobby is one of the most vigorous in Washington."[40]

Because import levels determined the survival of the industry, manufacturers and unions came together in a remarkable coalition to protect domestic production. In the early 1980s, the two sides combined into FFACT, an alliance that held together through three major legislative campaigns. Although there were tensions within the partnership, this story of cooperation between management and labor causes us to rethink much of what has been written about labor relations in the textile industry, an industry dominated by labor strife and failed strikes. The alliance was especially remarkable in the South, where executives who had fiercely opposed unionization proved willing to work with organized labor to try to ensure that the industry survived.[41]

As they fought against imports, industry supporters consistently used three main arguments. For several decades they stressed the industry's size, its importance to national defense efforts, and its role in employing large numbers of unskilled workers, particularly women and racial minorities. Working with the Congressional Textile Caucus—which brought together the industry's supporters from across the country—FFACT vigorously defended one of America's largest industries. In telling this little-known story of the industry's long battle against imports, this book uses previously unseen records, including those of the textile and apparel unions, several manufacturing associations, and political leaders. The papers of politicians who led the fight for import controls are particularly important. This study also draws on interviews with important participants, including workers affected by deindustrialization and federal politicians who championed the industry's cause.[42]

In 1985 to 1986, 1987 to 1988, and 1990, the industry came agonizingly close to winning strict import controls. These were crucial battles; according to Karl Spilhaus, the long-serving president of the Northern Textile Association, the bills "were very important," especially as they "demonstrated the clout of the industry in Congress." Overseen by FFACT, the campaigns were strongly supported at the grassroots level, as many workers and other citizens took part in demonstrations and letter-writing campaigns. On each occasion, textile import-restriction bills were easily passed by Congress but were vetoed by presidents Ronald Reagan (twice) and George H. W. Bush. In 1986, a massive effort to override the veto fell short by only eight votes, while in 1988 and 1990 similar campaigns failed by eleven and ten votes respectively. Thus, the 1985 to 1986 bill was the closest that the industry would come to winning vital import controls, making it a crucial battle to analyze in detail. While the trade issue cut across party lines, in each case Democrats were more helpful than Republicans. In 1986, for example, efforts to override the veto were supported by just seventy-one Republicans—compared to 205 Democrats—a pattern that was maintained in subsequent votes.[43]

These efforts ultimately failed because absolute limits on textile imports contravened America's long-standing economic policy of lowering global trade barriers. They aroused determined opposition from retailers, exporters, and the Reagan and Bush administrations. As the industry declined, these forces gradually gained the upper hand, and they consistently pushed trade policies that were detrimental to the textile and apparel complex.[44]

Led by Roger Milliken, a multimillionaire who owned the largest privately held textile company in the world, industry groups and unions also ran an innovative campaign to encourage consumers to buy American-made textiles and apparel. Launched in 1984, the "Crafted with Pride in the U.S.A." initiative ran for more than a decade and was an important part of the industry's response to deindustrialization. The program sponsored "Miss America" and won endorsements from leading celebrities, including Ted Danson, Bob Hope, O. J. Simpson, and Sally Struthers. It was also backed by Wal-Mart, the giant retailer who would later become a major importer. In the long term, the Crafted with Pride campaign could not save the industry, but it did draw attention to its problems and slowed the pace of its decline. It also reinforced FFACT's legislative fight.[45]

The failure of the import-restriction legislation was a turning point. In 1987, one federal study found that apparel imports had doubled over the previous ten years and that they made up half of the American market. Although penetration levels were lower in textiles, they were on the rise. The implications were clear. "Unless policy action is taken in the next few years," warned the report, "there is reason to be concerned about the very existence of many parts of the industry."[46] Once it was clear that the legislative fight had failed, the demise of the industry accelerated. As the first bill's chief sponsor later reflected, the industry's long-term future was at stake. "I was attempting in this piece of legislation to establish some quotas from the cheap labor countries that were exporting to us a lot of textiles," explained former congressman Ed Jenkins. "I knew that the textile industry could not survive if that prevailed."[47] Even at the time, both manufacturers and labor leaders recognized that the fate of the industry was on the line. As one South Carolina mill owner put it, "The future of the textile industry depends on the passage of this bill." In 1985, the treasurer of the West Point Pepperell Company, Marshall N. Norton, drove home the point in a letter to Senator Strom Thurmond of South Carolina. "The importance of this legislation cannot be overestimated," he declared, adding that there would be few mills left if imports were not reined in.[48]

The three textile bills were crucial if the industry was to survive, and we shall examine in detail why each was vetoed despite strong support from the public and Congress. Their failure paved the pay for new free trade initiatives and more imports. The industry was particularly affected by the passage of the North American Free Trade Agreement (NAFTA) in 1993. Although parts of the industry supported NAFTA in the hope that they could build a strong regional trading bloc, the dramatic rise of China squashed these aspirations. For China and other emerging economies, textile and apparel exports were lucrative, and access to the giant American market was vital. The domestic industry's divided response to NAFTA was also very damaging.[49]

The phase-out of the MFA, which took place in stages between 1994 and 2004, was also very important. Occurring at the end of 2004, the abolition of all remaining quotas devastated the domestic textile and apparel industry. Between December 2004 and July 2009, the Department of Labor recorded that the industry lost 256,300 jobs, or 38.2 percent of all its positions. Losses accelerated as soon as the quotas were removed. In the early months of 2005, for example, the rate of textile plant closings tripled when compared to the previous year. Responding to lobbying from the newly formed National Council of Textile Organizations, the Bush administration was able to get some "sensitive" textile items put back under quota in May, but the Chinese continued to make inroads. On January 1, 2009, moreover, all temporary safeguards were removed, and the United States was not allowed to reimpose them. In January 2012, the Commerce Department recorded that China was responsible for 47.04 percent of all textile and apparel imports into the United States, a remarkable level of market penetration. The figure was trending upward—in June 2010 it had stood at 45.75 percent. As a result, America's oldest industry stood on the brink of extinction.[50]

As the industry collapsed, the press carried scores of stories, most of them focused on closures of little-known mills. Some of the shutdowns, however, had a wider significance. One example was the 2003 closure of a towel-making plant in Roanoke Rapids, North Carolina. Thirty years earlier, it was at this factory that Crystal Lee Sutton had stood on a table and held up a crude, handmade sign saying "UNION" after her employer, J. P. Stevens, had fired her for talking about the union on the job. Sutton's life and actions later became the inspiration for the Oscar-wining movie *Norma Rae*. "If ever there was an icon of that industry, this was it," declared a union leader at the time of the shutdown. Also in 2003, Levi Strauss closed its last U.S. plants, ensuring that a product that was integrally associated with America would no longer be made there. Four years later Springs Industries announced that it was ending domestic production of its sheets. For more than a century, the sheets had been made in the United States, and they had become a household name under the Springmaid brand.[51]

Such was the pace of the decline that southern towns such as Roanoke Rapids were soon littered with vacant mills. As the town's *Daily Herald* summarized in 2004, "Since the industry has moved to Mexico, Pakistan, and China, textile mills in America have become empty tax burdens."[52] While empty mills were a relatively new phenomenon in Roanoke Rapids, they were a familiar sight further up Interstate 95. Thirty-eight years earlier, Rhode Island senator John O. Pastore had seen discarded textile plants as a defining feature of the northern landscape. "I see the ghosts of mills once a mainstay of such Rhode Island places as Providence, Pawtucket, Pascoag, and Woonsocket," he told his Senate colleagues as he urged them to help a forgotten industry. "Massachusetts sees the deserted mills of Metheun, Farnumsville, Worcester, Plymouth, and Uxbridge. Six great Philadelphia mills are missing and New Jersey no longer looks upon Passaic, Trenton, and Garfield giants of the past. Connecticut bids farewell to fine plants of Baltic and Putnam and the State of New York suffers the tragedy of great textile complexes that are no more." Overall, the industry's decline was a "dramatic and tragic story" that begged to be told. The first chapter of this story occurs in Pastore's New England, in the historic textile towns that the senator lucidly referred to.[53]

## NOTES

1. Jay Reeves, "Oldest Cloth Factory to Shutter Its Looms: Ala. Textile Mill That Employed Generations Loses Fight with Imports," *Akron Beacon Journal*, August 28, 2005, p. D1. This is an Associated Press story that is also available in several other newspapers.

2. U.S. Congress, Office of Technology Assessment, *The U.S. Textile and Apparel Industry: A Revolution in Progress—Special Report* (Washington, DC: U.S. Government Printing Office, 1987), p. 3.

3. Mark Mittelhauser, Employment Trends in Textiles and Apparel, 1973–2005," *Monthly Labor Review* 120:8 (August 1997), p. 24; BLS employment data at http://www.bls.gov/iag/tgs/iag_index_alpha.htm (accessed March 26, 2012). Under the BLS's North American Industry Classification System (NAICS), data for the textile and apparel sector is divided into three codes: Apparel (NAICS 315), Textile Mills (NAICS 313), and Textile Product Mills (NAICS 314). Throughout this work, I obtained overall industry employment data by adding the employment numbers in these three classifications together. See www.bls.gov/bls/naics.htm for more information about these classifications. The BLS is part of the federal Department of Labor, and its site provides a wealth of official employment data for all sectors of the American economy.

4. Richard Lezin Jones, "N.C. Plant Closing Indicative of Eroding Workforce in South," *Philadelphia Inquirer*, October 10, 1999, p. A20 (Raynor quotation).

5. Economists and sociologists have written some helpful work on the industry's demise, especially in essays or articles. See, for example, Lauren A. Murray, "Unraveling Employment Trends in Textiles and Apparel," *Monthly Labor Review* 188:8, August 1995, pp. 62–72; John Gaventa and Barbara Ellen Smith, "The Deindustrialization of the Textile South: A Case Study," and Rhonda Zingraff, "Facing Extinction?," both in Jeffrey Leiter, Michael D. Schulman, and Rhonda Zingraff, eds., *Hanging by a Thread: Social Change in Southern Textiles* (Ithaca: ILR Press, 1991), pp. 181–96 and pp. 199–216; Cynthia D. Anderson, Michael D. Schulman, and Phillip J. Wood, "Globalization and Uncertainty: The Restructuring of Southern Textiles," *Social Problems* 48:4 (November 2001), pp. 478–98. Much of this work is quantitative, and the impact of deindustrialization upon workers and community members is not explored in detail. For case studies that give limited coverage to individual mill closings, see Beth English, *A Common Thread: Labor, Politics, and Capital Mobility in the Textile Industry* (Athens: University of Georgia Press, 2006), esp. pp. 173–76; Douglas Flamming, *Creating the*

*Modern South: Millhands and Managers in Dalton, Georgia, 1884–1984* (Chapel Hill: University of North Carolina Press, 1992), pp. 307–27.

6. Barry Bluestone and Bennett Harrison, *The Deindustrialization of America: Plant Closings, Community Abandonment, and the Dismantling of Basic Industry* (New York: Basic Books, 1982); Barry Bluestone, "Foreword," in Jefferson Cowie and Joseph Heathcott, eds., *Beyond the Ruins: The Meanings of Deindustrialization* (Ithaca: ILR Press, 2003), p. xii; Testimony of Betty McGrath, Labor Market Information Division, Employment Security Commission of North Carolina, September 6, 2007, available at www.uscc.gov/hearings/2007hearings/transcripts/sept_6/betty_mcgrath.pdf (accessed December 8, 2008). As discussed specifically below (see p. 6), Bluestone and Harrison defined *deindustrialization* as "a widespread, systematic disinvestment in the nation's basic productive capacity" (Bluestone and Harrison, *The Deindustrialization of America*, p. 4).

7. Jack Sheinkman quoted in "Textile Trade Law a Must, Union Tells Senate Hearing," *Labor Unity*, August–September 1985, p. 3. Trade deficit data is taken from Herbert Koshetz, "Lag in Growth and Rise in Imports Decried at Meeting of Textile Makers," *New York Times*, April 15, 1977, p. 95; and Lawrence H. Kaufman, "US Textile Export Outlook Brightens, Gains May Help Cut Trade Deficit," *Journal of Commerce*, March 1, 1993, p. 3A.

8. For a sample of studies of deindustrialization with a northern focus, see: Thomas Dublin, *When the Mines Closed: Stories of Struggles in Hard Times*, with photographs by George Harvan (Ithaca: Cornell University Press, 1998); Terry F. Buss and F. Stevens Redburn, *Shutdown at Youngstown: Public Policy for Mass Unemployment* (Albany, NY: State University of New York Press, 1983); Steven P. Dandaneau, *A Town Abandoned: Flint, Michigan, Confronts Deindustrialization* (Albany, NY: State University of New York Press, 1996); Ruth Milkman, *Farewell to the Factory: Auto Workers in the Late Twentieth Century* (Berkeley: University of California Press, 1997); Kathryn Marie Dudley, *The End of the Line: Lost Jobs, New Lives in Postindustrial America* (Chicago: University of Chicago Press, 1994); William Serrin, *Homestead: The Glory and Tragedy of an American Steel Town* (New York: Vintage Books, 1993); Mark Reutter, *Sparrows Point: Making Steel—The Rise and Ruin of American Industrial Might* (New York: Summit Books, 1988); John P. Hoerr, *And the Wolf Finally Came: The Decline of the American Steel Industry* (Pittsburgh: University of Pittsburgh Press, 1988); Sherry Lee Linkon and John Russo, *Steeltown USA: Work and Memory in Youngstown* (Lawrence, KS: University Press of Kansas, 2002); Staughton Lynd, *The Fight against Shutdowns: Youngstown's Steel Mill Closings* (San Pedro: Singlejack Books, 1982). Apart from these case studies, Steven High has recently published a somewhat broader work on the entire North American Rust Belt. See Steven C. High, *Industrial Sunset: The Making of North America's Rust Belt, 1969–1984* (Toronto: University of Toronto Press, 2003).

9. For an excellent exploration of why so much has been written about deindustrialization in Youngstown, see John Russo and Sherry Lee Linkon, "Collateral Damage: Deindustrialization and the Uses of Youngstown," in Cowie and Heathcott, eds., *Beyond the Ruins*, pp. 201–18 (quotation on p. 203).

10. For some representative conclusions, see: Dudley, *The End of the Line*, esp. p. xi; David Bensman and Roberta Lynch, *Rusted Dreams: Hard Times in a Steel Community* (New York: McGraw Hill, 1987), esp. pp. 2–9; Steve Mellon, *After the Smoke Clears: Struggling to Get By in Rustbelt America* (Pittsburgh: University of Pittsburgh Press, 2002), esp. p. 7. On p. xi above, for example, anthropologist Kathryn Marie Dudley summarizes her study of the closure of a Chrysler plant in Kenosha, Wisconsin, by noting that "the loss of an industrial job can be so devastating. Friendships built up over twenty years on the shopfloor gradually fade away, and with them the sense of community that gives us all a meaningful place in the world". For a broader context in regard to these conclusions, see Richard Sennett and Jonathan Cobb, *The Hidden Injuries of Class* (New York: Knopf, 1972), pp. 267–68; Bluestone and Harrison, *The Deindustrialization of America*, pp. 11–12; John Russo and Sherry Lee Linkon, "The Social Costs of Deindustrialization," in Richard McCormack, ed., *Manufacturing a Better Future for America* (Washington, DC: The Alliance for American Manufacturing, 2009), pp. 187–98.

11. William E. Schmidt, "Future of 2 Southern Industries Raises Concern," *New York Times*, December 9, 1984; "Top Ten States—Total Textile and Apparel Employment (1994)," "Textile Industry Employment, By State" folder, box 2, Research Department Files, papers of

the Union of Needletrades, Industrial, and Textile Employees (UNITE), held at the Kheel Center for Labor-Management Documentation and Archives, School of Industrial and Labor Relations, Cornell University, Ithaca, New York, hereafter cited as "UNITE Papers-Cornell." The closing quotation is from Jefferson Cowie and Joseph Heathcott, "Introduction: The Meanings of Deindustralization" in Cowie and Heathcott, eds., *Beyond the Ruins,* p. 12.

12. John Leslie to the General Executive Board of the Amalgamated Clothing and Textile Workers Union, March 17, 1986, "Grassroots Campaign" folder, box 787, Amalgamated Clothing and Textile Workers Union Papers, held at the Kheel Center for Labor-Management Documentation and Archives, School of Industrial and Labor Relations, Cornell University, Ithaca, New York, hereafter cited as "ACTWU Papers-Cornell."

13. Sandra Salmans, "The Textile Industry Shakes Itself Up," *New York Times*, May 10, 1981; Jefferson Cowie, *Capital Moves: RCA's Seventy-Year Quest for Cheap Labor* (Ithaca: Cornell University Press, 1999), p. 5 (quotation); Ellen Israel Rosen, *Making Sweatshops: The Globalization of the U.S. Apparel Industry* (Berkeley: University of California Press, 2002), p. 2. Cowie's own study of the electronics industry, which employed large numbers of women, has helped to redress this imbalance to some extent.

14. U.S. Department of Commerce's Office of Textiles and Apparel, "U.S. Textile and Apparel Import Program," document, January 11, 1988, "U.S. Textile and Apparel Import Program" folder, Susan Lauffer files, OA16376, White House Staff and Office files, Ronald Reagan Presidential Library, Simi Valley, California, hereafter cited as "Reagan Library." For fine overviews of the recent scholarship on southern textile workers, including the debates about the distinctiveness of mill village culture and the reasons for the weakness of unions in the region, see Robert H. Zieger, "Textile Workers and Historians," in Robert H. Zieger, ed., *Organized Labor in the Twentieth-Century South* (Knoxville: University of Tennessee Press, 1991), pp. 35–59; Robert H. Zieger, "From Primordial Folk to Redundant Workers: Southern Textile Workers and Social Observers, 1920–1990," in Robert H. Zieger, ed., *Southern Labor in Transition, 1940–1995* (Knoxville: University of Tennessee Press, 1997), pp. 273–94. Influential works on southern textile workers include Hall et al., *Like a Family: The Making of a Southern Cotton Mill World* (Chapel Hill: University of North Carolina Press, 1987); David L. Carlton, *Mill and Town in South Carolina, 1880–1920* (Baton Rouge: Louisiana State University Press, 1982); James A. Hodges, *New Deal Labor Policy and the Southern Cotton Textile Industry, 1933–1941* (Knoxville: University of Tennessee Press, 1986); I. A. Newby, *Plain Folk in the New South: Social Change and Cultural Persistence, 1880–1915* (Baton Rouge and London: Louisiana State University Press, 1989); Michelle Brattain, *The Politics of Whiteness: Race, Workers, and Culture in the Modern South* (Princeton: Princeton University Press, 2001). An important history of the Textile Workers Union of America, Clete Daniel's *Culture of Misfortune: An Interpretive History of Textile Unionism in the United States* (Ithaca: ILR Press, 2001), also overlooks the industry's decline and the union's long fight for import controls, largely because it concentrates heavily on the TWUA's early history, especially its struggle to organize the South.

15. One important book that relates to this topic is Rosen, *Making Sweatshops*. An important study of the globalization of production in the apparel industry, this book gives little coverage to the political fight to avert job losses or to the effects of deindustrialization on U.S. workers, which are the central concerns of my work. It also focuses largely on apparel rather than the textile-apparel complex as a whole. For a case study of apparel workers in Pennsylvania that gives some coverage to deindustrialization, see Kenneth C. Wolensky, Nicole H. Wolensky, and Robert P. Wolensky, *Fighting for the Union Label: The Women's Garment Industry and the ILGWU in Pennsylvania* (University Park, PA: Pennsylvania State University Press, 2002), esp. pp. 219–34.

16. Mittelhauser, "Employment Trends in Textiles and Apparel, 1973–2005," pp. 24–25. While this book looks at both the textile and apparel industries, on some occasions in the text the term *textile industry* will be used to refer to both industries.

17. ACTWU General Executive Board Minutes, June 12, 1978, p. 5, untitled folder, box 854, ACTWU Papers-Cornell.

18. Mittelhauser, "Employment Trends in Textiles and Apparel, 1973–2005," p. 26. Throughout the period covered by this work, trade associations also referred to textiles and

apparel as one industry. See, for example, "1984 Worst Trade Year in History for American Textile and Apparel Industry" (ATMI Press Release), January 30, 1985, in "American Textile Manufacturers Institute (ATMI) 1984–1985" folder, box 1, MS 106.3.3.17.1, William S. Cohen Papers, held at the Special Collections Department, Raymond H. Fogler Library, University of Maine-Orono, hereafter cited as "Cohen Papers."

19. "Imports Affect Cannon People," *Cannon News*, July 1985, p. 2; Crafted with Pride in USA Council, Inc., Fact Sheet, ca. 1985, folder 22.12, box 22, Northern Textile Association Papers (MS2000.178.1), held at the American Textile History Museum, Lowell, Massachusetts, hereafter cited as "NTA Papers"; Congressional Textile Caucus Resolution, July 28, 1981, "Textiles, General" folder, box 14, MS 106.3.3.17.1, Cohen Papers; Murray, "Unraveling Employment Trends in Textiles and Apparel," p. 62.

20. George C. Langston to Ed Jenkins, July 24, 1986, "Textile" folder, box 6, series 329-92-138, Edgar L. Jenkins Papers, unprocessed collection held at the Richard B. Russell Library for Political Research and Studies, University of Georgia, hereafter cited as "Jenkins Papers"; Crafted with Pride in USA Council, Inc., Fact Sheet, n.d., folder 22.12, box 22, NTA Papers.

21. U.S. Department of Labor, "U.S. Textile and Apparel Wages—1983" document, "Trade-Textiles, Shoes, 1983–1991" folder, box 25, MS 106.3.4.3, Cohen Papers.

22. "Statement of Northern Textile Association before the Committee on Ways and Means," July 10, 1978, "Textile Industry, 1975–1978, 1 of 2" folder, box 13, MS106.3.3.17.1, Cohen Papers. Chace defined the mid-Atlantic states as New York, New Jersey, and Pennsylvania.

23. U.S. Department of Commerce's Office of Textiles and Apparel, "U.S. Textile and Apparel Import Program," document, January 11, 1988, "U.S. Textile and Apparel Import Program" folder, Susan Lauffer files, Reagan Library.

24. S. D. Chapman, *The Cotton Industry in the Industrial Revolution, Second Edition* (Basingstoke, UK: MacMillan, 1987), p. 17.

25. First quotation in "Textiles: America's First Great Industry," ATMI Board of Directors Meeting Minutes, November 20–21, 1986, box 20, series 1998/18, Harmony Grove Mills Papers, 1898–1994, held at the Richard B. Russell Library for Political Research and Studies, University of Georgia, hereafter cited as "Harmony Grove Mills Papers"; William E. Schmidt, "Textiles Defends Its Last Bastion," *New York Times*, June 23, 1985, p. A4.

26. Marilyn Lloyd et al. to Colleague, June 26, 1990, "Congressional Textile Caucus 1990" folder, box 69, Marilyn Lloyd Papers, held at the Special Collections Department, Lupton Library, University of Tennessee at Chattanooga, hereafter cited as "Lloyd Papers."

27. Thomas Dublin, *Women at Work: The Transformation of Work and Community in Lowell, Massachusetts, 1826–1860* (New York: Columbia University Press, 1979), pp. 15–16; "Who We Are," Slater Mill history available at http://www.slatermill.org/museum/about/ (accessed August 6, 2010, copy in author's possession); "Union Drive for Trade Bill Gets Off to a Rousing Start," *Labor Unity*, May 1985, p. 2; Ed Jenkins to William Bolger, January 5, 1983, "Trade-General" folder, box 43, series 329-86-0219, Jenkins Papers; William F. Sullivan to All Members of the Northern Textile Association and National Association of Cotton Manufacturers, September 5, 1956, vol. 1.28, 1956 Annual Meeting Files, NTA Papers.

28. William S. Cohen, American Textile Institute Speech, February 26, 1991, "Trade-1985-95" folder, box 11, MS 106.3.4.6, Cohen Papers; "Remarks by U.S. Commissioner of Customs William von Raab," April 12, 1985, "Textile/Trade (4)" folder, William B. Lacy files, OA13030, Reagan Library.

29. Mittelhauser, "Employment Trends in Textiles and Apparel, 1973–2005," p. 24.

30. Bluestone and Harrison, *The Deindustrialization of America*, p. 4; Bluestone, "Foreword," in Cowie and Heathcott, *Beyond the Ruins*, pp. viii–xiii, quotations on pp. x, xiii.

31. U.S. Chamber of Commerce, "What 100 New Jobs Means to a Community," 1985 pamphlet, pp. 4–6, in "Textile Bill FFACT Sheets" folder, box 788, ACTWU Papers-Cornell; Joseph R. Meisenheimer II, "The Services Industry in the 'Good' versus 'Bad' Jobs Debate," *Monthly Labor Review*, February 1998, pp. 22–23.

32. U.S. Congress, Office of Technology Assessment, *The U.S. Textile and Apparel Industry*, p. 6.

33. U.S. Department of Commerce's Office of Textiles and Apparel, "U.S. Textile and Apparel Import Program," document, January 11, 1988, "U.S. Textile and Apparel Import Program" folder, Susan Lauffer files, OA16376, Reagan Library.

34. Hall et al., *Like a Family*, pp. 140, 180.

35. "Fact Sheet: Women and Minorities in the Textile and Apparel Industries," undated but ca. 1987, "Woman and Minorities in the Textile and Apparel Industries" folder, box 793, ACTWU Papers-Cornell.

36. TWUA Executive Council Minutes, May 22–26, 1961, p. 30 ("earliest proponent" quotation), "1959–61" folder, box 1, Mss. 396, Textile Workers Union of America Papers, held at the Wisconsin Historical Society, Madison, Wisconsin, hereafter cited as "TWUA Papers"; TWUA Executive Council Minutes, July 9–13, 1956, p. 25 ("best approach" quotation), "1956–58" folder, box 1, Mss. 396, TWUA Papers.

37. George Perazich and W. T. Stone, "Economic Effect of Textile Mill Closings: Selected Communities in Middle Atlantic States" (Washington, DC: U.S. Government Printing Office, 1963), p. 1, copy cited in folder 24.10, box 24, NTA Papers; Statement of William F. Sullivan at the NTA Annual Meeting, September 27, 1956, vol. 1.28, 1956 NTA Annual Meeting Files, NTA Papers.

38. Herman E. Talmadge Press Release of May 20, 1959, "Column—Textile Industry Relief" folder, box 299, series II, Herman E. Talmadge Papers, held at the Richard B. Russell Library for Political Research and Studies, University of Georgia, hereafter cited as "Talmadge Papers." For another example of the same allegation being made, see ILGWU General Executive Board Minutes, October 15–17, 1991, p. 25, "ILGWU GEB Minutes 1991" folder, box 2, series 5780/150, International Ladies' Garment Workers' Union Papers, held at the Kheel Center for Labor-Management Documentation and Archives, School of Industrial and Labor Relations, Cornell University, Ithaca, New York, hereafter cited as "ILGWU Papers-Cornell." Here, the ILGWU leaders privately charge that the Bush administration wanted to "give the apparel industry away."

39. Stuart Auerbach, "Mexican Trade Pact Unravels the Once-Durable Textile Lobby," *Washington Post*, May 12, 1991, p. H1.

40. Clyde Farnsworth, "Trade and Favored Nations," *New York Times*, May 20, 1979, p. F18.

41. Many of the works cited in note 14 cover the textile industry's history of resistance to unionization and the many bitter strikes that resulted. See also: Janet Irons, *Testing the New Deal: The General Textile Strike of 1934 in the American South* (Urbana: University of Illinois Press, 2000); John A. Salmond, *The General Textile Strike of 1934: From Maine to Alabama* (Columbia: University of Missouri Press, 2002); Timothy J. Minchin, *"Don't Sleep with Stevens!": The J. P. Stevens Campaign and the Struggle to Organize the South, 1963–80* (Gainesville: University Press of Florida, 2005).

42. For this book I received special permission to use the voluminous papers of former U.S. Senator Ernest "Fritz" Hollings (D-SC), who was one of the industry's most powerful supporters. The chief sponsor of the 1985 textile bill, former Georgia congressman Ed Jenkins also gave me permission to use his unprocessed congressional papers, which contain a wealth of original material on the decline of the industry and legislative efforts to stop it. In a similar fashion, former congressman Butler Derrick (D-SC), the chief sponsor of the 1987 textile bill, gave me access to his restricted congressional files. In addition, I am grateful to UNITE HERE! (created by a 2004 merger of UNITE and the Hotel Employees and Restaurant Employees Union) for giving me permission to use the restricted files of both ACTWU and UNITE, including the minutes of the executive board meetings. The union's records are very detailed and are drawn on extensively in the pages that follow. With help from the staff of the American Textile History Museum in Lowell, Massachusetts, I also used the detailed papers of the Northern Textile Association, which are not processed and have been largely neglected by scholars. Other unprocessed collections that I draw on here include the papers of former senator John Pastore (D-RI) and Congresswoman Marilyn Lloyd (D-TN), who was the chief sponsor of the 1990 textile bill. My discussion of the 1985 and 1987 textile bills also draws heavily on more than four thousand pages of original documents that I obtained from the Ronald Reagan Presidential Library through a Freedom of Information Act request, while my coverage of the

1990 bill also draws on records obtained from the George Bush Presidential Library through a separate FOIA request. All of these papers are cited in the bibliography, as are the various interviews I conducted. Finally, the decline of the textile and apparel industry has generated thousands of articles in the press, especially the local press, creating a rich source that few scholars have yet to access in detail. I have drawn on this press coverage heavily here, especially in the later chapters.

43. "Textile Bill Override Vote Patterns," undated, "1990 Trade Bill" folder, box 13, 6000/023, UNITE Papers-Cornell; Karl Spilhaus interview with the author on April 26, 2011, in Boston, Massachusetts.

44. U.S. Congress, Office of Technology Assessment, *The U.S. Textile and Apparel Industry*, p. 3.

45. Sara U. Douglas and Michelle A. Morganosky, "Textile and Apparel Industry Support for the Crafted With Pride Campaign: A Systems Perspective," *Clothing and Textiles Research Journal* 9:1 (July 1990), pp. 37–44.

46. U.S. Congress, Office of Technology Assessment, *The U.S. Textile and Apparel Industry,* pp. iii, 3 (quotation).

47. Ed Jenkins interview with Bob Short, July 7, 2008, Jasper, Georgia, "Reflections on Georgia Politics" series, ROGP-037.

48. M. F. Thompson to Ernest F. Hollings, June 21, 1985, box 10, Ninety-Ninth Congress files, Ernest F. Hollings Papers, held at South Carolina Political Collections, University of South Carolina-Columbia, hereafter cited as "Hollings Papers"; Closing quotation in Marshall N. Norton to Strom Thurmond, April 25, 1985, folder 517, box 75, CMS Series, Strom Thurmond Papers, held at the Strom Thurmond Institute, Clemson University, Clemson, South Carolina, hereafter cited as "Thurmond Papers."

49. These points are explored more fully in later chapters, especially chapters 7 and 8.

50. BLS data cited in "Plant Closings and Job Losses," available at the National Council of Textile Organizations website at http://www.ncto.org/ustextiles/joblosses.asp (accessed August 17, 2009, copy in author's possession); "2005—The Quota Phaseout and NCTO Response," available at the NCTO website at http://www.ncto.org/tradejobs/index.asp (accessed August 20, 2009, copy in author's possession); Donald W. Patterson, "Calls Renew for Textile Curbs," Greensboro (North Carolina) *News and Record*, April 1, 2005, p. B8; "China Not to Blame for Textile Trade Disputes, Official Says," *BBC Monitoring International Reports*, March 22, 2005; Import data from the Office of Textiles and Apparel, International Trade Administration, U.S. Commerce Department, at http://otexa.ita.doc.gov/msrcty/a5700.htm (accessed August 13, 2010, and April 6, 2012). This import penetration figure refers to imports in "square meter equivalents."

51. Tony Mecia, "Plant Depicted in 'Norma Rae' to Close," *Charlotte Observer*, April 26, 2003 (Harris Raynor quotation); Hunter James, "Hard Times Follow Real 'Norma Rae,'" *Atlanta Journal Constitution*, June 9, 1985, p. C14; "The Very Fabric of America," *San Francisco Chronicle*, July 4, 1987, p. 11; "Faded Glory: An American Icon Is about to Become an Overseas Import," Watertown (New York) *Daily Times*, December 21, 2003, p. E1; Stella M. Hopkins, "Springs' Slashed Work Force in S.C., Will Now Be Without any Plants; 120 Years of Manufacturing Fades Away," *Charlotte Observer*, June 28, 2007, p. 1D.

52. Jennifer Heaslip, "Patterson Mill Worth Its Weight in Wood and Bricks," Roanoke Rapids (North Carolina) *Daily Herald*, June 11, 2004. For more information on the problem of empty mills in the South, see Charles Lunan, "Empty Mills Burden Carolinas: Cavernous Brick Hulks Can Drain Remaining Vitality of Small Towns," *Charlotte Observer*, July 22, 2002, p. 1A.

53. Senator John Pastore comments, *Congressional Record*, February 7, 1966, pp. 2193–94, in "Senator's Remarks on Senate Floor Re: Editorial in *Washington Post*, February 7, 1966" folder, Pastore General Files, John O. Pastore Papers, held at Phillips Memorial Library, Providence College, Providence, Rhode Island, hereafter cited as "Pastore Papers." Pastore's papers are unprocessed, and all citations given here are as detailed as possible.

## *Chapter One*

# A Troubled Industry in an Era of Prosperity

As Barry Bluestone has noted, the two-and-a-half decades after World War II were "glory days" for the American economy. For most of this period, the nation's gross national product grew by around 4 percent a year, and over the course of the 1960s it expanded by an impressive 50 percent.[1] In standard classroom works, prestigious American historians have celebrated this period, citing the unprecedented wealth that most citizens experienced. Many have taken their cue from the economist J. K. Galbraith, whose classic *The Affluent Society* (1958) helped to define the era. In the 1950s and early 1960s, writes Alan Brinkley, Americans basked in "a golden age" of national prosperity. "Affluent America," adds David Kennedy and Lizabeth Cohen, was a society where a sustained economic boom "wrought wondrous changes in American society," including more jobs and an expanding middle class. While Galbraith also tried to call for greater social spending to tackle ongoing inequalities, few Americans heeded his advice.[2]

The situation was very different for America's textile workers. Even in this supposed golden age, they toiled in a troubled industry, especially in the North, where many jobs were being lost. In New England, the textile industry declined sharply just as the national economy boomed. Between 1947 and 1957, for example, the region witnessed a 50 percent drop in textile employment, the number of workers tumbling from 288,500 to 144,100. Throughout the 1960s, the New England textile industry continued to struggle, and by 1977 just 68,400 workers remained in the region's mills. Across the country, even those textile workers who kept their jobs failed to share in the wider economic boom. Between 1946 and 1956, per capita personal consumption expenditure increased nationally by 49 percent, but in textiles it fell slightly. While the production index for all manufacturing rose by 40 percent over this decade, in textiles the increase was only 6 percent. The story of America's textile workers, declared TWUA president William Pollock in 1958, was "one of misfortune rather than fortune." Textile workers were, he declared, "the forgotten men and women of the 1950's."[3]

While the bulk of this first wave of mill closures occurred in the North, textile leaders argued that the industry's problems were national, not regional. As early as 1952, the TWUA's Executive Council held a "lengthy discussion" about "why there is a depression in the textile industry in an economy of full employment and high wages."[4] This depression persisted through the 1950s, a decade indelibly associated with economic growth. According to the TWUA, between 1951 and 1957 about 445 large mills were closed, throwing 350,000 people out of their jobs, while many more workers had their hours cut. "These developments," it added, "are without geographical limits and the rate of southern mill liquidations is accelerating." The union argued, with some justification, that it was an issue of national concern when "such a basic industry as textiles is sick." The following year, the TWUA's leaders called for improved unemployment insurance in order to help the "scores of textile communities both in the north and the south" who had been "hit hard" by plant closures and layoffs.[5] In short, textiles was "a deeply and chronically depressed industry." Supporting this, the union's figures showed that from February 1951 to July 1958 there had been a loss of 17 percent in textile employment in the South. While this was a significant drop, over the same period New England and New Jersey fared much worse, shedding 55 and 46 percent of their jobs respectively.[6]

Others agreed that this was an industry with national difficulties. "The basic textile problem," declared the *New York Times* in 1956, "extends beyond regional lines." Two years later, the Senate Committee on Interstate Commerce held special hearings to explore the "problems of the domestic textile industry." Chaired by Senator Pastore, the committee held hearings in Washington, D.C., and New York City, as well as in both northern and southern textile centers. In all, they compiled a record of more than 1,700 pages, including testimony from scores of witnesses. The central message that all of these observers gave was that theirs was a troubled industry and that imports were the primary culprit. According to southern executive Halbert M. Jones, "The lower costs of foreign production have already resulted in serious inroads into our domestic market." New York–based executive Edwin Wilkinson spoke of "the damaging effects of textile imports," adding that "the United States is not going to be the dumping ground for textile manufacturers around the world." Union leaders shared these sentiments. "They have given away millions of jobs of our American people due to the imports of foreign stuff into our country," declared John Arpino, a local union leader from Auburn, New York.[7]

In its final report, the committee concluded that textiles was one of the few industries that was failing to share in the broader economic prosperity. It also found that the industry's problems were so serious that Congress and the administration should carefully evaluate those public policies that had contributed to its decline and take necessary corrective action. According to Pastore, imports were imposing an "extraordinary burden" on domestic mills. Because the industry was so important to national security, the committee agreed that it could not be allowed to fade away.[8]

In the 1950s and 1960s, the industry's demise was most marked in New England, largely because it had already been occurring there for decades. The example of New England, the industry's American birthplace, offers an instructive initial case study. As economic historian William F. Hartford has claimed, "The collapse of textile production in New England is the story of the deindustrialization of America." Viewed in retrospect, New England's experience certainly offers wider lessons, especially for the subsequent demise of textile production. There are many similarities between the two waves of decline, especially the harsh impact of deindustrialization upon workers and the determined effort of mill owners to seek political assistance. Neither wave was, however, entirely regional specific, especially as many southern mills also closed or contracted during the 1950s and 1960s, while some northern mills only went out of business much later. Nevertheless, the early decline was centered in New England, and this generated significant tensions between northern and southern mill owners that only abated when they united to fight imports.[9]

New England's textile workers were in trouble well before World War II, and the key cause of their problems—at least initially—was not imports but competition from newer mills in the American South. As far back as the 1870s, southern economic and political leaders had started to develop a textile industry, partly because they were aware that it was the South's industrial weakness that had contributed to its defeat in the Civil War. Because most textile jobs could be learned easily, the industry was attractive to a region that possessed a large but unskilled native-born workforce. Just like the Asian economies decades later, the South used textiles as its first industry, a way of getting industrialization off the ground, absorbing a labor surplus, and generating income. As many scholars have pointed out, the South's early mills were indeed highly profitable, and mill owners became a powerful class in the New South. In the late nineteenth and early twentieth centuries, capacity tripled or even quadrupled in every decade, and by the 1920s the southern states had already surpassed the northern states in the number of spindles. By 1927, the South produced 82 percent of the coarse yarn and 71 percent of the medium yarn in the country, and only in fine goods did New England maintain a slight lead. This would soon disappear. "By 1933," concludes historian John Salmond, "the southern textile manufacturers had triumphed." While the Great Depression hurt both branches of the industry, it did not alter the fundamental advantages that the South possessed.[10]

The causes of the industry's migration have been studied a lot, with most scholars seeing the availability of low-cost, malleable labor in the South as crucial. Because wages were lower in the South, northern mills simply could not compete, especially in the cheaper-grade fabrics that the South specialized in. Crucially, rates of unionization were also significantly higher in the North, further encouraging the industry's migration. Although unions fought to maintain northern mills, they could do little as more and more mill owners moved their operations to the South to take advantage of cheaper labor. The move split the industry, as some executives tried to maintain production in the higher-wage labor market for as long as possible. The industry's shift to the South ultimately highlighted that textile capital was much more mobile than textile workers. This lesson was not lost on either mill owners or textile labor leaders, who were among the first Americans to recognize the threat posed by cheap imports. A generation or two later, the industry would move again, and mill owners would again be divided about whether to stay or go.[11]

From the start, the South's textile workers were paid less than their northern counterparts. Across the region, the steady decline of agriculture had created a large pool of workers who were hungry for factory jobs, whereas in New England workers had a wider range of opportunities. In the late nineteenth century northern textile workers were paid up to three times as much as their southern counterparts, and the differential was greatest for unskilled workers. As Alice Galenson has concluded in her detailed study of the relocation process, "the wage differential between the two regions was critical," especially as wages comprised about one-quarter of the cost of producing cotton textiles. According to Galenson, between 1880 and 1930 the differential did narrow, yet it remained decisive.[12] As late as 1952, in fact, the inaugural report of the New England Governors' Textile Committee, which was set up to explore the industry's problems and find solutions to them, concluded that the wage gap was crucial: "The major explanation of New England's decline in textiles is the large differential between wage costs here and those in the South." As the report explained, wages were not simply higher in New England; northern workers also received more generous fringe benefits, including paid holidays and shift differentials. More likely to belong to unions, they also had lower workloads. In the South, nascent efforts to protest against harsh working conditions were generally crushed by hostile and powerful employers.[13]

America's oldest trade association, the National Association of Cotton Manufacturers, was based in New England, and its members frequently discussed the industry's decline. At the 1922 annual meeting in Boston, President Robert Amory noted that the industry had operated in New England for over a century but was now being eclipsed by cheaper mills in the South. In

1900, he related, the key textile state of Massachusetts contained about half of all the spindles in the country, but by 1922 this had dropped to about one-third. During this time, four million spindles had been installed in Massachusetts, but 8,500,000 had been added in the Carolinas and Virginia. Amory predicted that the industry would continue to move to where labor was cheaper. "We have the skill and capital," he acknowledged. "But capital will always go where it can get the largest return and it can move easily." The industry's demise in its American birthplace was already established. "The record is clear enough," declared Amory sadly. "The cotton industry is gradually slipping away."[14]

The slippage was especially noticeable in the region's largest textile centers. In Fall River, for example, the number of manufacturing jobs fell from thirty-seven thousand in 1923 to twenty thousand in 1935, as most of the city's mills went bankrupt or moved South. During the 1920s and 1930s, no fewer than thirty-one cotton and rayon mills closed down in the city, while nearby New Bedford witnessed nineteen shutdowns.[15] Closures caused immense hardship in textile communities, many of which were wholly reliant on the industry. "There is great unemployment in many of the large textile centers," reported the *New York Times* from Fall River in 1925. "The cotton towns have been hit hardest and suffering and destitution prevail in Fall River, Lowell, Lawrence, the Pawtucket Valley of Rhode Island and Willimantic, Conn." Visiting Massachusetts five years later, journalist Louis Adamic found "tragic towns" and downcast residents. Because few jobs were available, displaced mill workers often stayed on public relief for years. The Great Depression only compounded the problems, and older workers were hit hard. In 1939, the Works Progress Administration found that 36 percent of textile workers in New Bedford were unemployed, but among those aged over fifty-five the rate was 52 percent.[16] By 1944, scholar Seymour Wolfbein had already published a book-length study of the industry's decline in New Bedford. "Heavily dependent on one industry upon which it concentrated most of its energies," he concluded, "it prospered as textiles prospered and it suffered from the industry's movement to the South."[17]

Occurring in the midst of the Great Depression, the shutdown of the giant Amoskeag Manufacturing Company in Manchester, New Hampshire, graphically illustrated the industry's problems and foreshadowed the harsh social and economic impact of its decline. After a century of operation the mills were liquidated, a victim of increasing domestic and international competition. In November 1935, 22.8 percent of Manchester's families were on relief, and about 70 percent of this load was attributed to the recent closing. Earlier in the year, New England's governors had visited President Franklin D. Roosevelt and sought concessions to protect the industry. They cited the example of Manchester, which faced "ruin" if its mile-long complex of mills went out of business. FDR, however, was reluctant to undertake sweeping policy changes, and the company duly collapsed. Once proudly proclaimed as "the world's greatest cotton textile plant," the huge, red-brick mills stood "grimly silent" when they were visited by a journalist after the closure, the time on the mill's large clock tower frozen forever on the figure "8." The mills had once employed sixteen thousand men and women, but now they were empty.[18]

The effects of the closure were long lasting. According to historians Tamara K. Hareven and Randolph Langenbach, the shutdown "destroyed the economic base" of Manchester, a city planned and developed by the company. "Most workers lost their jobs, their life savings, and the possibility of career advancement for themselves and their children," they concluded in their detailed study. Interviewed several decades later, former workers felt that the city had never recovered. "You can't imagine the impact that the shutdown had on a community like Manchester," recalled Virginia Erskine. "Complete families—fathers, sisters, everyone—were all out. There was nobody that you could turn to. I don't think before the Amoskeag closed I knew anyone that was on welfare during the Depression." The closure "was a terrible situation," added Thomas Smith. "Most of the workers couldn't go for other jobs. They didn't have the ability, and a lot of them were very old. . . . A lot died of broken hearts." For decades after the closure, displaced Amoskeag workers would rush to the gates of local mills whenever they were hiring, but these were small operations with a limited life span.[19]

Although it generated a widespread economic boom, World War II was only of temporary help to the textile industry, especially in New England. During the course of the war, the American economy experienced remarkable growth, as the gross national product rose from $97 billion in 1940 to $190 billion in 1944. The United States was alone among the major combatants in experiencing a rising standard of living as a result of the war.[20] The importance of the textile industry to national defense was highlighted during the conflict, as a substantial proportion of its production was given over to military and industrial needs. The war represented the industry's high point; the mills ran so well that there was a labor shortage of between fifty thousand and one hundred thousand workers, and the forty-eight-hour week became commonplace. Although the unions complained that textile wages were too low, mill workers still enjoyed several pay increases in these years.[21]

For most American industries, the war provided a stable platform for long-term growth, but not for textiles. In 1947, as peacetime economic conditions resumed, so too did the industry's problems. Over the next decade, the number of manufacturing jobs in New England fell by 16 percent, while in Massachusetts cotton mill employment plummeted from thirty-five thousand in 1946 to five thousand in 1960. By 1950, New Bedford mill owner Seabury Stanton reported that the war-related boom was truly over. The industry had excess capacity, he told Congress, and as a result "thousands" of workers were "walking the streets." The expansion of the service sector was of little help because it generally bypassed mill towns. In July 1952, the jobless rate in the wool center of Lawrence hit 52 percent, earning the city the dubious distinction of being the "#1 Labor Surplus area in the country."[22] Lawrence, however, was not alone; in the same year, for example, one Massachusetts judge declared that the state's textile industry was "very sick." Not long after the war, the plant closures resumed. Between 1949 and 1957, the NTA recorded that two hundred mills were liquidated in New England, with Massachusetts suffering the most.[23] In November 1951, the New England Governors' Textile Committee was established as a response to "serious unemployment and economic hardship in New England textile centers." Each state named one representative to the committee, and they included labor, management, and public figures.[24]

While the bulk of attention focused on New England, losses were also heavy in the mid-Atlantic states of New York, New Jersey, and Pennsylvania. In 1958, the TWUA's New York director, Jack Rubenstein, told the Senate hearings that the union had lost half of its members in the state over the previous six years. Plant closings had led to 24,255 jobs being wiped out, and because most of the affected factories were in small towns such as Jamestown, Fort Plain, Amsterdam, and Little Falls, they had created "serious and prolonged" unemployment. Feeling that most Americans were unaware of these layoffs, Rubenstein stressed that former textile centers stayed "in a crippled condition for years and years after a major mill closing."[25]

An upstate community of fifteen thousand people, Amsterdam illustrated these points particularly well. In 1957, the closure of the Bigelow-Sanford carpet mill, one of the town's main employers, caused the unemployment rate to double overnight. One of those laid off, forty-eight-year-old David McKnight, testified before the hearings eighteen months later. "The unemployment insurance is the only thing that is carrying the people in Amsterdam right now," he explained. Elsewhere, even New Yorkers with mill jobs were struggling. "We are out of work right now," testified Charlotte Marsh from the tiny town of Stottville, located south of Albany. "They laid us off due to bringing in imported yarn, so that leaves less work for us." Because of the industry's problems, the unemployment rate in some New York textile towns was 14 or 15 percent. As the state's deputy industrial commissioner explained, the industry's decline had been "devastating" for residents, and there had been numerous "personal tragedies." "Some of these communities have not yet recovered from the mill closings even though they have occurred 5 or more years ago," added Charles Hughes. Most Americans were oblivious to these conditions, however, and the union's efforts failed to change this. What made the closures particularly damaging for those involved—the isolated location of small towns where mills were located—also made them easy to overlook.[26]

In other parts of the mid-Atlantic region, it was a similar story. According to Sol Stetin, the TWUA's regional director for Delaware, New Jersey, and Pennsylvania, the industry had "shrunk to a shadow of its former self." Those affected—especially older workers—endured long spells of unemployment. "There is no work around I can find in our industry right now and it is difficult to find a job at my age," explained fifty-one-year-old Frank Kroger, a displaced weaver from Scranton, Pennsylvania. "Nobody will hire." More than a year after the shutdown, Kroger was jobless, and he worried that he would not be able to pay off his home.[27] In Passaic, New Jersey, the decline of local silk and wool mills had terrible consequences for a workforce that was highly experienced but lacked knowledge of other trades. Vera Malenda, for example, was still unemployed three-and-a-half years after losing her job at Botany Mills, a large wool manufacturer. "I haven't been able to get a job because the only thing I am qualified for is textile work," she explained in November 1958. "I have been taking jobs babysitting, anything I can get hold of because as far as getting a job in a different mill, I am not able to."[28]

Among the plant closures recorded in the TWUA's files was that of the A. and M. Karagheusian rug mill in Freehold, New Jersey. The closure was noted in a matter-of-fact manner, and it was just a small part of the broader demise of the struggling carpet and rug sector. This was, however, the mill that Bruce Springsteen would later sing about on his hit record "My Hometown," the mill "across the railroad tracks" that came to symbolize northern deindustrialization. It closed in 1961, when Springsteen was twelve years old, and as forecast in the song it never reopened. Moreover, the shutdown came shortly after A and M. Karagheusian had shifted most of its domestic production to Georgia. After describing the devastation that the closure had caused in Freehold, whose main street was now home to "whitewashed windows and vacant stores," the song ends with a grown-up Springsteen also considering "heading South" in search of more opportunity.[29]

Throughout the 1950s, America's largest textile union repeatedly documented the distressing impact of mill closures upon small towns, providing a very different picture of a decade often associated with prosperity and consensus. Although the media trumpeted that new industries were expanding, union leaders pointed out that they were not locating near old mill towns. Moreover, many dislocated textile workers were reluctant—or unable—to move. Labor leaders stressed the industry's role in offering jobs to women and older workers who found it particularly hard to find new positions. Speaking to these issues in 1957, one TWUA research paper concluded that "textile employment has been shrinking in most areas and the displaced workers have had great difficulties in finding jobs. A large proportion of those displaced have suffered long periods of unemployment and many are now permanently out of the labor market." Overall, many former textile communities continued to "suffer from chronic unemployment despite the high level of national employment."[30]

Reports from TWUA joint board managers illustrated the problems generated by the industry's decline. In 1957 to 1958, for instance, Felix P. Damore reported from the Central Massachusetts Joint Board that union membership had "dropped dramatically" due to "layoffs in the various mills." The closures had demoralized local people and hindered organizing. In other locations, deindustrialization hurt the union by negating its hard-won gains. As Irving Epstein of the Greater New York Joint Board explained, "Although we have organized approximately 125 workers during this five month period, August through December, we have lost approximately 150 employees by shops going out of business." Similar complaints came in from across New England and the mid-Atlantic region.[31]

Rather than signing up new members, TWUA representatives also found that they were consumed by trying to help laid-off workers. By the late 1950s, conditions were particularly bleak in Maine's Biddeford-Saco area, once a major center of textile production. At the Saco-Lowell mills, representative Michael Schoonjans related that layoffs were "occurring . . . every week." Most of the textile machinery was being "moved South," devastating the local economy and wiping out the union's membership base. Still, Schoonjans spent much of his time helping the unemployed, even using local union funds to buy food for workers' families. "Everything labor can do to help alleviate the distressed conditions in the area is being done," he explained in one 1958 report. "After having met with the City Welfare head (both in Biddeford and Saco) in regards to surplus commodities for the area, I have met with the Director of Surplus Commodity Relief in the State in regards to getting increased quotas for unemployed workers eligible for surplus food." Despite Schoonjans's best efforts, he felt that local political leaders and the media were reluctant to address the "serious plight" of the unemployed, preferring to turn a blind eye to their suffering.[32]

Clearly, the prosperity enjoyed by the American economy hurt the union's efforts to secure assistance for its members. At the 1958 Senate hearings, TWUA leader Victor Canzano related that the decline of the textile industry had caused "untold distress for many New England textile communities." A whole range of once vibrant towns, including Lowell and Lawrence in Massachusetts and Providence and Pawtucket in Rhode Island, were suffering from chronic unemployment and were "flat on their backs." According to the union's vice president, these communities were "sore spots in our industrial picture." However, because the national economy was still strong, Canzano complained that there was general "indifference" to the workers' plight.[33]

Bearing this out, national policy makers had little sympathy for the textile industry while the economy as a whole was thriving. In 1956, presidential assistant Sherman Adams told the NTA that while the industry's problems were genuine, the Eisenhower administration was committed to the "expansion of foreign commerce." Adams pointed to the strength of export-oriented industries and noted that America had a significant trade surplus. He would not be the first to suggest that dislocated textile workers could find work in industries that were doing well. In a similar vein, deputy assistant secretary of state, W. T. M. Beale, told executives that while their industry was "beset with many difficulties," the federal government would not change its policies. "It is, of course, the fundamental purpose of the trade agreements program to expand world trade," he added.[34] In a more sympathetic vein, other administration officials stressed that they were trying to minimize the "hardships" of dislocated mill workers. Still, Senator Pastore was not impressed, replying that the textile industry had become "the sacrificial lamb of our foreign policy."[35]

In a sign of things to come, Pastore's hearings also heard from importers and retailers who did not feel the domestic textile industry deserved help. In a 121-page submission, Mike Masaoka of the American Importers of Japanese Textiles argued that Japanese imports were "inconsequential to the giant American industry." Domestic mill owners, he argued, should focus on improving their competitiveness rather than blaming external enemies: "Indicting imports especially from Japan is an easy rallying cry for the domestic operators." Japanese imports were a "convenient scapegoat," agreed Noel Hemmendinger of the United States–Japan Trade Council, who reminded his audience that Japan stood on America's "side" in the Cold War. Unlike the industry's advocates—who generally tried to conceal regional differences—Masaoka stressed that "many liquidations" were related to southern competition, an argument that shifted attention away from imports. Although they made legitimate points, in the 1950s industry opponents found themselves outgunned by powerful domestic mill owners. According to Donald Comer, the owner of Alabama's large Avondale Mills, the American government should look after its own industries. "I raise cattle and I plant and develop pastures for my cows," he explained. "I know of no farmer who does not put a fence around such pastures to protect the grazing and keep out hungry cows from across the road." Over time, however, the balance of power would change.[36]

Produced under the aegis of the New England Governors' Committee on the Textile Industry, which operated throughout the 1950s, one special report investigated the fate of displaced textile workers in detail. In the process, it drove home the harsh impact of deindustrialization and exposed the flaws in the Eisenhower administration's approach. In 1955, Northeastern University economist William H. Miernyk published *Inter-Industry Labor Mobility: The Case of the Displaced Textile Worker*. Focused on the case histories of 1,700 dislocated workers from six New England communities, the study found most individuals suffered a lot when they lost their jobs. Almost one-half of the group were still unemployed more than a year later, while the majority of those who had found posts were earning less. Although growth industries such as electronics were often touted as a replacement for the mills, Miernyk found that they were not hiring many textile workers. Workers' strong "attachment" to the textile industry was also "striking," as most workers wanted to stay in the mills. Furthermore, Miernyk established that workers over forty-five had the greatest difficulty in finding new positions. Later, when the industry's collapse accelerated in the South, many of these findings were repeated.[37]

Published a few years later, a comprehensive study of mill closures in eight mid-Atlantic communities confirmed that these problems were not restricted to New England. Carried out by the U.S. Department of Commerce, the study found that more than thirty thousand textile workers had lost their jobs in the eight communities since 1950. The effects had been harsh, especially as most mills were the biggest employer in town. As the report concluded, overall there was "much evidence of hardship and suffering." It explained, "Many older workers were unable to find new jobs; many younger men left their home communities to find employment elsewhere. Long periods of unemployment were common, and many displaced textile workers were forced to seek assistance from relatives or public relief agencies, or eventually to take lower paying jobs in other industries." The problems were still acute in Amsterdam, New York, a carpet and rug center that lost over six thousand textile jobs between 1950 and 1962. Here, the closures had "serious and far-reaching" consequences, leading to cuts in community services and increased residential taxes. They also hurt the small towns of Gloversville, New York, a former center of leather glove production, and Kulpmont, Pennsylvania, which the report described as "a one-mill town in a declining coal and textile community." In these communities, suffering was exacerbated by the failure of local leaders to recruit replacement industries. In the bigger centers of Utica, New York, and Reading, Pennsylvania, the losses were partly offset by gains in other manufacturing industries, particularly machinery and electronics, and by growth in the service sector. The lesson was clear—small towns heavily dependent on textile mills were hurt the most as the industry declined. Even in bigger communities, however, closures caused painful adjustments for workers who were deeply attached to the industry.[38]

The main trade association for the northern textile industry, the NTA also collected a great deal of information that highlighted the harsh impact of mill closures upon workers. As association secretary William F. Sullivan wrote powerful congressman Wilbur Mills, the key point was that most textile mills were located in small communities where they employed a "high proportion" of local residents. "Our experience with the displacement of textile workers has taught us that the displaced worker finds it extremely difficult to secure any other employment, and then, only after months of unemployment," he summarized. "Because of age and other factors, many have to accept unskilled jobs at low pay."[39]

Subsequent scholarly work has advanced our understanding by showing that the consequences of job loss were not simply financial. Rather, workers derived a strong sense of identity from their work and were affected psychologically when plants closed. "Lowell mill workers," concluded historian Mary H. Blewett from her interviews in the city, "often demonstrated a commitment to and, for the relatively skilled, a fascination with their machines and work." Lowell workers who were interviewed for a separate local history project also illustrated this attachment. When he lost his job at a local upholstery factory in 1957, Victor Sherburne recalled that it was "quite a blow." Sitting in an empty mill more than thirty years later, he commented that "when I'm in a room like this, I can still feel the beat of the machinery." Hareven and Langenbach's classic study of the Amoskeag Company reached similar conclusions. Some four decades after the shutdown, many workers called themselves "Amoskeag men," and they described their co-workers as "like a family." Decades later, many southern mill workers would return to the family metaphor when their mills also closed.[40]

It is important not to romanticize mill jobs, and many workers recognized that conditions had been harsh, especially as mill owners had an enormous amount of power. In many ways, the close bonds that workers formed with one another were a way of surviving in this hostile environment. In his work on the early textile industry in Fall River, John T. Cumbler shows how an "insidious" system tied workers to the mills. Low wages forced workers into the factories at a young age and kept them there once they reached adulthood. Moreover, because each worker mastered a specific skill it was almost impossible to find work elsewhere. The situation was compounded by the textile industry's location in towns where it was the dominant employer. Many workers resented the mill owners' economic control, but they also needed the mills to survive. Similarly, Amoskeag workers were painfully aware of the company's absolute power, its ability to "blackball you for the rest of your days," yet they still formed what Hareven and Langenbach called a "deep attachment" to their work.[41]

The migration of mills to the South also divided executives, and some southerners were happy to prosper while their northern counterparts struggled. In public, northern mill owners tried to minimize these differences, stressing that the industry had national problems. Upon taking over the presidency of the NTA in 1950, William F. Sullivan called for unity. "A healthy industry in the North is of importance to the industry in the South," he declared, "and healthy and profitable southern operations can be of assistance to the North. Sickness in any part of the industry will impair the functioning of the whole body." By the end of the 1950s, moreover, Sullivan insisted that imports were hurting both regions. "A few years ago," he declared in 1958, "textile problems appeared to be a New England monopoly; now we have competition." Bearing this out, in 1958 the NTA claimed that more spindles had been liquidated in the Southeast than they had in New England, the first time this had ever occurred. Regional divisions were also downplayed by Harvard economist and Governors' Committee chair Seymour Harris, who told the hearings that southern plants were experiencing many of the same "difficulties" as their northern counterparts. While the industry's demise had started as a regional problem, it was turning into a national one.[42]

Within the North, there were also significant divisions between mill owners who wanted to keep old plants open and those who were keen to move to the South. This frustrated many executives, particularly New Bedford's Seabury Stanton. Like other supporters of the northern industry, Stanton hoped to use federal wage legislation to wipe out the wage differential. In early 1949, following the Democratic capture of both houses of Congress, he pushed for a minimum of ninety-seven cents an hour. This was considerably more than many southern workers earned. "In making this suggestion," he wrote Senator Henry Cabot Lodge Jr. of Massachusetts, "I am aware of the fact that many Northern mill men would not be in accord because of the large number who have Southern interests, as well as interests in New England, and who are planning the development of these Southern interests at the expense of the New England area." When the possibility of moving factories to a cheaper labor source overseas occurred much later, the same divisions resurfaced. Again, only part of the industry had the will to stand and fight.[43]

In order to build unity, industry lobbyists tried to focus attention on American mills that were being put out of business by foreign—rather than domestic—competitors. In a special textile supplement published by the *Boston Sunday Herald* in January 1958, for example, Sullivan emphasized the case of Lowell's Merrimack Manufacturing Company, which had recently shut its doors. He blamed the closure of the historic mill, which had operated on an uninterrupted basis since 1823, on foreign competition. Specifically, the mill made velveteens, a fabric that Japan was importing in large quantities. "It is unfortunate," he concluded, "that Lowell must lose 1200 jobs and the oldest established mill in the United States in order to satisfy Japan's desire for a few million extra yards of a particular fabric." Overall, policy makers saw the textile industry as "expendable." For Sullivan, the industry was "too important for national defense and domestic prosperity" for it to be destroyed by unregulated imports.[44]

Despite the NTA's efforts to keep the focus on foreign competition, the group's papers highlight that much of the northern industry was being undermined by competition from *within* the United States. In 1953, the association compiled a seven-page list of New England cotton or rayon mills that had been "liquidated or moved" over the previous thirty years. Overall, more than eleven million spindles had been lost from the region during this period. Examples included American Thread Company in Fall River, Massachusetts, where spindles were "removed South" in 1949, and Pepperell Manufacturing Company in Biddeford, Maine, which had shifted 290,000 spindles to Dixie. In Rhode Island, the historic Crompton Company had also relocated all of its manufacturing operations to the South.[45] Throughout the 1950s, the careful reports of the New England Governors' Textile Committee showed that domestic competition remained a source of conflict. In 1957, for example, the Committee's annual report proclaimed that the "industry's most pressing problem" was "the vigorous competition of new industrial areas."[46]

There were other differences between northern and southern mill owners. In particular, many northern executives called for federal intervention to help their troubled industry, but southerners argued that their companies would thrive if federal agencies left them alone. The difference was highlighted at Pastore's hearings in 1958, where Frederick B. Dent of South Carolina's Mayfair Mills testified that the textile industry had a "fine future" as long as "the fetters of Federal Government control, unfair tax policies and unfair competition" were removed. According to Dent, South Carolina's nonunion mills were successful because of "teamwork" between management and employees. In a diplomatic note to his members, Sullivan called Dent's testimony "an interesting presentation and . . . representative of the attitude taken by Southern Industry witnesses at the hearings." Indeed, some of the southern workers who testified agreed with Dent. "I believe we make better cloth than they could make in New England, which was the reason the mills came south," claimed Robert Edwards, a loom fixer from Enoree, South Carolina. Quality was higher, thought Edwards, because management and labor were willing to "work together."[47] At the hearings, even southern politicians tried to shift attention away from regional issues. "What we want to do is bring the North and South together here," warned South Carolina senator Strom Thurmond, a key member of Pastore's committee. Hoping to focus attention on the industry's problems, Thurmond reminded witnesses that the hearing was "not a regional investigation."[48]

This testimony hinted at broader differences between northerners and southerners. In the North, many companies had a cordial relationship with labor unions, and TWUA leader J. William Belanger sat on the New England Governors' Textile Committee alongside leading manufacturers such as Stanton. The TWUA's papers show that Stanton, who was president of Hathaway Manufacturing Company, corresponded closely with TWUA president Emil Rieve as both sought to raise southern wages. In 1948, Stanton also testified against a bill that would have banned the closed shop, or compulsory union membership. The Hathaway Company had been unionized for seven years, he explained, and the union shop had led to "harmonious relations" between management and labor. Illustrating their close relationship, Rieve subsequently thanked "Seabury" for his "very fine presentation," and both men also worked together as they sought import controls. As Stanton wrote Rieve in 1953, "It is . . . very encouraging to those of us who are working on protection for the textile industry to know that you and your organization are with us in this battle."[49]

In sharp contrast, most southern mill owners were fiercely antiunion, and the region also attracted northern executives who wanted to escape union influence. They included the Stevens family, who had operated unionized mills in the North but opposed organizing efforts in the South. Shortly after World War II, J. P. Stevens closed six large northern mills—all of them unionized—and expanded operations in the South. None of the southern plants were organized, and Stevens's management wanted to keep it that way. Rather than defending the closed shop, southerners—native and adopted—led opposition to it, and by the end of 1947 seven southern states had passed right-to-work laws, which forbade firms from making union membership a condition of employment. More states followed suit in the years that followed, and the South became the largest single area in the country with right-to-work laws.[50]

In a similar fashion, in 1954 New York native Roger Milliken moved his family textile firm to Spartanburg, South Carolina, partly to avoid union influence. In an address to the State Fiscal Survey Commission in 1955, Milliken explained that the Palmetto state offered a higher "quality of labor" than the northern states. The South Carolina worker, he noted, was willing to help managers reduce costs, which was essential in a competitive industry. "This same intelligent attitude," he added, "cannot be said to be held by New England workers who have been influenced and badgered by CIO propaganda to resist all management changes and to throw road blocks in the way of making improvements that will lower costs." Forty years old, the tall, red-haired Milliken epitomized the view that it was unions that were primarily responsible for the industry's problems in the North. Between 1921 and 1954, he explained, the southern textile industry had grown slightly, but the North had lost most of its mills. He concluded that "cooperation" between management and labor was the key reason for this outcome. Like Stevens, Milliken fervently opposed unionization in the South. In 1956, when workers at a company plant in Darlington, South Carolina, voted in the TWUA by forty votes, Milliken closed the mill rather than deal with the union. Because of the tycoon's hard line, it took more than two decades for the case to reach the Supreme Court, which ruled that the mill had been closed to "chill unionism" at other company facilities. The message was certainly not lost on Milliken's workers, who steadfastly avoided the union while the case sat in the courts. During this time, Milliken's empire grew steadily, making its chairman one of the most powerful figures in the industry.[51]

Like the subsequent migration off shore, the movement of the industry within the United States was deeply divisive. Rather than seeking to help their beleaguered northern colleagues, southern producers fought efforts to close the wage differential. In 1951 even the South's unionized mills rejected the TWUA's desperate pleas for a 12 percent wage increase that would have narrowed the regional pay gap, instead enduring a general strike that gravely weakened the union. After the strike the differential—which had narrowed under constant pressure from the union—widened again. While northern mills faced many other problems, including increasing competition from imports, the wage gap was a constant handicap. Northern mill owners were left frustrated with the union's inability to raise southern wages as much as it had promised. "How long must New England mills go on being destroyed by a double-standard—one for the South, another for New England?" asked one after the doomed strike.[52]

In 1952, the New England Governors' Textile Committee made several recommendations that illustrated the industry's divisions. The committee mandated that southerners should follow their northern counterparts and accept trade unionism as a "vital necessity," a suggestion that did not go down well. As both northerners and southerners realized, unions would raise southern wages. The committee also criticized the South's powerful congressional delegation, claiming that it fought for sectional interests. "It would be better," the committee suggested, "if Southern Congressmen emphasized the national interest to the extent that New England Congressmen do."[53] Further aggravating the issue, northern and southern mill owners belonged to separate professional associations. Although it had some northern members, the ATMI was southern-dominated, while the Northern Textile Association was the main lobby group for the rest of the industry.[54] The regional base of both groups reflected the industry's long history. The NTA's lineage dated back to 1854, when New England's mills were in the ascendancy, whereas the ATMI was not established until 1949, when the South had established itself as the dominant textile region. In its early years, moreover, the ATMI was based in Charlotte.[55]

Driven partly by a desire to protect its members' jobs in the North, the TWUA repeatedly tried to organize the South. The union played a central role in the CIO's "Operation Dixie," an ambitious effort to organize the entire region. Initiated in the summer of 1946, Operation Dixie ran into determined opposition from southern executives and politicians, and although efforts carried on until 1953, concrete gains were limited.[56] In the year that the drive ended, just 13.3 percent of textile workers in the Carolinas, Georgia, Alabama, and Tennessee were unionized, whereas in the key northern centers of Fall River and New Bedford workers had been solidly organized for decades.[57] Privately, TWUA leaders doubted that they would ever crack the South. As the union's Executive Council noted in November

1953, "In the South today there seems to be a greater desire for organizing than in the recent past but this desire seems to extend to about 25% of the workers in each mill." There would be no easy victories.[58]

Because the bulk of the TWUA's membership was in the North, deindustrialization had a devastating impact on the union, and its subsequent fight for import controls was largely motivated by self-preservation. Between 1951 and 1958, for example, the union lost 164,770 members. According to figures collected by the NTA, over three-quarters of the mills that closed in New England between 1949 and 1968 had been unionized.[59] At the time, many Americans blamed the union for the industry's demise. According to this line of argument, the union's desire for higher wages had forced manufacturers to move to the South. More recently, scholars have pointed out that these claims—which retain a hold in popular memory—have been exaggerated. According to David Koistinen, low-cost competitors that were "founded, managed, and financed" by southerners put most New England mills out of business. Only a minority of New England firms set up southern plants, or "runaway shops" as union leaders called them. Others have noted that in the early stages of the migration, unions were an insignificant presence in New England's mills, and they only become more common once the process was well underway. As Milliken's example shows, however, some prominent northern companies did run away from unions.[60]

Although they did not intend to hurt northern production, unions must bear some responsibility for the industry's decline. Since its foundation in 1939, the TWUA had argued that textile workers deserved much better pay. In 1959, for example, the union's executive council declared that "our goal is to bring textile workers up to par with all other industrial workers in our society."[61] This pressure to raise wages at a time when northern companies were facing severe competition from low-wage southern mills did contribute to the industry's problems. The union found itself caught in a horrible quandary; in order to survive institutionally, it needed to deliver benefits to its members, yet in doing so it inadvertently contributed to the industry's demise. As the New England Governors' Committee summarized in 1952, "The trade union leaders face a dilemma: if they allow other Northern wages to gain on textiles, they face discontent, challenges to their leadership and even loss of members. If they insist on keeping up with the Northern standards, while the South resists all pressure to raise its wages, they encourage the migration of the industry from New England."[62]

The TWUA faced other problems. Reports from its officials on the ground showed that many northern workers saw wage increases as compensation for the heavier workloads that they had to endure as companies tried to stay in business. Raising workloads was always difficult for the union. In 1952, for example, the union was forced to accept increased workloads at the Pequot Sheeting Mill in Salem, Massachusetts, because the company had already opened a plant in South Carolina. The move allowed the Salem plant to stay open, but it was not popular with workers, some of whom were required to tend as many as fifty looms. In February 1958, the TWUA's Edward Doolan similarly reported from Fall River, where local mills had either shut down or raised workloads. "The feeling of the people is that we should push for a wage increase because of the cost of living," he wrote, "along with the increased work loads makes them feel that they are deserving of something."[63]

Furthermore, in its battle to raise wages the union also popularized the industry's poor image, and opponents would later use this to claim that textile jobs were not worth saving. The TWUA constantly argued that southern textile workers, in particular, were the poor relations of their better-paid, unionized counterparts in the North. All textile workers, meanwhile, lagged behind their counterparts in industries such as steel and autos, which the union held up as its model. In 1961, for example, the TWUA's Executive Council declared in a resolution that "the backwardness of the textile industry in providing decent wages and economic security for its workers is a blot on our Great Society." For the TWUA, the industry's treatment of its workers was a "national disgrace."[64]

By the 1950s, much of the apparel industry, which had originated in the northeast, was also moving "out of town." The industry—which had been solidly organized by the ILGWU and the ACWA in big northern centers—was initially attracted by the cheaper wages available in rural areas of New York, Massachusetts, and Pennsylvania. In Pennsylvania's declining hard-coal region, for example, the garment industry gained a foothold as the mines closed, setting up plants in small, isolated communities. These factories offered valuable jobs to the wives and daughters of the displaced miners. By the 1960s, there were two thousand apparel factories in Pennsylvania, and they employed nearly 180,000 people. Although the ILGWU did eventually gain a foothold in the region, this only encouraged the industry to move again.[65]

It was not long, indeed, before companies were lured South by the even lower wages available there. In 1949, there were 339,000 apparel workers in the New York metropolitan area, but by 1960 this number had fallen to 271,200. Over the same period, the number of apparel workers nationally held steady—what was changing was where they were based. The "runaway shops" were attracted to Dixie by local elites who promised that they would keep unions out, even if they had to use violence and intimidation to do so. Like the TWUA, the ILGWU and ACWA found itself struggling to organize the South yet facing a backlash from northern members who were reluctant to endure wage freezes and higher workloads. "As an increasing number of apparel producers moved out of town," writes scholar Ellen Israel Rosen, "especially to the South, the labor-management accord began to fall apart."

In 1958 the ILGWU struck factories in seven Northeastern states in an effort to secure a 15 percent wage hike, but manufacturers refused to grant the increase, claimed that they could not absorb the higher costs and compete with the lower-wage South.[66]

Events in apparel highlighted how this labor-intensive, low-wage industry was particularly susceptible to capital flight and deindustrialization. As ILGWU leader Sol Chaikin later reflected, "Relocating the garment industry was not difficult since it is an industry on wheels. It can be moved overnight because capital investment is low, machines are easily transportable and materials are comparatively light. Clothes are not steel, not copper, not lumber, not brick." Through a study of the Allied Signal Seat Belt Company, sociologists John Gaventa and Barbara Ellen Smith illustrated the propensity of apparel makers to move. The firm originally shifted from Michigan to Knoxville, Tennessee, in search of lower wages, but within a few years it had moved to Greenville, Alabama, where wages were even lower. Later, the firm began to transfer most of the Alabama jobs to a new plant in Mexico, part of an emerging trend among apparel firms. In general, however, moving off shore did not become common until the 1970s. Prior to this, most textile and apparel companies relocated within the United States.[67]

For both managers and union leaders in the North, then, the issue of southern competition was highly divisive. While northerners supported interregional wage equalization and unionization, southerners strongly opposed both. In sharp contrast, the issue of import control united the industry. As imports gradually began to threaten all mills, the northern and southern branches came together to fight for stricter controls. Partly for these strategies reasons, the TWUA emphasized that imports were not simply a northern problem. At Senate hearings held in Charlotte in September 1958, for example, union data showed that many mills were also closing in the South. Between 1952 and 1958, 115 plants closed in eleven southern states, and 31,855 workers lost their jobs. North Carolina suffered more shutdowns than any other southern state, and the bulk of them occurred in small towns.[68]

The hearings also highlighted that there was plenty of genuine concern among southerners about the industry's future. As W. J. Erwin of Virginia's Dan River Mills complained, overseas mills had "invaded" the American market and were making important inroads. "Foreign producers," he explained, "in large measure because of their dismally low wage levels by United States standards, can and do undersell domestic textile manufacturers in the domestic marketplace." The president of a mill in Rock Hill, South Carolina, that had operated for over sixty years, W. J. Roddey Jr. had similar grievances. Recently, the Victoria Cotton Mill had been forced to close, and Roddey blamed imports, especially from Japan. "We in the carded gingham industry," he explained, "saw most of our customers and our market taken over by the influx of foreign goods with which we had no earthly chance to compete."[69]

By 1958, imports were a problem for the entire textile and apparel complex, and Pastore's hearings—which ended up recommending strict quotas—highlighted how manufacturers were fighting back. Even in New England, sizeable economic interests were at stake. The industry still provided many jobs, and the retail and service sectors also relied heavily on mill workers' purchases. According to the New England Governors' Committee on Textiles, the liquidation of the region's textile industry would be catastrophic, causing $1.5 billion of capital to be lost. In the South, the textile industry was the biggest employer, and its cultural and political influence was immense. As the *New York Times*'s Henry P. Leifermann put it, the industry was "the bedrock of the Deep South's economy, religion, politics, industry." The industry packed a sizeable punch, and as imports increased this became more and more evident.[70]

## NOTES

1. Barry Bluestone, "Foreword," in Cowie and Heathcott, *Beyond the Ruins*, p. viii (quotation); Bluestone and Harrison, *The Deindustrialization of America*, p. 4.

2. Mary Beth Norton et al., *A People and a Nation: A History of the United States, Sixth Edition* (Boston: Houghton Mifflin, 2001), p. 790; Alan Brinkley, *American History: A Survey, Volume II, since 1865, Eleventh Edition* (Boston: McGraw Hill, 2003), p. 799; David M. Kennedy, Lizabeth Cohen, and Thomas A. Bailey, *The American Pageant: A History of the Republic, Volume II, since 1865, Thirteenth Edition* (Boston: Houghton Mifflin, 2006), pp. xi (first quotation), 882–84 (second quotation on p. 882); John Kenneth Galbraith, *The Affluent Society* (Boston: Houghton Mifflin, 1958).

3. William F. Hartford, *Where Is Our Responsibility?: Unions and Economic Change in the New England Textile Industry, 1870–1960* (Amherst: University of Massachusetts Press, 1996), p. 151; "New England Textile Mill Employment, 1947–1977," NTA Data, January 1978, "Textile Industry 1975–78, 2 of 2" folder, box 13, MS 106.3.3.17.1, Cohen Papers; Statement of William F. Sullivan at the NTA Annual Meeting, September 27, 1956, vol. 1.28, 1956 NTA Annual Meeting Files, NTA Papers; Closing quotation in Testimony of William Pollock, July 9, 1958, p. 277, U.S. Congress, Senate, Committee on Interstate and Foreign Commerce, *Problems of the Domestic Textile Industry*, 85th Congress, 2nd Session, 1958.

4. TWUA Executive Council Minutes, September 8–11, 1952, "1952–55" folder, box 1, Mss. 396, TWUA Papers.

5. First three quotations in TWUA Executive Council Minutes, June 17–21, 1957, p. 9, "1956–58" folder, box 1, Mss. 396, TWUA Papers; Final two quotations in TWUA Executive Council Minutes, February 17–20, 1958, p. 23, "1956–58" folder, box 1, Mss. 396, TWUA Papers.

6. Testimony of William Pollock, July 9, 1958, p. 277, U.S. Congress, Senate, Committee on Interstate and Foreign Commerce (quotation); *New England Textiles and the New England Economy* (Report by the New England Governors' Textile Committee to the Conference of New England Governors), 1958–59, p. II-45, American Textile History Museum library in Lowell, Massachusetts, hereafter cited as ATHM.

7. Opening quotation in "Japan's Textiles Stir New Protest," *New York Times*, July 21, 1956, p. 19; "Remarks of U.S. Senator John O. Pastore at the Annual Dinner of the Market Committee of the ATMI," January 28, 1965, folder 10, box 24, Speech files, Pastore Papers; Testimony of Halbert M. Jones, July 8, 1958, p. 7, U.S. Congress, Senate, Committee on

Interstate and Foreign Commerce; Testimony of Edwin Wilkinson, November 12, 1958, p. 1213, U.S. Congress, Senate, Committee on Interstate and Foreign Commerce; Testimony of John Arpino, November 14, 1958, p. 1546, U.S. Congress, Senate, Committee on Interstate and Foreign Commerce.

8. R. Buford Brandis, "The Making of Textile Trade Policy, 1935–1981" (ATMI Study), pp. 16–17, copy in "Textiles: The Making of Textile Trade Policy, 1935–1981" folder, Michael A. Driggs files, Reagan Library; Pastore quoted in cross-examination of William F. Sullivan, July 9, 1958, p. 230, U.S. Congress, Senate, Committee on Interstate and Foreign Commerce.

9. Hartford, *Where Is Our Responsibility?* p. 1.

10. James A. Hodges, *New Deal Labor Policy and the Southern Cotton Textile Industry, 1933–1941* (Knoxville: University of Tennessee Press, 1986), pp. 9–12; Salmond, *The General Textile Strike of 1934*, p. 2 (quotation); Alice Galenson, *The Migration of the Cotton Textile Industry from New England to the South, 1880–1930* (New York: Garland Publishing, 1985), pp. 1–3.

11. Salmond, *The General Textile Strike of 1934*, pp. 2–4; David Koistinen, "The Causes of Deindustrialization: The Migration of the Cotton Textile Industry from New England to the South," *Enterprise and Society* 3 (September 2002), p. 484. For important works on the decline of the New England textile industry that explore the points made in this paragraph in greater depth, see Galenson, *The Migration of the Cotton Textile Industry*; Hartford, *Where Is Our Responsibility*?; Nancy Frances Kane, *Textiles in Transition: Technology, Wages, and Industry Relocation in the U.S. Textile Industry, 1880–1930* (Westport, CT: Greenwood Press, 1988); Laurence F. Gross, *The Course of Industrial Decline: The Boott Cotton Mills of Lowell, Massachusetts, 1835–1955* (Baltimore and London: The Johns Hopkins University Press, 1993); Seymour Louis Wolfbein, *The Decline of a Cotton Textile City: A Study of New Bedford* (New York: Columbia University Press, 1944); William F. Hartford, *Working People of Holyoke: Class and Ethnicity in a Massachusetts Mill Town, 1850–1960* (New Brunswick: Rutgers University Press, 1990), pp. 183–209; Mary H. Blewett, *The Last Generation: Work and Life in the Textile Mills of Lowell, Massachusetts, 1910–1960* (Amherst: The University of Massachusetts Press, 1990).

12. Galenson, *The Migration of the Cotton Textile Industry*, pp. 140, 190 (quotation).

13. *Report on the New England Textile Industry by the Committee Appointed by the Conference of New England Governors*, 1952, pp. 5–6, ATHM. On the difficulties of organizing unions in the early textile South, the literature is vast. For a useful summary, see Irons, *Testing the New Deal*, pp. 13–37.

14. "Transactions of the National Association of Cotton Manufacturers Annual Meeting," No. 112, April 27–28, 1922, pp. 288, 290, ATHM.

15. "NTA, New England Cotton-Rayon Mills Liquidated or Moved, 1924–1952," folder 24.12, box 24, NTA Papers; "Statement of Judge A. B. Cason on Behalf of the Massachusetts Rayon and Cotton Textile Mills," April 8, 1952, folder 24.13, box 24, NTA Papers.

16. David Koistinen, "The Political Economy of Deindustrialization: Business, Labor, and the State during the Decline of the New England Textile Industry," p. 11 (unpublished book manuscript in author's possession, cited with permission from David Koistinen); "Bay State Mills Seek 54-Hour Week," *New York Times*, November 16, 1925, p. 21 (quotations).

17. Wolfbein quoted in Salmond, *The General Textile Strike of 1934*, p. 2. For more detail on New Bedford, see Wolfbein, *The Decline of a Cotton Textile City*.

18. "Roosevelt Hears Textile Demands," *New York Times*, April 13, 1955, p. 6 ("ruin" quotation); Francis Brown, "A New England Chapter Is Closed at Amoskeag," *New York Times Magazine*, November 15, 1936, p. SM6 (other quotations).

19. Tamara K. Hareven and Randolph Langenbach, *Amoskeag: Life and Work in an American Factory City* (New York: Pantheon Books, 1978), pp. 26 (first two quotations), 305–06, 354–55 (Erskine quotation), 358 (Smith quotations).

20. Michael C. C. Adams, *The Best War Ever: America and World War II* (Baltimore and London: Johns Hopkins University Press, 1994), p. 6.

21. TWUA Executive Council Minutes, March 13 and 14, 1944, "1939–46" folder, box 1, Mss. 396, TWUA Papers.

22. Koistinen, "The Political Economy of Deindustrialization," chapter 6, pp. 2–3, quotation on p. 3; Stanton quoted in Joseph A. Loftus, "Minimum-Pay Rise in Textiles Urged," *New York Times*, November 1, 1950, p. 52.

23. "New England Mill Liquidations 1949–1957," folder 24.12, box 24, NTA Papers; Quotation in "Statement of Judge A. B. Cason on Behalf of the Massachusetts Rayon and Cotton Textile Mills," April 8, 1952, folder 24.13, box 24, NTA Papers; Roger Milliken, "Teamwork: The South's Secret Weapon," Presentation before the South Carolina Fiscal Survey Commision, October 12, 1955, folder 24.10, box 24, NTA Papers.

24. Sherman Adams et al. to Maurice J. Tobin, November 15, 1951, folder 516, box 42, National Association of Cotton Manufacturers/Northern Textile Association Papers, 1896–1970, MSS73/327, held at the American Textile History Museum, Lowell, Massachusetts, hereafter cited as "NACM/NTA Papers."

25. Testimony of Jack Rubenstein before the Pastore Subcommittee of the Senate Committee on Interstate and Foreign Commerce, November 13–14, 1958, "Pastore Hearings" folder, box 524, Mss. 396, TWUA Papers. For an important study of the pre–World War II textile industry in Philadelphia that throws light on the early problems experienced by the industry in the mid-Atlantic region as a whole, see Philip Scranton, *Figured Tapestry: Production, Markets, and Power in Philadelphia Textiles, 1885–1941* (Cambridge: Cambridge University Press, 1989), esp. pp. 1–16.

26. Testimony of David McKnight, November 14, 1958, p. 1422, U.S. Congress, Senate, Committee on Interstate and Foreign Commerce; Testimony of Charlotte Marsh, November 14, 1958, p. 1534, U.S. Congress, Senate, Committee on Interstate and Foreign Commerce; Testimony of John Arpino, November 14, 1958, pp. 1544–46; Testimony of Jack Rubenstein before the Pastore Subcommittee of the Senate Committee on Interstate and Foreign Commerce, November 13–14, 1958, "Pastore Hearings" folder, box 524, Mss. 396, TWUA Papers; Testimony of Charles Hughes, November 14, 1958, p. 1577, U.S. Congress, Senate, Committee on Interstate and Foreign Commerce.

27. Testimony of Sol Stetin, November 14, 1958, p. 1424, U.S. Congress, Senate, Committee on Interstate and Foreign Commerce; Testimony of Frank Kroger, November 14, 1958, p. 1451, U.S. Congress, Senate, Committee on Interstate and Foreign Commerce.

28. Testimony of Vera Malenda, November 14, 1958, p. 1466, U.S. Congress, Senate, Committee on Interstate and Foreign Commerce.

29. TWUA Executive Council Minutes, November 11–14, 1961, p. 1, "1959–61" folder, box 1, Mss. 396, TWUA Papers; Herman E. Talmadge Textile Speech ca. 1953, folder 10, box 36, Early Office files, Talmadge Papers. For more on "My Hometown," see Bruce Springsteen's website at http://brucespringsteen.net/songs/my-hometown (accessed January 25, 2011, copy in author's possession). As well as the mill closure, the song also links the town's problems to subsequent racial tensions at the local high school.

30. "American Cotton Textile Industry and Foreign Trade Policy," TWUA Research Paper I-197T, November 1957, "ILGWU, TWUA, and Other Union Statements on Imports" folder, box 532, ACTWU Papers-Cornell.

31. Felix P. Damore, "Area Activity Report," October 15, 1957 through June 10, 1958, "Central Massachusetts Joint Board Felix Damore" folder, box 14, Mss. 396, TWUA Papers; Irving Epstein to William Pollock, January 23, 1958, "Greater New York Joint Board 1958 Irving Epstein" folder, box 14, Mss. 396, TWUA Papers. For another similar example, see Sol Stetin, "Organizational Report—Wilkes-Barre-Scranton-Williamsport Area," March 29, 1958, "Sol Stetin Organizing Reports 1958" folder, box 14, Mss. 396, TWUA Papers.

32. Michael Schoonjans to William Pollock, November 14, 1958, and April 22, 1958 (closing quotation), "Biddeford-Saco Joint Board Michael Schoonjans 1958" folder, box 14, Mss. 396, TWUA Papers.

33. "Statement of Victor Canzano before the Committee on Interstate and Foreign Commerce of the United States Senate," September 17, 1958, "Pastore Hearings" folder, box 524, Mss. 396, TWUA Papers.

34. Address of Sherman Adams to the Annual Meeting of the Northern Textile Association, September 27, 1956, vol. 1.28, NTA 1956 Annual Meeting Files, NTA Papers; Testimony of

Hon. W. T. M. Beale, December 2, 1958, pp. 1714, 1716 ("difficulties" quotation), U.S. Congress, Senate, Committee on Interstate and Foreign Commerce.

35. Testimony of Hon. Frederick H. Mueller, December 2, 1958, pp. 1811–19, first quotation on p. 1818; "Northern Textile Group Warned on Competition and Instability," *New York Times*, September 26, 1958, p. 37 (Pastore quotation).

36. Testimony of Mike Masaoka, November 14, 1958, pp. 1617 (first two quotations), 1661 (final quotation), U.S. Congress, Senate, Committee on Interstate and Foreign Commerce; Testimony of Noel Hemmendinger, November 14, 1958, pp. 1697, 1698, U.S. Congress, Senate, Committee on Interstate and Foreign Commerce; Testimony of Donald Comer, December 2, 1958, p. 1891, U.S. Congress, Senate, Committee on Interstate and Foreign Commerce.

37. "A Study of Displaced Textile Workers," *Textile Age*, March 1955, p. 70; William H. Miernyk, *Inter-Industry Labor Mobility: The Case of the Displaced Textile Worker* (Boston: Bureau of Business and Economic Research, Northeastern University, 1955), pp. 17–22, quotations on p. 20. Miernyk studied the Massachusetts communities of Lowell, Lawrence, Fall River, and New Bedford, as well as Providence, Rhode Island, and one "non-textile" area.

38. George Perazich and W. T. Stone, "Economic Effect of Textile Mill Closings: Selected Communities in Middle Atlantic States" (Washington, DC: U.S. Government Printing Office, 1963), pp. 2 (first two quotations), 3, 17 (third quotation), 36 (final quotation), copy cited in folder 24.10, box 24, NTA Papers.

39. William F. Sullivan to Wilbur D. Mills, September 21, 1967, folder 1707, box 148, NACM/NTA Papers.

40. Blewett, *The Last Generation*, p. xix (first two quotations); Interview with Victor Sherburne in *The Workers Remember* (VHS produced by Lowell National Historical Park, Lowell, Massachusetts, 1994); Hareven and Langenbach, *Amoskeag*, pp. 11–12. For the use of the family metaphor in a southern context, see Hall et al., *Like a Family*, esp. pp. xvii–xviii. The use of the family metaphor by southern workers in the 1990s and 2000s is explored more fully in chapters 8 and 9.

41. John T. Cumbler, *Working-Class Community in Industrial America: Work, Leisure, and Struggle in Two Industrial Cities, 1880–1930* (Westport, CT: Greenwood Press, 1979), p. 145; Hareven and Langenbach, *Amoskeag*, p. 11 (first quotation by former weaver William Moul), p. 12 (second quotation).

42. "Remarks of William F. Sullivan, President," September 28, 1950, folder 401, box 34, NACM/NTA Papers; Statement of Northern Textile Association before the Committee on Interstate and Foreign Commerce of the U.S. Senate, p. 2, July 8, 1958, folder 787, box 72, NACM/NTA Papers (1958 quotations); Testimony of William F. Sullivan, July 8, 1958, p. 217, U.S. Congress, Senate, Committee on Interstate and Foreign Commerce; Harris quoted in Testimony of Seymour E. Harris, July 9, 1958, p. 441, U.S. Congress, Senate, Committee on Interstate and Foreign Commerce.

43. Seabury Stanton to Henry Cabot Lodge Jr., March 2, 1949, "Hathaway Manufacturing Company (1)," folder, box 53, Mss. 396, TWUA Papers (quotations); "Seabury Stanton (1892–1971)," profile available at the website of the National Textile Association at http://www.nationaltextile.org/people/stanton_seabury.htm (accessed February 9, 2011, copy in author's possession).

44. "Statement of William F. Sullivan, Counsel, Northern Textile Association, for *Boston Sunday Herald* Textile Supplement," January 19, 1958, copy in "Tariffs" folder, "General Files, RU-TN," Pastore Papers. The Merrimack Manufacturing Company closure is discussed in greater detail in chapter 9.

45. "New England Cotton-Rayon Mills Liquidated or Moved—1924–1952," folder 24.12, box 24, NTA Papers.

46. *Report on the New England Textile Industry by the Committee Appointed by the Conference of New England Governors*, 1952, pp. 5–6; *New England Textiles and the New England Economy* (Report by the New England Governors' Textile Committee to the Conference of New England Governors,) March 1957, p. I-1, both at ATHM.

47. William F. Sullivan to Member Mill Executives, October 24, 1958, and Testimony of Frederick B. Dent, September 29, 1958, both folder 24.11, box 24, NTA Papers; Testimony of

Robert Edwards, September 29, 1958, p. 1005, U.S. Congress, Senate, Committee on Interstate and Foreign Commerce.

48. Thurmond quoted in cross-examination of Seymour E. Harris, July 9, 1958, p. 465, U.S. Congress, Senate, Committee on Interstate and Foreign Commerce.

49. Seabury Stanton, "In Opposition to House Bill #1745," ca. 1948 (first quotation); Seabury Stanton to Emil Rieve, August 20, 1947; and Emil Rieve to Seabury Stanton, April 12, 1948 (Rieve quotations), all "Hathaway Manufacturing Company (1)" folder, box 53, Mss. 396, TWUA Papers; Seabury Stanton to Emil Rieve, November 25, 1953, "Hathaway Manufacturing Company (2)" folder, box 53, Mss. 396, TWUA Papers.

50. Minchin, *"Don't Sleep With Stevens!"* pp. 9–12; Timothy J. Minchin, *Fighting against the Odds: A History of Southern Labor since World War II* (Gainesville: University Press of Florida, 2005), pp. 45, 185.

51. Roger Milliken, "Teamwork: The South's Secret Weapon," Presentation before the South Carolina Fiscal Survey Commission, October 12, 1955, folder 24.10, box 24, NTA Papers (Milliken quotations); John Monk, "Roger Milliken: The Last Textile Giant," *The State*, October 7, 2001, p. D1; "Roger Milliken (1915–2010)," *Textile World*, January 4, 2011, obituary available at http://www.textileworld.com/Articles/2011/January/Roger_Milliken.html (accessed January 7, 2011, copy in author's possession). For the Darlington case, see Hodges, *New Deal Labor Policy and the Southern Cotton Textile Industry*, pp. 193–94; Bill Arthur, "The Darlington Mills Case: Or 17 Years Before the Courts," *New South* 28:3 (1973), pp. 40–47 (final quotation on p. 40).

52. Hartford, *Where Is Our Responsibility*? pp. 85–86; Timothy J. Minchin, *What Do We Need a Union For?: The TWUA in the South, 1945–1955* (Chapel Hill: University of North Carolina Press, 1997), pp. 65, 100–01, 156–57 (quotation on p. 157).

53. *Report on the New England Textile Industry by the Committee Appointed by the Conference of New England Governors*, 1952, p. 11, ATHM.

54. "ATMI Active Members," May 1, 1966–April 30, 1967, folder 1587, box 140, NACM/NTA Papers; Quotation in Herbert Koshetz, "Cotton Mills Told to 'Get Out of Rut,'" *New York Times*, September 26, 1952, p. 31.

55. William F. Sullivan to All Members of the Northern Textile Association and National Association of Cotton Manufacturers, September 5, 1956, vol. 1.28, 1956 Annual Meeting Files, NTA Papers; Stella M. Hopkins, "Textile Institute Continues Long-Term Battle with Imports: Organization Holding 50th Annual Meeting," *The State*, March 11, 1999, p. B6.

56. Barbara S. Griffith, *The Crisis of American Labor: Operation Dixie and the Defeat of the CIO* (Philadelphia: Temple University Press, 1988), esp. pp. 49–61; Minchin, *What Do We Need a Union For*? pp. 26–47.

57. *New England Textiles and the New England Economy* (Report by the New England Governors' Textile Committee to the Conference of New England Governors), March 1958, p. I-34, ATHM; Hartford, *Where Is Our Responsibility*? pp. 5–33.

58. TWUA Executive Council Minutes, November 9–12, 1953, "1952–55" folder, box 1, Mss. 396, TWUA Papers.

59. Hartford, *Where Is Our Responsibility?*, pp. 151–52, 239 (statistic); "New England Cotton and Synthetic Textile Mills Which Ceased Operations, 1949 to Present," folder 24.12, box 24, NTA Papers.

60. Koistinen, "The Causes of Deindustrialization," pp. 482–86, quotation on p. 482; Salmond, *The General Textile Strike of 1934*, p. 3; Hartford, *Where Is Our Responsibility*? p. 1; Hartford, *Working People of Holyoke*, pp. 183–84; Gross, *The Course of Industrial Decline*, pp. 95, 165.

61. TWUA Executive Council Minutes, February 2–6, 1959, "Executive Council Meeting, February 2–6, 1959" folder, box 8, Mss. 396, TWUA Papers.

62. *Report on the New England Textile Industry by the Committee Appointed by the Conference of New England Governors*, 1952, p. 5, ATHM.

63. John H. Fenton, "Work-Load Raised at Bay State Mill," *New York Times*, November 14, 1952, p. 15; Edward F. Doolan, "Area Activity Report," February 6, 1958, "Greater Fall River Joint Board Edward Doolan 1958" folder, box 14, TWUA Papers, Mss. 396 (Doolan quotations).

64. TWUA Executive Council Minutes, January 18–22, 1965, "1962–63" folder, box 2, Mss. 396, TWUA Papers.

65. Rosen, *Making Sweatshops*, p. 98 (quotation); Wolensky et al., *Fighting for the Union Label*, pp. 11–12.

66. Rosen, *Making Sweatshops*, pp. 98–102 (quotations on pp. 100–01); Testimony of Seymor E. Harris, July 9, 1958, p. 434, U.S. Congress, Senate, Committee on Interstate and Foreign Commerce.

67. Chaikin quoted in Wolensky et al., *Fighting for the Union Label*, p. 1; Gaventa and Smith, "The Deindustrialization of the Textile South," pp. 188–91; Rosen, *Making Sweatshops*, p. 99.

68. "Southern Textile Mills (Other Than Hosiery) Liquidated, 1956–1958," TWUA Data, September 1958, folder 24.11, box 24, NTA Papers.

69. Testimony of W. J. Erwin, July 8, 1958, p. 78 (second and third quotations), p. 82 (first quotation), U.S. Congress, Senate, Committee on Interstate and Foreign Commerce; Letter from W. J. Roddey Jr. to Strom Thurmond, June 26, 1958, extracted on pp. 242–43, U.S. Congress, Senate, Committee on Interstate and Foreign Commerce.

70. *Report on the New England Textile Industry by the Committee Appointed by the Conference of New England Governors*, 1952, p. 3, ATHM; Henry P. Leifermann, "Trouble in the South's First Industry: The Unions Are Coming," *New York Times Magazine*, August 5, 1973, p. 10.

## *Chapter Two*

# Mobilizing Against the Import Threat

For the textile and apparel industry, imports became a problem much sooner than they were for most other American industries. They first emerged as a major issue in the 1930s, when Japan became a large exporter of low-priced cotton goods. Following American complaints, Japan agreed to voluntarily restrict its textile exports to the United States in 1937, a pledge it repeated twenty years later. Responding to ongoing lobbying from mill owners, in 1962 the Kennedy administration oversaw the introduction of the Long-Term Agreement, the first multilateral controls over the textile trade. These were also aimed largely at Japan. They failed to satisfy the industry, however, largely because imports increasingly came from Hong Kong, Taiwan, and South Korea. This "Big Three" soon displaced Japan as the biggest suppliers of textiles and apparel to the American and European markets. Dissatisfied with the Long-Term Agreement, domestic manufacturers joined with union leaders and demanded mandatory import quotas, setting the stage for the major legislative battles of the 1980s. In the process, they illustrated the power of America's largest industrial complex and the way that its demise had wide-ranging consequences.[1]

The growth of imports reflected global changes. As early as 1958, for example, the New England Governors' Textile Committee had noted the rise of foreign competition, adding that "underdeveloped countries are taking strong protectionist measures in order to foster their textile industries."[2] In the wake of the economic devastation wrought by World War II, the textile industry was the pioneer industry for emerging economies, particularly Asian powers such as Japan, South Korea, and China. In 1958, the Northern Textile Association estimated that about sixteen million people were employed in the textile industry worldwide, and this number grew sharply in the decades that followed. By 1968, textile imports accounted for one-third of the U.S. balance of payments deficit.[3]

As a low-wage, unskilled industry where labor made up a significant portion of the production cost, textiles and apparel was particularly susceptible to import competition, something that both manufacturers and labor leaders were acutely aware of. From an early stage, the industry rallied against imports. The National Association of Cotton Manufacturers—the predecessor of the Northern Textile Association—played a particularly important role. In November 1918, the NACM formally demanded "adequate protection" for domestic mills. "Free trade and a low tariff will reduce our working people to the scale of wages and of living which exist in competing countries," it declared. A few years later, the Association warned that "an adequate protective tariff bill" was needed to guard against "the abnormally low costs of production abroad."[4] In calling for protection, the NACM occasionally drew on racial fears. In October 1936, the Association noted its concern about Japanese imports, which had reached more than forty-nine million yards in the first seven months of the year. It added that substantive action was required to protect American workers "from cheap Oriental labor." The following year, it declared that existing tariffs offered little protection against "coolie" wages. These precedents were significant; after World War II, opponents would accuse the industry of racism as it sought controls aimed at Asian nations, charges that undermined its legislative campaign.[5]

Japan certainly posed a real threat to American dominance of textile production. As economist Michael Smitka has shown, the cotton textile industry was "the first major 'modern' industry" to emerge in Japan, and it remained the largest manufacturing sector for over sixty years. In 1897, the Asian country became a net exporter of yarn, while thirteen years later it achieved the same status for cotton. As well as being a major employer, the textile industry also pioneered the development of efficient management techniques and mass manufacturing technology. In particular, Japanese mills prospered through the adoption of "ring" technology, which permitted greater operating speeds. As in New England, where early mills relied heavily on female labor, the Japanese industry's growth was inextricably linked to the recruitment of unmarried women from the countryside.[6] After World War II, textiles played a central role in Japan's remarkable recovery from military defeat and industrial devastation. As the *New York Times* reported in 1968, Japan had progressed "from complete ruin two decades ago to the front rank of industrial nations." Building on its strength as an industry before the war, textiles and yarn were Japan's chief exports, constituting 17 percent of the total. In the same year, ATMI official A. Lee Parsons reported from a field visit that Japan's textile industry was well organized and export oriented. Overall, Parsons concluded that "the spectre of the economic shadow of Japan is awesome."[7]

Almost as soon as Japan had cemented itself as a textile powerhouse, however, it was challenged by other Asian nations. Between 1962 and 1966, developing countries raised their share of the world market for cotton goods from 24 to 32 percent, yet the Japanese share actually fell. In one key policy paper, the U.S. Commerce Department's Office of Textiles and Apparel summed up the industry's importance to emerging economies: "For many developing countries, textile and apparel exports are one of the chief sources of employment and foreign exchange earnings." Because the United States had the world's biggest textile and apparel market, it was a key target for exporters.[8]

In the United States, management and labor agreed that the import problem had to be tackled, and they worked together at a time when there was little broader concern about import levels. In 1945—while most Americans were enjoying unprecedented prosperity—the TWUA asserted that import quotas on textiles were needed.[9] From the 1950s through to the 1970s, the textile and apparel unions laid the groundwork for the high-profile anti-import fight that followed. When the TWUA and ACWA merged in 1976, they had a shared history of fighting against imports. As the TWUA's Executive Council reflected, "For two decades the ACWA and TWUA have been working to impress upon the general public and on government the seriousness of the import situation and its devastating effect on the American job market. We have emphasized that we are not against trade, but only in favor of regulation of trade to avoid disruption and avoidable unemployment."[10] In industry circles, textile leaders also pioneered in raising concerns about imports. As the NTA's William F. Sullivan wrote in 1958, "The textile industries have borne a disproportionate share of the burden of foreign trade. Unlike some industries which have benefited from exports and prospered from sales financed with foreign aid funds and military procurement, the textile industries have borne the impact of increased imports and shrinking markets."[11]

In the basic textile industry, imports were clearly a problem even when the national economy was doing well. In 1957, for example, a TWUA paper on trade called for "an outright quota system on imports," a solution that few supported at the time, even in the labor movement.[12] In another paper written the following year, TWUA research director Solomon Barkin repeated the message. "Imports," complained the New Yorker, "have been particularly demoralizing because they have intensified the degree of price competition, as well as taken away a sector of the domestic market."[13] In 1961, a resolution passed by the TWUA's executive council expressed concern about the "disastrous impact of imports," particularly on northern carpet and rug workers.[14]

The other major textile union, the AFL's United Textile Workers, was much smaller than its CIO counterpart. The relationship between the two organizations was very poor, as in the wake of the 1951 strike TWUA vice president George Baldanzi resigned and joined the UTW, taking many local unions with him. Disillusioned with Emil Rieve's leadership, Baldanzi sought to turn the UTW into a genuine rival for the TWUA, especially in the South. Rather than seeking new members, the UTW and TWUA spent several years stealing them from each other. Ultimately, the bitter war for control achieved little. By 1960, the UTW had just forty-five thousand members, compared to the TWUA's 220,000.[15] The need to control imports was one of the few issues upon which the leaders of the feuding unions agreed. In 1960, for example, Baldanzi criticized the Eisenhower administration for its failure to protect domestic mills, claiming that five hundred thousand jobs had been lost since the war as a result. The former textile dyer from Paterson, New Jersey, saw serious trouble ahead if trade policies were not changed. "The whole subject of foreign trade and tariffs could spell disaster for the textile industry of the North American continent," he declared in New York, "unless the Government changes its thinking about the basic principles of reciprocal trade." Anticipating later developments, Baldanzi called for labor and management to work together on trade issues.[16]

These calls for import controls were especially significant because at the time the rest of the U.S. labor movement supported free trade. In 1955, the TWUA's Executive Council referred to the "normal CIO position in favor of liberalized trade," concluding that it was inappropriate for the textile sector. As Barkin wrote in 1957 in reference to an AFL–CIO policy statement, "Our position on foreign trade is sharply at variance with that expressed in the AFL–CIO paper." At this time, most American industries were booming, and labor leaders were not worried about imports—this only changed later. It was the textile and apparel industry that first experienced significant job losses as a result of international competition. As ILGWU leader Gus Tyler wrote in his memoirs, "The negative impact of apparel imports on the American garment workers was felt early—long before waves of imports of other products struck the United States."[17]

Imports did have a particularly marked impact on the labor-intensive apparel sector, and labor leaders expressed concern at a time when the economy was booming. In the decade after World War II, imports were facilitated by duty reductions, as well as by domestic entrepreneurs who began to develop factories abroad. In addition, some of the large retailers established buying offices in foreign countries. As early as October 1955, ILGWU president David Dubinsky noted his anxiety about "rapidly increasing" imports, particularly from Japan. "An unrestrained scramble for American markets by countries which utilize home workers and pay starvation wages can seriously threaten American labor standards," he cautioned. For Dubinsky, the answer lay in "regulated" trade, especially with Japan.[18]

Dubinsky's counterpart in the ACWA sounded similar warnings. With considerable foresight, President Jacob S. Potofsky cautioned in 1961 that imports threatened to wipe out the domestic apparel industry. In a speech to New York manufacturers, the Ukrainian-born leader declared that "the men's tailored clothing industry is confronted by one of the most dangerous threats to its continued existence in its long history in the U.S. . . . This threat arises from the ever growing volume of apparel imports which have been coming to our shores from low-wage countries. No section of the industry is immune. . . . My friends, the apparel industry of the United States will have to be particularly alert if it is to survive." Writing to Secretary of Labor Arthur J. Goldberg in the same year, Potofsky noted that it was the "special nature" of the clothing industry that made it vulnerable to import competition; the industry was labor intensive and was "particularly attractive" to low-wage countries that wanted to grow quickly through export-led industrialization.[19] Keen to respond, Potofsky called for a $1 million general fund to bankroll the fight for global textile quotas. In the early 1960s, he also threatened to call a "strike" against Japanese imports after the Asian nation refused to agree to new restraints on men's suits.[20]

Industry leaders echoed the unions' warnings. Led by the NTA, northern mill owners lobbied particularly hard for federal assistance. As the *New York Times* summarized in 1956, "The Northern Textile Association has been warning of increasing competition from Japanese imports for several years." In July 1958, William F. Sullivan told the Senate that the industry had "serious problems," adding that "assistance and understanding" must come from federal agencies. In particular, Sullivan complained that existing tariffs were not doing their job. "Government policies have contributed materially to the problems of the textile industry," he concluded. "A more fundamental reappraisal and comprehensive solution is necessary."[21]

Through Senate hearings and related lobbying, the industry was able to exert a significant amount of political pressure. In 1959, for example, the Rhode Island Textile Association informed Senator Pastore that employment in the state's textile industry had halved in just a decade. "This office has the results of innumerable Surveys, Studies, and reviews demonstrating that imports from foreign low-wage countries have had a depressive effect on our industry," it noted. Overall, the industry's "tragic" decline was responsible for widespread unemployment and suffering. As his papers reveal, these developments worried Pastore. America's first Italian-American senator, Pastore understood the way that the industry had provided jobs for generations of unskilled immigrants. In reply, Pastore told the Association that it had "friends at court," adding that Congress was sure to look after one of America's oldest and most important industries.[22] Finding that the textile industry was not sharing in the broader prosperity, Pastore's committee recommended that import quotas be established by category of product. It also insisted that these quotas should not be limited to cotton goods, as imports of wool and man-made fiber imports were also on the rise. Despite these recommendations, there was no immediate change in federal trade policies.[23]

Still, the NTA kept up the pressure. Highlighting the need for action, the group calculated that 128 U.S. textile mills had closed between 1958 and 1960. In March 1960, NTA chairman Seabury Stanton told the U.S. Tariff Commission that the industry needed a number of key changes, including the equalization of cotton prices and stricter controls on imports. "We urge the Tariff Commission to recommend quotas," he concluded.[24] In February 1961, Stanton and Sullivan returned to another round of hearings before the Pastore Committee and complained that its recommendations had been ignored. "The past two years," they declared, "have been marked by an almost complete lack of action on the substantive Recommendations of this Committee and specifically on your recommendations to limit imports by categories so that they will not further endanger existing textile capacity." Of particular concern, the "injustice" of two-price cotton continued, and no revision of depreciation rates on textile machinery had been adopted. The two-price system exacerbated the import problem because it meant that foreign manufacturers paid a lower price for American cotton than domestic manufacturers. On top of their wage advantage, this was a vital benefit.[25] At the hearings, northern and southern mill owners stressed that they faced a common import threat. As William I. Kent of the Kent Manufacturing Company in Clifton, Pennsylvania, put it, "While employment, production and plant installations have been receding, the tide of imports since 1957 has been surging in at storm levels."[26]

Following the second round of hearings, Pastore's committee released a report that called for "essential and urgent quotas" to be applied on all on textile and apparel products. Updating the findings of the original investigation, the report emphasized that conditions in the industry had "continued to deteriorate." As a result, the original recommendations needed to be "promptly" implemented. While the industry's frustration was understandable, federal officials had taken some action to help the industry. In January 1957, the Eisenhower administration announced a five-year limitation on Japanese textile imports. Negotiated between the two governments, the agreement came after industry officials had been unable to reach a deal. It did not satisfy American textile leaders, who pressed for further concessions. Despite continued complaints from the industry, in June 1960 the U.S. Tariff Commission voted four to two not to take any further action on textile import restrictions, and the two-price cotton system also remained in place.[27]

When John F. Kennedy ran for the presidency in 1960, the industry pressured him to address these issues. As a senator from Massachusetts, Kennedy had developed strong links with textile manufacturers and union leaders. He was friends with Bill Belanger, the TWUA's director in the Bay State, and the union had been one of Kennedy's main political supporters for over a decade. In 1952, when he had announced his candidacy for the U.S. Senate, Congressman Kennedy declared that his home state was suffering from an economic "crisis" that called for new political leadership. "Unemployment," he explained, "particularly in our textile and shoe centers is on the increase. For entirely too long the representatives of Massachusetts . . . have stood by helplessly while our industries and jobs disappear."[28] While in the Senate, Kennedy argued that urgent action was needed to assist the struggling textile industry. In April 1957, he was one of twelve New England senators who asked President Eisenhower to help an industry that was "extremely important to the economy of New England and of the Nation." The letter built on an earlier appeal by New England's governors, who had urged Eisenhower to do more to support America's "most troubled" industry.[29] In June 1960, Kennedy also addressed the TWUA's national convention. He again stressed the importance of the industry, declaring that "as the Textile Workers Union go, so goes the United States." Although the TWUA had faced "some of the most difficult problems" of any American union, including lockouts and liquidations, he was confident that it would survive. "I have been supported every time that I have run for office in Massachusetts by this union, and I have won," he added. It was clear that if Kennedy prevailed in November, his textile supporters would be rewarded.[30]

In a close election, JFK also needed as much support as he could muster in the South. There, one of his key supporters was South Carolina governor Ernest "Fritz" Hollings, who delivered crucial votes to the Democrats in the textile belt. Acting on complaints from his constituents, Governor Hollings used his friendship with Kennedy to good effect. In August 1960, for instance, he wrote Kennedy and urged him to do more to protect the textile industry from imports, particularly from Japan. Textile mills, he added, were "of critical importance to the economy of my region and, indeed, to the entire United States." In a sympathetic and warm response, Senator Kennedy noted that the decline of the textile industry had hurt his home state of Massachusetts. He chastised Eisenhower for failing to protect the mills and agreed that imports "should be within limits which will not endanger our own existing textile capacity and employment."[31]

Hollings was determined to ensure that Kennedy followed through on his commitment. While campaigning heavily in his home state, Hollings secured several meetings with Kennedy. At the gatherings, he reiterated that the industry should receive more federal assistance. On January 7, 1961, Hollings also had lunch with the president-elect and secured a commitment that "solutions" would be found to the industry's problems. After further meetings, on May 2 Kennedy announced a seven-point program to help the industry. Key provisions included extra federal funding to help mills to modernize and the promise of further assistance if the industry suffered "serious injury" from imports. Kennedy also promised to bring about "a basis for trade that will avoid undue disruption of established industries." Justifying the program, JFK insisted that the industry was such a large employer that its fate had a "direct effect" upon the health of the American economy.[32]

Hollings was delighted. "This is the best thing that has happened to the industry in decades," he wrote. "The jobs of the textile workers will no longer be considered expendable." Industry leaders, such as John K. Cauthen, a key official in the South Carolina Textile Manufacturers Association, were also optimistic. "Governor Hollings has opened the doors of the White House and all of the government departments, concerned with our problem, at the very top," he wrote. "We have not just gotten into the White House, but we have reached the President." Many SCTMA members sent similar letters of appreciation to their governor.[33]

The national press saw the situation very differently. Stealing Hollings's thunder, the *New York Times* and the *Washington Post-Times-Herald* quickly ran editorials against the restrictions. According to the *Post*, textiles and apparel was a "low-wage, low-investment industry." It was "suitable for the early stages of a nation's development" but was out of step with the "high-wage, mature economy of the rest of the nation." In a similar vein, the *Times* pressed for tariff cuts and lambasted the textile and apparel industry as "the giant of the protectionist camp."[34] These attacks were no temporary aberration. A few years later, for instance, the *Post* called textiles and apparel a "prosperous and politically powerful domestic industry" that did not deserve further protection. Rather than being a positive move, quotas would raise prices for American consumers and undermine "international amity."[35]

On the international stage, Kennedy's commitments to the industry led to the 1961 Short-Term Agreement Regarding International Trade in Cotton Textiles, which placed limits on certain imports in order to protect domestic producers from undue disruption. In 1962, the Long-Term Agreement replaced the Short-Term Agreement, and nineteen major trading partners signed it. The new, tighter accord allowed for the negotiation of temporary bilateral agreements if U.S. markets were significantly disrupted either by rapid increases in imports or by prices that undercut those of similar domestic goods. Over the next decade the United States negotiated thirty bilateral agreements, and they helped to restrict job losses, especially in cotton textiles. Domestic manufacturers, however, complained that a more comprehensive agreement was needed, especially as the LTA did not cover synthetic fabrics.[36] According to the industry, the exclusion of wool and man-made fibers from the LTA was a critical weakness. Over the course of the 1960s, world trade in synthetic fibers grew sharply. Between 1964 and 1971, for example, U.S. imports of man-made fibers doubled every two years. In 1969, the Nixon administration promised to seek a solution to this problem with the major importing countries, and in that year several comprehensive quota bills were introduced into Congress. The surge in synthetic imports also reflected changing consumer tastes. As fashions became less formal and more reliant on synthetic fabrics, many textile companies struggled to adjust.[37]

Over time, the industry's enthusiasm for the agreement waned. In particular, they complained that many of the provisions were not properly administered, particularly when Kennedy devolved the running of the program to State Department officials and pursued free trade policies elsewhere. In late 1962, Hollings counseled one frustrated executive that he was doing his best to influence the administration. "The 'force' approach is not a wise one," he advised.[38] Over time, however, dissatisfaction grew. In 1966, for example, Sullivan wrote a colleague that his members were "critical of the Administration for its failure to administer the LTA in accordance with expectations, for its failure to get anything done on wool, and for its failure to even try to do anything about blends and man-mades." At the NTA's Boston headquarters, Sullivan's files bulged with letters that called for more decisive federal action. Increasingly unhappy with the situation, the New Hampshire native came to the conclusion that foreign governments would not agree to new restrictions "unless the United States is ready to act or maybe until the U.S. has already acted." The issue drew the NTA and the southern-dominated ATMI together, giving Sullivan confidence to vocalize his members' complaints. At the end of 1966, he reported to the ATMI's Robert C. Jackson that "our disillusionment with the Textile Program is now outspoken and we are going to do all we can to work with everyone else to get a solution to this matter."[39]

Thus, in 1966 the NTA and ATMI both passed resolutions that called for tough action against imports. According to the NTA, since 1961 cotton textile imports had risen from 720 million square yards to 1,680 million square yards. Only "unilateral limitations" on all textile imports would address the problem.[40] In a similar vein, the ATMI called for the U.S. government to "establish controls on imports of all textile and apparel products, regardless of fiber." They complained that the LTA only covered one-half of the industry's production based on the weight of fibers consumed and only one-third based on dollar value. "Cotton, man-made fiber, and woolen textile imports currently are at the highest levels ever recorded," they explained. In October, Jackson reiterated to his ATMI colleagues that controlling imports was crucial. "Stated simply and directly, it now seems clear that the import pattern will go very far in determining the size, character and structure of the total textile industry complex of this country in the future," he warned.[41] The situation in the wool industry was particularly grave. The ATMI claimed that this historic industry, which was based largely in New England, had been "dangerously crippled by imports."[42]

Dissatisfied with the LTA, the textile and apparel unions voiced similar complaints. In 1966, the TWUA's Executive Council called imports "a serious threat to the job security of America's textile workers." The TWUA called for the LTA to be strengthened, and for immediate restraints to be imposed on wool and man-made fiber imports. Because these demands were not met, in 1969 the Executive Council passed another resolution; it declared that imports had "skyrocketed in the last 10 years" and that they threatened "the jobs and living standards" of all workers in the industry. Unless stricter international agreements were concluded, the only answer was domestic legislation.[43] Things were no better in apparel. In September 1968, the ILGWU's General Executive Board passed a resolution expressing its concern about "an ever-increasing tide of imported ready-to-wear from low wage countries." If international agreements could not stem the flow, then "unilateral" action by Congress was justified.[44] By the mid-1960s, the ACWA's research department was even collecting data on clothing imports on a monthly basis, paying particular attention to items from Japan and Hong Kong. The data was sent to the union's General Executive Board, where leaders also called for import quotas.[45]

Sullivan corresponded regularly with Senator Pastore, and both men worried that many Americans were not aware of the industry's problems. In an effort to address this, Pastore stressed the industry's importance to national defense, an argument that resonated at the time of the Vietnam War. In February 1966, for example, he told the Senate that "the country is experiencing astronomical growth in its gross national product; yet here is an industry classified as second only to steel in national security, which has gone down the hill." Pastore focused particular attention on the stricken wool sector. Supplying his colleagues with a list of wool plants that had closed since 1951, he argued that the industry was no longer big enough to meet defense needs, a clear worry for a country at war. "I am for the textile industry because I am for American security," he explained.[46] This argument built on the work of Pastore's committee, which had also stressed that a high level of textile capacity and employment must be maintained for national security reasons. Pastore's hearings prompted an investigation by the Office of Civil and Defense Mobilization, which concluded that textiles was "an essential industry" and "an essential part of the nation's mobilization base." Testifying to the hearings, procurement specialist Stephen Kennedy also admitted that the industry's decline could "jeopardize" the federal government's ability to provide "proper protection" to its troops.[47]

Because of the industry's size, national politicians responded to its grievances. The main industry in the South, textiles also remained vital in New England and the mid-Atlantic region. Illustrating this, presidents Kennedy, Johnson, and Nixon all took notice of the industry and tried to placate its calls for protection. In the lead-up to the 1964 presidential election, LBJ stressed his good intentions when he visited the textile centers of Providence, Rhode Island, and Macon, Georgia. "The textile industry plays a vital role in the health of the American economy," he commented. Defending the administration's record, Johnson claimed that the seven-point program was working and had proved to be "a classic example of the benefits of constructive cooperation between government and business." New bilateral and multilateral trade agreements were controlling imports, he asserted, while even in the wool area "unintended loopholes" had been closed. "We intend to keep cotton textile imports from disrupting the market," he added. Crucially, LBJ also pushed through legislation that made it possible to buy American cotton for the same price that it was sold abroad. Still, industry leaders reiterated that the seven-point program did not go far enough.[48]

When he ran for president in 1968, Richard M. Nixon also reached out to the industry. In a communication with Massachusetts senator Edward W. Brooke, Nixon accused Kennedy and Johnson of not carrying out the seven-point program effectively. Promising to take "prompt action," Nixon declared that he would extend the LTA to cover wool and man-made fibers. It was crucial, he explained, to help the "vast industrial-agricultural-fiber complex," especially as it was a major presence "in both rural and urban communities where jobs are needed most." Nixon sent the same message to other key supporters. South Carolina senator Strom Thurmond, for example, used the communication to consolidate support in the South, a region where the Republicans were making unprecedented gains. According to Thurmond, Nixon's telegram was the "most important policy statement" of the campaign because it promised to protect jobs in the region's biggest industry. The industry's power and importance was also highlighted by the actions of Democratic candidate Hubert Humphrey, who promised to extend the LTA to wool and man-made fibers and to "attack all arbitrary foreign barriers to our textile and apparel exports." Keen not to lose votes, Humphrey insisted that "it would be imprudent for us not to do all we can to strengthen and expand this vital sector of our industrial complex."[49]

It is clear that the industry's complaints had some legitimacy, as imports were responsible for shutdowns across the country. In the late 1960s, imports were blamed for a series of plant closings and layoffs in North Carolina and Georgia, two key textile states. In 1969 alone, Georgia lost 6,300 textile jobs. In New England—where the industry was now on its back—the situation was particularly dire. In the historic textile center of Wilton, New Hampshire, where the main mill was forced to close in 1970, a company spokesman summed up broader themes well: "We have withstood the challenge of low wage imports for the last 19 years while every other textile mill of our same type closed its door. Every appeal to our federal government from our own mill, from New England textile leaders, and from national textile leaders has been ignored and overlooked by those who could have given aid to our industry. We can no longer bridge the wage gap between ourselves and foreign imports and maintain a profit making business. Therefore, our regretful decision (is) to announce the phasing out of our production and business."[50]

Plant closures were often devastating, especially for small towns that depended on the industry. In 1966, a study of New England textile towns by economists W. Stanley Devino, Arnold H. Raphaelson, and James A. Storer found that closures caused "sharp, severe blows to the economic and social structures of the communities." In Sanford, Maine, for example, over 70 percent of the town's workforce of five thousand lost their jobs when the Goodall-Sanford plant closed, while in Adams, Massachusetts, the mills had employed half of the town's workforce when they disappeared. "Heroic adjustments were required to achieve some measure of recovery," concluded the authors, "and there were many workers who could not make the necessary transitions."[51]

These problems were not restricted to New England. In Aragon, Georgia, for example, Aragon Mills provided five hundred jobs in a town of 1,200 people, so when the company closed its doors in 1969, widespread unemployment resulted. Many of those that did find new work—including female breadwinners—ended up driving long distances. One woman who had used her mill job to raise three children summarized the consequences of the closure. "I'm taking home $51 a week at my new job," she explained. "I drive 35 to 40 miles a day. At my job in the mill here, I was taking home $100 to $103 a week. Textiles is all I know, and it's hard for all of us in this town to adjust to other jobs. . . . But most of all there were so many women here who made good livings. They were close to home and were able to cook supper after they got off work." Now, the commuting meant that women workers were no longer able to cook for their families or mind children after their day shift. They longed to get the plant back. Publicizing the Aragon shutdown as representative, Senator Herman Talmadge tried to make his colleagues aware of the human costs of the industry's decline. "What happened in Aragon," he asserted, "what has been taking place in Georgia and in many states throughout the country is the story of people. These are people who were trying to hold down a job, make a decent living, support their families, and educate their children." These were citizens who wanted to work, yet many now faced long spells of joblessness.[52]

Two recent scholarly studies have confirmed that southern workers were hurt by the industry's problems. Beth English's study of Dwight Manufacturing Company in Gadsden, Alabama, highlights how the textile industry was marked by a high degree of capital mobility, and this undermined workers' job security right across the country. In 1959 Dwight—which had closed its Massachusetts operations three decades earlier—also shut the Alabama mill. According to the company, foreign competition had caused "major losses" at the plant. As a result, an estimated ten thousand people in Etowah County who were "fed, sheltered, and clothed by mill money" lost their main source of income. A decade later, Crown Cotton Mill in Dalton, Georgia, also closed, another victim of the industry's troubles. Because the South was experiencing economic growth in general, however, few noticed these closures. As Douglas Flamming has written in his history of Crown Mills, "Basic cotton textile mills began to fold in Dalton and the South at the very time the regional economy as a whole was experiencing a major upswing." Despite this economic growth, dislocated workers struggled to find comparable jobs, and for both communities the shutdowns were devastating. "That's when Gadsden died," declared former Dwight employee Laura Beard.[53]

The papers of elected officials illustrate the pressure that the industry exerted as it confronted the import challenge. A senator for over twenty-five years, Pastore built up a warm relationship with textile executives. In April 1959, he told a gathering of textile manufacturers in Providence that his "years of contact" with them had been "very human" and had given him "great satisfaction." Illustrating these close links, Pastore's Senate hearings grew out of a resolution that was passed at the ATMI's annual meeting. Just two weeks later, Senate Resolution 287 authorized funds for a study of the American textile industry by the Committee on Interstate Commerce. Pulling no punches about the industry's power, a few years later Pastore told the ATMI that it was "one of the most effective industry organizations operating in Washington." The institute's leaders had "won the respect and confidence and cooperation of many of the gentlemen who occupy high places in our Government, in both the Executive and Legislative branches."[54]

The industry's immense political influence was illustrated particularly well in Georgia. In 1960, the state was the fifth largest producer of cotton textiles in the country, and one out of every three Georgians who were employed in industry worked in a cotton mill. In addition, more than eighty-five thousand Georgia cotton farmers depended on the industry as the market for their crops. As the Chamber of Commerce noted in 1969, the hundreds of textile plants located across the state were a "golden thread" that provided manufacturing jobs to around 114,000 people. A further sixty-eight thousand Georgians worked in the related apparel industry.[55]

Mill owners had close links with Georgia senators Herman Talmadge and Richard B. Russell, both of whom held office for long periods. In June 1966, for instance, Talmadge corresponded warmly with Willis H. Newton, a former college classmate who was now the president of the Georgia Textile Manufacturers Association. Accepting an invitation to speak at the GTMA's annual convention, Talmadge noted that his friendship with the Newton family filled him with "great pride." Since the 1940s, when Talmadge had served as Georgia's governor, the Newtons had financed Talmadge's political career. Willis H. Newton was also very grateful to Talmadge. "Our industry and the people of Georgia thank you for the integrity of your service to us in Washington," he wrote.[56] Talmadge's senior by sixteen years, Russell also corresponded closely with mill owners. "I shall continue to do everything within my power as one member of Congress to safeguard our domestic textile industry," he reassured them. Russell's friends included Robert T. Stevens, a former secretary of the army who was now leading the family textile company, J. P. Stevens, in its fight for tighter import controls. As he did so, Stevens stressed the industry's importance to national security, an argument that appealed to patriotic southerners. Both Talmadge and Russell also had close links with the ATMI. In June 1969, for example, G. Stewart Boswell from the ATMI's national headquarters wrote Russell to express "our sincere appreciation for your continuing interest in, and concern with, the textile import problem."[57]

The industry's lobbying power could be seen in Talmadge's actions, as he frequently used the Senate floor to press the industry's case. In 1967, he spoke out against "excessive" imports and called for "proper action by this government to preserve and strengthen this oldest of U.S. industries." Specifically, Talmadge demanded that U.S. trade negotiators in Geneva fight proposals to cut textile tariffs. Rather than duty reductions, the industry needed a stronger LTA, as the existing agreement was about to expire. The LTA—which Talmadge compared to a "leaky" dam that only covered half a river—needed to cover wool and man-made fibers. Partly because of this pressure, the LTA was renewed in that year. As he tried to help the industry, Talmadge rejected the idea that he was merely responding to local pressures. "Those who live in the heart of our textile-producing area sometimes overlook the fact that this is a *national* industry," he declared in 1969. "It is an industry which employs one out of every nine manufacturing workers in this country."[58]

Following the renewal of the LTA, Talmadge pressed on. In June 1969, he lashed out against the "uncontrolled expansion" of imports. Citing a "disastrous chain of events" that dated to the 1950s, Talmadge blamed imports for the closure of seven hundred mills and the loss of 330,000 jobs.[59] Rather than just repeating the industry line, the outspoken Talmadge brought an inimitable style to the issue. A native of the tiny town of McRae, Talmadge rejected the whole idea of free trade as abstract economic theory, arguing that it could never exist when other countries did not play by the same rules. As he wrote in one of his regular textile columns, "Free trade is supposed to be a two-way street where goods of all nations flow freely throughout the world for the mutual benefit of everyone. This is the way it should be, but insofar as the United States is concerned, it is not the way it is. The free trade streets of today consist of a four lane, super-highway leading into the United States and a narrow, winding country road leading practically nowhere for our goods."[60]

Elected to the Senate in 1956, at the height of "massive resistance" to the civil rights movement, Talmadge was a prominent segregationist. Although increased black voting caused him to moderate his views, some of his attacks on textile imports drew on xenophobic or even racist sentiments. Arguing that free trade with poorer nations was impossible, Talmadge insisted that America would "court its own destruction" if it allowed "the backward nations of the world to achieve their aspirations at the expense of its own economy." These "backward nations" included "greedy 'have-not' nations and unprincipled Communist slave states."[61] Talmadge, who had seen combat in the South Pacific during World War II, frequently used Japan to illustrate his point. "Japan has become the second largest industrial nation in the free world, thanks to United States aid, money, and equipment," he blasted. "Yet she wants more and more of our market. Most of the foreign textiles, including Japan's, come into our country not because they are any better or prettier, but because they are produced for wages and under working conditions that would be illegal in this country." Talmadge's attacks on "Red China" were also influenced by fears that the Chinese could dominate the global textile trade. "The United States does not want to be flooded with more cheap labor imports," he explained.[62]

Such rhetoric did not go unanswered. Indeed, industry officials and diplomats in other countries saw the American market as overprotected. In September 1967, for example, the Japanese textile union, Zensen Domei, formally protested against American efforts to restrict textile imports. President Minoru Takita rejected the picture of an American industry in trouble, writing to TWUA leader William Pollock that he could not understand "what actually necessitates import restrictions in the U.S." In response, Pollock informed Takita that he would not be changing his stance. "Imports are threatening the continued employment of our members and we are trying to protect our jobs," he admitted.[63]

Together with Senator Hollings, Talmadge led efforts to introduce mandatory import quotas. In April 1968, the friends worked together on a textile bill that was cosponsored by sixty-seven other senators. When the House passed a measure that regulated trade in cranberries, they seized their chance and introduced an amendment that authorized the president to impose import quotas on textile goods. "This bill," explained Talmadge, "would go a long way toward safeguarding the future of the domestic textile industry." Supporters came from every section of the country, and Hollings recalled that there was national concern about the textile situation. "My colleagues recognized that we had been hemorrhaging jobs because of the failure to adhere to the quota system established by Jack Kennedy's seven-point program," he wrote later. Facing a threatened presidential veto, the textile amendment was killed in the House, where Ways and Means Committee chairman Wilbur Mills was a powerful opponent. Still, Hollings had not given up, and neither had many of his congressional colleagues. They continued to express dismay about the direction of trade policy and constantly looked for opportunities to help the American textile worker, a figure that Talmadge termed "the forgotten man in the trade legislation debate."[64]

In July 1969, a large group of senators again threatened to introduce import-restriction legislation if foreign countries did not back down. As the Southbridge (Massachusetts) *News* reported, "The North and South have joined forces in an effort to restrain textile sales in this country." During an impassioned debate, northern senators voiced concern about the decline of the textile and shoe industries, especially in New England. They included Senator Edmund S. Muskie of Maine, the 1968 Democratic vice presidential nominee, who broke with his party's free trade leanings. "The bald truth is that our foreign trade policy is in effect giving jobs of American workers to their foreign counterparts," he declared. Like his predecessors, President Richard Nixon did not support strict quotas, although he did recognize the seriousness of the textile problem and called the industry a "special case." The industry's supporters remained skeptical. Senator Norris Cotton of New Hampshire declared that he was "very pessimistic" about getting voluntary agreements, while Pastore agreed with Talmadge that only the United States and Canada had real "free trade"; other countries protected their own interests. Pastore's position mirrored that of the Northern Textile Association, whose leaders wanted him to take "unilateral action" against imports.[65]

As the 1960s came to a close, the NTA and ATMI ratcheted up the pressure on legislators. In September 1969, an NTA resolution called import growth "excessive." If an international solution could not be found, then Congress had to take action to ensure that the influx was "moderated." In 1970, the NTA and ATMI pushed for a Trade Act that contained quota provisions for textile, apparel, and shoe imports; these could be applied through international agreements or through unilateral action. After the House passed the measure by a vote of 215 to 165 on November 19, the Senate Finance Committee reported it, but it was never brought to a vote because of threatened filibusters on this and other bills during the final days of the ninety-first Congress. Following this outcome, President Nixon resumed textile talks with Prime Minister Sato of Japan, who agreed to limits on some goods, with the new restrictions set to begin on July 1. Despite this commitment, Japanese shipments were allowed to increase by 5 percent a year, and the Japanese reserved the right to alter the restrictions if they wished. Industry and labor groups condemned the agreement, and President Nixon subsequently gave his backing to quota legislation. Reacting quickly, Wilbur Mills made it clear that congressional action would not be forthcoming. The NTA was undeterred; as Chairman Robert Booth commented in September 1971, the Association's "traditional position" called for import quotas, and nothing had happened to alter this. According to Booth, the textile industry was on the "front lines" of an "international economic war" that showed no signs of ending. Over the next decade, as textile imports continued to escalate, so too would political efforts to stem the industry's demise.[66]

## NOTES

1. United States International Trade Commission, "Emerging Textile-Exporting Countries," USITC Publication 1273, August 1982, p. 1 (quotation), p. 5, copy in "USITC Textile Reports (3)" folder, Wendell W. Gunn files, OA9646, Reagan Library; Timothy Warren Vanderburg, "Cannon Mills: A Case Study in Southern Industrialization" (PhD dissertation, Mississippi State University, 2001), pp. 265–66.

2. *New England Textiles and the New England Economy* (Report by the New England Governors' Textile Committee to the Conference of New England Governors), March 1958, p. I-38, ATHM.

3. "Statement of William F. Sullivan, Counsel, Northern Textile Association, for *Boston Sunday Herald* Textile Supplement," January 19, 1958, copy in "Tariffs" folder, "General Files, RU-TN," Pastore Papers; Herman E. Talmadge Press Release, August 15, 1969, "Textile Trade, 1969–71" folder, box 312, series II, Talmadge Papers.

4. Transactions of the National Association of Cotton Manufacturers, No. 105, October 31–November 2, 1918, p. 176, ATHM; Transactions of the National Association of Cotton Manufacturers, No. 111, November 2 and 3, 1921, p. 422, ATHM.

5. Transactions of the National Association of Cotton Manufacturers, No. 137, October 7, 1936, p. 208; Transactions of the National Association of Cotton Manufacturers, No. 138, October 6–7, 1937, p. 280.

6. Michael Smitka, "Introduction," in Smitka, ed., *The Textile Industry and the Rise of the Japanese Economy* (New York: Garland, 1998), pp. xiv–xv (quotation on p. xiv).

7. Robert Trumbull, "Japanese Growth Slows to a Gallop" (first quotation), and "'Made Elsewhere' Label Irking Japan," *New York Times*, January 19, 1968, p. 51; A. Lee Parsons to Robert C. Jackson, January 3, 1968, folder 1778, box 152, MS.73/327, NACM/NTA Papers.

8. Trumbull, "Japanese Growth Slows to a Gallop," and "'Made Elsewhere' Label Irking Japan"; U.S. Department of Commerce's Office of Textiles and Apparel, "U.S. Textile and Apparel Import Program," document, January 11, 1988, "U.S. Textile and Apparel Import Program" folder, Susan Lauffer files, OA16376, Reagan Library (quotation).

9. TWUA Executive Council Minutes, May 22–26, 1961, p. 30, "1959–61" folder, box 1, Mss. 396, TWUA Papers; TWUA Executive Council Minutes, July 9–13, 1956, p. 25, "1956–58" folder, box 1, Mss. 396, TWUA Papers.

10. TWUA Executive Council Minutes, May 24–28, 1976, p. A35, M78-173, TWUA Papers.

11. "Statement of William F. Sullivan, Counsel, Northern Textile Association, for *Boston Sunday Herald* Textile Supplement," January 19, 1958, copy in "Tariffs" folder, "General Files, RU-TN," Pastore Papers.

12. "American Cotton Textile Industry and Foreign Trade Policy" (TWUA Research Paper I-197T), September 3, 1957, "ILGWU, TWUA, and Other Union Statements on Imports, 1950" folder, box 532, ACTWU Papers-Cornell.

13. Solomon Barkin, "Textile Development Agency Vital to Industry's Growth," November 13, 1958, "Pastore Hearings" folder, box 524, Mss. 396, TWUA Papers.

14. TWUA Executive Council Minutes, August 21–24, 1961, "Executive Council Meeting August 21–24, 1961, Monticello, New York" folder, box 8, Mss. 396, TWUA Papers.

15. For the Rieve-Baldanzi spilt, see Minchin, *What Do We Need a Union For*? pp. 168–75; "U.S. Textile Policy Scored by Union," *New York Times*, October 4, 1960, p. 58.

16. "U.S. Textile Policy Scored by Union."

17. TWUA Executive Council Minutes, February 21–23, 1955, p. 7, "1952–55" folder, box 1, Mss. 396, TWUA Papers; Solomon Barkin to Research Directors of AFL–CIO International Unions, November 4, 1957, "ILGWU, TWUA, and Other Union Statements on Imports, 1950" folder, box 532, ACTWU Papers-Cornell; Gus Tyler, *Look for the Union Label: A History of*

*the International Ladies' Garment Workers' Union* (Armonk, NY: M. E. Sharpe, 1995), p. 319 (closing quotation).

18. David Dubinsky to "All Affiliated Unions," October 31, 1955, "ILGWU, TWUA, and Other Union Statements on Imports, 1950" folder, box 532, ACTWU Papers-Cornell.

19. Speech of Jacob S. Potofsky at the Manhattan Merchant Tailors Association, Inc., January 26, 1961, and Jacob S. Potofsky to Arthur J. Goldberg, March 17, 1961, both "ACWA Statements on Foreign Trade—1961" folder, box 532, ACTWU Papers-Cornell. For similar discussions among the leaders of the ILGWU, see ILGWU General Executive Board Minutes, September 9–11, 1968, p. 14, "GEB 1968" folder, box 1, series 5780/084, ILGWU Papers-Cornell.

20. A. H. Raskin, "Union Threatens to Boycott Japan," *New York Times*, December 29, 1960, p. 41; Rosen, *Making Sweatshops*, pp. 108–09.

21. "Japan's Textiles Stir New Protest," *New York Times*, July 21, 1956, p. 19 (first quotation); "Statement of Northern Textile Association before the Committee on Interstate and Foreign Commerce of the U.S. Senate," July 8, 1958, pp. 1, 6–7, 11–12, folder 787, box 72, MS.73/327, NACM/NTA Papers.

22. Rhode Island Textile Association, "Statement for the Committee for Reciprocity Information," ca. 1959, "Tariffs" folder, General files RV-TN, Pastore Papers; "Address of U.S. Senator John O. Pastore at the 40th Annual Dinner of the Rhode Island Textile Association," April 16, 1959, folder 18, box 9, Speeches files, Pastore Papers (Pastore quotation).

23. R. Buford Brandis, "The Making of Textile Trade Policy, 1935–1981," ATMI Study, pp. 16–17, copy in "Textiles: The Making of Textile Trade Policy, 1935–1981" folder, Michael A. Driggs files, Reagan Library.

24. NTA, "Fact Sheet: U.S. Textile Mill Liquidations and Imports," June 15, 1961, folder 24.13, box 24, NTA Papers; Statement of Seabury Stanton before the U.S. Tariff Commission, p. 5, March 3, 1960, folder 1085, box 99, NACM/NTA Papers.

25. "Statement of Seabury Stanton before the Special Subcommittee of the Committee on Interstate and Foreign Commerce" (accompanied by William F. Sullivan), February 6, 1961, folder 1137, box 105, NACM/NTA Papers.

26. "Textile Group Urges Congress to Save Industry from Imports," *New York Times*, February 7, 1961, p. 45.

27. NTA Memo to Member Mills re: "Pastore Report," March 15, 1961, folder 1138, box 105, NACM/NTA Papers (quotations); Vanderburg, "Cannon Mills," pp. 266–67, 274–76.

28. Kennedy quoted in "Statement of Judge A. B. Cason on Behalf of the Massachusetts Rayon and Cotton Textile Mills," April 8, 1952, folder 24.13, box 24, NTA Papers.

29. Theodore Francis Green et al. to Mr. President, April 18, 1957, "Tariffs" folder, General Files RU-TN, Pastore Papers; "Troubled" quotation in "Japan's Textiles Stir New Protest."

30. "Kennedy's Speech to Textile Union," *New York Times*, June 3, 1960, p. 7.

31. Ernest F. "Fritz" Hollings with Kirk Victor, *Making Government Work* (Columbia: University of South Carolina Press, 2008), pp. 101–02; Ernest F. Hollings to Senator John F. Kennedy, August 26, 1960, and John F. Kennedy to Governor Ernest Hollings, August 30, 1960, both box 21, Gubernatorial files, Hollings Papers.

32. Ernest Hollings to Z. L. Sanders, January 14, 1961, and White House Press Release, May 2, 1961 (Kennedy quotations), both box 21, Gubernatorial files, Hollings Papers.

33. Statement by Ernest F. Hollings, May 2, 1961; John K. Cauthen to W. F. Robertson et al., May 8, 1961, and W. Gordon McCabe Jr. to Ralph Cuthbertson and E. F. Hollings, May 4, 1961, all box 21, Gubernatorial files, Hollings Papers.

34. *Washington Post-Times-Herald* quoted in TWUA Executive Council Minutes, May 22–26, 1961, p. 30, "1959–61" folder, box 1, Mss. 396, TWUA Papers; John D. Morris, "Protectionists Gird for Tariff Battle," *New York Times*, November 19, 1961, p. E10.

35. "Pulling the Wool," *Washington Post*, February 7, 1966, in *Congressional Record*, February 7, 1966, pp. 2193–94, copy in "Senator's Remarks on Senate Floor Re: Editorial in Washington Post, February 7, 1966" folder, Pastore General Files, Pastore Papers.

36. U.S. Congress, Office of Technology Assessment, *The U.S. Textile and Apparel Industry*, p. 86; Grace I. Kunz and Myrna B. Garner, *Going Global: The Textile and Apparel Industry, Third Edition* (New York: Fairchild Publications, 2007), p. 206.

37. U.S. Department of Commerce's Office of Textiles and Apparel, "U.S. Textile and Apparel Import Program," document, January 11, 1988, "U.S. Textile and Apparel Import Program" folder, Susan Lauffer files, Reagan Library.

38. J. M. Cheatham et al. to John F. Kennedy, June 29, 1961; Robert Stevens to Fritz Hollings, July 28, 1961; and Ernest Hollings to William A. L. Sibley, August 23, 1962, all box 21, Gubernatorial files, Hollings Papers.

39. William F. Sullivan to Robert C. Jackson, September 21, 1966, folder 1587, box 140, NACM/NTA Papers (first quotation); William F. Sullivan to Robert C. Jackson, July 29, 1966 (second quotation), and October 3, 1966 (closing quotation), folder 1587, box 140, NACM/NTA Papers.

40. Northern Textile Association Annual Meeting (Press Release), September 29, 1966, "Textiles—Materials from Bill Sullivan 1965–1966" folder, Pastore General Files ("Textiles-General"), Pastore Papers.

41. "Proposed 1966 Resolutions," ATMI 17th Annual Meeting, March 24, 1966, folder 1586, box 140, NACM/NTA Papers; ATMI quotations in "Statement Adopted by ATMI Board of Directors at Its Meeting at Point Clear, Alabama," October 19–21, 1966, folder 1587, box 140, NACM/NTA Papers; "Robert C. Jackson Report to the Board of Directors," October 20, 1966, folder 1587, box 140, NACM/NTA Papers (closing quotation).

42. "Statement Adopted by ATMI Board of Directors at Its Meeting at Point Clear, Alabama," October 19–21, 1966, folder 1587, box 140, NACM/NTA Papers.

43. TWUA Executive Council Minutes, October 17–20, 1966, p. 13, "1965–66" folder, box 2, Mss. 396, TWUA Papers; TWUA Executive Council Resolution, "Imports of Textiles and Apparel," October 8, 1969, in box 8, Ninety-First Congress files, Hollings Papers.

44. ILGWU General Executive Board Minutes, September 9–11, 1968, pp. 13–14, "GEB 1968" folder, box 1, series 5780/084, ILGWU Papers-Cornell.

45. "July 1966 Imports," Report from ACWA Research Department to General Executive Board, September 8, 1966, folder 6, box 246, Amalgamated Clothing Workers of America Papers, held at the Kheel Center for Labor-Management Documentation and Archives, School of Industrial and Labor Relations, Cornell University, Ithaca, New York, hereafter cited as "ACWA Papers-Cornell."

46. Senator John Pastore comments, *Congressional Record*, February 7, 1966, pp. 2193–94, in "Senator's Remarks on Senate Floor Re: Editorial in Washington Post, February 7, 1966" folder, Pastore General Files, Pastore Papers.

47. R. Buford Brandis, "The Making of Textile Trade Policy, 1935–1981," (ATMI Study), pp. 16–17 (first two quotations on p. 17), copy in "Textiles: The Making of Textile Trade Policy, 1935–1981" folder, Michael A. Driggs files, Reagan Library; Closing quotation in Testimony of Dr. Stephen J. Kennedy, December 2, 1958, p. 1792, U.S. Congress, Senate, Committee on Interstate and Foreign Commerce.

48. "Statement by President Lyndon B. Johnson Regarding Textile Industry and Cotton Matters," October 26, 1964 (first three quotations), and "White House Statement by the President," September 28, 1964 (closing quotation), both folder 1703, box 147, NACM/NTA Papers.

49. Richard Nixon to Edward W. Brooke, August 21, 1968, folder 22.16, box 22, NTA Papers; "Nixon Promises Firm Textile Action: Announces Move to Sen. Thurmond," *Southern Textile News*, August 26, 1968, p. 1 (Thurmond quotation); Hubert H. Humphrey to John O. Pastore, September 19, 1968, folder 1780, box 153, NACM/NTA Papers.

50. Quotation in Herman E. Talmadge Press Release, December 15, 1970, "Textile Trade, 1969–71" folder, box 312, series II, Talmadge Papers.

51. W. Stanley Devino, Arnold H. Raphaelson, and James A. Storer, *A Study of Textile Mill Closings in Selected New England Communities* (Orono, ME: University of Maine Press, 1966), pp. 28, 145 (quotations). This study focused on six New England communities, and in four of them—Sanford, Maine; Adams, Massachusetts; Wauregan, Connecticut; and Nashua, New Hampshire—the mills dominated the local economies and their closures had a harsh impact. In the two other communities studied, West Warwick, Rhode Island, and Brattleboro, Vermont, closures were less devastating because the mills involved only employed a small proportion of the local labor force.

52. Herman E. Talmadge Press Release, December 15, 1970, "Textile Trade, 1969–71" folder, box 312, series II, Talmadge Papers. The worker who is quoted is referred to in the document as "Mrs. Smith," which is apparently a pseudonym.

53. English, *A Common Thread,* pp. 174–75; Douglas Flamming, *Creating the Modern South: Millhands and Managers in Dalton, Georgia, 1884–1984* (Chapel Hill: University of North Carolina Press, 1992), pp. 307–09 (quotation on p. 308).

54. "Address of U.S. Senator John O. Pastore at the 40th Annual Dinner of the Rhode Island Textile Association," April 16, 1959, folder 18, box 9 (Speeches files), Pastore Papers (first two Pastore quotations); "Remarks of U.S. Senator John O. Pastore at the Annual Dinner of the Market Committee of the American Textile Manufacturers Institute," January 28, 1965, "Speeches, January 1, 1965–June 30, 1965" folder, box 24, Pastore Papers (third and fourth Pastore quotations); John O. Pastore to William F. Sullivan, December 3, 1957, William F. Sullivan to John O. Pastore, December 9, 1957, and Theodore Francis Green et al. to Mr. President, April 18, 1957, all "Tariffs" folder, "General Files, RU-TN," Pastore Papers.

55. Herman Talmadge Newsletter, February 24, 1960, "Column—Cotton Textile Import Duties" folder, box 296, series II, Talmadge Papers; Chamber of Commerce quoted in Herman Talmadge Press Release, August 15, 1969, "Textile Trade, 1969–71 (4)" folder, box 312, series II, Talmadge Papers.

56. Willis H. Newton to Herman E. Talmadge, June 8, 1966, and Herman E. Talmadge to Willis H. Newton, June 10, 1966, "Georgia Textile Manufacturers Association" folder, box 268, Talmadge Papers.

57. Richard B. Russell to B. G. Stumberg Jr., November 21, 1967 (Russell quotation); Robert T. Stevens to Richard B. Russell, November 17, 1967, and Richard B. Russell to Robert T. Stevens, November 21, 1967, all "Textiles—May–December 1967" folder, box 122, series 15, Richard B. Russell Papers, held at the Richard B. Russell Library for Political Research and Studies, University of Georgia, hereafter cited as "Russell Papers"; G. Stewart Boswell to Richard B. Russell, June 19, 1969, "Textiles—1969" folder, box 69, series 15, Russell Papers.

58. Herman E. Talmadge Press Release, March 1, 1967, "Textile Import Speech U.S. Senate" folder, box 268, Series II, Talmadge Papers; Herman E. Talmadge Remarks before an Institutional Seminar, Atlanta, August 15, 1969, "Textile Trade, 1969–71 (4)" folder, box 312, series II, Talmadge Papers (closing quotation).

59. Herman E. Talmadge Press Release, June 30, 1969, "Textile Imports Speech" folder, box 252, series II, Talmadge Papers.

60. Herman Talmadge Press Release, September 10, 1969, "Column—Free Trade and Textile Imports" folder, box 250, series II, Talmadge Papers.

61. Herman E. Talmadge, "Special to Southern Textile News," ca. 1962, "Article for Southern Textile News" folder, box 291, series II, Talmadge Papers.

62. Herman E. Talmadge Press Release, September 10, 1969, "Column—Free Trade and Textile Imports" (first two quotations); Herman Talmadge Press Release, June 2, 1971, "Column-Red China," folder, box 232, series II, Talmadge Papers (final two quotations). For information on Talmadge's background, including his service in the war, see Herman E. Talmadge with Mark Royden Winchell, *Talmadge: A Political Legacy, A Politician's Life* (Atlanta: Peachtree Publishers, 1987), pp. 43–56.

63. "Statement on International Trade," in TWUA Executive Council Minutes, March 4–7, 1968, M78-173, TWUA Papers.

64. Herman E. Talmadge Press Release, March 13, 1968, "Column—Textile Imports" folder, box 256, series II, Talmadge Papers; Hollings with Victor, *Making Government Work*, p. 130 (Hollings quotation).

65. "North, South Band Together to Seek New Import Quotas," Southbridge (Massachusetts) *News*, July 1, 1969 (first quotation); "Lawmakers Push for Barriers Against Imports of Textiles," Lebanon (New Hampshire) *Valley News*, July 1, 1969 (next four quotations), both clippings in "Textile Imports Speech" folder, box 252, series II, Talmadge Papers; Bill Sullivan to John O. Pastore, October 7, 1966, "Textiles—Material from Bill Sullivan, 1965–66" folder, Pastore General files ("Textiles—General"), Pastore Papers.

66. "Resolution Adopted by Northern Textile Association Board of Government," September 16, 1969, vol. 1.29, NTA 1969 Annual Meeting Files, NTA Papers; "Report of the Chair-

man and President to the Annual Meeting of the Northern Textile Association," September 16, 1971; NTA Press Release, September 16, 1971; "Remarks of Robert Booth, Chairman, Northern Textile Association Annual Meeting," September 16, 1971 (Booth quotations), all vol. 1.31, NTA 1971 Annual Meeting Files, NTA Papers.

## *Chapter Three*

# Import Escalation and the Buildup to H.R. 1562

In the 1970s, America's long economic boom came to an end, with the first oil crisis of 1973 being a key marker of the shift. This was an era in which the media regularly carried stories of plant closings and layoffs, documenting a transformation that would soon be dubbed "deindustrialization." For Barry Bluestone and Bennett Harrison, the scholars who would do so much to popularize this concept, the 1970s were "different altogether," but for the textile industry there was no sharp change of direction. Instead, its existing problems simply got worse. The northern industry's collapse accelerated, partly because of increasing imports. Imports also began to displace more southern workers, and both management and labor demanded stricter controls. Pressure from the industry helped to ensure that the MFA was adopted in 1974 and that it was renewed in 1977 and 1981. Despite this, imports continued to surge, and both managers and labor leaders argued that quota legislation was the only solution. In 1978, Congress passed a bill to protect the industry from tariff cuts, but President Carter vetoed the legislation. Emboldened rather than chastened, the industry's supporters fought on, and they drew encouragement from the actions of Carter's successor, Ronald Reagan. The legislative buildup to H.R. 1562—the Textile and Apparel Trade Enforcement Act of 1985—had begun.[1]

The import surge reflected the continued global expansion of the industry. Published in 1982, a detailed study of textile-exporting countries by the United States International Trade Commission summarized the broad changes that lay behind the domestic industry's problems. The ITC found that while international trade in textiles and apparel had expanded substantially in the 1970s, the "fastest growth" had been experienced by "developing countries," as they relied on the industry to generate export income. Between

1973 and 1980, exports from twelve key emerging countries increased by 223 percent. The United States was the biggest consumer market for textiles in the world, and importers were keen to gain access to it. China experienced a particularly rapid rate of expansion; in 1976, it was only the twelfth largest textile producer among developing countries, but by 1980 it had risen to fourth. Overall, the ITC's findings were particularly significant because the federal agency had no links with the domestic industry. Moreover, textile executives generally saw the ITC as a supporter of free trade.[2]

For emerging nations, textiles was the first industry that they established as they moved from an agrarian to an industrial economy. As it was labor intensive, the industry allowed these new economies to fully use their chief resource—an ample supply of workers. As had been the case in nineteenth-century New England, the main group recruited into the mills were young women. In order to reduce turnover and to secure a reliable labor supply, employers housed many of these workers near the plants. Again, there were striking similarities with the Lowell or boarding house system, which had been used in nineteenth-century New England to house women workers.[3]

By the late 1970s, the textile industry was a vital source of export income for emerging Asian economies, particularly Hong Kong, South Korea, and Taiwan. In South Korea, for example, textiles represented one-third of total exports. "Our textile trade makes the difference between prosperity and recession and unemployment," admitted a government spokesman in 1978. South Korea's textile industry employed 750,000 workers, the bulk of them young women. Most had moved to Seoul, the key production center, from poor, rural areas, and they regularly sent money back to their families. Once again, there were striking similarities with the earlier recruitment of American workers. The industry's rapid growth in Asia generated serious problems for mature economies. By 1978 Asian textile output was increasing by 25 percent a year, but demand in the developed world—which consumed 70 percent of global production—was rising by just 3 percent. Dubbed "little Japans," the burgeoning economies of Singapore, South Korea, and Taiwan relied heavily on textiles. The same was true of Hong Kong. By 1982, the textile industry was the largest single employer in Hong Kong, and its exports made up one-third of the global textile trade.[4]

Textiles and apparel was also one of the first industries to emerge in China, and it was a large employer before communist leaders initiated market-based economic reforms in the late 1970s. From an early stage, industry insiders worried about Chinese competition. On a trip through several Asian nations in 1968, the ATMI's A. Lee Parsons identified the massive potential of the Chinese textile industry. "All through the Orient," he reported back to his superiors, "one hears of the good condition of the Chinese textile industry and its product. The cotton textiles are of excellent quality and the cooperation of the Japanese and British has provided quality and increasing quantity production of man-made fibers." The Chinese had access to a massive supply of cheap labor, and they were able to ship their products through Hong Kong and Singapore. Other observers were soon expressing concern about the Chinese threat. In 1978, U.S. trade representative Robert Strauss reported privately that Chinese textile imports were increasing at a "very accelerated pace" and were becoming "a serious political and economic problem." By 1979 China was the sixth largest exporter of textiles to the U.S. market, and they were crucial exports. As Clyde Farnsworth noted in the *New York Times*, the Chinese were "counting on textile exports to earn the foreign exchange necessary to finance heavy capital goods for industrialization." In 1979, ACTWU secretary-treasurer Jacob Sheinkman also visited several Chinese textile mills. He reported back to his colleagues that the Chinese saw the industry as a "major hope," largely because it was relatively easy to start up and had the potential to employ huge numbers of people. The Chinese had modern equipment, Sheinkman warned, and a "very impressive" work ethic.[5]

By 1983, China was the world's biggest textile producer and the fourth largest exporter of textiles and apparel to the United States. Still, the Chinese pressed for more. When the United States unilaterally imposed import quotas on thirty-three categories of Chinese textile goods, the Chinese responded by refusing to buy American cotton, soybeans, and chemical fibers. The dispute dragged on for six months before the two sides agreed to compromise. American mill owners were not happy. According to powerful executive Roger Milliken, the Chinese had "outwitted" the Americans by threatening to reduce their purchases of cotton and grains. In reality, he argued, the Chinese would always buy these items "wherever they can get them cheapest." These decisions had "nothing to do with the reciprocal nature of their exports to the United States." American mill owners also complained that the Chinese were unfairly subsidizing their textile exports, an allegation that they would repeat in the years ahead.[6]

The industry's global expansion caused grave problems for the American textile industry. According to data collected by ACTWU's Research Department, between 1970 and 1979 some 604 textile plants were liquidated, causing the loss of 113,779 jobs. Of these closures, 246 occurred in the South and 358 in the "non-South," although the plants that shut in the South employed more workers. Reported to the union's General Executive Board, these figures did much to drive ACTWU's trade policy.[7] In the early 1980s, moreover, the rate of import penetration accelerated sharply, prompting Sheinkman to declare that the industry and its workers were in "crisis."[8]

Federal data confirmed the industry's demise, a decline that worsened during the economic downturn of the early 1980s. One thorough study prepared by President Reagan's Interagency Working Group—a special body set up to explore the industry's problems—reported that between 1972 and 1983, employment "declined steadily" at a rate of 3.3 percent per annum in textiles and 2.3 percent per annum in apparel. In textiles, employment dropped from 900,000 in 1978 to 750,000 in 1982, while in apparel it fell from 1,332,000 to 1,164,000 over the same period. At the end of May 1983, unemployment in textiles was 9.7 percent, while in apparel it was 14.4 percent. While the industry's problems were partly related to the general recession, the administration itself saw imports as the main cause of job losses.[9] Figures supplied to the administration by the Department of Labor also showed that in the leading state of North Carolina, employment in the textile industry tumbled from 253,500 in 1979 to 217,800 at the start of 1983, and there were similar drops in South Carolina and Georgia. The growth of other industries only partially offset these falls. In January 1983, South Carolina had an unemployment rate of 11.6 percent while in North Carolina the figure was 10 percent.[10]

As free-traders pointed out, some jobs were lost to automation rather than imports. Prior to 1970, the industry had relied on decreased handling of materials in order to raise productivity, yet this changed as new technology became available. In particular, open-end spinning and shuttleless looms dramatically reduced the time and number of workers needed to produce fabric. Open-end spinning could produce yarn four times faster than the antiquated ring-spinning technique, and it also reduced the number of steps involved in manufacturing some types of yarn. In the 1970s, textile manufacturers invested heavily in these new technologies. The results were obvious; during the 1970s labor productivity, expressed in terms of output per hour, rose 56 percent, while constant dollar shipments rose by $11.5 billion annually. According to the BLS, automation was responsible for many of the jobs that textile companies lost in the 1970s, although it was impossible to determine a precise number. The situation was complicated by the fact that automation was partly a response to import pressures, which pushed firms to modernize or die. For mill owners, the fundamental problem was rising imports, and it was this issue that would decide their fate.[11]

Press reports confirmed that imports were causing plenty of plant closures, especially in apparel. As early as October 1971, the *U.S. News and World Report* investigated the impact of textile imports, concluding that "there is real distress among people in many American mill towns—particularly those in which the mill is the only major employer."[12] Newspapers carefully documented many shutdowns. In February 1973, the "once-flourishing" Troy District Shirt Company in Troy, New York, shut its doors, with manager Mortimor Solomon blaming "imports which have killed us." In November 1975, workers at Louis Goldsmith, Inc., in Souderton, Pennsylvania, also lost their jobs, and the ACWA claimed that "increased imports" were responsible. While most of the closures occurred in the northern states, the South was not spared. In April 1975, for instance, Friedman-Marks Clothing Company shut its factory in Richmond, Virginia. Over 1,200 workers lost their jobs, and most of them women. As the Richmond *News Leader* reported, it was one of the biggest plant closures the city had ever experienced, and it came just a few years after the shutdown of the large Liggett & Myers Tobacco Factory. Aware of the weak local economy, laid-off workers worried that they would not find comparable jobs. "I need to work because my husband is unable to work," explained Clara Walker, who had started with Friedman-Marks as a youngster. "But when you are 59 years old, there are very few places you can go."[13]

In 1975, the closure of the Chicopee Company in Manchester, New Hampshire, was particularly notable. The mill had opened in 1937, just a year after the Amoskeag Company's shutdown. Although it was a small operation, the Chicopee mill had taken on some displaced textile workers and had given residents hope. "When the Amoskeag closed, there was nothing in Manchester until the Chicopee came," recalled Lottie Sargent, a child of Amoskeag workers who lost her job when the Chicopee shut down. The closure again hurt women and older workers the most. "It's terrible trying to find a job now," explained Sargent in the late 1970s. "You would think that being on the same job twenty-five years, they would say, 'You must be good; you must be a nice, steady person.' But it's not that way at all. . . . [A]t fifty years old, they figure you're dead. I keep telling them I'm not, but they don't believe me." With the closure of the last functioning cotton mill in Manchester—a city that had once been one of America's biggest textile centers—it was truly the end of an era. The vast mill buildings along the Merrimack River gradually fell into disrepair. "Today, everything is falling down," recalled another former worker. "If our old parents, who worked so much in these mills, if they'd come back today and see how these mills are, it would really break their hearts."[14]

Union files also provide insights into the hardships caused by deindustrialization. In a sign of the times, executive board members now spent a lot of time discussing how to dispose of union buildings that were no longer needed after plants had closed. In May 1974, for example, the TWUA's leaders heard a report from representative R. L. Roper about Converse, South Carolina, where it had proved impossible to sell the hall belonging to defunct Local 325, located in the heart of the struggling textile belt. "The realtor has not been back in touch," he noted. Of more concern to union leaders, however, were the frequent reports that there was also little demand for displaced mill workers. As the TWUA/ACWA merger convention minutes summarized, "Apparel and textile workers who lost their jobs are among the hardest of the unemployed to retrain and place in new occupations."[15]

Observing these developments, the unions gradually escalated their demands for action, setting in motion a chain of events that would culminate in the massive campaign for H.R. 1562. The roots of the campaign went back many years, and the apparel unions were particularly innovative. In August

1971, for instance, ILGWU officer Sol C. Chaikin proposed a "massive national campaign" against imports. The apparel sector, he explained, had been the first in the country to suffer enormous damage as a result of foreign competition. "The problem of imports from shockingly low wage countries," he explained, "has been ever present for many years since the conclusion of World War II." By the early 1970s, "huge chunks" had been "ripped out" of the industry, and dramatic action was called for. In particular, Chaikin insisted that members should be mobilized more, especially in demonstrations outside large retail stores. A few months later, ILGWU assistant president Gus Tyler also urged an anti-import crusade. "Personally," he wrote, "I believe that this campaign should be a do or die thing for the ILGWU." Action soon followed. On November 16, 1972, the ILGWU coordinated anti-import demonstrations at locations across the country, with most attention focused on big department stores. The largest protests were in Los Angeles and New York City, although "several thousand" members also took part in demonstrations in Newark, Boston, and Philadelphia. In an "Open Letter to Retailers," Louis Stulberg appealed for support. "We have a mutual interest: the workers whose jobs you help to save are your very own customers," he declared.[16]

As Chaikin's reference to "shockingly low wage countries" implied, at this time much of the ILGWU's concern was directed at overseas workers, who were seen as threats rather than allies. As union flyers put it, it was important to stem a "disastrous flood" of goods from "sweatshop countries." The ILGWU's "Fair Trade Practices Department" linked the union's earlier fight against sweatshops to its current battle against low-wage imports. As one union flyer put it, "Half a century after the ILGWU had won its battle against sweatshop conditions, its members were now confronted by sweatshop conditions. The decent work and pay conditions they have won through collective bargaining . . . are being undermined by products made, for example, at 9 cents an hour in Korea, 11 cents in India, and 18 cents in Portugal." The ACWA took a similar line.[17]

The ILGWU also highlighted that women employees were especially vulnerable as the industry declined. In the mid-1970s, research director Lazare Teper wrote a detailed paper that traced the import problem back to the early 1950s. It argued that the labor-intensive nature of the apparel industry made it impossible for American producers to compete with foreign suppliers. It was a conclusion that had stark consequences for America's apparel workers. The union's data showed that 80 percent of them were women, and of these around one-third were widowed, single, divorced, or separated. For every one hundred women apparel workers, sixty-four had to wholly or partially support dependents. These family ties meant that workers lacked "geographic mobility" and had "few alternative job opportunities." A professional economist, Teper concluded that "for women workers, the industry provides a real and continued source of livelihood. . . . When employment opportunities are eroded by rising imports, many workers sorely in need of work are deprived of employment opportunities. This alone justifies every measure federal authorities can take to safeguard jobs in this field."[18] Although the ILGWU highlighted how female workers were being hurt by imports, the bulk of its leaders—like Teper—were white men. In public, the union argued that it was hard to recruit female leaders because they were too busy raising their families. "We have difficulty getting people out of the rank and file," declared Chaikin. It was clear that the union could have done more to encourage female leadership, and this would have strengthened its campaign. Between 1967 and 1981, the ILGWU's membership fell from 457,000 to 300,000, and leaders claimed that imports and outsourcing were the main culprits.[19]

The import issue led to alliances between the textile and apparel unions, who had operated independently since the early twentieth century. This separation reflected historic differences between the related industries; textiles originated in New England and spread to the South, whereas apparel began in New York City and gradually shifted to both urban and rural locations across the country.[20] The import issue, however, brought the unions together. In 1976, the TWUA and ACWA merged, partly to ensure that they could pool resources and fight against imports. In that year, the merger convention of the new ACTWU passed a detailed "Resolution on Imports," which contended that a "rising tide" of foreign-made goods was "continuing to cause disruption and unemployment." The union issued a six-point program to deal with the problem, which it blamed for the loss of twenty thousand clothing jobs in 1975 alone. In particular, it called for a stronger MFA and tougher bilateral agreements with major exporting nations.[21] In the following year, an ILGWU/ACTWU memorandum on "Apparel and Textile Imports" demanded stricter controls.[22]

The import issue also led to alliances with employers, many of whom were otherwise reluctant to work with labor unions. By the start of 1978, the ACTWU and the ILGWU had joined with a number of industry groups, including the ATMI, the NTA, and the American Apparel Manufacturers Association (AAMA), in a national "Textile/Apparel Import Steering Group." The Steering Group was a forerunner of FFACT, and it rehearsed many of its arguments. In a letter to President Carter, for example, the group opposed any cut in import duties because foreign goods had already caused serious damage. "The undersigned organizations representing all segments of this industrial complex are completely opposed to any reduction in these tariffs," they declared. To justify this position, the letter stressed the size of the industry and its record of providing jobs to women and racial minorities.[23]

For southern textile companies, this alliance was particularly significant because most of these firms had repeatedly fought with unions. One key member of the Steering Group was Burlington Industries, a giant firm that subsequently supported FFACT and the Crafted with Pride initiative. Just a few years earlier, however, the TWUA had slammed Burlington for its fervent opposition to unionization. To keep unions out, managers threatened to close plants, a very effective deterrent and one that resulted in numerous NLRB charges. In 1961, the TWUA claimed that Burlington was spearheading the industry's "massive resistance" to unionization. In that year, the union's International Executive Council pulled no punches. "Burlington Industries," it alleged in a resolution, "is defacing the American image in the eyes of the rest of the world, for its cynical suppression of the right of textile workers to organize mocks the democratic process and besmirches the nation's image as a society of genuinely free men and women."[24]

Relations were even more strained with J. P. Stevens, America's second largest textile company and a key member of the import restriction movement. In the 1960s, the TWUA undertook a major drive to organize Stevens's plants in the South, a move that the company resisted by firing union supporters and openly flouting labor laws. The union's fight with Stevens continued into the 1970s, when organized labor launched a high-profile boycott against the company. In the process, the AFL–CIO castigated Stevens as "the nation's No. 1 labor law violator." It was not until October 1980 that a truce was finally reached. Relations had also traditionally been poor with Cannon Mills and Milliken and Company, as both firms were able to keep the unions out. While Milliken was able to work with labor on the import issue, Cannon refused to cooperate, partly because unions continued to try to organize its workforce. Instead, the company fought against imports on its own.[25]

The organization of the Steering Group reflected mounting desperation in the industry, and this forced both sides to realize that they would need to put historic animosities aside. In the late 1970s, the industry's long campaign for import protection certainly escalated. In April 1977, for example, Burlington Industries published a full-page statement to express its concern about the "rising tide" of imports. As the industry's largest company, Burlington's example was important, and the advertisement—which appeared in newspapers across the country—amounted to a rallying cry for American manufacturers. "We cannot stand silently watching our own industry's *decline*," it declared. In September, Burlington also issued a detailed "position paper" on the problem. It called for imports to be linked to the annual rate of growth in the domestic market, a key feature of the subsequent textile legislation. Both documents were sent to influential political leaders, including many members of Congress. "Some 2.3 million jobs are at stake," explained Burlington chairman William A. Klopman, "as well as one of this country's most important industries."[26]

The following year, Cannon Mills also issued an import statement. Based in Kannapolis, North Carolina, Cannon called itself the "Largest Manufacturer of Household Textiles" in the country, and these products were vulnerable to foreign competition. Emphasizing that imports were causing "widespread" unemployment, the company again demanded tighter restrictions.[27] While Burlington and Cannon were based in the South, there were similar efforts from northern companies. In the summer of 1978, representatives of the Northern Textile Association testified before Congress on the need for more effective import controls. "The increasing levels of imports which began in the late 1950's has caused serious injury and loss of jobs in our industry in the North," declared Kenneth V. Chace. Again, the NTA argued that only a change in federal policy could address the problem.[28]

Seeking to gain the backing of key legislators, the industry's leaders developed important new arguments. In the South, the textile industry had traditionally hired whites for production jobs. Less than 5 percent of the workforce, African Americans were restricted to a small range of laboring positions, usually outside the plants. As *Atlanta Journal* columnist Lee Walburn put it, "Until the passage of the Civil Rights Act, the only thing whiter than a textile mill was the Ku Klux Klan." With the passage of the landmark legislation, the South's largest industry came under significant pressure to change, especially as most companies were sued by African Americans who wanted a better deal. Over the course of the 1960s, the industry made rapid progress in integrating its mills, and black employment increased four times faster than the national average for all manufacturing. In 1968—a year often regarded as an end point for the civil rights movement—about one-third of the workers hired by the nation's textile companies were African American, and further integration occurred in the years that followed. By 1978, blacks held a quarter of all production jobs in the southern textile industry. While much of this progress was the result of black activism, it was a genuine turnaround, and industry leaders soon grasped that they could use the diversity of their workforce to their advantage.[29]

Lobbying Congress, the ATMI started to highlight the industry's diversity and the important role that textile companies could play in solving racial problems. In the wake of Martin Luther King's assassination on April 4, 1968, race riots broke out in 125 U.S. cities, resulting in forty-three deaths and more than twenty thousand arrests. Over seventy-two thousand Army and National Guard troops were used to quell the riots, the largest domestic deployment of military forces since the Civil War. At the time, many Americans worried that racial divisions would split their country into two.[30] Cities in both northern and southern textile areas were affected by the violence, a fact not lost on the industry's leaders. As the ATMI's Robert C.

Jackson noted, the textile industry was a major employer of blacks and could help to avert future riots. "We are told that many of the problems of our cities and towns will be alleviated when Negroes can find and hold decent jobs," he wrote in a May 1968 press release. "Considering the fact that so much of the textile industry is located in areas where the Negro population is heavy . . . it should be clear to anyone that this industry is uniquely situated to make a contribution. It is my understanding that 40 percent of the new hirings in South Carolina's textile industry during the past 12 months have been Negroes." Jackson cleverly added that the textile industry could only play a major role in assuaging racial tensions when imports were brought under "reasonable control."[31]

Corporations that had fiercely opposed the 1964 Civil Rights Act were soon using similar arguments. Before the passage of the law, Burlington Industries had opposed integration. Across the firm's sprawling southern operations, black men were restricted to a small range of nonproduction jobs, while black women found it hard to get even these positions. In September 1969, however, Burlington chairman Charles F. Myers Jr. told a professional gathering that rapid integration had occurred recently. "Employment of minority races and the disadvantaged has increased rapidly," he noted proudly. "No other industry has been more successful in providing jobs for Negroes."[32] In the years that followed, Burlington's managers continued to capitalize on these changes. In 1977, the company's "position paper" on imports expressed concern that "free trade" policies were taking away the jobs of vulnerable Americans. Because minorities filled 23 percent of posts, the impact of job loss was "more severe" than would otherwise have been the case. "The displaced workers are frequently entry-level people from minority groups and the job market is inelastic," it explained. In the same year, the company made similar points in its full-page newspaper statement.[33]

While they used the industry's diversity for strategic value, executives also knew that African Americans and women were being genuinely—and disproportionately—hurt by the industry's decline. In both textiles and apparel, the passage of civil rights legislation had led to more jobs for women and blacks, and these workers lacked seniority when the mills contracted. Ongoing discrimination in hiring also meant that these workers found it harder to land skilled posts, and they were concentrated in lower-level jobs that were more likely to be automated in response to import competition. Acknowledging these problems, in 1979 Roger Milliken wrote Senator Hollings that "blacks and women seem to be most adversely affected by the jobs that are lost through the tremendously increasing amounts of textile and garments coming into this country." In his reply, Hollings expressed his concern about black poverty, a problem he termed "one of our great needs in South Carolina." Because southern blacks desperately needed greater economic power, the decline of the region's largest industry was particularly tragic.[34]

The industry's arguments certainly got through to crucial political supporters, even though some of them—especially Georgia's Herman Talmadge and South Carolina's Strom Thurmond—were conservatives who had led opposition to the civil rights legislation. By August 1969, however, Talmadge was even lecturing the Senate about the industry's importance to African Americans. The man who had once called the *Brown v. Board of Education* school desegregation decision "a mere scrap of paper" now highlighted that black employment in textiles and apparel was increasing faster than the national average. "This pattern of increasing minority employment in the textile industry is of particular interest to the Congress," he added. "It represents an immediate and practical opportunity to combat problems of chronic poverty and unemployment." Talmadge noted that the industry provided vital jobs for blacks in the rural South, where poverty was rife. It was also an important employer in the large northern cities, where the recent riots had been concentrated. Overall, an emphasis on racial diversity soon became a central plank of the industry's legislative campaign. In February 1977, for example, the Informal House Textile Committee wrote President Carter that it was vital to preserve the 2.2 million jobs that the textile sector provided. "No other industry in America offers as many jobs to non-whites and females," they asserted. Increasingly working together, management and labor groups took up similar arguments.[35]

The largest trade association in the industry, the ATMI helped to coordinate the anti-import fight. By April 1977, the Institute claimed that 65 percent of the world's spindles were in developing or Communist bloc countries. The textile trade deficit had reached $3 billion—about 30 percent of the U.S. trade deficit—and it was rising all the time. "No industry should be expected to absorb that much of our national trade deficit," asserted ATMI chairman James D. Finley. "We must have import controls and tighter administration of these controls."[36] Working out of its Washington office, the ATMI lobbied politicians from textile districts, and they responded. In July 1978, for example, Maine congressman William Cohen organized hearings that provided a platform for textile supporters. Testifying before the House Ways and Means Committee, Cohen stressed that the industry was "worth saving," especially as it was a major employer of disadvantaged Americans. Allowing imports to increase would kill an important economic sector. It was a message echoed by the ATMI's Robert Small. "This industry stands at the precipice as never before in its almost 200 years of service to our country," he declared.[37]

The increased pressure from the industry yielded other important results. In 1978, for example, the Congressional Textile Caucus was officially organized. According to the group's constitution, its purpose was "to promote and expand the economic viability of the American textile/apparel/fiber industry and the jobs of its workers." Operating funds came from annual dues of $100, while staff salaries were paid on a clerk-hire basis. The Caucus's Constitution pledged it to look for "legislative solutions to the textile trade problem," increasing the likelihood of future battles between Congress and the administration. Within a few years, the Caucus had sixty paid-up members, and just over half were southerners. Democrats were overrepresented, although Georgia Republican Newt Gingrich was one of several notable exceptions. A separate Caucus operated in the Senate, where veterans Strom Thurmond and Fritz Hollings played leading roles. Both caucuses stressed that they were bipartisan.[38]

The Caucus built on the work of the Informal House Textile Committee, which was chaired for many years by South Carolina Democrat James R. Mann. "We have been in existence since the early 1960s," explained Mann in 1976, "and have continuously worked for the goal of achieving orderly international trade in textiles." By the mid-1970s, the Committee claimed that its activities were supported by over half of the House's members, including representatives from both political parties and from "every part of the country." The Committee certainly mobilized an impressive amount of support. In November 1975, for example, 130 congressmen wrote President Gerald Ford and demanded that the MFA be extended. Although it was "not a perfect agreement," the MFA still protected the industry, and the Committee's letter helped to ensure that it was renewed and strengthened. In the closing days of the Ford administration, some 229 members of Congress also signed a policy resolution that called for the industry to be preserved. After the 1976 presidential election, the Committee quickly exerted pressure on Ford's successor. "It is folly," declared Mann in a letter to Jimmy Carter, "to allow the lion's share of American market growth to benefit foreign industry at the expense of this country's largest employer in manufacturing."[39]

The papers of key Caucus members highlight why the group was able to mobilize so effectively. In Mann's home state, for example, around half of all manufacturing jobs were in textiles, and the industry's pull was enormous. It affected both Democrats and Republicans. As Senator Hollings candidly explained to one of his constituents, "Since coming to the United States Senate I have spent the majority of my time in legislation and programs to assist and protect our textile industry and employees." In a similar vein, Senator Thurmond called the loss of textile jobs "one of the major problems facing the Nation" and devoted a large portion of his time to the industry. "Ever since coming to the United States Senate in 1954," he explained to one of his many constituents who worked in the mills, "I have worked to stabilize our domestic textile industry." According to Butler Derrick, a South Carolina congressman for over twenty years, "Textile mills were the dominant force in South Carolina politics, for many, many generations."[40] While the New England textile industry had already declined significantly, its influence was still considerable. A key member of both the Congressional Textile Caucus and its predecessor, William Cohen, understood as much. "The textile and apparel industry," he wrote President Ford in 1975, "plays a vital role in the economy of the State of Maine as well as in the other New England states." Following his election to Congress in 1972, Cohen consistently asked his Republican superiors to endorse industry demands. His papers reveal that his letter to Ford was even drafted with the "assistance" of Doug Horstman, the NTA's Washington representative. Cohen also sent copies to local mill owners and the ATMI.[41]

Cohen's example was not unusual. Throughout the 1970s, ATMI officials in Washington corresponded closely with key members of Congress, helping to coordinate the actions of the Informal Textile Committee and the Textile Caucus. Even before the Caucus was organized, ATMI leaders knew that the Committee had real power. As two top Institute officials wrote Cohen in 1975, "We know firsthand of the important role this (Informal Textile) Committee plays in the formulation of U.S. textile trade policy and your participation in its activities adds greatly to its influence. . . . (A) communication from the Committee to our top trade policy-makers will have a significant impact."[42]

The industry's power had helped to bring about the MFA, and in the years that followed executives mobilized to build on their achievement. Signed by the United States, the European Economic Community, and developing countries, the MFA was a broad—and complex—framework for determining the conditions under which the textile and apparel trade was controlled. Like the Short- and Long-Term Agreements, the MFA was basically an exception to the General Agreement on Tariffs and Trade (1947), a multilateral trade agreement that had been designed to promote free trade. Under the MFA, countries could enter into bilateral agreements to restrict the textile and apparel trade. The MFA also allowed for unilateral trade restraints if bilateral agreements were not secured. Furthermore, it established the norms for bilateral export restraint agreements and provided for annual import growth of 6 percent.[43] In both 1977 and 1981, the industry put up a strong fight to ensure that the MFA was renewed and strengthened. Indeed the MFA, which was originally designed as a short-term measure to allow developed countries to adjust to imports, eventually lasted for over thirty years. While they often criticized the MFA's inadequacies, industry executives knew that the arrangement offered them some protection. As the NTA's William F. Sullivan wrote to his members in 1977, "If the MFA goes out of existence, the industry will face the formidable task of securing legislation requiring or permitting the President to impose quotas on imports of textiles and textile products."[44]

Still, the MFA had many weaknesses. Considerable flexibility was built into the arrangement, including the ability to carry over unused export ceilings from one year to the next and the facility to use part of the unfilled ceiling of one category for another category. Although the United States signed scores of bilateral agreements, imports continued to surge. "Interestingly," concluded scholars Grace I. Kunz and Myrna B. Garner in one study, "the MFA really didn't work." In spite of the MFA, U.S. imports of textiles and apparel rose from $2.3 billion in 1973 to $68 billion in 2000. The industry continued to expand globally, a move supported by American retailers and some apparel manufacturers, who could move to countries where no bilaterals were in effect. At this time, however, most of the industry remained in the United States.[45]

Aware of the MFA's flaws, industry supporters continued to push for domestic legislation. In September 1978, during the closings days of the ninety-fifth Congress, Caucus members played a key role in passing H.R. 9937, a bill that prohibited U.S. trade negotiators in Geneva from reducing textile tariffs. Sponsored by Senator Ernest Hollings and Representative Ken Holland, both from South Carolina, the provision was tacked onto a minor bill authorizing further sales of Carson City silver dollars. The bill built on Cohen's work to protect the industry from tariff cuts, as he had sponsored a similar effort a few months before. Now, Hollings claimed that the industry was in a "distraught condition" and needed urgent help. "When a man is hemorrhaging, you don't cut another vein," he declared. According to the bill's supporters, imports were "flooding" in, and the president had to act. In a strongly worded telegram, they reminded Carter of the industry's size and economic importance, especially in his native region. "More than 2 million workers, their families, and the communities in which they work are counting on you to sign the bill," they proclaimed.[46]

Caucus members expected a lot from Carter, who had made encouraging pledges to Hollings on the eve of the 1976 election. "The American textile industry is national and not regional in scope," he wrote in October. "The textile industry provides employment opportunities in every state, particularly to minority workers who deserve a place in the economic mainstream of our country." Soon after taking office, Carter also invited textile leaders to a special briefing at the White House, raising hopes that he would respond to their needs. By 1978, Carter had followed through on his promise to renew the MFA, and the industry hoped that his administration would also provide the "orderly marketing conditions" that he had spoken of.[47]

The bill was the culmination of a national lobbying effort by the industry. One of the first to petition the president, New Jersey governor Brendan T. Byrne blamed imports for heavy job losses in his state. In December 1977, meanwhile, Massachusetts congressmen James A. Burke and Thomas P. O'Neill wrote Carter to express "deep concern" about "increasing" imports and the effect they were having on domestic mills. "We are speaking for 2,300,000 employees whose jobs will be further threatened by reductions in tariffs on incoming goods," they concluded. The following month, the newly organized Textile/Apparel Import Steering Group pressured Carter in a similar vein. "We unanimously oppose any reductions in the import duties on any of the products of our industry," they declared. In an impressive show of unity, thirteen industry and labor groups signed the group's petition. Once H.R. 9937 was introduced, other members of Congress joined the fray. Citing job losses within his Pennsylvania district, Raymond F. Lederer advised Carter that "the U.S. Government has a duty not to allow any industry to be destroyed by unfair trade competition."[48]

From his office in Boston, the NTA's William F. Sullivan also coordinated a campaign to get members involved. He carefully instructed them what to include in letters to their political representatives: "You may wish to mention your employment, the seriousness of imports to you directly as well as indirectly because of the impact of imports on the whole textile industry and the apparel industry. . . . In any event, please take the time to put it in your own words." Many NTA members responded, and by April 1978 Sullivan reported that 251 members of Congress had signed a resolution declaring that it was the "sense of the House" that textile products should be excluded from the tariff negotiations. Support was strong along the East Coast but was limited in western states, where the industry had less influence.[49]

Hollings's papers confirm that mill owners and workers were pressing him for help. From right along the eastern seaboard, worried mill executives wrote the South Carolinian, who was known to be one of the industry's most forceful supporters. In February 1978, for example, mill owner Robert G. Laidlaw wrote from Stamford, Connecticut. The industry, he explained, carried an "unfair burden," as it tried to compete with countries where wages were much lower. As a result, "equitable restraints" upon imports were justified. Scores of workers also petitioned Hollings, and many lived in his home state. "Recently I was laid off from MAFO Textured Fabrics, located here in McBee, South Carolina," wrote James Rodgers in late 1977. "It was a result of too much foreign import. We enjoy free enterprise and foreign import(s) but not as opposed to our jobs. Please stop it now." Hard-working citizens were hurting, and something had to be done. "Please be advised that we here in S. Carolina are much concerned about tariff cuts in the textile and apparel goods," added John R. Nash from Spartanburg. "Those who are employed now are lucky. What in the world is going to happen to the generation to follow?"[50]

It was a question that also troubled Hollings. In late October, the Charleston native met with Carter and urged him to sign a bill that would help to secure the industry's future. According to Hollings, the president was "attentive," even allowing the senator to stuff a flyer into his pocket. Despite this, Carter was careful to avoid firm commitments. As Hollings knew, most of Carter's aides were telling him to veto the bill. They included U.S. trade representative Robert Strauss, who politely rebuffed numerous appeals to support the legislation. The administration, he insisted, had the industry's best interests at heart.[51]

In private, Carter's advisers were more forthright. H.R. 9937, they insisted, was a protectionist piece of legislation that would prevent American negotiators from extracting concessions from their trading partners. As Chief Domestic Policy Adviser Stuart Eizenstat wrote the president, excluding textiles and apparel from tariff cuts would lead to "retaliatory withdrawals" from other countries and "damage the overall climate for international economic cooperation." Contending that "negative reaction" on the home front could be contained by a sympathetic presidential message, Eizenstat recommended that the bill be vetoed. Carter's advisers also worried about setting what Office of Management and Budget director James T. McIntyre Jr. called a "seriously undesirable precedent," as other industries would expect similar treatment. Finally, one of Carter's top priorities was to combat inflation, and advisers opposed textile import restrictions because they would raise prices, thus undermining the "basic policy thrust" of the administration.[52]

Outside administration circles, strong opposition also came from the press, export-oriented industries, and foreign governments. It helped tip the balance. Although he received many petitions from textile workers and mill owners, Carter vetoed the bill. In his veto message, delivered on November 11, Carter stressed that he did care about the textile industry but insisted that it could not be protected at the expense of other parts of the economy, especially export-oriented industries. "If the two and a quarter million workers in the textile and apparel industry are to survive in their jobs," he asserted, "we must work to keep the world economy strong and international trade free."[53] As the *Southern Textile News* reported, the veto shook the industry and generated "deep concern" about the future. Carter, however, softened the blow by pledging to help the "beleaguered textile industry." As Eizenstat had predicted, the conciliatory language assuaged criticism, especially from labor unions. Thus the leaders of both the ILGWU and the ACTWU wrote that while they would have preferred the bill to be signed, the president's "concern" for the industry was "a positive step in the right direction." Nevertheless, Carter's veto was an important turning point, especially as several scholars have located the roots of industrial decline in this period. According to Judith Stein, the 1970s was a "pivotal decade" where policy makers "traded factories for finance," ushering in a long period of deindustrialization.[54]

The veto certainly highlighted that while elected officials were aware of the textile industry's political power, the free trade philosophy held sway within the federal bureaucracy. Here, officials argued that consumers would benefit from a relaxation of import controls, a view that predominated within the State Department and the U.S. trade representative's office. As State

Department aide Robert J. McCloskey wrote Congressman Mann, it was in the national interest to consider the views of "producer and consumer groups." Prior to the veto, State Department official Joan Braden even informed the American Apparel Manufacturers Association that the department had "generally tried to discourage protectionist pressures" because they disadvantaged the American consumer. While Braden's speech drew complaints from the House Textile Committee, it served as a warning that the industry's efforts to secure protective legislation were unlikely to be supported by any administration.[55] In 1978, Robert Strauss also informed Congressman Cohen that he would go ahead and "reduce duties on certain textile products" in the Geneva negotiations. It was possible, he argued, to pursue both "freer and fairer trade."[56]

The veto was also significant because it carried considerable political risks for a president whose popularity was on the wane, especially in the South. As the *Washington Post* highlighted, many textile workers lived in the "politically volatile" Deep South, where the Democrats had been losing support for more than a decade, particularly among white voters.[57] Prior to the veto, some of these voters had made it clear that they were losing faith in the Democrats because the party was not doing enough to help the textile industry. Writing Senator Hollings on November 3, District Judge Robert W. Hemphill spoke for many: "I just hope you will let Mr. Carter know that there are a hell of a lot of us down here who resent the fact his trade negotiator ignores the people and jobs in Carolina and the Carter section of this nation. . . . If he vetoes your magnificent effort, he will lose even more votes down here than he has already lost." When the veto was applied, many southerners felt betrayed. In the northeast—where the President retained more support—some executives were also angry. "There is a good deal of indignation among our friends in the Congress about the President's veto," reported Sullivan to the NTA's officers.[58]

Carter's veto was linked to a package of measures that were designed to help domestic textile manufacturers. While full details of the changes were not publicized, Carter promised to act against "harmful surges" in textile imports and to "negotiate strenuously" for the removal of nontariff barriers to American exports. As most mill owners realized, the real question was whether Carter would enforce these pledges over the long haul. "A vigorous implementation of President Carter's new program is a must," summarized Spartan Mills president Walter S. Montgomery Jr. In fact, over the coming months executives complained that the administration had not fulfilled its commitments. Moreover, the papers of the Carter White House reveal that the program was opposed by powerful figures within the administration. In particular, Council of Economic Advisers chairman Charles Schultze—who consistently pressed for trade liberalization—criticized the program as "a significantly restrictive international trade measure." Schultze also worried that further limitations on textile imports would cause inflation.[59]

In a confidential document that was released to Hollings, however, Carter promised the industry even more. He pledged to eliminate "import surges" that caused "market disruption" and promised to set up a "high-level Industry-Labor-Government Policy Group" to assist domestic producers. The president acknowledged the economic importance of the industry and expressed concern about the textile-apparel trade deficit, which had climbed to $5 billion. Crucially, he also promised that U.S. officials would seek tighter "restraint levels" with the Chinese.[60]

These were major commitments, and industry advocates claimed that the administration did not deliver on them. By September, Hollings was complaining to the USTR's office that many of the "Textile Program" pledges had "not yet been fulfilled." In particular, the high-level policy group had not even held its first meeting, and administration aides had not consulted fully with the industry as they negotiated amendments to bilateral agreements. Hollings also worried that intervention by retailers and other free-traders had caused the administration to backtrack on its promises to take tough action against China. Indeed, policy makers were concurrently seeking to grant "Most Favored Nation" trading status to China. In an effort to keep the pressure on the administration, industry and labor groups issued a White Paper that called for many changes, including import quotas in particular categories. All the members of the Textile/Apparel Steering Group, including the ACTWU, the ATMI, and the AAMA, signed the paper. Over the coming months, however, these organizations became increasingly dissatisfied.[61] Aware of this, Carter's aides worked through Hollings and tried to allay industry fears. In February 1979, Strauss reported to Eizenstat that several telephone calls with Hollings had "got him settled down."[62]

Although many textile executives and workers were already leaning toward the Republicans, Carter's veto helped to accelerate the trend. In the 1980 presidential election campaign, Reagan's overtures to the industry were also crucial. To win the presidency, the Republicans needed solid support in the South, and the textile issue provided an excellent way of achieving this. In January 1980, Reagan told South Carolina congressman Carroll A. Campbell Jr. that he would help the industry more than Carter had. "I share your concern for the well-being and continued viability of the American textile-apparel-fiber industry, and its more than two million workers," he wrote. Crucially, Reagan declared that he would link "import growth to the growth of the American market," fulfilling a key industry demand. This commitment—which Reagan also made in writing to Senator Thurmond—was widely publicized, and it helped the Republicans to win every southern state apart from Georgia (Carter's home state). Helped by other factors, especially Reagan's opposition to busing and affirmative action, white textile workers turned to the Republicans in droves. Once in office, Reagan repeated his pledges to the industry. In October 1982, he wrote Thurmond that he stood by his "commitment" to "relate total import growth to the rate of growth in the domestic market." A year later, the Reagan administration also promised to protect the textile and apparel industry from "market disruption" caused by imports.[63] Widely publicized, these promises would come back to haunt the administration.[64]

Crucially, these assurances raised expectations among the industry's congressional supporters and encouraged them to push for import restriction legislation. Written by Secretary of Commerce Malcolm Baldrige, one private memorandum to the president captured the bind that Reagan found himself in. "You have pledged to Senator Thurmond and others to relate the growth of textile imports to growth in the domestic market. However, import growth continues at unprecedented levels." A clash was brewing, especially as aides privately viewed many of the industry's demands as "protectionist." In April 1984—a year before H.R. 1562 was introduced— Carroll Campbell and James Broyhill (R-NC) told USTR William Brock that the textile industry was in "crisis." They warned: "We cannot sit by and watch the textile/apparel/fiber import situation deteriorate month by month, as imports continue to skyrocket. . . . Be advised that we are preparing legislation to implement a freeze in the event strong action is not forthcoming from the Executive Branch." The stage was set for a showdown between the administration and one of the biggest industries in the country.[65]

## NOTES

1. Bluestone and Harrison, *The Deindustrialization of America*, p. 4 (quotation), p. 5; Bluestone, "Foreword," in Cowie and Heathcott, eds., *Beyond the Ruins*, pp. viii–ix; Kunz and Garner, *Going Global*, p. 206.

2. United States International Trade Commission, "Emerging Textile-Exporting Countries," USITC Publication 1273, August 1982, pp. 1–8 (quotations on p. 3), copy in "USITC Textile Reports (3)" folder, Wendell W. Gunn files, OA9646, Reagan Library. The twelve countries covered by this study were Brazil, China, Colombia, India, Macau, Malaysia, Mexico, Pakistan, Philippines, Singapore, Sri Lanka, and Thailand.

3. Gross, *The Course of Industrial Decline*, pp. 9–10, 83–85; Don Johnson interview with author on June 23, 2010, in Athens, Georgia. In the southern United States, employers hired workers through a "family labor system" that had also been used previously in New England, rather than recruiting single women from farming backgrounds. Under this system, whole family groups were hired rather than just women, although these groups also included many women. See Hall et al., *Like A Family*, pp. 51–53 (quotation on p. 52).

4. Pamela G. Hollie, "Tensions in Textiles: A Challenge from Asia," *New York Times*, February 5, 1978, International Economic Survey, p. 21 (first quotation); Henry Scott Stokes, "Seoul Textile Plant's Closing Becomes Political Issue," *New York Times*, August 15, 1979, p. A2; Henry Scott Stokes, "The Industrious East Asians," *New York Times*, February 3, 1980, p. SM214 ("little Japans" quotation); Pamela G. Hollie, "Curb on Hong Kong's Textiles," *New York Times*, April 17, 1982, p. 29.

5. A. Lee Parsons to Robert C. Jackson, January 3, 1968, folder 1778, box 152, NACM/NTA Papers; Robert S. Strauss to Stuart L. Eizenstat, June 14, 1978, "Textiles (O/A6237)"

folder, box 291, Stuart Eizenstat files, held at the Jimmy Carter Presidential Library, hereafter cited as "Carter Library"; Clyde Farnsworth, "Trade and Favored Nations," *New York Times*, May 20, 1979, p. F18; ACTWU GEB Minutes, May 30–June 1, 1979, p. 10, untitled folder, box 854, ACTWU Papers.

6. Christopher S. Wren, "U.S. Curbs Chinese Textiles after Trade Talks Fail," *New York Times*, January 14, 1983; Christopher S. Wren, "China, Upset by U.S. Trade Curb, Halting Imports of 3 Commodities," *New York Times*, January 20, 1983, p. A1; "China and the U.S. Said to Near End of Trade Dispute," *New York Times*, July 31, 1983, p. 1; Roger Milliken to Edwin Meese III, November 3, 1983, "Textile Working Group (8)" folder, OA11723, Sherrie M. Cooksey files (Office of Counsel to the President), Reagan Library (quotations).

7. "Textile Plant Liquidations: Non-South and South, 1970–1979," ACTWU Research Department data, September 5, 1980, "Textile Plant Liquidations: Non-South and South" folder, box 2, series 6000/020, UNITE Papers-Cornell. These figures excluded apparel. ACTWU defined the South as the states of Maryland, Virginia, West Virginia, North Carolina, South Carolina, Georgia, Florida, Tennessee, Alabama, Mississippi, Louisiana, Arkansas, Oklahoma, and Texas.

8. "Textile Trade Law a Must, Union Tells Senate Hearing," *Labor Unity*, August–September 1985, p. 3.

9. "Textiles: Interagency Working Group Report," May 1983, p. 11, "Textiles: Interagency Working Group Report" folder, OA12242, Michael A. Driggs files, Reagan Library.

10. Irving I. Kramer to James F. Taylor, November 22, 1983, "Textiles 1983 (1)" folder, Wendell W. Gunn files, OA9663, Reagan Library.

11. Murray, "Unraveling Employment Trends," p. 63.

12. "Story behind the 'Textile War' with Japan," *U.S. News and World Report*, October 11, 1971, pp. 47–50, quotation on p. 48.

13. "Troy Shirt Set to Shut Down," Troy (NY) *Times Record*, January 12, 1973 (first two quotations); "Goldsmith Firm Closed; Workers File for Aid," Souderton (Pennsylvania) *Independent*, November 5, 1975 (third quotation); "'No One's Hiring': Clothiers Facing Bleak Future," Richmond (Virginia) *News Leader*, April 9, 1975 (Walker quotations); "Cluett's Phasing Out Operations at Plant," Fitchburg (Massachusetts) *Sentinel*, May 24, 1971, all clippings in "Plant Shutdown 1973–75" folder, box 631, ACTWU Papers-Cornell.

14. Hareven and Langenbach, *Amoskeag*, pp. 11, 373, 376.

15. TWUA Executive Council Minutes, May 20–24, 1974, p. A16, and April 22–25, 1975, pp. A13–A14, A16, both M78-173, TWUA Papers; TWUA Executive Council Minutes, May 24–28, 1976, p. A35, M78-173, TWUA Papers (closing quotation).

16. Sol C. Chaikin to President Stulberg, August 2, 1971; Gus Tyler to Henoch Mendelsund, December 21, 1971; "Demonstration Sites," n.d., and Louis Stulberg, "An Open Letter to Retailers," ca. 1972, all in "Import Activities, 1972–73" folder, box 12, 6000/023, UNITE Papers-Cornell.

17. Louis Stulberg, "An Open Letter to Retailers," ca. 1972 (first two quotations), and ILGWU Fair Trade Practices Department Sample Press Release, November 16, 1972, both in "Import Activities, 1972–73" folder, box 12, 6000/023, UNITE Papers-Cornell (other quotations). For an illustration of the ACWA's activism in this regard, as early as 1961 its submission to the Senate Commerce Committee declared that while the union supported improved trade links, "That objective is not served by permitting the competition of sweated labor to destroy a basic American industry like apparel." "Statement of ACWA to the Subcommittee of the Senate Interstate and Foreign Commerce Committee to Investigate Problems of the Textile Industry," February 20, 1961, "ACWA Statements on Foreign Trade—1961" folder, box 532, ACTWU Papers-Cornell.

18. Lazare Teper, "Women's and Children's Apparel and the Multifiber Arrangement," April 12, 1977, pp. 11–12, "Textile Industry 1975–78, 2 of 2" folder, box 13, MS106.3.3.17.1, Cohen Papers.

19. William Serrin, "Ailing Garment Workers Union Faces More Problems," *New York Times*, November 29, 1981, p. 56.

20. For a good summary of these historic differences, see: Rosen, *Making Sweatshops*, pp. 96–98.

21. TWUA Executive Council Minutes, May 24–28, 1976, pp. A35–37, M78–173, TWUA Papers.

22. ACTWU and ILGWU, "Apparel and Textile Imports," February 1977, "Textile Industry 1975–78, 2 of 2" folder, box 13, MS106.3.3.17.1, Cohen Papers.

23. Murray H. Finley et al. to Mr. President, January 31, 1978, "Textile Industry 1975–78, 2 of 2" folder, box 13, MS106.3.3.17.1, Cohen Papers.

24. TWUA Executive Council Minutes, November 11–14, 1961, p. 28, "1959–61" folder, box 1, Mss. 396, TWUA Papers.

25. 1978 ACTWU Convention Proceedings, p. 200, held at the Kheel Center for Labor-Management Documentation and Archives, School of Industrial and Labor Relations, Cornell University, Ithaca, New York. For a full insight into the J. P. Stevens campaign, see Timothy J. Minchin, *"Don't Sleep with Stevens!": The J. P. Stevens Campaign and the Struggle to Organize the South, 1963–80* (Gainesville: University Press of Florida, 2005).

26. "Jobs in Textiles: Another Endangered Species—A Statement from Burlington Industries," April 11, 1977, in "Textiles (C/F, O/A 24)" folder, box 291, Stuart Eizenstat files, Carter Library; Burlington Industries, "Are Textile Jobs Expendable?" September 19, 1977; and William A. Klopman to William S. Cohen, September 19, 1977, both "Textile Industry 1975–1978, 2 of 2" folder, box 13, MS106.3.3.17.1, Cohen Papers.

27. Norris Dearborn, "The Famous Cannon Mill Sign," "Cannon Mills," folder (drawer item), and "Cannon's Position on Textile Imports," November 1978, folder 267 ("Textile Imports"), #9501, both held at the Cannon Mills Papers, Cabarrus County Library, Kannapolis, North Carolina, hereafter cited as "Cannon Mills Papers."

28. "Statement of Northern Textile Association before the Committee on Ways and Means," July 10, 1978, "Textile Industry, 1975–1978, 1 of 2" folder, box 13, Cohen Papers (MS106.3.3.17.1).

29. Lee Walburn, "Shutdown of Mill Affects Union and Non-Union Alike," *Atlanta Journal*, September 29, 1986, p. A6 (quotation); Timothy J. Minchin, *Hiring the Black Worker: The Racial Integration of the Southern Textile Industry, 1960–1980* (Chapel Hill: University of North Carolina Press, 1999), p. 3; *Southern Textile News*, December 23, 1968, p. 1.

30. Michael K. Honey, *Going Down Jericho Road: The Memphis Strike, Martin Luther King's Last Campaign* (New York: W. W. Norton, 2007), pp. 445–47; "Memorandum for the President: Civil Disturbances," April 8, 1968, part 1, reel 4, Civil Rights during the Johnson Administration microfilm collection, held at the Borchardt Library, La Trobe University, Melbourne, Australia (microfilmed from the Lyndon Baines Johnson Library, Austin, Texas).

31. ATMI Press Release, May 18, 1968, folder 1779, box 152, NACM/NTA Papers.

32. Charles F. Myers Jr., "Are We Ready for the Seventies?" September 16, 1969, vol. 1.29, NTA 1969 Annual Meeting Files, NTA Papers.

33. James D. Finley to Herman E. Talmadge, February 25, 1977, "ATMI" folder, box 87, series II, Talmadge Papers; Burlington Industries Statement, April 11, 1977, and Burlington Industries, "Are Textile Jobs Expendable?" September 19, 1977 (quotations), both "Textile Industry 1975–1978, 2 of 2" folder, box 13, MS106.3.3.17.1, Cohen Papers. For Burlington's opposition to integration prior to 1964, see Minchin, *Hiring the Black Worker*, esp. pp. 92–96.

34. Roger Milliken to Fritz Hollings, January 5, 1979, and Ernest F. Hollings to Roger Milliken, January 16, 1979, both box 9, Ninety-Sixth Congress files, Hollings Papers.

35. Juan Williams, *Eyes on the Prize: America's Civil Rights Years, 1954–1965* (New York: Penguin, 1987), p. 34 (first quotation); Herman Talmadge Senate Speech, August 15, 1969, "Textile Trade, 1969–71" folder, box 312, series II, Talmadge Papers (Talmadge quotations); James T. Broyhill et al. to President Jimmy Carter, February 2, 1977, "Informal House Textile Committee" folder, box 4, James R. Mann Papers, held at South Carolina Political Collections, University of South Carolina-Columbia, hereafter cited as "Mann Papers" (House Textile Committee quotation); Murray H. Finley et al. to Mr. President, January 31, 1978, in NTA *Bulletin*, vol. 69 (1978), NTA Papers.

36. Quotations in Herbert Koshetz, "Lag in Growth and Rise in Imports Decried at Meeting of Textile Makers," *New York Times*, April 15, 1977, p. 95.

37. William S. Cohen to William Frenzel, July 26, 1978; Statement of William S. Cohen before the Committee on Ways and Means, July 10, 1978 (Cohen quotation); and Testimony of

Robert S. Small before the Committee on Ways and Means, July 10, 1978, all "Textile Industry, 1975–1978, 1 of 2" folder, box 13, MS106.3.3.17.1, Cohen Papers.

38. "Constitution and By-Laws of the Congressional Textile Caucus," n.d. (quotations), Carole Ayers to James C. Tuttle, March 16, 1984, and "Congressional Textile Caucus Membership for 1984," all "Textile Caucus 1983" folder, box 38, series 329-92-39, Jenkins Papers.

39. James R. Mann et al. to President Gerald Ford, April 14, 1976 (first, second, and fourth quotations); James R. Mann to President Jimmy Carter, May 24, 1977 (third quotation); James R. Mann et al. to President Gerald Ford, November 20, 1975; "Textile Trade Policy Resolution of the Informal House Textile Committee," September 21, 1976; and James R. Mann to President Jimmy Carter, May 24, 1977 (closing quotation), all "Informal House Textile Committee," folder, box 4, Mann Papers.

40. Ernest F. Hollings to A. Lowe Cook, June 17, 1968, box 7, Ninetieth Congress files, Hollings Papers; Strom Thurmond to Ken Pritchett, September 19, 1988, folder 503, box 61, CMS Series (first Thurmond quotation); and Strom Thurmond to Blair Rice, September 6, 1984, folder 523, box 70, CMS Series (second and third Thurmond quotations), both Thurmond Papers; Closing Derrick quotation in Butler Derrick interview with author on April 13, 2011, in Easley, South Carolina.

41. William S. Cohen to Gerald R. Ford, December 3, 1975 (first and second quotations), and William S. Cohen to Doug Horstman, December 4, 1975 (third quotation), both "Textile Industry 1975–78, 2 of 2" folder, box 13, MS106.3.3.17.1, Cohen Papers. For Cohen's efforts to send copies of his letter to other textile manufacturers and the ATMI, see William S. Cohen to H. W. Close, December 4, 1975, and William S. Cohen to Louis Strier, December 4, 1975, both in the same folder.

42. W. Ray Shockley and G. Stewart Boswell, November 12, 1975, "Textile Industry 1975–78 2 of 2," folder, box 13, MS 106.3.3.17.1, Cohen Papers.

43. Kunz and Garner, *Going Global*, pp. 102–05.

44. William F. Sullivan to Member Mill Executives, July 26, 1977, NTA *Bulletin*, vol. 66 (1977), NTA Papers.

45. Kunz and Garner, *Going Global*, pp. 104–05, quotation on p. 104.

46. "Hollings Wins Senate Approval of Textile Tariff Amendment," Senator Ernest F. Hollings Press Release, September 29, 1978 (first two quotations), and "SC Democrats Urge Carter to Sign Textile Bill Now," November 3, 1978 (other quotations), both box 8, Ninety-Fifth Congress files, Hollings Papers; Art Pine, "Carter Veto Expected on Textile Tariffs," *Washington Post*, October 19, 1978, p. F1. For a useful overview of the complicated battle to pass the 1977 bill, see Hollings, *Making Government Work*, pp. 194–97.

47. Jimmy Carter to Fritz Hollings, October 2, 1976, "MC3-3 1/20/77–2/10/77" folder, box M12, White House Central Files, Carter Library (quotations); W. Ray Shockley to Steve Selig, February 15, 1977, and James D. Finley to Midge Constanza, February 10, 1977, both American Textile Manufacturers Institute Name File, Carter Library.

48. Brendan T. Byrne to The President, October 12, 1977, "TA4-14 1/20/77–12/31/77" folder, box TA29, White House Central Files, Carter Library; James A. Burke and Thomas P. O'Neill to Jimmy Carter, December 15, 1977, NTA *Bulletin*, vol. 67 (1977), NTA Papers; Murray H. Finley et al. to Mr. President, January 31, 1978, NTA *Bulletin*, vol. 69 (1978), NTA Papers; Closing quotation in Raymond F. Lederer to Mr. President, November 6, 1978, "TA 4-14 1/1/78–12/31/78," folder, box TA29, White House Central Files, Carter Library. For another example of the congressional letters received by Carter, see Marilyn Lloyd to Jimmy Carter, October 27, 1978, ibid.

49. William F. Sullivan to Member Mill Executives, April 24, 1978, NTA *Bulletin*, vol. 69 (1978), NTA Papers.

50. Robert G. Laidlaw to Ernest F. Hollings, February 17, 1978; James Rodgers to Ernest F. Hollings, November 14, 1977; and John R. Nash to Ernest Hollings, November 17, 1977, all box 8, Ninety-Fifth Congress files, Hollings Papers.

51. Ernest F. Hollings to Leslie W. Levy, October 30, 1978 ("attentive" quotation), and Ernest F. Hollings to Roger Milliken, October 25, 1978, both box 8, Ninety-Fifth Congress files, Hollings Papers; Robert S. Strauss to William Cohen, March 21, 1978, "TA 4-14 1/1/78–12/31/78" folder, box TA29, White House Central Files, Carter Library.

52. Stu Eizenstat to the President, November 11, 1978, and James T. McIntyre Jr. to the President, November 6, 1978, both "TA 4-14 1/1/78–12/31/78" folder, box TA29, White House Central Files, Carter Library; Closing quotation in W. Michael Blumenthal to the President, February 6, 1979, "Textiles (CF O/A 539)" folder, box 291, Stuart Eizenstat Files, Carter Library. Blumenthal was Secretary of the Treasury.

53. Jimmy Carter, "Memorandum of Disapproval," November 11, 1978 (Carter quotations), box 8, Ninety-Fifth Congress files, Hollings Papers. For an example of textile workers' petitions to President Carter, see J. Roscoe Cauthen et al. to President Jimmy Carter et al., February 6, 1978, in the same box.

54. "Veto Shakes Industry," *Southern Textile News*, November 27, 1978, p. 1 (first quotation); Jimmy Carter, "Memorandum of Disapproval," November 11, 1978 (Carter quotation), box 8, Ninety-Fifth Congress files, Hollings Papers; Murray H. Finley and Sol C. Chaikin to Jimmy Carter, November 8, 1978, "TA4-14 1/1/78–12/31/78" folder, box TA29, White House Central Files, Carter Library (union quotations); Last two quotations in the title of Judith Stein, *Pivotal Decade: How the United States Traded Factories for Finance in the Seventies* (New Haven: Yale University Press, 2010). For another important recent work that locates the roots of industrial decline in the 1970s, see Jefferson Cowie, *Stayin' Alive: The 1970s and the Last Days of the Working Class* (New York: The New Press, 2010), esp. pp. 1–19.

55. Robert J. McCloskey to James R. Mann, July 9, 1976, and Joan R. Braden speech to the AAMA, May 24, 1976, both "Informal House Textile Committee" folder, box 4, Mann Papers.

56. Robert S. Strauss to William Cohen, March 21, 1978, "Textile Industry 1975–78, 2 of 2" folder, box 13, MS106.3.3.17.1, Cohen Papers.

57. There is a massive literature on the rise of the Republican Party in the South. For a recent overview, see James C. Cobb, *The South and America since World War II* (New York: Oxford University Press, 2011), pp. 121–23, 137–39. For a guide to much of the literature on the rise of the Republicans in the South, see Numan V. Bartley, *The New South, 1945–1980: The Story of the South's Modernization* (Baton Rouge: Louisiana State University Press, 1995), pp. 484–86.

58. Art Pine, "Carter Veto Expected on Textile Tariffs," *Washington Post*, October 19, 1978, p. F1; Robert W. Hemphill to Fritz Hollings, November 3, 1978, box 8, Ninety-Fifth Congress files, Hollings Papers; William F. Sullivan to Officers of the Association, December 22, 1978, NTA *Bulletin*, vol. 69 (1978), in NTA Papers.

59. Mary Russell, "Ways and Means Passes Countervailing Duties Bill," *Washington Post*, February 22, 1979, p. F1; Carter quoted in Jimmy Carter, "Memorandum of Disapproval," November 11, 1978, box 8, Ninety-Fifth Congress files, Hollings Papers; Walter S. Montgomery Jr. to Fritz Hollings, February 27, 1979, box 9, Ninety-Sixth Congress files, Hollings Papers; Schultze quoted in Charlie Schultze to the President, February 6, 1979, "Memos to President 2/79" folder, box 53, Charles L. Schultze Subject File, Council of Economic Advisers Files, Carter Library.

60. "Proposed Presidential Textile Program," January 17, 1979, box 9, Ninety-Sixth Congress Files, Hollings Papers.

61. Ernest F. Hollings to Reubin Askew, September 13, 1979, box 10, Ninety-Sixth Congress Files, Hollings Papers; "Comprehensive Fiber/Textile/Apparel Trade Program," (Industry/Labor White Paper), December 13, 1978, NTA *Bulletin*, vol. 69 (1978), NTA Papers.

62. "Joanne to Stu (Eizenstat)," February 1, 1979, "Textiles (CF O/A 539)" folder, box 291, Eizenstat Files, Carter Library.

63. Reagan to Campbell quoted in W. G. Hefner and Butler Derrick to Colleague, September 22, 1988, "Textile Trade Act," folder, box 24, series 1, Charles F. Hatcher Papers, held at the Richard B. Russell Library for Political Research and Studies, University of Georgia, hereafter cited as "Hatcher Papers"; Ronald Reagan to Strom Thurmond, September 3, 1980, and October 4, 1982; and White House Press Secretary Press Release, December 16, 1983, all "FFACT Book: 1986 Override Vote" folder, box 1019, ACTWU Papers-Cornell. For an overview of Reagan's success in the 1980 presidential election, see Brinkley, *American History*, p. 903.

64. For copies of these pledges in Reagan's files, see: Ronald Reagan to Strom Thurmond, October 4, 1982, "Textile Working Group (7)" folder, OA11723, Sherrie M. Cooksey files

(Office of the Counsel to the President), Reagan Library; Ronald Reagan to Carroll A. Campbell Jr., January 18, 1980, "Textiles: Miscellaneous Letters (2)" folder, OA12242, Michael A. Driggs files, Reagan Library. For Reagan's stance on racial issues and its role in helping him win the South, see Timothy J. Minchin and John A. Salmond, *After the Dream: Black and White Southerners since 1965* (Lexington: University Press of Kentucky, 2011), p. 205.

65. Malcolm Baldrige to Ronald Reagan, undated but ca. 1983, "Textiles (2)" folder, Geoffrey O. Carliner files, OA10697, Reagan Library (first two quotations); Carroll A. Campbell and James T. Broyhill to William Brock, April 26, 1984, "Textiles (1)" folder, Geoffrey O. Carliner files, OA10697, Reagan Library.

## *Chapter Four*

# The Most Important Battle: The Fight to Pass the 1985 Textile Bill

By the mid-1980s, the textile industry was experiencing a national crisis. According to the U.S. Customs Service, between 1980 and 1985 textile and apparel imports grew by 86 percent, and in 1984 alone they exceeded $15 billion in value.[1] As the Woonsocket *Call and Reporter* noted, mill closings were now harming southern communities just as much as their northern counterparts. "The locations are different . . . but the results are the same," wrote reporter Dave Lavallee. "Textile plants across the country are being hurt severely, and union and industry officials cite one major reason—imports."[2]

Formally known as the Textile and Apparel Trade Enforcement Act of 1985, H.R. 1562 was a bold effort to protect the domestic textile industry from this import surge. According to a Reagan administration analysis, the bill placed "stringent limits" on textile imports from twelve countries, most of them in Asia. Imports from South Korea and Taiwan, for example, would be instantly reduced by 30 percent, while those from Hong Kong would be cut by 14 percent. Imports from the remaining countries would be frozen at 1984 levels. Future imports would also be strictly limited, in most cases to a 1 percent growth rate.[3] Overall, the Commerce Department estimated that the bill would limit textile imports to seven billion yards a year, much less than the 1984 import level of around ten billion yards.[4]

For the industry's supporters, a huge amount was at stake in the fight to secure the bill's passage. As FFACT consultant John Leslie wrote during the campaign, "We are facing perhaps the most important battle this union has ever fought."[5] In January 1986, ACTWU president Murray Finley also reported to his General Executive Board on the bill's importance. "Every one of us must understand that this issue is vital for the survival of our members and industries," he warned.[6] The bill's opponents, however, also recognized how much was on the line, and H.R. 1562 provoked strong opposition from retailers, exporters, and other free-traders. According to Loyd Hackler of the American Retail Federation, the trade in textiles and apparel was "as politically charged as any economic issue facing the Administration." During a prolonged and exhausting legislative battle, the power of the bill's opponents was decisive.[7]

The industry's troubles were clear. Between 1980 and 1985, federal figures indicated that over 142,000 jobs were lost in the textile and apparel industry; textile employment dropped by 15 percent, while in apparel the fall was 11 percent. Although the industry had been experiencing problems for some time, these were particularly discouraging figures. By the mid-1980s, profitability had tumbled, a victim of the rising dollar, a substantial drop in textile exports, and two recessions. In an effort to stay afloat, textile manufacturers took part in mergers and acquisitions, further reducing the number of small and midsized firms. Job losses were caused by these mergers, as well as by changing consumer preferences, automation, and imports. Often, the reasons were linked. In apparel, for example, there was a switch toward casual clothing that tended to be imported. The rise of discount-minded retailers such as Wal-Mart and K-Mart was also important, as clothing increasingly came to be seen as a short-term purchase rather than a long-term one. While imports were not the only difficulty facing the beleaguered industry, they were its major problem. They were also an issue that could be tackled through domestic legislation.[8]

Independent studies confirmed that imports were increasing and that they were causing job losses. In a careful analysis of IMF data, the Congressional Office of Technology Assessment documented that imports had made rapid gains. Measured in square yards, in 1985 some 33 percent of the U.S. textile market and 48 percent of the apparel market was imported, shares that had more than doubled in a decade. Between 1980 and 1986, the U.S. trade deficit in textiles and apparel rose fourfold, reaching more than $21 billion. Industry advocates pointed to the example of the EEC, where restrictions imposed in 1983 had ensured that textile and apparel imports had actually fallen. The situation was very different in the United States. As the OTA report concluded, "The United States is one of the few nations that has left its markets largely open to foreign sales of textiles and apparel, and one of the few that has paid little attention to the research needs of its domestic industry. As a result, imports have flooded domestic markets." The impact of imports was also magnified by the fact that American textile and apparel companies were not big exporters, although manufacturers responded that this was because overseas competitors had closed their markets. In 1980, for example, apparel exports reached an all-time high, yet they still only constituted 3 percent of domestic production. The industry's critics, however, charged that mill owners had relied on the domestic market for too long and should have modernized their plants rather than seeking protection.[9]

Privately, the Reagan administration acknowledged that most of the industry's problems were related to imports. As the U.S. trade representative's office reported to the president in 1985, since 1980 imports of textiles had grown at an annual rate of 19 percent. This was "far greater than the orderly growth objectives of the Multi-Fiber Arrangement and far in excess of the 1 percent average growth of the U.S. market during that period." In a joint memorandum to the president, USTR William Brock and Commerce Secretary Malcolm Baldrige admitted that textile imports had surged 25 percent in 1983 and 32 percent in 1984. "Imports have continued to increase despite our quota actions and bilateral agreements because only 60 percent of current trade is covered by quotas," they acknowledged. The rise in imports was partly related to the strong U.S. dollar. As Brock and Baldrige admitted, however, Reagan's promises to the industry gave the situation "sharp political significance," especially as imports were causing "a large number of mill closures."[10]

Occurring at the end of 1984, the collapse of the Crompton Company was particularly illustrative. Founded in 1807 in Providence, Rhode Island, Crompton was the oldest textile company in the United States to remain in operation.[11] Managers of the historic company, moreover, blamed imports for its demise. In corduroy, the main product manufactured by Crompton, imports increased 240 percent between 1979 and 1984, and by the latter date they controlled 42 percent of the U.S. market. According to company president William G. Lord II, the firm had been unable to cope with "drastically increased levels of foreign garment imports, primarily from the Far East." Imports, agreed the *New York Times*, were Crompton's "nemesis."[12] As a result of Crompton's collapse, 2,400 workers lost their jobs, and Lord accused the Reagan administration of selling these employees short. Responding to these accusations, Brock stressed that the administration was trying to control imports, which were "at an unusually high rate," but he argued that the strong dollar was undermining their efforts. "I can assure you that no one dealing with textiles in this Administration remains unmoved when a firm with Crompton's history and reputation ceases operation," he added.[13]

As the administration was aware, the MFA was not containing import growth effectively. The arrangement, aides noted, did not include a mechanism for relating import growth to the expansion of the domestic market, a central industry demand. In addition, it contained an obligation to allow for annual growth in quotas and to demonstrate a threat of market disruption before any restrictive action could even be contemplated. As Brock and Baldrige had acknowledged, bilateral agreements negotiated under the aegis of the MFA also covered less than 60 percent of textile and apparel imports, so many goods were circumventing the arrangement. In addition, transshipments were common. As presidential aide John A. Svahn explained in March 1985, some exporters had been "able to circumvent their country's export quotas by transhipping goods through a third country to the United States." Overall, the problem of textile fraud was immense; between October 1983 and July 1984, for example, U.S. Customs officials seized $19.6 billion in illegally shipped textile products. Because customs lacked the resources to catch most offenders, transhipments usually arrived undetected.[14]

While the administration recognized the industry's problems, it felt unable to fulfill the pledges it had made. In the fall of 1983, Brock admitted in a private memorandum to presidential counselor Edwin Meese that the administration was "having so much difficulty meeting the President's commitment," chiefly because they involved fundamental changes in trade policy. Apparently written by Brock, an administration paper confirmed that aides felt that establishing quotas that were linked to the growth or contraction of the domestic market would "run afoul" of the U.S.'s obligations under both the MFA and twenty-six bilateral agreements. Brock hoped that "quiet conversations" with mill owners offered the best solution, although he also referred to an "unavoidable conflict" with the industry.[15] Brock's colleagues were also apprehensive. As deputy chief of staff M. B. Oglesby Jr. summarized in one memorandum, "The textile issue is an extremely volatile one having both economic and political ramifications."[16]

Aware of the industry's political influence, Reagan and his advisors tried to pacify the textile lobby without making fundamental policy changes. In March 1983, Vice President George H. W. Bush accepted an invitation to speak at the ATMI's annual meeting, pleasing executives such as Mayfair Mills president Frederick B. Dent, who admitted to Bush that ATMI members were "generally politically active and . . . supporters of the Reagan Administration." At the gathering, Bush told mill executives that their industry mattered. In July, following a White House meeting on the textile problem that was hosted by Meese, Reagan established an interagency White House Working Group to review implementation of the textile import program. As a result of this appraisal, on December 16 the president announced additional criteria for taking action to impose quotas on individual categories of imports from particular countries.[17]

The task of applying these quotas fell to the Committee for the Implementation of Textile Agreements (CITA). Established by Executive Order on March 3, 1972 to supervise the implementation of bilateral agreements and to apply import restraints under the LTA, the CITA was comprised of members from the commerce, state, labor, and treasury departments, as well as the Chief Textile Negotiator in the USTR's office. By 1985 Reagan claimed that the CITA had established 125 new quotas, yet executives argued that these were inadequate. Import levels, they reiterated, should be linked to the growth of the domestic market. Responding to the industry's pressure, in

May 1984 Reagan issued Executive Order 12475, which authorized regulations to deter circumvention of the textile and apparel quota program. In particular, the order aimed to tighten country-of-origin rules—a source of grievance to the industry—yet mill owners claimed that U.S. Customs lacked the resources to implement the order. Still, the administration used these actions to sell its record. "This Administration has done more than any other to assist the textile and apparel industry," it boasted.[18]

As imports continued to surge, however, so too did discontent within the industry. In October 1983, the administration's own figures showed that textile and apparel imports had increased 45 percent compared to the same month in 1982, setting an all-time monthly record and putting the 1983 figures at the highest point ever recorded for a ten-month period.[19] In November, mill owner Roger Milliken—a big GOP donor and a key supporter in the South—told Meese that the figures were a "disaster." According to Milliken, much stronger import controls were needed. "The main purpose for my writing is to let you know that there is really total dissatisfaction with the way this Administration is handling the textile situation," he concluded. Strident criticism also came from the chairman of Burlington Industries, who spoke for the industry as a whole. "Mr. President," wrote William A. Klopman, "it was with great hopes that we welcomed you to the White House. Our industry has been a strong supporter of yours, so I am sure you can appreciate the disillusionment we now feel." Taking a more conciliatory tone than Milliken, Klopman appealed to the president to make an "earnest effort" to honor his commitments and win back the industry's goodwill.[20]

Leading politicians also expressed the industry's frustration. None was more forceful than South Carolina senator Strom Thurmond, who used his senior status within the Republican Party to press his case. As president pro tempore of the U.S. Senate, Thurmond was one of the industry's most influential supporters. In 1983, Thurmond wrote that the textile and apparel industry had an unemployment rate of 16 percent, and he cited imports as the main culprit. "Action now is urgent," he scrawled in hand on a letter to presidential assistant Wendell Gunn. Dissatisfied with the lack of response, Thurmond then reminded Chief of Staff James A. Baker III of the president's promises to the industry. "I cannot overemphasize how important this entire issue is to South Carolina, the Southeast, and the Nation as a whole," he concluded. In 1984 Thurmond also headed a letter to Reagan from fourteen U.S. senators that claimed that the "very survival" of the industry was at stake.[21] A former presidential candidate, Alabama governor George Wallace, was another high-profile politician who pressed the administration on this issue. Citing the rising textile trade deficit and claiming that current policies were costing the industry over two hundred thousand jobs a year, Wallace demanded change. "It is not fair," he concluded, "to put Americans out of work so someone in a foreign country can have a job."[22] Responding to this pressure, Baker and Meese reiterated their concern, yet they also sought to lower expectations by advising that the president's original commitments to the industry had been "ambitious."[23]

The Congressional Textile Caucus also responded to the demands of an increasingly angry industry. Most Caucus members were Democrats, and they were keen to seek confrontation with the Republican administration. The Caucus gathered strength after December 1982, when Edgar Lanier ("Ed") Jenkins became its chair. Described by the *New York Times* as "a soft-spoken conservative Democrat from Georgia," Jenkins was a deceptively skillful political operator. As the *USA Today*'s Lacrisha Butler concluded when Jenkins retired from politics, "During his eight terms in Congress, the bespectacled, gray-haired Jenkins has earned a reputation as a shrewd bargainer who is not afraid of a fight."[24]

One of Jenkins's biggest confrontations began in the spring of 1985, when he took on the administration over textiles. In explaining why he led this fight, Jenkins was fond of quoting House Speaker Thomas ("Tip") O'Neill's dictum that "all politics is local."[25] Jenkins's papers certainly highlight the enormous influence that the industry exerted in his north Georgia district, where it was by far the biggest employer. By the early 1980s, his files were bulging with pleas for help from textile workers and executives, and his mail ran forty to one in favor of import restriction legislation. In 1982, one letter from a plant manager in Calhoun, Georgia, was typical. "Foreign textile imports are continuing to strangle the textile industry," wrote Obie Mason, and Washington had to act. Similar cries came from both workers and concerned citizens. As Mr. and Mrs. Joel Young wrote from the textile town of Gainesville, Georgia, "Imports are America's biggest problem." A key member of the House Ways and Means Committee, Jenkins concluded that the problem could only be solved by legislation. "As a member of the Trade Subcommittee," he wrote as early as May 1982, "I am continuously striving to protect some of our domestic industries being harmed by foreign imports."[26]

Jenkins's concern for the industry, however, was not simply political. Born in 1933, he had been raised in Young Harris, a tiny community near the Tennessee state line where the only local industry was a small apparel plant. Jenkins's mother had worked at the factory, and he understood how vital the job had been in allowing her and other local women to raise their families. "I was familiar with that operation and what it meant to the people of that small county, Union County, as the only industry available," he recalled later.[27] When he entered politics, Jenkins worked as an aide for Congressman Phil Landrum, an early chair of the Informal House Textile Committee, and in the process he developed close links with the industry. The 1985 bill was strongly associated with Jenkins, who was known as "Mr. Textiles" in his home state. Realizing that being a "protectionist" carried negative connotations,

Jenkins insisted that he was an "orderly marketeer" intent on restoring fair competition. Free trade, he argued, could only work in cases where wage scales were comparable in competing territories. He championed the industry's cause with genuine zeal, insisting that domestic manufacturers were spending millions on modernizing and just needed a fair chance to compete. His bill was designed to provide this opportunity.[28]

In early 1985, Jenkins's congressional staff consulted with industry groups and put the bill together. "I asked my legislative assistant to commence working with the associations, other members of the caucus, and the union groups, to try to reach a consensus on a final bill to be drafted," recalled Jenkins. "Once a consensus was reached, we requested House counsel to draft the legislative language for the final bill." With the industry squarely behind him, Jenkins felt confident as he launched the biggest fight of his career. Aware that passage of the bill would be difficult, he reasoned that a strong campaign would at least pressure the Reagan administration to strengthen the MFA. Jenkins was "very close" to powerful Ways and Means chairman Dan Rostenkowski, who did not support the bill but nevertheless allowed his Democratic colleague to pursue it.[29]

Jenkins received strong support from an industry that had been brought together by the import crisis. In the months prior to the bill's introduction, both the NTA and the ATMI carefully documented that their members were hurting. In January 1985, for example, the NTA compiled a list of seventeen New England textile and apparel mills that had closed over the previous two years, while earlier shutdowns were also carefully collated in its files. Between January and June of 1985, the ATMI similarly listed forty-eight closings and twenty layoffs, with most of the affected mills located in the South, where the Institute's membership was concentrated. Both groups shared data with one another and stressed that actual job losses were higher than their figures showed, especially as some layoffs or plant closures were not reported.[30]

Most of the closures occurred in small towns, and the effects were frequently devastating. An apt example was provided by Ware Shoals, South Carolina, a nondescript community of a couple of thousand people. When the mill that had built the town closed in early 1985—a move the owners blamed on imports—the whole community was hurt. Visiting the area a few months later, *Boston Globe* reporter Bruce Mohl noted that "it's as if the heart of the town just stopped beating after the layoff earlier this year of 900 people. Ware Shoals still exists. It's still on the map between Greenville and Columbia. But there is little sign of life." As Mohl reported, since the shutdown almost all the young people had left to find jobs elsewhere, restaurants had been boarded up, and the local hotel had closed. Workers who had taken the mill for granted were still in shock, their mood captured by a sign outside the local Baptist church. "Remember," it warned, "Jesus suffers when we suffer."[31]

Both the NTA and ATMI played important roles in pushing for the bill. At the NTA's annual meeting in October 1984, President Ames Stevens Jr. commented that "our traditional nemesis, the import of textile products, is stronger than ever this year." The industry was facing "nothing short of extinction," and it was time for a "radical policy change." Used to lobbying the industry's corner, the group was ready for a new legislative battle. The NTA's official in Washington, Doug Horstman, had what Stevens termed "good relations with state and federal officials and U.S. Senators and Congressmen." As the bill took shape, Horstman was a crucial point of contact between the industry and its congressional supporters. NTA leaders also urged their members to get involved in the fight. As executive director Seth M. Bodner wrote, "My message is that it is time for people in this industry to start raising hell in a way that they never had to before."[32] Constant pressure also came from the ATMI, and H.R. 1562 was by far the group's top legislative priority. According to President E. S. McKissick Jr., passage of the bill was the "only way" for the federal government to address the import problem and stem deindustrialization.[33]

Building on their prior efforts to fight imports, the unions also came together to push for the legislation. In January 1985, for example, the leaders of the ILGWU and the ACTWU outlined plans for "working on import problems" together, and they subsequently organized joint demonstrations.[34] More remarkably, the import crisis caused both unions to strengthen their ties with corporations that remained fiercely opposed to unionization, particularly Milliken and Company, J. P. Stevens, and Burlington Industries. By early 1985, both the ILGWU and ACTWU were part of the American Fiber, Textile, and Apparel Coalition, an industry-based group that sought import controls. AFTAC soon morphed into FFACT, and both organizations were based in Washington, D.C. Union leaders explained that their actions were motivated by self-preservation. As former ACTWU leader Art Gundersheim recalled, "Every other union used to say, 'You guys are crazy. How do you possibly deal with this on one side and then hate him on the other?' And I say, 'We don't have a choice.'" It was, added the ILGWU's Susan Cowell, a strategic alliance based on economic necessity. "They [the unions] were very consciously getting in bed with the enemy. This was the way that together they could win."[35]

The chances of victory certainly looked good, at least initially. On March 15, 1985, the bill already had 106 cosponsors; forty-six came from former Confederate states while most of the others were drawn from New England and the mid-Atlantic region. No state had more sponsors than Pennsylvania, where a wave of plant closings had convinced thirteen congressmen to support the bill.[36] On March 19, Jenkins introduced H.R. 1562 into the House. "I know of no other industry or group of workers that has suffered more hardships than has the textile industry, as a direct result of cheap foreign imports," he explained. Aware of the opposition of the Reagan administration, Jenkins pledged to do everything he could to ensure the bill's passage. Within two months, the bill had over 260 cosponsors.[37]

In the Senate, prospects were also encouraging. On May 13, the bill had forty-one sponsors, and within five weeks this had increased to fifty-two.[38] The key sponsors of S. 680—the Senate version of the bill—were senators Hollings and Thurmond. Both were important figures within their parties and long-standing industry allies. In April, for example, Hollings wrote his "friends" in the Carolina Yarn Association that he was "doing everything" he could "to obtain passage of this bill." The Association was a powerful coalition of textile companies in the Carolinas; it dated back to 1930 and had 179 members.[39]

Northern senators also played prominent roles. William Cohen, the former congressman from Maine who was elected to the Senate in 1978, provided an apt example. Cohen's senatorial papers again illustrated the industry's economic importance and the wisdom of O'Neill's dictum that "all politics is local." In a memo analyzing the bill for Cohen, adviser Robert Porter described it as "highly protectionist" and noted that it would attract opposition from retailers, importers, farm groups, and the Reagan administration. Nevertheless, Porter recommended that Cohen should support the legislation in order to "save what is left of a very important part of the state's manufacturing base." These "Maine considerations" were crucial. As Cohen noted when he announced his cosponsorship, fifteen thousand people were employed in Maine's textile and apparel industry, and import controls were needed to help them. Cohen was also acutely aware of the plight of the footwear industry, which had already moved offshore, hurting local people. "As a politician," he candidly admitted in early 1986, "my first duty is to represent the constituency which elected me." Many other representatives adopted the same reasoning. As New Jersey senator Frank R. Lautenberg explained, "New Jersey's apparel and textile industry is a vital part of our state economy. We must do all we can to slow the influx of textile and apparel goods into our markets."[40]

The broad support behind the bill showed that the industry had national significance. Most of the larger textile companies, for example, had plants in both the North and the South, and they were equally affected by imports. The fate of textile and apparel makers was also inextricably linked. These points were illustrated by the case of Cranston Print Works, the largest printer, finisher, and dyer of textiles in the country. By the summer of 1985, the company's large plant in Fletcher, North Carolina, was under threat just as much as its factories in Rhode Island and Massachusetts, as all of them supplied American garment manufacturers. "The way we look at it, if the

American manufacturer doesn't stay in business," explained Fletcher plant manager Tony Palazzo, "there'll be nobody here to buy our goods." With thirty-three factories located throughout the country, apparel maker Hartmax was in a similar position. As vice chairman John R. Meinart told the U.S. Senate, the company's plants had provided "jobs, benefits, and dignity" for generations of Americans, including many immigrants. If imports were not curbed, future generations would not have the same opportunities.[41]

The campaign to pass the bill was marked by a remarkable degree of grassroots mobilization, and supporters were optimistic. In November 1985, Senator Hollings noted that although Reagan might veto the bill, which had passed the Senate by a vote of sixty to thirty-nine, its popularity with voters made this difficult. "I believe President Reagan will sign the bill," he asserted. "He has received over three million letters concerning the legislation—the largest mailing ever sent by the private sector over any one issue. Surely the President will realize its importance."[42] The popular response to the bill was truly impressive, even for seasoned observers. As white-collar employee James Blair wrote from a Burlington Industries plant in Rabun Gap, Georgia: "I am an employee in the textile industry in North Georgia and have been for twenty years. In all these years I've never seen fellow employees more concerned about their jobs than this day and time, and this concern stems from the large amounts of imports entering our Country." Apart from the president, leading friends of the industry in Washington were bombarded with letters. Over the course of 1985, for example, South Carolina congressman Butler Derrick received seventeen folders of letters in support of the bill. Many came from a Burlington Industries plant in Calhoun Falls that Derrick had visited, and the plant's manager reported in October that 2,700 of his employees had also written President Reagan.[43]

The main thrust of the campaign was indeed directed at the president, and by early 1986 Derrick claimed that the number of letters received by Reagan had increased to 3.5 million.[44] While some of these were form letters produced using early computer technology, many were personal, handwritten efforts. Writing from Dalton, Georgia, textile worker Hubert Parrott explained how the mills were the economic lifeblood of the rural South. "The south is just now catching up with the industrial sections of the U.S. and this is largely due to the textile industry," he declared. After twenty-seven years in the industry, Parrot was afraid that the mills would disappear, shattering his dream of sending his twelve grandchildren to college. In order to protect this hope, Parrott pleaded with Reagan to "do whatever necessary to curb these imports." Writing from Pageland, South Carolina, textile worker Alex McCallum admitted that he had voted for Reagan partly because of his promises to the industry, which were now being ignored. McCallum warned the president that textile workers were "not going to let this issue die."[45]

Many companies also organized letter-writing campaigns or sponsored petitions. Before the measure was voted on, South Carolina–based Greenwood Mills mailed Reagan a petition signed by 5,300 of its employees. "We are appalled that you have allowed textile imports to flood this nation at the expense of thousands of American workers," explained company president Mat Self. Even more striking was the example of Burlington Industries, which claimed in October that its employees had sent 335,300 letters to the president.[46] Worried that Reagan might ignore mailed letters, some representatives took matters into their own hands. On September 25, 1985, James Broyhill (R-NC) traveled with some of his constituents to the White House and hand-delivered seven thousand letters from his district, all of them urging passage of H.R. 1562.[47] Because of the industry's broad importance, it was not just those who worked for textile firms that put pen to paper. Rather, many letters came from concerned citizens, including suppliers to the mills and community leaders. As Milliken's Washington Counsel noted, the industry's campaign had "created a firestorm" that had spread well beyond the plant gates. "We must not forget," added John F. Nash Jr., "people are truly concerned and they are watching closely to see what the President is going to do."[48]

A few examples illustrate Nash's point. The manager of a bearings maker with operations in South Carolina and Ohio, M. F. Thompson was one of many Americans who understood the threat that imports posed to domestic manufacturing. "The textile industry like the bearing industry is suffering from imports," he explained. "With the present trend and without some curtailment, the bearing and textile industry can be imported with the domestic manufacturers sitting idle."[49] Other correspondents were suppliers to the mills. Like Pure Water Testing, an engineering and contracting firm, suppliers urged help for "all of the peripheral businesses which depend on a healthy textile and apparel industry."[50] In the South, the industry's economic reach was especially great, and this meant that the bill received community backing. In Georgia, for example, several chambers of commerce passed resolutions in support of the legislation, including those in Dahlonega, Griffin, and Rome.[51]

Women composed many of the letters written by workers, and they were particularly adept at describing employees' fears of job loss. The prominent role that women played in the campaign highlighted broader themes. In the post–World War II period, increasing numbers of women entered the workforce, an important change that had wide-ranging consequences. Significantly, these women were more likely to be wives rather than single women. Between 1940 and 1980, the number of married women who worked jumped from 15 percent to over 50 percent, and these national changes affected textiles. In her work on the textile community of Central Falls, Rhode Island, anthropologist Louise Lamphere traced how "working mothers" replaced the "working daughters" that the industry had initially relied upon. An increasingly important part of the workforce, women textile workers mobilized behind H.R. 1562.[52]

The letters illustrated how the industry provided vital jobs to women, especially family heads. In all, well over half of the hundreds of letters written to Jenkins and Congressman J. Roy Rowland, another Georgia Democrat, came from women.[53] "I am sole support of 4 people," wrote Ann Chester from a carpet mill in Dahlonega, Georgia. "My husband is disable to work. . . . There are several hundred who work here, who depend on this as their only means of livelyhood." Chester ended with a plea for Jenkins's assistance. "America has always helped the underdog or someone in trouble," she declared. "I feel like we are in trouble now." In a similar vein, Mrs. Glyndon Robinson wrote from Jasper, Georgia, to express her "real concern" about increasing imports. "I am even afraid of losing my job if something is not done to slow down foreign imports of apparel," she concluded.[54] Other correspondents were indignant rather than apprehensive. "It is time we started looking at this situation in the light of *the people* of our Country that are affected greatly," declared Mrs. Clyde Holloway from Elijah, Georgia, another struggling mill town. The flood of mail clearly affected Jenkins, who wrote back sympathetically to every worker that contacted him. "I shall use every ounce of my energy to try to pass this bill," he vowed.[55]

The vital importance of textile jobs to women was also evident in letters sent to Senator Hollings. "I work in textiles," explained Daisy Byrd from Society Hill, South Carolina. "I am 52 years old. This kind of work is all I know. I am too old to learn a new trade. My husband is disable, so you see I need my job." A widow in her fifties, Miriam Allison wrote from Gaffney in a similar vein. "I need this job because of the money and the health insurance. No one would give me a job if I got laid off. All I ask is that you consider people with needs, who want to work." Others spoke to their hopes for their children. "It scares me when I think my job at Burlington Industries (twelve years) may not be here in five years," wrote Brenda McCaskill from Bennettsville. "I wonder if my children will have the funds to even get to go to College." Imports had to be controlled, she urged, or her family would have no future.[56] In an effort to help his constituents, Hollings wrote Reagan and reminded him of his promises to help the industry. The president had a "callous disregard" for the suffering of textile workers, he charged.[57]

As the vote on H.R. 1562 approached, supporters stepped up their lobbying efforts. In October 1985, ACTWU's *Labor Unity* reported that members had been mobilized from "coast to coast" in a variety of activities, including letter writing, conducting demonstrations, and calling lawmakers. As part of this drive, in September the union brought a selection of witnesses to testify before the Senate Finance Committee's Subcommittee on International Trade. A resident of eastern Pennsylvania, union representative Eleanor

Kuhns likened the impact of imports on the area to "economic murder." She spoke on behalf of one thousand workers who had been recently laid off from Arrow Shirt plants in Lewiston and Elysburg. "Dedicated employees were discarded like broken-down machines with very little notice, no time to adjust and no other place to go because garment factories have been closing one after the other for the last decade or so," declared Kuhns, who had worked at Arrow for twenty-four years. While her public testimony was composed, Kuhns admitted privately that the plight of the Arrow workers had left her with "tears running down my cheeks." Over a third of the group were more than fifty years old, and most had been unable to find jobs in an area with high unemployment. "I'm feeling very blue these days because things are so gloomy for the Arrow Shirt workers," she wrote ACTWU's Liz Smith.[58]

While deindustrialization hurt all textile and apparel workers, the Senate hearing highlighted the disproportionate impact on women. A resident of the small city of Decatur, Illinois, Beverly Reed described how she had used her job at the R. and M. Kaufman Garment Company to raise three young children after her husband died. The job was not well paid but it had provided her with security, especially as it came with health insurance and other benefits. Her experience was representative. "We in the garment industry are basically a working women's industry," she testified. "We don't make a lot of money and we work very hard. But what we do have is our children; they are our future and our hope that life will be better. In the past our industry has always guaranteed that future." This changed in the 1970s, however, as garment shops in Illinois were hit hard by imports. By 1984, all five clothing plants in Decatur had gone. Reed drew on the language of motherhood to explain how her co-workers had responded by becoming more outspoken. "The members of Local 120 are not normally an aggressive bunch," she cautioned. "But when you back a mother into a corner, and when the future of her children is at stake, we'll fight back."[59]

Similar testimony was also heard from southern garment workers. A resident of McAllen, Texas, Nilda Quintanilla described how she was afraid of losing her job at the local Levi Strauss plant. Quintanilla depended on the factory to support her four children because her husband's work was irregular, a common predicament. "There is a lot of fear among my friends of plant closings," she related. "Especially people who have been working here at Levi's. . . . There isn't much alternative employment available in the area. And what is available has bad conditions and low wages." In the years that followed, Levi's gradually shut most of its U.S. plants, validating workers' fears.[60] As Quintanilla's testimony also touched on, the apparel industry provided an important gateway for new immigrants, particularly Latinos and Asians. A Chinese American garment worker from New York City, Wing Fong Chin spoke to some of these issues at the Senate hearing. "I want you to understand how difficult it is for an immigrant from an Asian country to find work in America," he explained. "If you don't speak English, there are almost no places outside of Chinatown where a Chinese immigrant can get a job." Although wages in the garment shops were low, generations of Asian immigrants had used them to raise their families. "If you let imports destroy the garment industry, where will people like myself find work?" pondered Chin.[61]

Developed jointly by the ILGWU and the ACTWU, campaign posters built on these themes. Large pictures of individual workers spotlighted the industry's racial diversity, with care being taken to represent African Americans, Asian Americans, Latinos, and whites in different versions of the same advertisement. Under each image was the slogan "I Don't Want Welfare . . . I Want to Work." The message was clear; regardless of their racial background, female breadwinners could end up on welfare if they lost their jobs. In a similar vein, the unions' print advertising sought to identify the reader with individual workers, humanizing trade issues that were often debated in abstract terms. "These aren't just jobs," declared one newspaper advertisement. "We're talking about two million people. And look who they are: 7 out of 10, women. Sitting at sewing machines, standing on their feet in the mills. Supporting their families alone, or making the difference so that the family can live a little better, the kids get a little better chance." If readers wrote their representatives, they could save an industry that was "hanging by a thread."[62]

**"The campaign to pass the 1985 textile bill mobilized textile and apparel workers in both the northern and southern states. It also illustrated that many women and racial minorities depended on the industry for their livelihoods." (Photo courtesy of the Kheel Center for Labor-Management Documentation and Archives, Cornell University)**

(Photo courtesy of the Kheel Center for Labor-Management Documentation and Archives, Cornell University)

**(Photos courtesy of the Kheel Center for Labor-Management Documentation and Archives, Cornell University)**

The industry's supporters presented a powerful case, yet their opponents were equally articulate. The bill attracted forceful opposition from free-traders, especially retailers and importers. One notable foe was Esprit, a clothing merchant that pioneered the use of imports to undercut domestic apparel makers. By 1984, Esprit sold $220 million of clothing in the U.S. market, and around 95 percent of it was imported. "We cannot obtain the same quality goods in the United States at competitive prices," insisted retail president Roger Kase. Esprit was based in California—where the bill struggled—and the company was a leading player in the American Free Trade Association, a group of import-focused companies and retailers that was based on the West Coast.[63]

While the opposition of retailers and importers was hardly surprising, it was more remarkable to find domestic apparel manufacturers breaking ranks with the industry and testifying against the bill. Revealingly, Nilda Quintanilla's own employer, Levi Strauss, was among the corporations that spoke out. According to company executive Peter Phillipes, the legislation would "prevent apparel companies from operating in the American consumer's best interests." The industry was already sheltered by "a heavy blanket of protectionism," and it needed to adopt a more "international approach." Because Levi's was the largest employer of apparel workers in the United States, its opposition undermined the campaign. Unlike most textile and apparel manufacturers, Levi's was based on the West Coast, and this helped to explain its different approach. Over time, however, many apparel firms invested in overseas production facilities, and they consequently sided with importers rather than domestic manufacturers.[64]

Of most concern to the bill's supporters, however, was the antagonism they encountered from the Reagan administration. In June 1985, five top administration officials outlined their opposition to the bill in a letter that was sent to every member of Congress. Led by Secretary of State George P. Schultz, they claimed that H.R. 1562 proposed a level of protection that was "contrary to the free-market principles which have made our economy the envy of the world." They also asserted that it would raise prices and provoke retaliation against important American exporters.[65] The newly appointed U.S. trade representative, Clayton Yeutter, was a particularly formidable adversary. A native of Nebraska who held a PhD in agricultural economics, Yeutter's sympathies lay with export-oriented farming interests. Writing in the *Washington Post*, Yeutter attacked H.R. 1562 as a deeply flawed piece of legislation that would turn America into a "protectionist fortress." Worried by these criticisms, staff at the ACTWU even collected "Dirt on Ambassador Yeutter." The file mainly contained reports of comments where Yeutter had claimed that weaker industries should be "phased out" rather than assisted. Led by Senator Thurmond, industry supporters criticized Yeutter's remarks. In response, Yeutter told the industry's *Daily News Record* that he had no intention of backing down, largely because he knew that the administration was behind him.[66]

The administration's opposition to H.R. 1562 was unyielding. As one memorandum that was prepared for the president summarized, "The Administration has maintained a strong and consistent record of opposition to H.R. 1562 at every stage of congressional consideration." As early as May, aide Roger B. Porter reported that an unequivocal position was needed in order to "hold those Republicans that are not yet committed to supporting the legislation." In addition to the key letter sent to all members of Congress in June, five months later the administration sent slightly revised position statements to both the House and Senate. Republican representatives were left in no doubt where their party stood, and this made a difference. As the *Daily News Record* acknowledged, the backing of the Reagan administration also meant that the industry's opponents had "a strong psychological edge."[67]

The administration's determination to fight back showed that the bill posed a real threat to its policies. Just before H.R. 1562 was introduced, Vice President George H. W. Bush wrote privately that he was "concerned that administration is about to get in a real bind on textiles," presumably because he knew that the industry's arguments struck a chord.[68] The bill undoubtedly reflected genuine concerns that many Americans had about the mounting trade deficit and the loss of manufacturing jobs. Key industry supporters thus doubted whether Reagan could risk a veto. "I didn't think Reagan would veto the bill because of the political fallout it would cause," remembered Hollings. "Public opinion was with us." At the end of 1985, even the administration's private polling reported "widespread concern about our trade policy and a somewhat protectionist sentiment." Still, aides reasoned that these worries would dissipate as the economy strengthened.[69]

The records of the Reagan administration also highlight that advisers worried that the twelve countries targeted by the bill would retaliate, especially as these nations were "heavily indebted" and "economically dependent on their textile industries." As adviser Alex Dimitrief warned, "These countries were not sit idly by . . . they will retaliate against American exports. These twelve countries are important trading partners, and we have much to lose from a trade war." Overall, Dimitrief estimated that the affected nations purchased over $13 million of farm goods from the United States each year. Sharing these fears, State Department official Denis Lamb related that CITA's actions to tighten textile agreements had already damaged America's "standing in the international trading community" and had hurt poor countries for whom textiles was "the first rung of the ladder of industrialization."[70]

A variety of farm groups, including the influential American Farm Bureau Federation and the National Association of Wheat Growers, strongly opposed the bill. These groups were assisted by powerful Kansas senator

Bob Dole, who argued that lucrative wheat sales to China should not be "held hostage" to the interests of the domestic textile industry.[71] In the agricultural states of the Midwest, most senators agreed with Dole, while West Coast senators worried that a decline in trade with Asia would hurt their region's export-oriented economy. In mid-November, the administration estimated that twenty-eight Republican and eleven Democratic senators supported its position, and virtually all of them came from states located west of the Mississippi River.[72]

The retail lobby was a powerful and sophisticated adversary. Thus, while FFACT sent out form letters, the retail stores went one better and used computer technology to prepare letters that employees could send to politicians on "personalized stationery."[73] As the records of the Reagan administration make clear, these efforts built on earlier lobbying efforts by retailers. From its headquarters in Michigan, K-Mart liaised with the White House on behalf of several retail groups, including the American Retail Federation and the National Retail Merchants Association. Using the language of freedom to great effect, it urged the administration to uphold free trade policies and castigated the textile industry as backward looking and "protectionist." In one typical letter from K-Mart executive Robert Dewar, the *p* word was used to describe the textile industry on no fewer than four occasions. In meetings with administration aides, store owners pressed the need for what the American Retail Federation termed "a re-examination of the long-standing protectionist program for the textile and apparel industry."[74]

The national press was also very hostile to the bill, partly because they needed advertising revenue from retailers. Even in textile areas, many papers were not supportive. In South Carolina, the *Greenville News* slammed the bill, declaring that automation was "the real cause for most of the shrinkage in the textile workforce."[75] As NTA president Ames Stevens Jr. privately admitted, however, it was at national level that the industry actually lost the battle in the media. "The National Press is really our enemy," he explained. "The National Press such as NEWSWEEK, such as the NEW YORK TIMES, such as the WALL STREET JOURNAL, continually take up the cry of our friendly importing nations."[76] Furthermore, economists generally supported free trade and opposed the textile bill. As Heritage Foundation writer Warren T. Brookes summarized, "Economists don't agree on much, but on one subject there is almost no debate: protectionism, the deliberate prevention of imports, is the most economically destructive and cruelly regressive 'tax' policy a government can pursue." Even liberal economist Robert B. Reich criticized the industry's calls for additional protection. Reich—who would later serve as Secretary of Labor in the Clinton White House—argued that textiles and apparel was bound to decline as international competition increased. "In a world economy becoming increasingly integrated," he wrote, "advanced industrial nations must learn to divest themselves of their least competitive industries."[77]

As well as combating external opposition, the campaign was also dogged by internal problems. Despite the public alliance forged between companies and unions, there were damaging tensions behind the scenes. The differences were especially apparent at North Carolina's Cannon Mills, where managers were fighting an ACTWU organizing drive just as the import bill was being debated. The ACTWU campaign was the latest effort by unions to organize the giant southern firm; since "Operation Dixie" in the 1940s, the company had used its considerable power to discourage its workers from supporting organized labor.[78] While Cannon Mills supported the bill, it did so without involving the union. In May 1985, for example, owner David H. Murdock presented Ronald Reagan with a petition in favor of the legislation that was signed by over 14,700 Cannon workers. In addition, the company launched a "massive letter writing campaign" among their employees. Within a month, managers claimed that thirty-six thousand letters had been sent to the president and other key politicians, helped by the fact that the company provided writing supplies and paid for postage.[79] In August, Cannon also organized a "Rally against Textile Imports" that attracted over three thousand workers, or "associates" as the company termed them. Congressman Jenkins spoke at the gathering, but union representatives were clearly not welcome.[80]

As the union election neared, the company mobilized its workers to fight imports *and* the union, even though ACTWU was a central member of the anti-import coalition. The company's *Cannon News* insisted that voting for ACTWU would put workers under the "control of union bosses in New York," leading to "strikes and other disruptions" that could hurt the plants. Workers were told that with the industry in trouble, they must support the company to keep their jobs. On the eve of the October vote, they were bombarded with antiunion material, much of it conveyed by company supporters. "The unions have caused many companies larger than Cannon Mills to close their doors for good," claimed worker Myrtle E. Hartsoe. "I feel this could happen here in Kannapolis." The campaign paid off, and on October 10 workers rejected ACTWU by a vote of 5,982 to 3,530, or 62.9 percent to 37.1 percent. It was, declared union organizer Chris Chafe, "one of the union's worst defeats," although for the company it was cause for celebration. Ironically, the defeat came just as FFACT's union representatives were working to get the textile bill through the Senate.[81]

The main trade publication in the region, the *Southern Textile News*, also disliked labor unions. Published in Charlotte—a city where unions had little influence—the *News* reported on the anti-import campaign without mentioning the involvement of organized labor. Furthermore, the *News* editorialized against unions on several occasions, including on the eve of the Cannon vote. A vote for the union, warned the *News*, "could very definitely lead to more union votes in more major mills and eventually cause the demise of not only those mills but the certain death of many smaller, family-owned companies." In particular, the *News* suggested that ACTWU's desire for higher wages, which it claimed were needed to fill union coffers, could push Cannon Mills over the edge.[82]

As they fought for the bill's passage, the unions also mobilized their workers separately from the companies. Shortly after H.R. 1562 was introduced, ACTWU and the ILGWU held a joint rally in New York City that attracted over 1,500 textile and apparel workers, as well as the leaders of both unions. Most of the participants came from the New York metropolitan area, where the garment industry had declined dramatically. "There used to be 500 people in my shop," explained marcher Louisa Burgos, "and now we're down to as few as 50 sometimes. I guess I'll be able to finish up and get my pension but I feel so sorry for the younger workers." In June, the unions also held rallies in cities across the country, including New York, Chicago, and Los Angeles. One of the largest demonstrations occurred in Philadelphia, where Mayor Wilson Goode joined around three thousand marchers. Wearing a union cap, Goode endorsed "Roll Back Imports Week," which was designed to dramatize the union's demands. In Los Angeles, where 1,200 people attended a joint ACTWU/ILGWU demonstration in front of City Hall, another African American mayor, Tom Bradley, enthusiastically approved the rally's message of "More Imports = More Unemployment."[83]

From Lawrence, Massachusetts, to Andalusia, Alabama, union members also rallied in support of the bill. In Asheville, North Carolina, where a June march attracted ACTWU members "from all over the South," workers buried a pile of imported goods in a coffin. Vietnam veteran Bill Pressly captured the mood of the group: "I risked my life to protect my country and so did many of my fellow workers. Now my country owes it to us to protect our jobs. If there were a military invasion, we'd all take up arms and do something about it. Well, there is an imports invasion, and something must be done about that, too!"[84] Drawing on these patriotic sentiments, some labor leaders expressed hostility to foreign goods and even the workers that made them. In Pennsylvania, ACTWU members pressed merchants to establish separate racks for clothing made in "slave labor countries." Some stores agreed with the move, but bigger retailers refused. "Not surprisingly, the chain stores are not cooperating—they sell mostly foreign made junk if you've shopped K-Mart lately," declared one labor paper.[85] Because these efforts frequently targeted foreign countries, critics charged that the bill's supporters were xenophobic or even racist. Again, residents of western states led the opposition. In November 1985, for example, Senator Malcolm Wallop (R-WY) told the Senate Finance Committee that S. 680 was "one of the most racist bills this house has ever passed. If your eyes are round, you're out from under." Wallop criticized the way that the bill aimed to reduce imports from three Asian countries yet exempted Canada and the EEC.[86]

Wallop had a point. Thus, the bill did alienate foreign leaders, especially in the Asian countries that were most affected by its provisions. In November 1985, the ILGWU's Sol Chaikin responded to criticism from South Korean union leader Oh Seok, who had complained that his country was being unfairly targeted. Chaikin highlighted how American union leaders were still thinking primarily in national terms. "While we are sympathetic to the needs and aspirations of our brothers and sisters overseas," he wrote, "we also have a responsibility to assist workers in the United States."[87] The bill also drew protests from the Taiwan Textile Federation, which argued that its provisions would have a "devastating impact" on Asian producers. The Federation told the House Ways and Means Committee that the bill would require textile production to be cut by 10 percent in Taiwan, causing the loss of forty-five thousand jobs. They also threatened that they would retaliate against the United States if this occurred.[88] In a similar vein, Indonesian ambassador A. Hasnan Habib protested to the Reagan administration. "My government wishes to convey to you its continued grave concern over any measure that imposes quotas on imports of textiles and apparel," he noted. According to Habib, Asian countries received "unequal treatment" under the bill compared to their European counterparts.[89]

In the United States, many workers also drew on nationalist sentiments as they expressed support for the legislation, and they were frequently hostile to other countries. Letters written by workers to their members of Congress illustrate this well. "I'm writing to voice my objections to foreign countries flooding our market with their cheap poorly made products," wrote Ruby Quarles from Ellijay, Georgia. "My family and friends want to keep their jobs." From Gaffney, South Carolina, Lena Martin similarly petitioned Senator Hollings: "Through the years I've worked here, I have watched the Japanese and foreign trade snatch peoples homes, cars and jobs from under them. We have all suffered a great loss in working hours. Haven't we sacrificed enough?"[90]

Congressman Jenkins rejected the racism allegations. Part Cherokee himself, Jenkins stressed the racial diversity of the textile workforce. He did acknowledge, however, that his bill was aimed at developing countries. "The problems that we had," he recalled later, "were from the countries that . . . had the cheap labor, and they had manipulated the currency, and Canada was not in that situation, nor the European countries, because they too had had textiles for generations." Overall, it is clear that the racism allegations hurt the bill. As Congressman Derrick admitted, industry advocates were consistently told that their legislation was "anti-Asian," and for this reason Derrick changed the 1987 bill so that quotas were set by category, rather than by country.[91] The charges of racism also hurt efforts to secure backing from civil rights groups. Support did come from the National Puerto Rican Coalition, which argued that the Hispanic community would suffer if the textile industry disappeared, but the Congressional Black Caucus was ambivalent, concerned that Caribbean and African countries were being victimized by the legislation. Led by Cardiss Collins, a black congresswoman from Illinois, bill supporters stressed that the most important thing was to help African Americans who relied on the industry. "The textile and apparel industry has given opportunity and a decent living to minorities and women in the South and in our major Northern cities to an extent no other industry can claim," wrote Collins to Caucus colleagues who opposed H.R 1562.[92]

Weakened by the opposition they encountered, Jenkins and his allies were unable to secure an outright victory. On November 13, 1985, the bill passed the Senate by a comfortable margin of twenty-one votes. A very similar bill had already got through the House, but rather than going to conference with the Senate, the House brought the Senate bill to the House floor under a special rule. On Tuesday, December 3, the House duly approved the Senate version of H.R. 1562 by a vote of 255 to 161. For bill supporters, the outcome confirmed that the majority of the public wanted to help the industry. Because the votes fell short of the two-thirds majority needed to overturn a veto, however, the Reagan administration was also confident. "The votes both indicate strong veto support," declared deputy chief of staff M. B. Oglesby Jr. Two days after the House vote, Oglesby told Reagan that his cabinet recommended a veto "unanimously."[93]

While some industry supporters still hoped that Reagan would fulfill his election promises, this was little more than wishful thinking. Just a week before Christmas, Reagan vetoed H.R. 1562 on the grounds that its "economic and human costs" were too high. In particular, the president claimed that the bill would lead to retaliation against American exporters and cause "damage to the world trading system upon which our prosperity depends." Acknowledging that the pain of workers in "troubled industries" was "very real," the president promised to renegotiate the MFA and to vigorously enforce trade laws. In a worrying sign for the industry's supporters, however, he also insisted that free trade policies were creating jobs for all Americans and suggested that dislocated workers could simply retrain for new positions in other sectors.[94] The veto reflected the actions of Reagan's advisers, who warned him that Congress could not be allowed to derail the administration's free trade agenda. According to Office of Management and Budget director James C. Miller III, H.R. 1562 was "the first significant protectionist trade bill this Congress has passed." Miller explained that all of the executive agencies, including the OMB, felt that Reagan had to block the legislation. "A veto will be a crucial action in our continuing effort to see that Congress does not alter this Administration's trade policy and seriously damage the nation's economic interests," he declared.[95]

For the bill's supporters, the veto was a huge blow. According to ACT-WU leaders Murray Finley and Jacob Sheinkman, it was a "major defeat for American workers." The union could not conceal its bitterness and anger. Thus, Finley and Sheinkman declared that there would be "dancing in the streets of foreign cities," while *Labor Unity* contended that the president had told union members "To Drop Dead." The veto, added the ILGWU's *Justice*, was "a bitter holiday message" for America's struggling textile and apparel workers. Speaking on behalf of FFACT, industry executive John N. Gregg was "shocked" by the veto but was more guarded in his criticism of the president.[96]

Although they were wounded, the industry's supporters agreed to fight on. In response to the veto, the bill's congressional leaders deliberately held up the override vote until August 6, 1986, largely because they wanted to put pressure on the administration during the renegotiation of the MFA, which was due to expire on July 31. In addition, Jenkins recalled that he selected August 6 because of its proximity to the forthcoming congressional elections. "I discovered that you could have a certain date for the override, under the House of Representatives, and I did that, to place it right before the election in November, to try to impact some of the members in their vote," he related.[97]

By delaying the override vote, the industry's supporters were able to launch a massive campaign to fight for the extra support they needed. According to the *Southern Textile News*, this effort was "the largest legislative initiative ever undertaken by the textile, apparel, and fiber industries."[98] The bill's adherents insisted that public opinion was on their side, and certainly a clear majority of Congress ended up backing the bill. In May 1986, for example, 302 representatives and seventy senators wrote Reagan and expressed their support for the legislation. They also urged the president to negotiate a tougher MFA and warned him that his veto could be overridden.[99] On the eve of the vote, some congressmen reminded their colleagues of the industry's size and geographical spread. As South Carolina Republican Carroll Campbell explained to Texan Tom DeLay, "Politically, even though President Reagan with his tremendous personal popularity may be able to afford to concede the textile trade issue, congressional Republicans cannot. Textiles and apparel are a significant employer in almost every state. . . . The fact is that congressional seats are won and lost in many districts on the basis of textile industry support."[100]

Across the country, workers and executives again put pen to paper as they tried to gain the extra votes they needed. At Eastland Woolen Mills in Corinna, Maine, CEO Norman Kominsky was especially active. Several years earlier, Kominsky had written Senator Cohen and urged him to take action against imports, especially in the troubled wool sector. Now, Kominsky launched a letter-writing campaign among his employees. "It is up to us to make sure that the politicians in Washington know that we are not going to roll over and die," he explained, "and that we are going to let everyone know how each of them has voted on this issue next November." One of Kominsky's employees who took up the challenge, David Dean, spoke on behalf of all workers whose jobs were threatened by imports, especially in the struggling shoe-making sector. "For us in the footwear and textile industries," he wrote, "as well as other industries whose markets are encroached upon or dominated by foreign imports, the loss of our jobs is turning the American Dream into the Un-American Nightmare." Dean urged Reagan to help American workers rather than focusing so much on the Cold War. "While you throw billions into weapons, you throw millions into unemployment, and American business into ruin," he charged.[101]

As the crucial vote neared, thousands of workers bombarded their members of Congress with pleas for support. In Georgia, Congressman J. Roy Rowland received several hundred letters from constituents in his eighth district, where he estimated that at least 1,500 mill workers had been laid off recently. A trained physician who had been elected to Congress in 1982, Rowland had few direct links with the industry, but the correspondence helped to make him a committed supporter of the legislation.[102] The letters drove home the importance of the industry to residents of small towns, particularly women. A self-described "American textile worker," Lexie L. Brewer from Barnesville, Georgia, wrote on the eve of the vote. "I fear that my job is in jeopardy from increased foreign textile imports," she explained. "I can not afford to look for another job. I support my family through the American textile industry. Please help us to keep it strong by voting to override the Presidents [*sic*] veto of the Textile and Apparel Trade Enforcement Act." Despite the impressive mobilization, an air of desperation infused much of the correspondence. As Kimberly J. Cravey appealed to Rowland, "Prayer may be our only answer, so couldn't we set aside a day to pray for the textile companies?"[103]

**"Campaigning to override President Reagan's veto of the textile bill, August 1986." (Photo courtesy of the Kheel Center for Labor-Management Documentation and Archives, Cornell University)**

The records of the Reagan White House confirm that the override campaign did have a considerable impact. Five days before the vote, aide

William L. Ball III reported to the president that he could not guarantee that his veto would be sustained. "There has been some apparent erosion due to continued Congressional frustration with the unrelenting trade deficit and to aggressive industry/labor efforts," he admitted. As a result, Ball arranged for Reagan to meet with GOP members of Congress who were leading the fight to sustain the veto, including Trade Subcommittee chairman Sam Gibbons and senior free-trader Bill Frenzel. At the meeting, Reagan stressed the importance of the vote "to our ability to secure more open markets for U.S. products and services in the future." Attendees were left in no doubt that the administration must prevail.[104]

On August 5—the day before override vote—Reagan made similar points in a "GOP Leadership Meeting" that was attended by aides, cabinet members, and members of Congress. Before the meeting, Ball warned Reagan that "the entire trade posture of the administration is being questioned by some members of the House." As result, the president stressed that his veto had to be sustained. Reagan also reached out to those in the "Republican family" who came from states that had experienced textile job losses. He reassured them that his administration was taking action to stem imports, as the renewal of the MFA and the negotiation of tougher bilateral agreements with Taiwan, South Korea, and Hong Kong indicated. Overall, both meetings shored up Republican support on the eve of the crucial vote.[105]

The renewal of the MFA was particularly important. Five days before the override vote, the administration announced that it had successfully negotiated a tougher MFA that would help the domestic industry compete "more fairly" in the international marketplace. The new, five-year agreement expanded coverage to include fibers such as ramie, linen, and silk blends, and strengthened provisions to combat fraud. The administration also trumpeted a new mechanism that was designed to prevent "destructive import surges." While the ATMI complained that the agreement was still inadequate, there is no doubt that it helped to appease moderates in Congress. It also gave fresh ammunition to the administration. On August 1, Clayton Yeutter boasted in a press conference that "we've been saying for months and months that the right way to handle any textile and apparel problems we have here in the United States is through negotiations rather than through legislation. And the Multifiber Arrangement is the heart of that argument."[106]

Negotiated eighteen months before they were due to expire, the new bilateral agreements with Hong Kong, South Korea, and Taiwan—three nations targeted by Jenkins's bill—were also significant. According to the administration, these agreements "expanded coverage and impose[d] the toughest limits ever on import growth." Industry opponents complained that these agreements pandered to domestic manufacturers, and they had a point. Concluded on August 4, the agreement with South Korea allowed imports to grow by no more than 0.8 percent a year, and the two other accords contained similar provisions. Bolstered by the MFA and the new bilaterals, the administration went on the offensive. In all, the administration claimed that it had negotiated 550 textile quota agreements since Reagan had taken office, including 250 in 1985 alone. As a result, quotas now applied to over 80 percent of textile and apparel imports from low-wage countries. The textile bill, aides insisted, was not required.[107]

On the day of the vote, there was impassioned debate in the House, and both sides appealed to patriotism. "We have to have some action to save basic industry in the United States," declared Ed Jenkins. Sam Gibbons disagreed, asserting that "no nation has ever risen its standard of living by restricting its imports." A native of Tampa who had been in Congress since 1963, Gibbons passionately promoted free trade and undermined support for the bill among House Democrats. As Jenkins later acknowledged, Gibbons was a formidable opponent.[108] To ensure that it prevailed, the administration took important last-minute actions. An influential body, the President's Council of Economic Advisers attacked the bill as a classic example of the evils of "protectionism." Reagan's advisers sent the CEA's analysis to several powerful members of Congress, including Gibbons and Ways and Means chair Dan Rostenkowski.[109] In the hours before the vote, Reagan also applied personal pressure on key congressmen. In a letter to House Republican leader Robert H. Michel, Reagan related that his concerns about the legislation had "not diminished" in the seven months since his veto. Reagan warned that many of the "achievements" of his presidency would be "negated" if the veto was overridden, especially his personal commitment to "increasing trade by opening markets abroad—not by closing them at home."[110] The administration's records also highlight how it worked through its "friends" in the retail and service sectors to lobbying intensively on the eve of the vote.[111]

The pressure worked. According to Roger Milliken, Reagan's last-minute actions were decisive. "We had it won in the House of Representatives until the full force of the Administration and President Reagan himself came in and peeled off votes that we had during the last 24 hours," he stated. "We won it on merit." In a thorough analysis of the vote, the *U.S. News and World Report* agreed that the president's intervention had been crucial. "Victory didn't come easy for Reagan, who spent two days telephoning House members," it noted. A Reagan Republican who had been elected to the Senate in the 1980 landslide, Mack Mattingly stressed the difficulties of taking on a well-regarded and charismatic president. Because he represented Georgia, Mattingly supported the "big push" to overturn the veto, but the president played a vital role in thwarting the effort. "Reagan was very popular," he recalled, "and he did everything with a smile, also, which is different than some people who get elected."[112]

The defeat certainly hurt. According to the ATMI's Dewey L. Trogdon, the industry was "bitterly disappointed," a sentiment that was shared by the unions.[113] "It was a tough fight to lose," agreed Milliken in a private note to Strom Thurmond. In a warm reply to his long-time political ally, Thurmond admitted that he was "deeply disappointed" with the administration's failure to help an industry that was so important nationally. The fight, he added, was not over. Butler Derrick agreed, reflecting that only victory would suffice. "When we're talking about affecting people's livelihoods, close doesn't count," he wrote.[114]

Despite the failure, the bill's proponents reasoned that their hard-fought campaign had pushed the administration to respond to their concerns. "We got a lot of small victories out of the big losses," thought Karl Spilhaus. Supporters argued that Reagan's advisers could not ignore the 276 congressmen who had voted to overturn the veto, and they were especially encouraged that all sixteen House members from the Carolinas had chosen to do so. Jenkins's allies were also proud that House Speaker Tip O'Neill had backed them, casting only his second vote since taking up his position nine years earlier.[115] Both the ATMI and FFACT made clear that they would fight on for a "legislative solution" to the industry's problems. As John N. Gregg put it, "America's fiber, textile and apparel industry and its two million workers have lost the battle, but not the war, against unfair trade."[116] Crucially, the powerful executives who funded much of the campaign wanted to fight on. Writing after the vote, the CEO of J. P. Stevens admitted that although the defeat was a setback the campaign had generated a lot of momentum. "It is difficult to accept the denial of simple justice," wrote Whitney Stevens, "but we are comforted by the fact that we have a continuing broad base of support in the House of Representatives." Rather than being demoralized, industry leaders were defiant. "We will be back," vowed Burlington Industries chairman William Klopman. Although the defeat had caused him "great grief," Roger Milliken had no intention of giving up. "An enormous coalition was forged in industry to battle for the override," he wrote Carroll Campbell, "and it will not be dismembered."[117]

The Reagan administration also knew that its battle with the textile and apparel industry was far from over. The import problem had not gone away, and such a large industry would continue to fight for government support. In September, the president was careful to send a thank-you note to "key supporters" of his veto. "The fight against protectionism is by no means over," he warned, "and thus I ask for your ongoing assistance as we work to open markets abroad, not to close ours at home." Both sides were ready to carry on the battle.[118]

## NOTES

1. U.S. Customs Service, "Textile Fraud Initiatives," January 1986, "Textile/Trade (5)" folder, OA13030, William B. Lacy files, Reagan Library.

2. Dave Lavallee, "Textile Import Restrictions Urged," Woonsocket (Rhode Island) *Call and Reporter*, July 27, 1985.

3. Alex Dimitrief to Mitch Daniels et al., November 21, 1985, "Textiles (3)" folder, White House Office of Political Affairs Records, OA19397, Reagan Library.

4. John A. Svahn to Ed Rollins, March 5, 1985, "Textiles: Textile Trade Paper for Ed Rollins 03/05/1985" folder, Michael A. Driggs files, OA12242, Reagan Library.

5. John Leslie to ACTW GEB, March 17, 1986, "Grassroots Campaign" folder, box 787, ACTWU Papers-Cornell.

6. ACTWU General Executive Board Minutes, January 13, 1986, p. 10, "GEB Minutes January, March, July, October 1986" folder, box 1006, ACTWU Papers-Cornell.

7. Loyd Hackler to Craig L. Fuller, June 23, 1983, "Textile Working Group (12)" folder, OA11723, Sherrie M. Cooksey files (Office of the Counsel to the President), Reagan Library.

8. Murray, "Unraveling Employment Trends," p. 63; U.S. Congress, Office of Technology Assessment, *The U.S. Textile and Apparel Industry*, p. 7.

9. U.S. Congress, Office of Technology Assessment, *The U.S. Textile and Apparel Industry,* pp. 3 (quotation), 4, 86.

10. "Textile and Apparel Trade Enforcement Act of 1985 Fact Sheet" (USTR Fact Sheet), March 4, 1985 (first quotation), and William E. Brock and Malcolm Baldrige to the President, March 12, 1985 (other quotations), both "Textiles (1)" folder, M. B. Oglesby files, Office of Legislative Affairs, OA13000, Reagan Library.

11. Although the Slater Mill in Pawtucket predated the company's foundation, there had been a break in that mill's operations, whereas when it went out of business Crompton had operated continuously for over 178 years. See "150th Anniversary of Crompton Company," ca. 1957, booklet in folder 35, box 11, Crompton Company Papers (MS1990.187.1), held at the American Textile History Museum, Lowell, Massachusetts, hereafter cited as "Crompton Company Papers"; William G. Lord II to William E. Brock III, October 24, 1984, folder 43, box 8, Crompton Company Papers.

12. "Analysis of Corduroy Apparel Imports," 1979–1984, folder 10.8, box 10, Crompton Company Papers; Lord quoted in Bryan Doherty, "Crompton Files Chapter 11, Seeks Time to Sell Assets," *Women's Wear Daily*, October 24, 1984, p. 48, clipping in folder 10.39, box 10, Crompton Company Papers; Pamela G. Hollie, "Crompton's Nemesis: Imports," *New York Times*, November 21, 1984, p. D1.

13. William G. Lord II to Ambassador William E. Brock III, October 24, 1984, folder 43, box 8, Crompton Company Papers; William E. Brock to William G. Lord II, November 9, 1984, folder 43, box 8, Crompton Company Papers (quotations).

14. Wendell W. Gunn to Jack Svahn, December 5, 1983, "Textiles 1983 (1)" folder, Wendell Gunn files, OA9663, Reagan Library; U.S. Department of Commerce's Office of Textiles and Apparel, "U.S. Textile and Apparel Import Program," January 11, 1988, "U.S. Textile and Apparel Import Program" folder, Susan Lauffer files, OA16376, Reagan Library; Svahn quoted in John A. Svahn to Ed Rollins, March 5, 1985, "Textiles: Textile Trade Paper for Ed Rollins 03/05/1985" folder, Michael A. Driggs files, OA12242, Reagan Library; Stuart Auerbach, "Customs Says Textiles Pose Serious Problem," *Washington Post*, July 25, 1984, p. C1.

15. William E. Brock to Edwin Meese, November 17, 1983 (first, third, and fourth quotations) and "Textile and Apparel Trade Issues (Update)," undated (other quotation), both "Textile and Apparel Trade Issue (4)" folder, Michael A. Griggs files, OA12242, Reagan Library.

16. M. B. Oglesby Jr. to Fred Ryan, May 8, 1984, "Textiles (2)" folder, M. B. Oglesby files, Office of Legislative Affairs, OA13000, Reagan Library.

17. Quotation in Frederick B. Dent to George Bush, September 15, 1982, "Address Final Session of the American Textile Manufacturers Institute's Annual Meeting 4/9/83" folder, Daniel Sullivan and Jennifer Fitzgerald Files, George Bush Presidential Library, College Station, Texas, hereafter cited as "Bush Library"; U.S. Department of Commerce's Office of Textiles and Apparel, "U.S. Textile and Apparel Import Program," document, January 11, 1988, "U.S. Textile and Apparel Import Program" folder, Susan Lauffer files, OA16376, Reagan Library.

18. U.S. Department of Commerce's Office of Textiles and Apparel, "U.S. Textile and Apparel Import Program," document, January 11, 1988, "U.S. Textile and Apparel Import Program" folder, Susan Lauffer files, OA16376, Reagan Library; Closing quotation in "Textile Bill—Talking Points," August 2, 1986, "Textile/Apparel (1)" folder, Michael L. Mussa files, OA17732, Reagan Library.

19. M. B. Oglesby Jr. to Ronald Reagan, December 12, 1983, "Textile Working Group (12)" folder, OA11723, Sherrie M. Cooksey files (Office of the Counsel to the President), Reagan Library.

20. Roger Milliken to Edwin Meese III, November 3, 1983, "Textiles: Miscellaneous Letters (1)" folder, OA12242, Michael A. Driggs files, Reagan Library; William A. Klopman to The President, May 17, 1983, "Textiles: Miscellaneous Letters (2)" folder, OA12242, Michael A. Driggs files, Reagan Library.

21. Strom Thurmond to Wendell Gunn, July 26, 1983, "Textiles: Miscellaneous Letters (1)" folder, OA12242, Michael A. Driggs files, Reagan Library; Strom Thurmond to James A. Baker III, June 12, 1984, "Textiles (1)" folder, M. B. Oglesby files, Office of Legislative Affairs, OA13000, Reagan Library; Strom Thurmond et al. to Mr. President, April 9, 1984, "Textiles (1)" folder, M. B. Oglesby files, Office of Legislative Affairs, OA13000, Reagan Library. For an example of Thurmond using his position as president pro tempore to put pressure on the president, see Jesse Helms et al. to Ronald Reagan, August 13, 1984, folder 522, box 70, CMS Series, Thurmond Papers. Written on Thurmond's pro tempore letterhead, this appeal to Reagan to help the industry is cosigned by twelve U.S. senators.

22. George C. Wallace to Ronald Reagan, December 20, 1984, "Textiles: Miscellaneous Letters (2)" folder, OA12242, Michael A. Driggs files, Reagan Library.

23. James A. Baker III to Strom Thurmond, October 27, 1983, and Edwin Meese III to Roger Milliken, October 19, 1983, both in "Textiles (2)" folder, M. B. Oglesby files, Office of Legislative Affairs, OA13000, Reagan Library. Both of these letters contain the "ambitious" quotation.

24. Susan F. Rasky, "Rep. Jenkins Wins a Philosophical Victory," *New York Times*, September 15, 1989, p. D2 (first quotation); Lacrisha Butler, "Jenkins Prepares to Leave Congress—with $300,000," *USA Today*, September 11, 1992.

25. Ed Jenkins interview with author on June 25, 2010, in Jasper, Georgia. For the history of this quotation, see http://en.wikipedia.org/wiki/All_politics_is_local (accessed November 22, 2010, copy in author's possession).

26. Obie O. Mason to Ed Jenkins, December 23, 1982, Mr. and Mrs. Joel Young to Ed Jenkins, December 11, 1982, and Ed Jenkins to W. C. Langford Jr., May 25, 1982, all "Trade-General" folder, box 43, series 329-86-0219, Jenkins Papers; Kenneth T. Walsh, "Two Sides of the Street in Trade Battle," *U.S. News and World Report*, September 23, 1985, p. 52 (forty to one statistic).

27. Ed Jenkins interview with author on June 25, 2010, in Jasper, Georgia.

28. "Mr. Textiles," *South China Morning Post*, July 5, 1985, clipping in untitled folder, box 787, ACTWU Papers-Cornell (all quotations in this article).

29. First two quotations in Ed Jenkins to author, September 9, 2010 (letter in author's possession); John A. Svahn to Ed Rollins, March 5, 1985, "Textiles: Textile Trade Paper for Ed Rollins 03/05/1985" folder, Michael A. Driggs files, Reagan Library; Jenkins interview with author (last quotation).

30. NTA, "New England Textile Mill Closings," January 1985, folder 27.11, box 27, NTA Papers; NTA, "Mill Liquidations, 1975–1982" folder 27.12, box 27, NTA Papers; ATMI, "1985 Permanent Plant Closings and Permanent Layoffs (January-June)," folder 27.5, box 27, NTA Papers.

31. Bruce Mohl, "Despite Fight, South May Not Rise Again," *Boston Sunday Globe*, October 20, 1985, clipping in folder 27.5, box 27, NTA Papers (MS2000.178.1).

32. Remarks by Ames Stevens Jr., October 1, 1984, and Remarks by Seth M. Bodner, October 1, 1984, both vol.1.34, NTA 1984 Annual Meeting Files, NTA Papers.

33. "Textile and Apparel Imports Reach Record Levels; Industry Calls for Legislative Solution" (ATMI Press Release), July 30, 1985, "ATMI, 1984–1985," folder, box 1, MS106.3.3.17.1, Cohen Papers.

34. ACTWU General Executive Board Minutes, January 9–10, 1985, p. 2 (quotation), and March 11–15, 1985, p. 2, both "GEB Minutes January–March 1985," folder, box 1006, ACTWU Papers-Cornell.

35. AFTAC Newsletter, February 1985, "Crafted with Pride" folder, box 35, ACTWU Papers-Cornell; Gundersheim and Cowell quoted in Dana Frank, *Buy American: The Untold Story of Economic Nationalism* (Boston: Beacon Press, 1999), p. 198.

36. "Textile and Apparel Trade Enforcement Act of 1985—Cosponsor List (106)," March 15, 1985, box 10, Ninety-Ninth Congress files, Hollings Papers.

37. Ed Jenkins to Larry Rodgers, May 28, 1985, "Textile" folder, box 6, series 329-92-138, Jenkins Papers.

38. Jack McDonald to Ernest F. Hollings, May 13, 1985, and Evelyn Dubrow to Ernest F. Hollings, June 21, 1985, both box 10, Ninety-Ninth Congress files, Hollings Papers.

39. Ernest F. Hollings to Carolina Yarn Association, April 22, 1985, box 10, Ninety-Ninth Congress files, Hollings Papers.

40. Robert Porter to William S. Cohen, January 25, 1985 (first three quotations), and "Statement of Senator William S. Cohen," March 19, 1985, both "Trade-Textiles, Shoes, 1983–1991" folder, box 25, MS106.3.4.3, Cohen Papers; "Speech of Senator William S. Cohen before the New England Council," February 5, 1986 (fourth quotation), "Trade-1985–95" folder, box 11, MS106.3.4.6, Cohen Papers; Frank R. Lautenberg to Jay Mazur, December 2, 1985, "Textile and Apparel Trade Enforcement Act 1985" folder, box 7, President's files, series 5780/154, ILGWU Papers-Cornell.

41. Joy Franklin, "Cranston Print Works Hurt by Textile Imports," Hendersonville (North Carolina) *Times-News*, July 17, 1985; John R. Meinart to U.S. Senate Finance Committee, July 15, 1985, "Letters to Congress on Bill" folder, box 787, ACTWU Papers-Cornell.

42. Hollings quoted in "Senate Passes Bill," *Southern Textile News*, November 18, 1985, p. 1. My Freedom of Information Act request to the Reagan Library failed to unearth these letters, presumably because they were not retained. Many of the letters to Reagan were copied to local congressmen, however, and I have used these records instead, along with many other records on the 1985 bill that were obtained from the Reagan Library. Subsequent efforts to locate the letters at the library were unsuccessful.

43. James Blair to Ed Jenkins, May 2, 1985, "Textile" folder, box 6, series 329-92-138, Jenkins Papers; "Volume Mail Sampling Sheet," September 24, 1985, folder 518, box 75, CMS Series, Thurmond Papers; Donald H. Smith to Butler Derrick, October 4, 1985, Butler Derrick to Donald H. Smith, May 6, 1985, and Christine Tucker to Butler Derrick, May 3, 1985, all box 27, Derrick Papers. The letters that Derrick received about the 1985 bill are contained in this box of his papers. When Butler Derrick gave me permission to use it, the Derrick collection was still being processed, and no folder citations were available.

44. See, for example, Jay R. Amber to Butler Derrick, January 12, 1986, box 31, Derrick Papers; "Senate Passes Bill," *Southern Textile News*, November 18, 1985, p. 1.

45. Herbert Parrott to Ronald Reagan, April 26, 1985, "Textile" folder, box 6, series 329-92-138, Jenkins Papers; Alex McCallum to President Reagan, February 21, 1986, box 31, Derrick Papers.

46. Mat Self to Ronald Reagan, March 13, 1985, box 10, Ninety-Ninth Congress files, Hollings Papers; Donald H. Smith to Butler Derrick, October 4, 1985, box 27, Derrick Papers.

47. "BK" to "AMK," September 25, 1985, "Tom Donnelly to Accept 7000 Textile Letters from Broyhill" folder, OA17439, White House Office of Legislative Affairs Records, Reagan Library.

48. John F. Nash Jr. to Carroll Campbell, December 4, 1985, "Textile and Apparel Trade Enforcement Act, October 24–December 1985" folder, box 32, Campbell Papers.

49. M. F. Thompson to Ernest F. Hollings, June 21, 1985, box 10, Ninety-Ninth Congress files, Hollings Papers.

50. J. Larry Lengel to Ed Jenkins, May 10, 1985, "Textile" folder, box 6, series 329-92-138, Jenkins Papers.

51. Larry Rodgers to Ed Jenkins, May 16, 1985; David Bolton to Ed Jenkins, April 1, 1985, and Tom Lloyd to Ed Jenkins, May 7, 1985, all "Textile" folder, box 6, series 329-92-138, Jenkins Papers.

52. Nancy Woloch, *Women and the American Experience: A Concise History* (New York: McGraw Hill, 1996), p. 328; Louise Lamphere, *From Working Daughters to Working Mothers: Immigrant Women in a New England Industrial Community* (Ithaca and London: Cornell University Press, 1987), pp. 15–16.

53. Most of the letters to Jenkins are in the large "Textile" folder, box 6, series 329-92-138, Jenkins Papers, as cited in the next two notes. There are also many similar letters in boxes 23-25 (series III) of the J. Roy Rowland papers, held at the Richard B. Russell Library for Political Research and Studies, University of Georgia, hereafter cited as "Rowland Papers." The letters written by female workers to Rowland are discussed further below.

54. Ann Chester to Ed Jenkins, May 3, 1985, "Textile" folder, box 6, series 329-92-138, Jenkins Papers; Mrs. Glyndon Robinson to Ed Jenkins, May 10, 1985, "Textile" folder, box 6, series 329-92-138, Jenkins Papers.

55. Mrs. Clyde Holloway to Ed Jenkins, May 16, 1985, and Ed Jenkins to Ms. Vivian Stanfield, August 30, 1985, both "Textile" folder, box 6, series 329-92-138, Jenkins Papers.

56. Daisy Byrd to Ernest Hollings, May 17, 1985; Miriam Allison to Ernest F. Hollings, May 7, 1985; Brenda McCaskill to Ernest F. Hollings, ca. May 1985, all box 10, Ninety-Ninth Congress files, Hollings Papers. Hollings's Republican counterpart in South Carolina, Strom Thurmond, also received many similar letters. See, for example, Lora Harris to Strom Thurmond, September 27, 1985, folder 518, box 75, CMS Series, Thurmond Papers.

57. Ernest F. Hollings to The President, June 21, 1985, box 10, Ninety-Ninth Congress files, Hollings Papers.

58. "Imports = Economic Murder, Members Tell Senate Panel," *Labor Unity*, October 1985, p. 3 (first two quotations); "Elli" to Elizabeth Smith, May 1, 1985, "Testimony to Trade Subcommittee" folder, box 787, ACTWU Papers-Cornell.

59. "Statement of Beverly Reed before the Subcommittee on International Trade, U.S. Senate Committee on Finance," September 12, 1985, pp. 2, 4, 7, "Testimony to Trade Subcommittee" folder, box 787, ACTWU Papers-Cornell.

60. "Statement of Nilda Quintanilla before the Subcommittee on International Trade, U.S. Senate Committee on Finance," September 12, 1985 (quotation on p. 3), "Testimony to Trade Subcommittee" folder, box 787, ACTWU Papers-Cornell. The subsequent Levi's closures are detailed further in chapter 8.

61. "Statement of Wing Fong Chin before the Subcommittee on International Trade, U.S. Senate Committee on Finance," September 12, 1985, p. 1, "Testimony to Trade Subcommittee" folder, box 787, ACTWU Papers-Cornell.

62. "I Don't Want Welfare . . . I Want to Work" (first quotation), and "Uncontrolled Imports," April 10, 1985 (final three quotations), both in untitled folder, box 787, ACTWU Papers.

63. "Testimony of Roger Kase before the Subcommittee on Trade, U.S. House Committee on Ways and Means," July 15, 1985, "Testimony to Trade Subcommittee" folder, box 787, ACTWU Papers-Cornell.

64. "Statement of Peter Phillipes before the Subcommittee on International Trade, U.S. Senate Committee on Finance," September 12, 1985, pp. 1, 2, 4, "Testimony to Trade Subcommittee" folder, box 787, ACTWU Papers-Cornell.

65. George P. Shultz et al. to Senator Hollings, June 19, 1985, box 10, Ninety-Ninth Congress files, Hollings Papers.

66. Clayton Yeutter, "It's So Bad, the Sponsors Must Want It Vetoed," *Washington Post*, May 18, 1986 (first quotation); Jan Greene, "Phasing Out of Weaker Industries," *Daily News Record*, November 15, 1985; Strom Thurmond to Clayton Yeutter, November 15, 1985, all in "Dirt on Ambassador Yeutter" folder, box 789, ACTWU Papers-Cornell.

67. James C. Miller III to Ronald Reagan, December 13, 1985, "Textiles (2)" folder, White House Office of Political Affairs Records, OA19397, Reagan Library; Porter quoted in Roger B. Porter to Donald T. Regan and Alfred H. Kingon, May 20, 1985, "Textiles and CRB (3)" folder, Roger B. Porter Files, OA15007, Reagan Library; Closing quotation in Richard Wightman, "Congress Battle Looms on Textile Trade Bill," *Daily News Record*, April 15, 1985, p. S3.

68. George H. W. Bush to Ed Rollins, February 27, 1985, "Textiles: Textile Trade Paper for Ed Rollins 03/05/1985" folder, OA12242, Michael A. Driggs files, Reagan Library.

69. Hollings, *Making Government Work*, p. 218 (Hollings quotation); William B. Lacy to Alan Woods, December 10, 1985, "Textile/Trade (1)" folder, William B. Lacy files, OA13030, Reagan Library. The polling referred to here was conducted by D/M/I.

70. Alex Dimitrief to Mitch Daniels et al., November 21, 1985, "Textiles (3)" folder, White House Office of Political Affairs Records, OA19397, Reagan Library (Dimitrief quotations); Testimony of Denis Lamb, March 6, 1985, pp. 114, 121, U.S. Congress, House, Government Operations Committee, *Federal Enforcement of Textile and Apparel Import Quotas (Part 2)*, 99th Congress, 1st Session, 1985.

71. American Farm Bureau Federation et al. to Ed Jenkins, July 30, 1986, "Textile" folder, box 6, series 329-92-138, Jenkins Papers; Dole quoted in Bob Dole to Ronald Reagan, July 26, 1983, "Textiles: Miscellaneous Letters (1)" folder, OA12242, Michael A. Driggs files, Reagan Library.

72. Alex Dimitrief to Mitch Daniels et al., November 14, 1985, "Textiles (3)" folder, White House Office of Political Affairs Records, OA19397, Reagan Library.

73. See Howard Young to Owen Bieber, September 30, 1985, "Textile and Apparel Trade Bill Opposition—Retailers Employees' Letters Against" folder, box 789, ACTWU Papers-Cornell.

74. Robert E. Dewar to Craig Fuller, June 27, 1983, "Textiles: Miscellaneous Letters (2)" folder, OA12242, Michael A. Driggs files, Reagan Library; Closing quotation in Loyd Hackler to Craig L. Fuller, June 23, 1983, "Textile Working Group (12)" folder, OA11723, Sherrie M. Cooksey files (Office of the Counsel to the President), Reagan Library.

75. *Greenville News* editorial reported in *Southern Textile News*, April 2, 1984, p. 4.

76. Remarks by Ames Stevens Jr., October 1, 1984, vol.1.34, NTA 1984 Annual Meeting Files, NTA Papers.

77. Warren T. Brookes, "Textile Quotas—The Cruelly Regressive Tax," Heritage Features Syndicate, July 27, 1986, in "Textiles" folder, OA14574, Mari Maseng files (Office of Public Liaison), Reagan Library; Robert B. Reich, "Industries in Distress: We're Protecting Ourselves Right out of the Market," *New Republic*, May 9, 1981, pp. 19–23, quotation on p. 23.

78. On previous struggles to organize Cannon mills, see Griffith, *The Crisis of American Labor*, pp. 46–61; Minchin, *Fighting against the Odds*, pp. 46–47, 179. Cannon's resistance to unionization is also explored further in chapter 10.

79. "Message Delivered to President," *Cannon News*, May 1985, p. 1; "Letter-Writing Campaign Launched," *Cannon News*, August 1985, p. 1 (quotation); "Letter-Writing Campaign Response Excellent," *Cannon News*, September 1985, p. 6; "Letters to the Editor," *Cannon News*, October 1985, p. 3, all in Cannon Mills Papers.

80. Branson C. Jones to Ed Jenkins, August 27, 1985, "Textile" folder, box 6, series 329-92-138, Jenkins Papers.

81. "ACTWU Union Facts Listed" (first quotation), "Teamwork Spells Survival—ACTWU Spells Trouble," and "Why Cannon Opposes ACTWU" (second quotation), all *Cannon News*, September 1985, pp. 1, 2, 3; "Associates Support Cannon Mills Company," *Cannon News*, October 18, 1985, p. 1; "Letters to the Editor," *Cannon News*, October 1985, p. 3 (Hartsoe quotation); Christopher Chafe interview with author on June 21, 2010 (telephone interview).

82. "Yes or No?" *Southern Textile News*, October 7, 1985, p. 4. For an example of how the *News* covered the campaign for the bill without mentioning the involvement of unions, see "Textile Employees Launch Letter Writing Campaign," *Southern Textile News*, September 23, 1985, p. 7. When ACTWU's successor, UNITE, finally won bargaining rights at Kannapolis in 1999, the *News* also reacted with great hostility to the union. See "Two Teenagers in a Movie House," *Southern Textile News*, November 29, 1999, p. 4.

83. "Union Drive for Trade Bill Gets Off to Rousing Start," *Labor Unity*, May 1985, p. 2 (Burgos quotation); "Pressure to Pass Textile Trade Bill Gaining Momentum," *Labor Unity*, June 1985, pp. 10–15, quotations on p. 11 (Philadelphia), p. 15 (Los Angeles).

84. "Pressure to Pass Textile Trade Bill Gaining Momentum," *Labor Unity*, June 1985, pp. 10–15, quotations on p. 13.

85. "Merchants Should Separate U.S./Union-Made from Foreign," *Colorado Labor Advocate*, January 24, 1986, clipping in "Imports" folder, box 447, ACTWU Papers-Cornell.

86. Jan Greene, "Phasing Out of Weaker Industries," *Daily News Record*, November 15, 1985, in "Dirt on Ambassador Yeutter" folder, box 789, ACTWU Papers-Cornell.

87. Sol C. Chaikin to Oh Seok, November 15, 1985, "Textile and Apparel Trade Enforcement Act 1985" folder, box 7, President's files (series 5780/154), ILGWU Papers-Cornell.

88. "Statement of the Taiwan Textile Federation in Opposition to HR 1562," July 12, 1985, Subcommittee on Trade of the U.S. House Ways and Means Committee, "Testimony to Trade Subcommittee" folder, box 787, ACTWU Papers-Cornell.

89. A. Hasnan Habib to M. B. Ogelsby Jr., October 4, 1985, "Textiles (1)" folder, M. B. Oglesby files, OA13000, Reagan Library.

90. Ruby Quarles to Ed Jenkins, May 30, 1985, "Textile" folder, box 6, series 329-92-138, Jenkins Papers; Lena Martin to Ernest Hollings, May 8, 1985, box 10, Ninety-Ninth Congress files, Hollings Papers. For another similar example, see Bobby J. Dove to Ed Jenkins, April 24, 1985, "Textile" folder, box 6, series 329-92-138, Jenkins Papers.

91. Ed Jenkins interview with author on June 25, 2010, in Jasper, Georgia; Butler Derrick, "Textile and Apparel Trade Act of 1987," *Congressional Record*, February 19, 1987, in box 33, Derrick Papers.

92. L. Fernando Milan to Edolphus Towns, July 29, 1985, "Letters to Congress on Our Bill" folder, box 787, ACTWU Papers-Cornell; Cardiss Collins to Caucus Member, n.d., "Textile and Apparel Trade Bill Opposition: Congressional Black Caucus" folder, box 789, ACTWU Papers-Cornell.

93. Alex Dimitrief to Mitch Daniels et al., November 21, 1985, "Textiles (3)" folder, White House Office of Political Affairs Records, OA19397, Reagan Library; M. B. Oglesby Jr. Memo re: Meeting with Senators Jeremiah Denton et al., December 5, 1985 (Oglesby quotation), "Textiles (3)" folder, White House Office of Political Affairs Records, OA19397, Reagan Library.

94. Ronald Reagan Press Release, December 17, 1985, "Textiles (2)" folder, White House Office of Political Affairs Records, OA19397, Reagan Library.

95. James C. Miller III to Ronald Reagan, December 13, 1985, "Textiles (2)" folder, White House Office of Political Affairs Records, OA19397, Reagan Library.

96. "Reagan Vetoes Textile Bill," *Labor Unity*, January 1986, p. 1 (Finley and Sheinkman quotations); "Reagan Vetoes Textile, Apparel Bill: ILG Vows to Continue Fight on Imports," *Justice*, January 1986, p. 3; "Industry Expresses Reaction to Presidential Veto," *Southern Textile News*, December 23, 1985, p. 1 (Gregg quotation).

97. Warren T. Brookes, "Textile Quotas—The Cruelly Regressive Tax," Heritage Features Syndicate, July 27, 1986, in "Textiles" folder, OA14574, Mari Maseng files, Reagan Library; Jenkins interview with author (Jenkins quotation).

98. "House Rejects Override By 276–149 Margin," *Southern Textile News*, August 11, 1986, p. 1.

99. David Pace, "Congress Urges Reagan to Strengthen Textile Trade Agreements," May 7, 1986 (AP Story); and Mary Beth Franklin, UPI Press Release, May 6, 1986, both in "MFA" folder, box 461, ACTWU Papers-Cornell.

100. Carroll A. Campbell Jr. to Tom DeLay, July 22, 1986, "Textiles (3)" folder, Richard Prendergast files, OA17432, Reagan Library.

101. Norman Kominsky to Senator William Cohen, February 25, 1983, "Eastland Woolen Mill, 1981–85" folder, box 15, MS106.3.3.17.1, Cohen Papers; Norman Kominsky to "Phil," n.d., NTA 1985 Annual Meeting files, NTA Papers (Kominsky quotations); David Dean to Ronald Reagan, n.d., NTA 1985 Annual Meeting files, NTA Papers.

102. Congressman J. Roy Rowland Floor Statement, October 10, 1985, "HR 1562 Folder 4," box 164, series 2, Rowland Papers.

103. Lexie L. Brewer to J. Roy Rowland, August 1, 1986, "Textile Bill Veto Override folder 1," box 25, series 2, Rowland Papers; Kimberly J. Cravey to J. Roy Rowland, July 31, 1986, "Textile Bill Veto Override folder 2," box 25, series 2, Rowland Papers.

104. William L. Ball III to Ronald Reagan, August 1, 1986 (first quotation), and "Talking Points" both "Friday 08/01/1986 9.45am Textile Meeting" folder, OA17438, White House Office of Legislative Affairs Records, Reagan Library.

105. Alan M. Kranowitz and Pamela J. Turner to David Chew, August 5, 1986 (first quotation); William L. Ball III to Ronald Reagan, August 5, 1986 (second quotation); Reagan quotation in "Talking Points," August 5, 1986, all in "Thursday 08/05/1986 9.30am GOP Leadership" folder, OA17438, White House Office of Legislative Affairs Records, Reagan Library.

106. "Statement by the Principal Deputy Press Secretary," August 1, 1986, "Textiles (1)" folder, Richard Prendergast files, OA17432, Reagan Library (first two quotations); Yeutter quoted in "Press Briefing by U.S. Trade Representative Clayton Yeutter," August 1, 1986, p. 3, "Textiles (1)" folder, Richard Prendergast files, OA17432, Reagan Library.

107. "Textile Talking Points," August 2, 1986, "Textiles" folder, OA14574, Mari Maseng files, Reagan Library.

108. "House Rejects Override By 276–149 Margin," *Southern Textile News*, August 11, 1986, p. 1 (quotations); Ed Jenkins interview with author on June 25, 2010, in Jasper, Georgia.

109. "Economists' Statement on Protectionism," August 3, 1986, "Textiles (1)" folder, White House Office of Political Affairs Records, OA19397, Reagan Library (quotation); Beryl W. Sprinkel Memorandum for the Economic Policy Council, August 5, 1986, "Textile/Apparel (1)" folder, OA17732, Michael L. Mussa files, Reagan Library.

110. "Ron" Reagan to "Bob" Michel, August 5, 1986, "Textiles (1)" folder, Richard Prendergast files, OA17432, Reagan Library.

111. "Dan" to Mari Maseng, July 25, 1986, "Textiles" folder, OA14574, Mari Maseng files, Reagan Library.

112. "House Rejects Override By 276–149 Margin," *Southern Textile News*, August 11, 1986, p. 1; "An *STN* Exclusive Interview: Roger Milliken," *Southern Textile News*, November 3, 1986, p. 9 (Milliken quotations); Richard Alm, "Death of a Bill, Birth of an Issue," *U.S. News and World Report*, August 18, 1986, p. 6; Mack Mattingly interview with author on June 13, 2010, in St. Simon's Island, Georgia.

113. "House Rejects Override By 276–149 Margin," p. 1 (Trogdon quotation); "Override Loses by 8 Votes; Battle Over, War Continues," *Labor Unity*, September 1986, p. 1.

114. Roger Milliken to Strom Thurmond, August 7, 1986, and Strom Thurmond to Roger Milliken, August 7, 1986, both folder 346a, box 49, CMS Series, Thurmond Papers; Butler Derrick quoted in *Congressional Record*, February 19, 1987, copy in box 33, Derrick Papers.

115. Karl Spilhaus interview with author on April 26, 2011 in Boston, Massachusetts; "Override Hopes Dashed," *Fieldcrest Cannon Today*, August 13, 1986, p. 1; "Override Loses by 8 Votes; Battle Over, War Continues," *Labor Unity*, September 1986, p. 1; "House Rejects Override By 276–149 Margin," p. 1.

116. "House Rejects Override By 276–149 Margin"; Gregg quoted in "Statement by John H. Gregg, Chairman, Fiber, Fabric, and Apparel Coalition for Trade," *Southern Textile News*, August 11, 1986, p. 1.

117. Whitney Stevens to Carroll Campbell Jr., August 15, 1986, "Textile and Apparel Trade Enforcement Act, August 11, 1986" folder, box 33, Campbell Papers; Bill Klopman to Butler Derrick, August 12, 1986, box 31, Derrick Papers; Roger Milliken to Carroll A. Campbell Jr., August 11, 1986, "Textile and Apparel Trade Enforcement Act, August 11 1986" folder, box 33, Campbell Papers.

118. White House Staffing Memorandum, September 17, 1986 (supporters quotation), and Ronald Reagan to supporter letter, September 17, 1986, both "Textiles" folder, Mary Dewhirst files, OA17788, Reagan Library.

*Chapter Five*

# A Resounding Blow: The 1987 and 1990 Textile Bills

Following the failure to override Reagan's veto, the textile industry's supporters lost little time in pushing for new import restriction legislation. In both the North and South, executives agreed that passage of this legislation was vital if their industry was to survive in the long term. As the ATMI's Carlos Moore reported to the Northern Textile Association in March 1988, a new bill was a "necessity" for "the health of the domestic textile and apparel industries in the next decade."[1] From the spring of 1987 through to the fall of 1988, the industry undertook another massive campaign, but it was again thwarted by the Reagan administration. Reasoning that George H. W. Bush might give them a more sympathetic ear, the Congressional Textile Caucus tried again in 1990, but the result was the same. Bush's veto proved decisive. As the *Southern Textile News* admitted, the failure of the 1990 campaign was a "resounding blow." Coming after the two previous failures, the defeat finally put a stop to the industry's hopes of passing protective legislation. In an interview in 2002, the ATMI's president indeed linked subsequent mill closures to the doomed fight to overturn Bush's veto. "Had we not lost that vote, I think we would see quite a different situation in the industry today," insisted Edward P. Schrum.[2]

Both the 1987 and 1990 campaigns had strong similarities with their predecessor, especially in the degree of grassroots mobilization that they produced. Despite growing fissures, the alliance between management and unions also endured. The powerful Roger Milliken provided another continuity, constantly pushing for legislation to restrict imports. "We are not an industry against imports," he explained at the end of 1986, "but we are against eliminating an industry that together employs two million jobs and an industry once lost is not easily recovered. . . . (T)o make sure of our market and our jobs are not taken away, there has to be a legislated effort."[3]

There were, however, many unique features of these later bills, which attracted fresh congressional leadership and emphasized new arguments. Anxious to avoid the mistakes of the 1985 campaign, the bill was changed to avoid charges of racism. In addition, the bill's proponents now emphasized the ethnic and racial diversity of the industry's workforce. As ACTWU's leaders grasped, this argument had strategic advantages, allowing congressional members to support an "entry industry for new immigrants" even when there were few mills in their districts. The pitch carried considerable weight, yet ultimately the economic recovery of the late 1980s played the key role in torpedoing both bills. With renewed prosperity, FFACT's opponents argued that the industry was recovering and that there was plenty of work available for those who did lose their jobs.[4]

It was no surprise that the new bill was championed by representatives from South Carolina, where Milliken's textile empire remained the state's largest privately held business. The key sponsor of the bill, South Carolina congressman Butler Derrick, had replaced Jenkins as chair of the Congressional Textile Caucus. At the end of 1986, Jenkins stood down in order to relieve his heavy committee load. "I had my hands full as I got a lot of seniority," recalled Jenkins, "and a lot of members from Carolina, Georgia, needed the exposure." Although he was a Democrat, Derrick was close to Milliken, a prominent Republican who had several plants in Derrick's third district. Characterized by what *The State* called a "civil, low-key nature," Derrick had a reputation as an effective legislator.[5] In 1984, he played a leading role in passing the textile labeling law, a measure that tried to help domestic manufacturers by tightening labeling regulations. Derrick was so proud of this achievement that he subsequently called himself the "Made in the USA" congressman. In 1985, the third-ranking Democrat on the House Rules Committee also took the lead in persuading his colleagues to send the textile bill to the House floor under rules that limited amendments, a move that proved crucial to its passage. Reagan's veto left Derrick "amazed and disappointed," yet he vowed to try again. "The textile industry hangs by a thread," he commented in early 1987, "but the fight is far from over."[6]

A graduate of the University of South Carolina, Derrick was a trained lawyer and had been in Congress for over a decade. His district was largely rural but included the textile centers of Anderson and Greenwood, as well as numerous small towns that were dependent on the industry. From his earliest days in Congress, Derrick forged close links with mill owners; in February 1977, for example, he wrote Greenwood Mills president Jim Self that he was "vitally concerned with issues affecting the textile industry." The following year, Derrick "pushed hard" to try to secure passage of Hollings's textile bill, even helping to arrange a breakfast meeting at the White House that was attended by a large number of industry executives. After Carter's veto, he vowed to keep up the "good fight" for import restriction legislation.[7]

Looking back, Derrick remembered that his actions were partly a response to the economic power of local mill owners, although he also stressed his genuine concern for the well-being of textile workers, many of whom he knew personally. "You either farmed or you worked in the textile mill," he recalled of the South Carolina of his youth, "or a lot of people did both. I mean the women, when I was a young man you couldn't walk across the main street in these little towns at 3:30 in the afternoon when the women got out of the sewing rooms, because there was a steady line of cars." By the time that he won his seat in Congress, Derrick estimated that "over 50 percent" of the people he represented either worked in the industry or depended on it. His course of action was clear, especially as there was no obvious replacement for the mills. "They were my constituents," he explained, "and that became one of my major concerns, about what to do about the textile industry. . . . It was about the only source of a cash income that most of these small towns could provide."[8]

**"Butler Derrick as a young congressman, ca. late 1970s." (Photo courtesy of the South Carolina Political Collections, University of South Carolina)**

"Wearing his trademark suspenders, Congressman Butler Derrick meets with constituents (date unknown)." (Photo courtesy of the South Carolina Political Collections, University of South Carolina)

"Congressman Butler Derrick (center) tours the Swirl, Inc. apparel factory in Easley, SC, January 1986. Also pictured are company officials Bob Olson (L) and Larry Nachman (R) and worker Ervie Lee McNeely (seated). McNealy had worked at the plant since the day it opened in 1953." (Photo courtesy of the South Carolina Political Collections, University of South Carolina)

Once elected as chair of the CTC, Derrick quickly got to work. Building on the "outstanding" work of his predecessor, Derrick called a meeting between the Caucus and FFACT to discuss "options for new legislation." He believed that a quota bill was desperately needed. "Our domestic textile industry is far from realizing the rosy recovery that President Reagan predicted," he wrote Caucus members in January 1987. "Despite the falling dollar on the international trade market, textile workers in our districts are still out of work due to the continuing flood of imported goods. We can—and must—take immediate legislative action to remedy this situation."[9] From the meeting came a new bill, which Derrick introduced to the House on February 19, 1987. According to Derrick, the bill was designed to "bring much needed relief to the industries that have played a key role in making our country the strong industrial competitor it is today." Over the weeks that followed, he worked hard to drum up support for the Textile and Apparel Trade Act. Much of his time was spent arranging for congressional hearings, which were designed to demonstrate the "dire straits" that the industry was in.[10] By May, H.R. 1154 had more than 230 congressional backers, and Derrick felt confident to take on Reagan, who had already dismissed the bill as "protectionist." "Mr. President," he wrote, "I challenge you to reflect on the thousands of jobs that have been lost as a direct result of our permissive import practices." According to Derrick, a president that had pledged to help the industry was now ignoring "the suffering of jobless textile workers in my district and across the nation."[11]

The 1987 bill differed from its predecessor in a number of key respects. Importantly, the new bill specified a global limit on imports but did not pick out individual nations. Quotas were established on each category of textiles from all sources, a change that signified how the racism allegations had undermined support for the previous effort. As the *New York Times* explained, "Unlike the 1985 bill, the present legislation does not single out big exporters such as Taiwan and South Korea, instead applying global import quotas that would also restrict shipments from industrial countries." The global quotas were also an effort to meet allegations that trade rollbacks would provoke retaliation against U.S. exports. Instead of rollbacks, each quota was based on the level of imports in that category in 1986. Addressing other criticisms of the previous bill, backers insisted that their legislation was now consistent with the stipulations of the GATT and the MFA.[12] Derrick insisted that the bill was "far more generous to our trading partners than past legislation," explaining that the industry had made "significant concessions" to win over its opponents. Because the bill was "reasonable," the outcome would be different.[13]

The bill received strong backing, especially in the heavily Democratic northeast. Operating out of Boston, NTA president Karl Spilhaus worked hard to bring congressional supporters on board. "Most members of Congress from the Northeast are co-sponsors of HR. 1154/S. 549 and it is important that they be present and vote in favor of the bill," he explained. The NTA knew that a lot was at stake, writing that the legislation would "prevent the continued deterioration of an important manufacturing industry which has been an integral part of America's industrial history since Colonial days."[14] The effort paid off, and on September 16, 1987, the House passed the bill by a vote of 263 to 156, with strong backing coming from East Coast legislators. Rhode Island Democrat Claiborne Pell, for example, saw himself as a free-trader but backed the bill because there was "no other way to cope with the circumstances which confront the industry." Now the battle switched to the Senate, where the bill was not voted on until the following year. On September 15, 1988, the Senate passed the bill fifty-nine to thirty-six, with strong support again coming from New England members. The House followed eight days later, but Reagan then vetoed the bill. Shortly afterward, the effort to override the veto fell short by eleven votes, three more than had been the case in 1986.[15]

To get this close required a massive effort. The campaign for Derrick's bill had a strong grassroots component, as labor unions strove to involve their members and humanize the import issue, which was often outlined in cold statistics by the media. "Trade is not just a bunch of numbers," summarized ACTWU's *Labor Unity*. "It is *People* who live and work in towns all across America, it is families, it is communities." The union launched a "Faces of Trade" campaign, with key congressmen being sent large pictures of unemployed mill workers who had recently lost their jobs. It was a deliberate attempt to put a human face on the three hundred thousand textile and apparel workers who had lost their jobs since 1979, to show "the people behind the numbers." In addition, the union circulated "displaced workers' stories," providing personal accounts of deindustrialization. One of those featured was Norma Thomas, an African American woman from Los Angeles who did not expect to find another job after her employer had moved offshore. "I'm 62, too old to start over again," she declared.[16] In addition, many workers wrote letters in support of the bill, often as part of campaigns that were coordinated by FFACT. "I work for Monsanto, Greenwood, SC, and we are up against a lot of unfair foreign competition," wrote Becky Timms to Congressman Derrick. "In every community that depends on these basic U.S. industries, people are hurting."[17]

As they fought for H.R. 1154, supporters also stressed the industry's importance as a military supplier. They pointed out that the Department of Defense ranked textiles as second only to steel in its importance to national security, and they noted that Reagan's administration had striven to "improve America's defense capabilities." They cited a recent report by the Industrial College of the Armed Forces that found that U.S. textile mills would not be able to fully supply the military in a national emergency. There were, for example, only four domestic manufacturers of the protective clothing that the military required. When the bill's supporters publicized this report, the American Security Council announced that it would support H.R. 1154. Led by John M. Fisher, Council leaders explained in a letter to Congress that "we all served in combat during World War II, and we know an essential element of our victory was the technology and productivity of our incomparable national base. This base is shrinking rapidly, and it has profound consequences for our leadership position in the Free World." In Congress, the bipartisan National Security Caucus also endorsed the bill on similar grounds.[18]

Led by ACTWU legislative director Elizabeth M. Smith—one of the few women to hold a top post in the union—the bill's advocates also emphasized the diversity of the textile workforce. As Smith wrote in a form letter to members of Congress, "The two million workers in the American textile and apparel industry are very special. These workers are overwhelmingly women, one-third are black, 17 percent are Hispanic-American, and 8 percent are Asian-American." Smith stressed the importance of textile jobs to these workers, many of whom had not graduated from high school and did not speak English well. She also emphasized that mill jobs were not expendable or undesirable; employees valued them dearly and took "pride in their work."[19]

The industry's diversity gave it some important lobbying advantages. In 1988, the Department of Commerce's Office of Textiles and Apparel reported that women comprised 65 percent of the workers in the industry, compared with 32 percent for the manufacturing sector as a whole. Racial minorities made up 29 percent of employees, again significantly more than the manufacturing average of 18 percent.[20] It was well documented that women and racial minorities found it particularly hard to find new jobs when textile plants closed. As the OTA report in 1987 had shown, this was the case because many of these workers lacked formal educational qualifications and had only ever worked in the industry. Moreover, because these groups were overwhelmingly concentrated in lower-paid positions, they lacked the savings that they needed to cope with unemployment. Furthermore, they faced ongoing hiring discrimination. Industry supporters now emphasized all of these points. As the campaign's well-circulated "FFACT sheets" put it, women and minorities were "hardest hit" by mill closures, and the textile and apparel sectors were also "the nation's greatest manufacturing employers of women and minorities." FFACT indeed stressed the industry's size, claiming that textiles and apparel employed more Americans than the steel and auto industries combined.[21]

Although these appeals resonated in eastern states, the situation across the Mississippi was very different. In the Midwest, many farming groups supported free trade because they wanted greater access to overseas markets, while the West Coast was an important conduit for textile imports. Thus the *Seattle Times* opposed the bill, pointing out that ports in Washington handled more than $2 billion worth of textile and garment imports a year. In the fall of 1987, the ATMI's Board of Directors discussed this issue, its minutes recording that it was "imperative to have congressional support from areas west of the Mississippi river" if the campaign was to succeed. To try to build support in the West, the ATMI worked through wool growers, yet their lobbying power was not decisive. Looking back, Butler Derrick felt that the western states had played an important role in stopping his bill. "The west *never* voted for it, and never did anything to help us with it," he recalled, "because they thought it was going to affect their imports."[22]

Very much a product of the industry's heartland in the Carolinas, Derrick was perhaps not the best leader to build a national coalition. As the *Charlotte Observer* commented, even the name Butler Derrick was "seemingly plucked from the pages of 'Gone With the Wind' or a Tennessee Williams play," and Derrick also had a fondness for wearing suspenders in the House chamber and for delivering speeches in a "quiet drawl." Furthermore, he did not try to disguise the fact that the economic interests of his constituents were his prime concern. "Protectionism doesn't bother me," he commented, stressing that textile workers "back home" needed his help. While he was an able congressman, Derrick struggled to reach out beyond the industry's core base.[23]

Behind the scenes, tensions within FFACT simmered away, and the unions complained that some employers were not pulling their weight. The harsh union-busting climate of the Reagan years, a time when organized labor declined precipitously, affected the coalition, as it was hard to cooperate at a time when labor-management relations were otherwise adversarial. Private records acknowledged the problems. As the ILGWU's General Executive Board noted in early 1987, "The employers continue to rely on us to solve all their outside problems—imports, homework, etc.—but still seem to think that cutting union rates and standards are the only ways to solve their immediate business problems."[24]

A related problem was that the unions who supported the bill were declining and becoming weaker. In the spring of 1987, when H.R. 1154 was introduced, the ILGWU's General Executive Board noted that the union had lost 22,556 members over the previous year. Because of declining revenues, the union had a net operating loss of $12.5 million just at the time when it was undertaking a major legislative fight. This compared to a shortfall of $5 million in 1985.[25] At the end of 1985, the ILGWU had 219,001 members, but three years later the number had tumbled to 165,710. The union thus hemorrhaged almost a quarter of its membership at a critical time. Although the decline was evident in every part of the country, it was most acute in the northeast and mid-Atlantic regions.[26] Overall, the ILGWU's membership had been falling since 1970—when it had peaked at 457,517—and leaders blamed imports as the primary cause. Operating with falling revenues, it was very difficult for the union to combat the well-funded retail lobby, which was becoming stronger—and richer—all the time.[27]

Behind the scenes, moreover, divisions *within* the industry also undermined the campaign. In particular, some companies had already established operations overseas, weakening their commitment to fight imports. At the NTA's annual meeting in September 1987, ATMI president Robert Laidlaw candidly commented on these problems, noting that executives "all say yes, yes, yes, but then what do they do, then they in fact take the stuff abroad. The same people who are making the comments." Laidlaw concluded that it was going to take a "Herculean effort" for the industry to work together and "overcome the problems that we face." Over time, an increasing number of executives—especially in the apparel industry—reasoned that it was more lucrative to move operations overseas rather than fighting to maintain domestic production. Every defeat strengthened the hand of those who advocated going offshore.[28]

The national press unanimously opposed the bill, and the strength of the economy gave it extra ammunition. Some of the country's most popular newspapers were particularly hostile. In his widely read weekly column in the *Washington Post*, for instance, Robert J. Samuelson castigated the bill as "dreary legislation." Samuelson insisted that the industry was well protected and argued that textile workers who did lose their jobs could simply move over to growing sectors of the economy. "The sooner this legislation is killed, the better," he concluded. An editorial in the high-circulation *Chicago Tribune* was even more damaging. Titled "The Costs of Coddling Textiles," it argued that foreign competition was healthy and called the industry "insular and lazy." Even in Massachusetts—where the textile industry still had considerable pull—the *Boston Globe* criticized the state's congressional delegation for supporting the bill. Import controls, it argued, would raise prices for consumers.[29]

The press drew off and shaped public perceptions that textiles was a low-wage industry that was not worth fighting for. For many years, the industry had suffered from a serious image problem. In the North, many citizens had a poor opinion of an industry that had fled to the low-wage South and then opposed workers' efforts to improve their lot through unionization. Thus, in 1970 a *New York Times* interviewer asked five leading textile executives whether they could overcome the industry's "stigma of being a low-profit, low-wage industry." In response, the executives stressed the amount of money that they were spending on raising wages and modernizing their plants.[30] The poor image stuck, however, and the J. P. Stevens campaign of the 1970s stigmatized the industry as backward and reactionary just at the time when it was trying to win public support. Referring to the industry's "illegal blacklisting and firing of union members," practices that the Stevens campaign had helped bring to the nation's attention, New York physician Peter E. Schrag argued in one letter to the *New York Times* that the industry's demands for import quotas should be rejected. These attitudes also informed the actions of policy makers, particularly USTR Clayton Yeutter, who reasoned that low-wage manufacturing jobs could be given up in exchange for economic benefits for other sectors.[31]

In the 1970s and 1980s much of the publicity about the prevalence of brown lung disease was also focused on the textile industry. Officially known as byssinosis, brown lung was a crippling disease that resulted from prolonged exposure to cotton dust. As early as 1940, the British government recognized the disease and began compensating victims, but in the United States lack of research and opposition from the industry delayed any action against the illness for more than three decades. Thus, the disease—and the way that the industry had tried to cover it up—received a great deal of publicity just at the time when executives were seeking public sympathy over trade issues. Leading mill owners insisted that the negative attention was not justified, but they acknowledged that it was damaging. As Burlington Industries chairman Charles F. Myers Jr. asserted, "'Brown Lung' is our latest, and exclusive, Albatross," a disease that was "almost synonymous with textiles."[32]

A fictionalized account of the Stevens campaign that depicted dirty and dusty mills, the hit movie *Norma Rae* (1979) exacerbated the industry's problems. As journalist Sandra Salmans summarized, "Propagated by *Norma Rae*, the movie based on the Stevens labor dispute, the industry's reputation for backwardness has clung as persistently as cotton dust." More than seven years after the movie's release, executives and educators complained that it was difficult to attract students into white-collar textile careers. "All the textile schools have had to hire recruiters because the negative image has impacted us so badly," admitted Al Turbak, the director of the School of Textile Engineering at Georgia Tech.[33] Defending their corner, mill owners insisted that the film projected an outdated image because most textile plants were now clean and modern. For several decades, they argued, executives had spent huge sums on capital expenditures to try to compete with imports, changes that themselves entailed significant job losses. By the late 1980s the industry was investing about $1.5 billion per year in new plants and equipment, and great leaps in productivity resulted. "'Norma Rae' came out 25 years too late," charged mill owner Marshall Chapman.[34]

Seizing on these investments, the bill's opponents argued that the impact of imports was exaggerated and that many job losses were actually caused by technological changes. They had a point, as by the late 1980s the U.S. textile industry was among the most productive in the world. The industry was representative of broader changes in the U.S. economy, where manufacturing productivity rose as employment fell. For more than a decade, in fact, the productivity growth of textiles and apparel had been double the average for manufacturing as a whole. Apart from shuttleless looms, other new technologies included robots to deliver materials and computers to design fabric. In addition, automation was helped by more uniformity in the quality of natural materials and by increased use of synthetic fibers. Automation was also a response to increasing awareness of brown lung, which ensured that machines were increasingly used to perform the dirtiest jobs.[35]

Automation continued to have its greatest impact on textile manufacturing, partly because it was much more difficult to mechanize labor-intensive apparel jobs. Because the new technology was expensive, it was also easier for large textile firms—rather than small apparel shops—to invest in it. According to the U.S. International Trade Commission, in the late 1980s the textile industry spent about four times as much on investment in new plants and equipment as its apparel counterpart. Ultimately, however, it is very difficult to put precise figures on how many jobs were lost because of automation or imports, especially as it was often a combination of both factors that were responsible for layoffs. Moreover, imports themselves spurred developments in technology. As the OTA report concluded, "Job losses resulting from imports cannot be easily disentangled from those resulting from rising domestic productivity." What was clear was that while imports were a major cause of job losses, the industry's supporters concealed the important role that was also played by automation, largely because there was no obvious political solution to it.[36] Conversely, avid free-traders exaggerated the impact of automation and tried to undermine the industry's fight for import controls. As one Heritage Foundation writer charged, "Most of the 'job losses' incurred by textile industries are the direct result of rising productivity, not imports." For workers who lost their jobs, of course, it made little difference whether imports or automation were to blame.[37]

The biggest obstacle for the 1987 bill to surmount, however, remained the Reagan administration's opposition. Although Derrick privately acknowledged these difficulties, he was not a member of the influential House Ways and Means Committee, as Jenkins had been, and this was an additional weakness. In July, when Clayton Yeutter told the committee that the bill was "an enormous rip-off of the American consumer," Derrick was not there to respond.[38] In a new shift, the administration also used the economic recovery to argue that the bill was not needed. By 1987, Reagan was taking credit for a sustained economic turnaround that was being enjoyed by many Americans. As the historian James T. Patterson has summarized, "The economy of the mid- and late 1980s was obviously ushering in a more glittering material world for a great many people." By the time that H.R. 1154 was considered, the administration boasted that the economy was generating two hundred thousand jobs a month, and even the textile industry was reaping some of the benefits.[39] Sent to every member of Congress, a letter from key administration figures—including Yeutter and Secretary of State George P. Shultz—was particularly important. It declared that there was "absolutely no economic justification" for the bill because the industry was "prospering." Fiber consumption had reached "record levels," and the industry simply did not have a case for further protection.[40]

Ironically, the gains that the campaign had already secured also made it harder to pass a new bill. The bilateral trade agreements that the Reagan administration had negotiated in 1986 were clearly influenced by the industry's legislative efforts, but they hurt efforts to pass Derrick's bill. The agreements did help to stem imports; in the first eleven months of 1987, imports grew by only 3 percent, compared with rates of 18 to 20 percent a few years earlier. Along with improved profitability and volume, critics pointed to these statistics and asserted that further protection was not needed. Some went further and lambasted wealthy mill owners as avaricious protectionists. "There's no protection from greed," blasted columnist Dick Youngblood in the *Minneapolis Star Tribune*.[41]

Sent to every member of Congress on September 15, 1988, a letter from the bill's corporate opponents highlighted the powerful forces that were arraigned against H.R. 1154, which its foes dubbed the "Textile Quota Bill." The signers included powerful retailers such as Gap, JCPenney, K-Mart, and Montgomery Ward, as well as farm groups and export-oriented service and manufacturing companies. In all, ninety-two companies or industry associations signed the letter, a formidable coalition.[42] Working diligently, Derrick tried to fight back. Within five days, the South Carolinian had dispatched a personal appeal to his congressional colleagues, reminding them that the jobs of two million Americans were at stake. Further appeals followed, including a last-minute letter to Vice President George Bush. As he campaigned for the presidency, Bush visited many textile areas, and Derrick urged him to inform Reagan of the "true state of the textile industry." Although there was no record of a direct response from Bush, during the Republican presidential debate the vice president reiterated his support for the administration's textile policies and insisted that the "answer" to the industry's problems was better "enforcement" of existing trade agreements. "I want to see us go forward with opportunity and without protection," he declared.[43]

On September 28, President Reagan duly vetoed H.R. 1154 on the grounds that it would have a negative impact on the American economy. In particular, he claimed that it would increase prices for consumers, threaten jobs in export industries, and hurt the nation's overseas farm sales. The economic recovery provided new ammunition, allowing Reagan to claim that his trade policies were working and that there were plenty of jobs available. "Our free and fair trade policies have created 17 million new jobs in the past 6 years," he boasted. "Increased trade means more jobs and a better standard of living." The "difficulties" of the textile and apparel industry were now pictured as "the inevitable result of a dynamic, expanding economy," and the president suggested that displaced workers could easily retrain for other posts.[44] Reagan was clearly influenced by his Council of Economic Advisers, which informed him that textile import restrictions would raise prices for consumers and harm the economy.[45]

Prior to the override vote, which was scheduled for October 4, Republican leaders lobbied hard. Administration aides made lists of the GOP members who had voted for the bill the previous September and highlighted more than thirty individuals who "should be talked to on the party loyalty issue." In addition, twelve members were to be leaned on in the "48 hours" before the vote.[46] When the vote came, Minnesota free-trader Bill Frenzel drove home the party line, insisting that American consumers should not have to pay more to "subsidize" a "greedy industry." Refuting these claims, Derrick insisted that the United States would no longer be a great power if it allowed its basic manufacturing industries to collapse. "I stand before this body today and I cry out for our country," he declared in an impassioned speech that was a defining moment of his political career. "What has happened to us? We are giving away our birthright. We are giving away our economic base." Frenzel's points got through, however, and when the vote came there were 272 yeas and 152 nays, with seven abstentions. Because two-thirds of members had not voted in favor of the bill, it was duly rejected.[47] In the end, Derrick actually lost the votes of two Democrats and two Republicans. In a letter to a constituent, the South Carolinian admitted that he was "deeply disappointed," but he had no regrets. "We must not continue to give away this industry to our foreign competitors," he explained.[48]

In the presidential election a few weeks later, George Bush's victory sealed the fate of Derrick's bill. Although Democratic candidate Michael Dukakis gave only lukewarm endorsement to the legislation, most of his party were behind it. As a result, Dukakis's comprehensive defeat was a severe blow. As the ILGWU's General Executive Board noted after the election, "A Dukakis win would have virtually guaranteed the passage of the bill; Bush's victory leaves little hope that a re-introduced bill would not be vetoed." The fight was gradually draining out of the industry, yet it would mount one more major effort to pass import restriction legislation.[49]

Crucially, the administration was able to fight the bill without enduring heavy political costs. This was particularly true in the South, a region that supported the Republicans in both the 1984 and 1988 presidential elections despite the administration's opposition to both textile bills. There were many broader reasons for this, including the GOP's appeal to white voters on racial issues, as well as its opposition to abortion and its support of gun ownership. In the ultrapatriotic South, the party was also seen as a stronger supporter of the military and was given credit for American successes in the Cold War. A former actor, Reagan had consummate political skills and was known for his geniality. On the ground, Reagan remained popular with voters, including mill workers who seemed unaware of the president's opposition to the textile bills. Some workers, such as Georgia's David Chastain, thus urged passage of the bill *and* advised their congressman to "support *our* President" who was "trying to do good for our country." Others were aware of Reagan's stance on the bill but still stuck with him. In October 1988, the *Daily News Record* interviewed six workers from Dixie Yarns in Gastonia, North Carolina, who were attending a Washington, D.C., rally organized by the industry on the eve of the override vote. Although they held banners that read "textiles-jobs-votes," all six declared that Reagan had generally done a good job and that they would still vote Republican. It was clear that the GOP could make a few concessions, rebuff the industry's core demands, and still carry the region where the textile industry remained the biggest employer, partly because most white southerners could not conceive of voting for the Democrats. Such was the impact of Reagan on the region that in 1980, only 40 percent of southern white conservatives identified themselves as Republicans, yet by 1988 that figure stood at 60 percent.[50]

Mirroring the broad support that the GOP received from the corporate world, most mill owners also stuck with the Republicans. Even when executives protested to Reagan about his opposition to the textile legislation, many made it clear that they still supported him. A resident of La France, South Carolina, textile manager Brenda J. Sewell complained to Reagan about his hostility to the textile bills but stressed that he could still count on the industry's support. "We are the ones who put you where you are and will be supporting you for the rest of your very comfortable life," she wrote. "Don't make it impossible for us." Another manager, Gregory B. Catoe from Greenwood Mills, urged Reagan to do more to help the industry but generously praised the president's record in general. "Your tenure as President has brought the United States back from financial chaos and military embarrassment to a strong stable economy now on the move and respect for us and our military once again," he declared. Reagan needed to act against textile imports, thought an executive from Dan River, Inc., but he was still "the best thing that's happened to the United States in a long, long time." Only occasionally did angry managers pledge to stop supporting the GOP because of the textile issue.[51]

Following the second veto, relations between the industry and the GOP remained cordial, even in the North. In September 1989, President Bush sent a message of congratulations to the Northern Textile Association, whose members were gathered in Harwich Port, Massachusetts, for the group's 135th annual meeting. Noting that the NTA was "the oldest trade association in the United States," Bush warmly praised it as "an outstanding example of the entrepreneurial spirit essential to America's continued leadership in the international marketplace." When the NTA's members sat down to business, however, they pursued policies that were very different from those of the Bush White House. In particular, delegates passed a resolution that called for "government action to halt the increases in textile and apparel imports." Within a year of Bush's Harwich Port address, he had vetoed a bill that one leading executive termed "the only solution" to the import problem. For the industry, it was a grave defeat that drove home the impossibility of passing an import restriction bill. In their hearts, executives now realized that the industry's decline would accelerate, and that the decade ahead would be very difficult.[52]

Designed to provide for "orderly imports of textiles, apparel, and footwear," the 1990 bill aimed to relate the growth of imports to the expansion of the domestic market, which had been a central goal of the ATMI for some time. Because domestic producers were threatened with "serious injury," this was to be achieved by allowing imports to increase by just 1 percent a year, which was the current rate of U.S. market growth. Answering criticisms that these provisions would undermine or even derail the tariff-cutting provisions of the Uruguay Round of international trade talks—which had been carried out under the framework of the GATT since 1986—the bill's supporters argued that a global quota with a 1 percent growth rate could be obtained as a separate law or as part of the Round's implementing legislation.[53] In 1990, the industry put up a good fight, and the Textile, Apparel, and Footwear Act passed the House by a bigger margin than its two predecessors. In addition, the override effort fell short by just ten votes, a slightly better result than the industry had achieved two years earlier.[54]

Members of FFACT decided to push for the bill because they were not satisfied with the outcome of meetings that they had with top officials in the Bush administration, including USTR Carla Hills and the Chief of Staff John Sununu. Throughout 1989, FFACT tried to work out an agreement with the administration to limit imports. The talks exposed divisions between companies and unions, largely because most employers supported the GOP and believed that working with the administration could secure results, a view that was not shared by labor leaders. As early as April 1989, President Jay Mazur told the ILGWU's Executive Board that "several Republican members of the FFACT coalition" had met with Bush to discuss the import problem. Mazur suggested that the unions, who supported the Democrats, were being sidelined. In October, Mazur agreed to a request from the "Republican FFACT members" to extend the talks, but he expressed his "impatience" with the process. In January 1990, ILGWU research director Herman Starobin reported to the board that the frustration of union delegates had increased: "Although the manufacturers in the coalition would not agree to introduce a new trade bill, and kept assuring us that an agreement was imminent, negotiations have continued for a year without satisfactory results."

According to the ILGWU, a new trade bill was the only answer.[55] When no agreement was forthcoming, other FFACT members came to the same conclusion. As ACTWU's Liz Smith reported privately, "In light of the fact that we can get no commitments out of the Administration on the future of the industry, we feel we have no alternative but to ask Congress to help us." The opposition of the Bush administration was critical, forcing the industry down the difficult path of seeking redress in Congress. This time, some union leaders privately doubted whether they could succeed. As the ILGWU board concluded, however, it was important to "keep the issue alive in the minds of Congress and the public."[56]

Although they were bruised from their earlier defeats, industry advocates also felt that they had a powerful case. They insisted that textile and apparel imports had tripled over the previous decade, causing more than 350,000 workers to lose their jobs. According to the ATMI, imports were at a "record level," and action had to be taken. "We are encouraging our supporters in the Congress to move quickly to enact textile legislation," declared President Edward P. Schrum shortly before the bill was introduced.[57] By 1989, the escalating trade deficit gave the bill's supporters a powerful weapon. Between 1980 and 1989, the textile and apparel trade deficit increased by over 500 percent, rising from $4.7 billion to a record $26.4 billion. This latter figure meant that textiles and apparel represented 24 percent of the U.S. trade deficit, and this had risen to 26 percent by the time that the bill was debated in the House.[58] The bill's footwear provisions also attracted support, as this industry had declined even more than textiles and many of the same areas of the country had been affected. In 1989, imports made up over 80 percent of nonrubber footwear sales, a figure that had increased fivefold within two decades. The House Footwear Caucus was determined to protect the eighty thousand manufacturing jobs that the industry had left, especially in the leading shoe-producing states of Missouri, Pennsylvania, Maine, and Tennessee. The bill promised to do this by holding nonrubber footwear imports to 1989 levels.[59]

On April 4, 1990, Congresswoman Marilyn Lloyd rose and introduced the bill to her colleagues. When she had taken over the leadership of the Congressional Textile Caucus a few months earlier, Lloyd had pledged that she would address the "severe crisis" that faced the industry. The first woman ever elected to Congress from Tennessee for a full term, Lloyd was a respected and experienced lawmaker who was well placed to deliver on her promise. A pastor's daughter from Arkansas, she had been in Congress for over fifteen years. As a conservative Democrat, she was able to mobilize both employers and labor groups. Through her service on the House Science Committee and the House Armed Services Committee, Lloyd had also developed valuable legislative experience. In building support for the textile bill, Lloyd emphasized the industry's national importance more than Derrick had done. "This issue joins people from North Carolina and Tennessee with New York and Massachusetts," she explained. "Many people think textiles are just a 'southern' industry. But we know that's not true. This industry provides nearly 2 million jobs." She advised her followers to publicize the industry's size and reach. "We've just got to keep talking about how important the American textile industry is to this country," she urged.[60]

As Lloyd acknowledged, her interest in the industry stemmed partly from the fact that her district in east Tennessee contained over twenty thousand textile and apparel workers and she wanted to preserve these jobs, especially as most mills were located in small towns. Lloyd was also moved, however, by the industry's importance to national security; as a member of the Armed Services Committee, she had seen "how vital" textiles were to national defense, and increasing tensions in the Persian Gulf now drove home this importance. "American troops should not be dependent upon foreign markets for uniforms and the many weapons parts which include fibers," she explained. "I want to see this industry survive." Insisting that she was a free-trader, Lloyd argued that stronger "guidelines" were needed to help American industries compete internationally. She saw the industry's expenditures on modernization, which had allowed it to partially share in the economic recovery, as proof of its willingness to compete in a fair marketplace. She also reasoned that George H. W. Bush was easier to work with than Reagan, largely because he had served in Congress. Thus, although the bill was "nearly identical" to its 1987 predecessor, Lloyd insisted that it stood more chance of success.[61]

More than a domestic effort, the 1990 bill was also designed to ensure that the U.S. textile companies got a fair deal in the Uruguay Round of international trade talks. The reasoning was that Congress could send a strong message to American negotiators in Geneva that textile jobs should not be traded away. As Lloyd explained to her congressional colleagues, "We are particularly concerned that the talks will result in a Uruguay Round textile agreement which could further jeopardize the domestic industry and its workers by putting the United States in an even more precarious position vis-à-vis our foreign competitors. We believe that without pressure from the Congress our negotiators may feel compelled to make further concessions to our trading partners just for the sake of achieving an agreement by the end of the year." The domestic bill would therefore "serve as an alternative" to Uruguay Round agreements that could harm the domestic industry.[62]

There were other distinguishing features of the 1990 campaign. Because the year marked the two-hundredth anniversary of the domestic industry's birth, supporters argued that it was an opportune time to celebrate "America's first basic industry." As Lloyd eloquently put it, "The American Industrial Revolution was born in the textile mills and the textile industry has been a mainstay of our nation's economy for two hundred years." Caucus members declared that October 13 to 20 would be "American Textile Industry Bicentennial Week," a move that allowed them to publicize the industry's historic importance as the bill's fate was being decided. With the upsurge in tensions in the Persian Gulf, especially after Iraq's invasion of Kuwait in early August, the industry's importance to national security also took on a new relevance. In September, twenty-seven House members wrote a letter of support for the bill on national defense grounds. They pointed out that over ten thousand military items were made entirely or partially from textiles, and three hundred of these were essential to combat. "There are critical shortages in a number of areas, and many of these items are crucial to our mobilization in the Persian Gulf," they concluded. During the House vote on the bill that month, Georgia congressman Newt Gingrich even brought out a box of military equipment that contained a uniform made of desert camouflage and a pair of green boots. The textile and footwear industries, he stressed, deserved legislators' help.[63]

Under Lloyd, the Congressional Textile Caucus gained renewed vigor. Prior to introducing the bill, Lloyd carried out a membership drive, so that by the time the legislation was ready the Caucus had ninety-three members. Most were concentrated along the East Coast, with the populous states of New York, Pennsylvania, and North Carolina being well represented.[64] Lloyd motivated Caucus members by reminding them of their duty to their constituents. "There are a great many people depending on us," she implored. "We can't let them down." Caucus leaders were also successful at securing backing for the bill outside of traditional textile states, and by May 23 Lloyd claimed to have "almost 230" House supporters. In the Senate—where Ernest Hollings and Jesse Helms provided forceful bipartisan sponsorship—there were some important victories. One notable catch was Utah senator Orrin Hatch, a senior free-trader who nevertheless pledged his assistance, largely because he was concerned about the trade deficit. Other prominent Senate supporters included Massachusetts's Edward Kennedy, Maine's William Cohen, and West Virginia's Robert Byrd. By June 8, 1990, continued hard work by Lloyd and others had yielded 231 cosponsors in the House and 55 in the Senate.[65] The amount of the support for the bill concerned Bush's advisers, with legislative assistant Frederick D. McClure writing the president in July that "the Geneva negotiations will be undermined if the textile bill gets majority votes in both Houses of Congress." McClure further advised Bush that "in light of the importance of the issue, you will be informed on all major developments."[66]

Lloyd also cooperated closely with the leaders of FFACT, and the Washington-based coalition continued to coordinate important lobbying efforts. In 1990, FFACT's campaign slogan was "It's Time to Stop Trading Away the U.S.A.," and it was widely distributed on letters, flyers, and other materials. Like its predecessor, "Give America a Fighting Chance: Stop Unfair Imports," the new slogan drew on patriotic sentiment, yet it focused fresh attention on the role of American policy makers rather than outside enemies. These domestic politicians and bureaucrats were accused of "trading away" American mills in the global arena. As Liz Smith wrote privately in 1990, the fear was that the industry would be given up "for services or intellectual property rights" in international trade talks by the Bush administration, which had brought textiles into the Uruguay Round even though the industry was covered by the MFA, which did not expire until 1991. The slogan forecast a major theme of the 1990s, a decade that would see the United States negotiate an unprecedented number of free trade agreements and commit to the abolition of worldwide textile quotas.[67]

The textile and apparel unions also mobilized their members in support of the bill. The ILGWU, for example, undertook what it termed "an extensive grass roots campaign" to try to secure passage. In late August, the union ran telephone banks that placed eighteen thousand calls to key members of Congress, and legislative director Evelyn Dubrow termed these efforts "very successful."[68] On September 12, more than four thousand ILGWU and ACTWU members rallied at the U.S. Capitol and outside the White House in support of the legislation. Drawn from across the country, they exhibited what the ILGWU General Executive Board called "tremendous zeal." The march also highlighted that union members had collected over 250,000 signatures in favor of the bill.[69]

The rally was well timed, as six days later Congress passed the Textile, Apparel, and Footwear Trade Act of 1990 by a vote of 271 to 149. On July 17, the Senate had already approved the legislation sixty-eight to thirty-two, the first time in the three attempts that the bill had achieved a veto-proof margin. Bearing out Lloyd's optimism, the bill also passed the House by a higher margin than that achieved by the previous House votes for initial passage. Some industry leaders believed that it really would be different this time. "Hardworking friends like you are treasures, and I know we would not have obtained the vote we did yesterday without your going the extra mile for us," wrote Burlington Industries executive Donna Lee McGee to Lloyd. "I want you to know that we at Burlington are your admirers and are very grateful to you." Now, a new stage of the campaign began as Lloyd strove to overcome the expected veto. Impressive as it was, the House vote fell nine votes short of being veto-proof. The administration's hostility was not in doubt, especially as President Bush personally called several members of Congress on the eve of the "extremely important" vote. The night before the ballot, Bush also wrote House Speaker Tom Foley and Republican House leader Robert H. Michel and stressed the need to stop a "damaging piece of legislation" that constituted "a threat to the stability of the world trading system."[70]

Many textile workers, however, also expressed their views in print. Congresswoman Lloyd received a large stack of letters from mill workers, most of them handwritten pleas for help. "We have 1,300 textile employees in my County," wrote Kyle Lee from Nicholls, Georgia, "but our jobs are threatened each day by the increasing number of imports. Two plants closed last month in our neighboring County and 840 people lost their jobs." Feeling that their jobs were indeed being traded away, most workers were apprehensive. "I think that unless legislative action is taken, we will lose the domestic textile/apparel industry," explained another. "I also think that the manufacturing jobs are critical to America's economic survival."[71] Drawing on this correspondence, Lloyd stressed the harsh impact of layoffs, especially as most mills were located in small towns. She also reminded her congressional colleagues that they had to defend "the 2 million hardworking Americans in all fifty states who labor in these very important industries."[72]

In New England, Lloyd's pleas found a sympathetic audience. Although there were few mill workers left to lobby politicians, residents insisted that their region had never recovered from the loss of its first industry. Despite the region's success in attracting high-tech industries—gains that free-traders emphasized—many locals pointed out that former mill towns had not benefited. As New Englander Edward D. Scullen wrote in August 1990, "If Dickens were to walk through the back streets of Lowell or New Bedford in 1990, he would instantly recognize the urban poor and a choking wave of despair." Indeed, for many residents the region's economic "miracle" had been "elusive and illusory." Former mill towns such as Lowell and Ludlow were now home to many immigrants from Asia, Latin America, and Eastern Europe. As old mill workers died or moved away, immigrants built new communities in the shadows of the empty mills. Although declining textile towns offered cheap housing, well-paid industrial jobs were in short supply.[73]

As they lobbied for the bill, textile executives and union leaders also argued that their industry epitomized the broader problems suffered by American manufacturing industries, which had lost 1.6 million jobs over the course of the previous decade. This had contributed to a rising trade deficit, and the industry's problems were a central reason for this. In a decade in which press reports and academic studies concentrated on the steel and auto industries, proponents tried to show that the textile industry was also in crisis. FFACT stressed that job loss was devastating for many textile and apparel workers. The group highlighted Labor Department data that showed that when these workers lost their jobs, around one-third of them got work at lesser wages, while another third suffered long-term unemployment. Despite this effort, the bulk of attention continued to focus on heavy industries, especially in the press.[74]

Lloyd's papers reveal that she had close links with industry groups, and these assisted her efforts. In June 1990, for example, Roger Milliken wrote "Marilyn" and thanked her for her "great leadership." Overall, Milliken was confident that the industry could find cosponsors who would "stick with us to the bitter end." Lloyd was also on first-name terms with ATMI leaders, especially Washington lobbyist Douglas W. Bulcao and President Don Trotter (who had replaced Schrum). Trotter headed SCT Yarns, which was based in Chattanooga, and he corresponded closely with his congresswoman. "We still have a long way to go," he wrote Lloyd in mid-June, "but the support you are providing is positively vital to the successful passage of this legislation and is very much appreciated."[75] Lloyd was greatly assisted by the NTA, which reported that it had "dedicated substantial resources" to this legislative fight. The northern group's efforts included meetings with key congressmen, public relations and educational programs, and support for FFACT's broad-ranging activities.[76]

Once again, however, there were damaging industry divisions, and they were getting worse. Following Reagan's second veto, even more companies—especially in the apparel sector—concluded that the chances of passing import restriction legislation were slim. Many refused to back H.R. 4328, a critical weakness that the bill's advocates privately acknowledged. The move also reflected other changes. At its General Executive Board meeting in May 1990, ILGWU president Jay Mazur related that the influential American Apparel Manufacturers Association would not support the bill "because many of their members are leading importers." This was a "change in position" that "represented a loss of resources for our efforts." Many of the AAMA's members now had plants overseas, a shift that the unions were powerless to stop. Although the ILGWU tried to use contract negotiations to maintain domestic production, these efforts were resisted by companies and usually ended in "failure."[77]

Among the companies that had embraced globalization was Liz Claiborne, Inc., a leading women's apparel producer that was based in New York City. Founded in 1976, the company was a rising force in the apparel industry but very little of its clothing was made domestically. Not surprisingly, its executives vehemently opposed H.R. 4328. "You can't protect yourself from imports and you can't turn the tide," charged chairman Jerome Chazen. Brushing off union criticism, Chazen even instructed his workers to fight the bill.[78] Industry divisions were also apparent in the textile industry, where one unnamed company complained to the *Southern Textile News* that they were tired of hearing the "whimpers and crys [*sic*] of textile executives about imports." The complainant asked, "When will these same executives wake up and discover real world class manufacturers compete in the real world?" While this was a minority voice, it showed that not all of the industry supported the anti-import campaign.[79]

Powerful resistance again came from retail and consumer groups, who argued that the bill would raise prices and provoke international retaliation. In particular, opponents insisted that the legislation would undermine American efforts to gain a fair deal in the Uruguay Round. Worried by the bill's passage, a diverse range of interests quickly coalesced. In August 1990, the Pro-Trade Group, a Washington-based lobby organization, circulated a letter against H.R. 4328 that was signed by ninety different corporations or industry associations, including major retailers, farm groups, and export-oriented manufacturers. Within the retail industry, opposition was coordinated by the Retail Industry Trade Action Coalition (RITAC), which insisted that the textile and apparel industry was already overprotected. "The next time textile industry lobbyists come asking for help," blasted RITAC's William Kay Daines to Lloyd, "we hope you'll ask them what you can do to promote their competitive position in the world." Led by American Express chairman James D. Robinson III, the Business Roundtable was another formidable opponent. A coalition of major corporations, the Roundtable argued that the Uruguay Round needed to open up markets for American service sector companies. Established in 1972, the Roundtable believed that businesses should "play an active and effective role in the formation of public policy," and the group steadily gained influence as its membership grew.[80]

Individual retailers also spoke out. In late August, for example, Target executive Paul Carroll, who managed a store in Lloyd's district, argued that the bill would hurt low-income Americans who needed access to "affordable clothing." Working tirelessly to refute such claims, on October 1 Lloyd even displayed two suits in the House chamber, explaining to members that she had bought both from a major retailer in her district. The two suits had the same brand, cut, and price, yet one was made domestically and one overseas. The memorable episode illustrated the industry's contention that retailers preferred imports not because they saved customers money but because they delivered bigger margins. As Lloyd concluded, "So, Members be the judge: Is it an anticonsumer bill? Certainly not."[81]

Lloyd still faced an uphill battle. After the Senate approved the legislation, the national press attacked with unprecedented venom, partly because they had been emboldened by the failure of the earlier bills. According to the *Los Angeles Times*, the bill was a product of "myopic legislators" that would result in consumers paying more for clothing. It would only benefit domestic textile makers, who would "get fat, happy and complacent because of less competition from imports." The *Chicago Tribune* called the bill "bad," while the *New York Times* termed it "awful." All of these national, mass-circulation newspapers devoted lengthy editorials to the legislation, which they urged Americans to fight. As the *Times* concluded, by raising consumer prices and provoking international retaliation, the bill would cause "an astounding amount of harm." In *Newsday*, wealthy retailer Leslie H. Wexner was given free rein to assail the legislation, which he claimed would cost consumers "something like $85 billion over the next few years." This attack caused concern among the bill's supporters, who realized that playing on consumer fears of higher prices was an effective "scare" tactic.[82]

There were other problems. During the Bush presidency, labor unions faced a hostile political climate. The new president continued his predecessor's practice of appointing conservative judges and National Labor Relations Board members, undermining legal protections for unions. In September 1990, Jay Mazur told his executive board that "these are the most difficult times which the Union has faced . . . Not only has the labor movement been opposed by Republican administrations in the White House, but has also had to contend with the conservative judges and NLRB board members appointed by those administrations." Bush's tenure continued a disastrous period for organized labor; between 1980 and 1991, union membership declined from 23 percent of the workforce to just 16.1 percent, and both the ACTWU and ILGWU shared in these losses.[83] The bill also had to compete with legislative efforts to ban employers from hiring permanent replacements during a strike, another key priority for the embattled unions. In the 1980s and early 1990s, an increasing number of employers were emboldened by the anti-union climate and hired permanent replacements, a move that threatened organized labor's viability. The unions responded by sponsoring legislation to ban the tactic; these bills eventually passed the House in 1992 and 1994 but were thwarted by Republican-led filibusters in the Senate.[84] By the spring of 1990, both the ILGWU and the ACTWU were taking part in this "major campaign," and it inevitably drained time and resources away from the trade battle.[85] Legislative director Evelyn Dubrow spoke to these difficulties, asking her union's executive board a pertinent question: "Can we tell a congressman who supports the striker replacement bill that the ILGWU will nevertheless refuse to back his candidacy if he also fails to support our Trade Bill?" Overall, labor had a "full and broad agenda," especially as unions were also pushing for health care reform, and this undermined the fight for import controls.[86]

Hopes that the Bush administration would be more supportive than its predecessor evaporated, and key officials mobilized to thwart the bill. Of particular importance, Secretary of State James Baker proved to be a fierce opponent of the legislation; as Lloyd acknowledged, Baker was "intractable on this issue." Baker consistently argued that the bill would jeopardize American relationships with crucial foreign allies, especially Egypt and Turkey, who had stood with the United States during the Gulf Crisis even though their economies had been hurt by the sanctions imposed upon Iraq. In response, Lloyd insisted that the administration still had "full power to allocate the country quotas" as it saw fit, yet Baker's prestige and profile ensured that his message got through.[87] Strong resistance also came from Carla Hills, who argued that the bill would hurt her efforts to ensure that the MFA was phased out in an equitable manner. According to Hills, the legislation was "protectionist" and would only encourage other countries "to take a more rigid stance." The Secretary of Commerce, Robert A. Mosbacher, and the Secretary of Agriculture, Clayton Yeutter, also spoke out in a similar vein.[88]

These fears of international retaliation were not unfounded. In August 1990, the ambassadors of Colombia, Ecuador, Venezuela, Bolivia, and Peru all spoke out against the bill. They claimed that "textile exporting countries" were already being "blocked from taking maximum advantage of their export potential because of the restrictions imposed on the textile trade." Textiles could produce much needed "export revenues," and it was therefore important to expand international trade, not restrict it. The same point of view was held by textile-exporting nations around the world. As Mosbacher and Hills reported to Bush, "We are under pressure in the Uruguay Round from many of our trading partners who desire a liberalization of textile trade."[89]

On October 5, the administration's hostility culminated in President Bush's veto of H.R. 4328. Advisers had told Bush that he needed to take a stand. As chief economic assistant Roger B. Porter put it, "the textiles story" illustrated "the difficulty of stopping protectionist actions once they are begun." The administration's opposition to the bill, summarized Office of Management and Budget director Richard G. Darman, was "consistent and strong."[90] Repeating the arguments of his top staff, in his veto statement Bush dismissed the bill as "blatantly protectionist, unwarranted, economically harmful, and internationally unviable." In particular, it would hurt consumers and jeopardize the progress of the Uruguay Round. Unlike Reagan, Bush failed to express any sympathy for American textile workers. Instead, he used the economic recovery to claim that the industry had "done well," adding that "the problems this bill is intended to address do not exist." In a hint of what was to come, Bush made clear his commitment to expanding free trade, insisting that this was the best way of building a strong economy. The key Senate sponsor, Ernest "Fritz" Hollings, was particularly disappointed. "If he had gone on the road to South Carolina and elsewhere around the country and talked to people who once held jobs in textile factories, Bush would surely have reached a different conclusion," he wrote. Hollings later wrote that the episode had strengthened voters' perceptions that Bush was detached from the concerns of ordinary Americans, a key reason for the president's failure to win a second term.[91]

Although they launched a short campaign to try to overturn the veto, FFACT's leaders privately doubted that they could prevail. As Mazur reported to his Executive Board, "Our opponents have advanced a variety of lies about the industry's situation and the impact of our bill . . . we have disseminated our own literature refuting these lies, but at this point, the votes will not be made on the merits, but rather based on politics and lobbying."

Validating these concerns, on October 10 the House voted 275 to 152 to override Bush's veto, ten votes short of the two-thirds majority that was needed. As FFACT's Daniel Frierson admitted, the campaign had not attracted enough support in the "wheat-growing states," a perennial weakness. In addition, the opposition of wealthy retailers and fears that the bill would endanger the Uruguay Round talks had undermined the effort. While thanking Marilyn Lloyd for her "leadership and energy," Frierson hinted at a change in tactics as he pledged to "work with" the administration to ensure that the American textile industry could compete on the global stage.[92] The lack of support in the West had been crucial. The economy of that region was dominated by service industries and export-oriented manufacturing, and the textile and apparel firms that did exist were mainly nonunion companies that had embraced offshore production. At a General Executive Board meeting in early 1991, the ILGWU's western director, Steven Nutter, reported on these difficulties and admitted that the union's influence in the region was on the wane. In particular, the opposition of California's representatives to the override campaign had been "devastating."[93]

The failure of Lloyd's bill was a grave blow to the struggling unions. Both the ACTWU and the ILGWU had spent millions of their scarce resources on the campaign, and they had again come up empty-handed. In June 1991, Mazur gloomily reported to his general executive board that the head office had suffered a net operating loss of $14.9 million over the previous year. He warned that the union could not continue to sustain these unprecedented losses, especially as its outlook was bleak. As the minutes summarized, "Mazur warned that the Union is on the threshold of a very difficult period, with imports continuing unabated and little hope that U.S. trade policy can be altered for the better. Our problems will not go away . . . they must be challenged."[94]

The union also complained that its inability to restrict imports was leading to a return of sweatshop conditions in the United States, especially in large cities such as New York, Los Angeles, and San Francisco. As early as 1970, the ILGWU's executive board had warned that "imports could reinstate the sweatshop," a prediction that proved to be accurate. By October 1989, the U.S. General Accounting Office estimated that fifty thousand garment workers were employed in sweatshops in New York City alone. As an investigation by the *New York Times* concluded, the problem was integrally linked to the decline of organized labor. In the 1950s, around 80 percent of the garment industry was unionized, but within thirty years this had dropped to 25 percent. It was also related to a surge in immigration to the nation's cities, which allowed unscrupulous employers to take advantage of desperate arrivals, especially when they were undocumented. In the area of Roosevelt Avenue and 108th Street in Queens, sweatshops had emerged that were "hot, cluttered, airless places." Labor laws were regularly flouted, and a workforce of new immigrants from Asia and Latin America could do little about it. In one Chinatown sweatshop, for instance, workers took home just $9 or $10 a day but employers altered their checks so that they appeared to receive the minimum wage of $3.35 an hour. "They see how much you make, and then they fix the hours to make it look correct," explained one worker. "Isn't that ridiculous?"[95]

As union leaders argued, sweatshops were also a reflection of the increase in imports, as the need to compete with cheap overseas goods encouraged employers to cut wages and violate federal labor standards. As Susan Cowell declared in 1990, "Imports not only export U.S. jobs, but they import third world conditions." Retailers, explained New York–based apparel manufacturer Chaim Feder, could bring in knit sweaters from Asia for $20 a dozen, whereas in the U.S. it cost $25 just to buy the yarn for a dozen sweaters. "And they don't sell it for less money," added Feder. "They just make more profit."[96] Cowell wanted the union to give more emphasis to the sweatshop angle as it pushed for the 1990 bill, but traditional trade-based arguments were used instead. A vice president, Cowell remained one of the few women at the top of the ILGWU, and she sometimes clashed with her male colleagues. In January 1987, even an internal task force acknowledged that the ILGWU had not always recognized "issues of special concern to women." In the 1990s, however, the ILGWU and UNITE did participate in campaigns that exposed the existence of sweatshop conditions in clothing factories owned by U.S. retailers. In particular, the union helped reveal that clothing endorsed by celebrity Kathie Lee Gifford was actually made in a Central American sweatshop. Some of these efforts also focused on Wal-Mart, which was now importing most of its textile products.[97]

The failure of the 1990 bill also derailed the industry's hopes of securing a more favorable deal in the Uruguay Round, instead paving the way for the abolition of the MFA. As early as January 1991, the ILGWU's Herbert Starobin reported on the GATT talks, which were about to resume, noting with concern that "the U.S. would be looking to gain an agreement on agriculture at the expense of apparel."[98] Organized labor responded and tried to prevent the Bush administration from gaining fast-track authority, which it was seeking to apply to both GATT and the U.S.-Mexico Free Trade Agreement. This would mean that Congress could not amend or filibuster trade agreements negotiated by the president, only approve or reject them. In June 1991, however, labor lost the fast-track vote, blaming defections from key Democratic leaders for the outcome. Although most House Democrats opposed fast track, much of the leadership supported it. Following this, the ILGWU worried that the Bush administration would now seek to "wipe out" the domestic apparel industry. In October 1991, Starobin again discussed the GATT talks, telling his superiors that "a prime purpose of the U.S. in these trade talks is to abolish the MFA, which provided some basis for control of imports." As the Cold War ended, Starobin worried that the United States would use apparel quotas to reward countries that joined the free market or became American allies. These fears were not unfounded, as foreign policy goals frequently influenced trade negotiators.[99]

The defeat of the bill also accelerated a fundamental shift in the industry's attitude to globalization, as executives grasped that they could not win the fight for tighter import controls. Illustrating this change, after 1990 NTA meetings increasingly stressed the need to grow export markets and engage in a global marketplace. In May 1990, President Karl Spilhaus foreshadowed these themes when he wrote a colleague that at the forthcoming meeting, "We intend to emphasize quality control, exporting, and the necessity to adapt in the increasingly internationalized textile and apparel business." In the years that followed, the transition continued. In 1991, the theme of the association's annual meeting was "Hitting to the Opposite Field—The Global Marketplace." Now, NTA leaders admitted that most of their members had been overreliant on the domestic market. As the 1991 minutes noted, there was "an increasingly common perception that textile manufacturers have export opportunities which have not been explored." Because imports were here to stay, a new approach was required.[100]

This shift in thinking had important consequences for the industry's "Crafted with Pride in the U.S.A" campaign, a high-profile public relations effort that had complemented the fight for import restrictions. Since 1984, the campaign had done much to raise the industry's profile, yet the failure of the textile bills robbed it of momentum. As the 1990s began, the new mood in the industry threatened to derail the program. Reflecting on the legislative defeats, Senator Hollings wrote in his memoirs that "textile executives who had long taken pride in making products that were 'crafted with pride in the U.S.A.' were now talking about outsourcing."[101]

## NOTES

1. NTA "Board of Government Meeting," March 23, 1988, NTA 1988 Annual Meeting files, NTA Papers.
2. "Textiles Standing Tall," *Southern Textile News*, October 22, 1990, p. 4 ("resounding blow" quotation); Devin Steele, "Industry Icon Schrum Retires after 50 Years," *Southern Textile News*, March 18, 2002, pp. 13–15 (Schrum quotation on p. 15).
3. "An STN Exclusive Interview: Roger Milliken," *Southern Textile News*, November 3, 1986, p. 14.
4. Liz Smith to Jack Sheinkman, June 12, 1990, "It's Time to Stop Trading Away the USA" folder, box 793, ACTWU Papers-Cornell.
5. Butler Derrick interview with author on April 13, 2011, in Easley, South Carolina; Ed Jenkins interview with author on June 25, 2010, in Jasper, Georgia (Jenkins quotations); Bill Arthur, "S.C.'s Derrick Amassing Power Quietly in House," *Charlotte Observer*, November 10, 1985, p. 1A; "Derrick's Retirement Loss to S.C., Congress," *The State*, February 18, 1994, p. 12A; Ben Szobody, "Roger Milliken, Textile Titan, Dies," *USA Today*, December 30, 2010.

6. Martha M. Hamilton, "Drug Bill Approved by House; Huge Savings Seen for Consumers in Generics Measure," *Washington Post*, September 7, 1984, p. A1; "Congressman Butler C. Derrick Jr. Third District—South Carolina," February 10, 1993, box 1, Derrick Papers ("Made in USA" quotation); "Additional Biographical Notes," ca. 1987, box 1, Derrick Papers (final three Derrick quotations).

7. Butler Derrick to Jim Self, February 16, 1977, box 7, Derrick Papers; Butler Derrick to Joseph Lee, October 27, 1978, box 10, Derrick Papers ("pushed hard" quotation); Butler Derrick to Vera Murray, April 5, 1978, box 10, Derrick Papers; Butler Derrick to Thomas B. Hogan III, October 25, 1978, box 10, Derrick Papers (closing quotation).

8. Butler Derrick interview with author on April 13, 2011, in Easley, South Carolina.

9. Butler Derrick to Textile Caucus Colleague, January 30, 1987, "Textile Caucus" folder, box 10, series I, Rowland Papers.

10. Butler Derrick, "Textile and Apparel Trade Act of 1987," *Congressional Record,* February 19, 1987, in box 33, Derrick Papers (first quotation); Butler Derrick to J. Roy Rowland, May 11, 1987 (second quotation), and March 2, 1987, both "Textile Caucus" folder, box 10, series I, Rowland Papers.

11. Butler Derrick to Ronald Reagan, May 19, 1987, box 33, Derrick Papers.

12. "Commerce Official Fights Textile Import Limits," *New York Times*, September 16, 1987, p. D7 (quotation); "The New Approach: How the Textile and Apparel Trade Act of 1987 Improves on Last Year's Bill," and "Fact Sheet: Textile and Apparel Trade Act of 1987," both "Textile and Apparel Trade Act of 1987: Assorted Fact Sheets" folder, box 793, ACTWU Papers-Cornell.

13. "Derrick Touts 'Global Quota' in New Textile Bill," Derrick Press Release, February 17, 1987, box 33, Derrick Papers (first and second quotations); Butler Derrick to George Seefeld, December 11, 1987, box 33, Derrick Papers (final quotation).

14. "Special Notice—Textile Bill Vote Set for September," September 4, 1987, NTA *Bulletin*, vol. 72 (June 1982–September 1987), NTA Papers (Spilhaus quotation); NTA Statement in Support of the 1987 Textile Bill, July 30, 1987, folder 533, box 59, CMS Series, Thurmond Papers.

15. Pell quoted in Robert Trautman, "Textile Bill Moves to Senate Floor," *Washington Post*, July 31, 1987, p. B3; "Union Gears Up for Trade Bill Fight in Senate," *Labor Unity*, October 1987, p. 3; Hollings, *Making Government Work*, p. 229.

16. "Union to Show Congress the Face of Trade," *Labor Unity*, May 1987, pp. 1, 3; "'I Blame the Imports': Displaced Workers' Stories," *Labor Unity*, April 1988, p. 7.

17. Mrs. Becky Timms to Butler Derrick, May 15, 1987, box 33, Derrick Papers.

18. Bill Gooding to Colleague, September 22, 1988 (first quotation), and John M. Fisher et al. to Charles Hatcher, September 21, 1988, both "Textile Trade Act" folder, box 24, series I, Hatcher Papers; Buddy Darden et al. to Colleague, September 28, 1988, "Textile Issues 101st" folder, box 24, series I, Hatcher Papers.

19. Elizabeth M. Smith to Representative, September 10, 1987, "Textile and Apparel Trade Act of 1987: Assorted Fact Sheets" folder, box 793, ACTWU Papers-Cornell.

20. U.S. Department of Commerce's Office of Textiles and Apparel, "U.S. Textile and Apparel Import Program," document, January 11, 1988, "U.S. Textile and Apparel Import Program" folder, Susan Lauffer files, OA16376, Reagan Library.

21. "Women and Minorities Hardest Hit by Textile, Apparel Layoffs," (FFACT Fact Sheet), and "Women and Minorities in the Textile and Apparel Industries," n.d. (second quotation), both in "Textile and Apparel Trade Act of 1987: OTA Report—Women and Minorities Hardest Hit" folder, box 793, ACTWU Papers-Cornell.

22. "Unneeded Protection: A Wrong-Way Bill" (editorial), *Seattle Times*, October 15, 1987, p. A14; ATMI Board of Directors Meeting Minutes, October 25–27, 1987, item 12, box 20, series 1998/18, Harmony Grove Mills Papers; Closing Derrick quotation in Butler Derrick interview with author on April 13, 2011, in Easley, South Carolina.

23. Bill Arthur, "S.C.'s Derrick Amassing Power Quietly in House," *Charlotte Observer*, November 10, 1985, p. 1A; Brigid Schulte, "Whipping Up Support after 19 Years, Derrick Still Using Soft Sell," *The State*, October 17, 1993, p. 1A (drawl quotation); Closing Derrick quotations in Cross Examination of Richard H. Imus and Walter C. Lenahan, March 6, 1985, p.

132, U.S. Congress, House, Government Operations Committee, *Federal Enforcement of Textile and Apparel Import Quotas (Part 2)*, 99th Congress, 1st Session, 1985.

24. ILGWU GEB Minutes of January 29–30, 1987, p. 3, "ILGWU GEB Minutes 1986–89" folder, box 2, series 5780/150, ILGWU Papers-Cornell. For an overview of the harsh labor-management climate of the 1980s, an era characterized by bitter labor disputes and the permanent replacement of strikers, see Robert H. Zieger, *American Workers, American Unions, Second Edition* (Baltimore: The Johns Hopkins University Press, 1994), pp. 193–202.

25. ILGWU General Executive Board Minutes, March 17–20, 1987, pp. 1–2, 9–10, "ILGWU GEB Minutes, 1986–89" folder, box 2, series 5780/150, ILGWU Papers-Cornell.

26. ILGWU General Executive Board Minutes, April 4–6, 1989, p. 1, "ILGWU GEB Minutes, 1986–89" folder, box 2, series 5780/150, ILGWU Papers-Cornell.

27. ILGWU General Executive Board Minutes, June 8–11, 1970, p. 2, "GEB-1970" folder, box 1, series 5780/084, ILGWU Papers-Cornell.

28. Remarks of Robert Laidlaw, September 28, 1987, 1987 NTA Annual Meeting files, NTA Papers.

29. Robert J. Samuelson, "The Peril of Protectionism: Why 'Managed Trade' Is a Sham," *Washington Post*, September 21, 1988, p. F3; "The Costs of Coddling Textiles," *Chicago Tribune*, September 12, 1988, in Harris W. Fawell to Colleague, September 22, 1988, "Textile Trade Act" folder, box 24, series I, Hatcher Papers; "Flirting with Protectionism," *Boston Globe* editorial cited in Karl Spilhaus, "Protecting Trade Means More US Employment," *Boston Globe*, September 1, 1986.

30. "Word in Fibers: 'Manmade,'" *New York Times*, January 11, 1970, p. 29 ("stigma" quotation); "Import Quotas for Southern Textile Mills," *New York Times*, October 7, 1971, p. 46.

31. "Import Quotas for Southern Textile Mills," *New York Times*, October 7, 1971, p. 46 (Schrag quotation); FFACT Backgrounder, May 1986, p. 8, "Textile Bill Fact Sheets" folder, box 788, ACTWU Papers-Cornell.

32. Hall et al., *Like A Family*, p. 81; Address by Charles F. Myers Jr. to the Northern Textile Association, September 16, 1969, vol. 1.29, NTA 1969 Annual Meeting Files, NTA Papers.

33. Sandra Salmans, "The Textile Industry Shakes Itself Up," *New York Times*, May 10, 1981 (first quotation); Chris Burritt, "Textile Industry Trying to Stitch Up a Ragged Image," *Atlanta Journal Constitution*, July 21, 1986, p. C1 (Turbak quotation). For an excellent analysis of *Norma Rae* and its broader impact, see James A. Hodges, "The Real Norma Rae," in Zieger, ed., *Southern Labor in Transition*, pp. 251–72.

34. Elizabeth M. Fowler, "Careers; Job Outlook in Textile Industry," *New York Times*, January 26, 1983, p. D19; Chris Burritt, "Textile Industry Trying to Stitch Up a Ragged Image," p. C1 (Chapman quotation).

35. Murray, "Unraveling Employment Trends," p. 63; U.S. Congress, Office of Technology Assessment, *The U.S. Textile and Apparel Industry*, pp. iii, 3, 7.

36. U.S. Congress, Office of Technology Assessment, *The U.S. Textile and Apparel Industry*, p. 7; Mittelhauser, "Employment Trends in Textiles and Apparel," p. 27.

37. Warren T. Brookes, "Textile Quotas—The Cruelly Regressive Tax," Heritage Features Syndicate, July 27, 1986, in "Textiles" folder, OA14574, Mari Maseng files, Reagan Library.

38. Butler Derrick to Eugene E. Stone III, April 13, 1987, box 33, Butler Derrick Papers; Yeutter quoted in Robert Trautman, "Textile Bill Moves to Senate Floor," *Washington Post*, July 31, 1987, p. B3.

39. James T. Patterson, *Restless Giant: The United States from Watergate to* Bush v. Gore (New York: Oxford University Press, 2005), p. 169.

40. George P. Shultz et al. to Representative, September 22, 1988, "Textile Trade Act" folder, box 24, series I, Hatcher Papers (quotations); "The Costs of Coddling Textiles," *Chicago Tribune*, September 12, 1988, in Harris W. Fawell to Colleague, September 22, 1988, "Textile Trade Act" folder, box 24, series I, Hatcher Papers.

41. Jenkins interview with author; Leslie Wayne, "U.S. Textile Industry's Turnaround," *New York Times*, February 15, 1988, p. D1; Dick Youngblood, "There's No Protection from Greed," *Minneapolis Star Tribune*, September 26, 1988, clipping in "Textile Trade Act" folder, box 24, series I, Hatcher Papers.

42. Textile Group Letter, September 15, 1988, "Textile Trade Act" folder, box 24, series I, Hatcher Papers.

43. Butler Derrick to Colleague, September 20, 1988, and Bill Hefner et al. to Colleague, September 22, 1988, both "Textile Trade Act" folder, box 24, series I, Hatcher Papers; Derrick quotation in Ed Jenkins et al. to George Bush, September 27, 1988, box 35, Derrick Papers; Bush quoted in Transcript of the Republican Presidential Debate (Atlanta), February 28, 1988, "Textiles (1)" folder, George H. W. Bush Vice Presidential Records, Bush Library.

44. Ronald Reagan veto message, September 28, 1988, "Textiles (1)" folder, Roger Bolton files, OA18689, Reagan Library.

45. Douglas Irwin to Steven Husted, April 28, 1987, "Trade-Multifiber Arrangements (MFA)—Textiles" folder, OA18895, Thomas G. Moore files, Reagan Library.

46. Greta R. Scott to Jim, Chuck, and Nancy, undated, "Textiles" folder, Chuck Greener files, OA18138, Reagan Library.

47. *Congressional Record*, October 4, 1988, H9497 (quotations), H9498, clipping in "Textiles (1)" folder, Roger Bolton files, OA18689, Reagan Library.

48. "Veto Override Yea Votes," n.d., "Whip Information" folder, box 68, Lloyd Papers; Closing Derrick quotations in Butler Derrick to Hugh Harris, October 13, 1988, box 35, Derrick Papers.

49. ILGWU General Executive Board Minutes, November 29–December 1, 1988, p. 2, "ILGWU GEB Minutes 1986–89" folder, box 2, series 5780/084, ILGWU Papers-Cornell.

50. David Chastain to Ed Jenkins, May 1, 1985, "Textile" folder, box 6, series 329-92-138, Jenkins Papers (first two quotations); Robert LaRussa, "Override Vote Falls Short on Textile Bill," *Daily News Record*, October 5, 1988, p. 1 (third quotation); Cobb, *The South and America since World War II,* pp. 177–80 (closing statistic on p. 179).

51. Brenda J. Sewell to Ronald Reagan, October 1, 1985, folder 518, box 75, CMS Series, Thurmond Papers; Gregory B. Catoe, May 30, 1985, folder 520, box 75, CMS Series, Thurmond Papers; Closing quotation in Salvador Alcina to Ronald Reagan, October 30, 1984, folder 10.8, box 10, Crompton Company Papers. For an example of an executive who does pledge to stop supporting Reagan in the wake of the veto override campaign, see Joe S. Fulmer to Strom Thurmond, August 7, 1986, folder 346a, box 49, CMS Series, Thurmond Papers.

52. George Bush message to NTA, September 22, 1989, NTA 1989 Annual Meeting files, NTA Papers; "NTA Resolution," September 22, 1989, NTA 1989 Annual Meeting files, NTA Papers ("government action" quotation); NTA Press Release of October 3, 1990, NTA 1990 Annual Meeting files, NTA Papers ("only solution" quotation from Donald R. Hughes).

53. "Textile, Apparel, and Footwear Trade Act of 1990," March 29, 1990, p. 1 (first quotation), pp. 2, 7 (second quotation), p. 8, "Textile Bill—Parts A and B," folder, box 68, Lloyd Papers; Marilyn Lloyd to Ronald J. Sorini, June 20, 1990, "Letters from ML" folder, box 68, Lloyd Papers. For more detail on the history and provisions of the complex Uruguay Round, which the WTO describes as "probably the largest negotiation of any kind in history," see the overview guide on the WTO's website: "Understanding the WTO: The Uruguay Round," available at http://www.wto.org/english/thewto_e/whatis_e/tif_e/fact5_e.htm (accessed March 7, 2011). The Round is also covered more fully in chapter 7.

54. "Textile Bill Override Vote Patterns," undated, "1990 Trade Bill" folder, box 13, series 6000/023, UNITE Papers-Cornell.

55. ILGWU GEB Minutes, April 4–6, 1989, p. 3 (first Mazur quotation), and October 11–13, 1989, p. 4 (second and third Mazur quotations), both "ILGWU GEB Minutes 1986–89" folder, box 2, series 5780/150, ILGWU Papers-Cornell; Starobin quoted in ILGWU GEB Minutes, January 8–11, 1990, p. 17, "ILGWU GEB Minutes 1989–90" folder, box 2, series 5780/150, ILGWU Papers-Cornell.

56. Liz Smith to Jack Sheinkman, June 12, 1990, "It's Time to Stop Trading Away the USA" folder, box 793, ACTWU Papers-Cornell; ILGWU General Executive Board Minutes, May 8–10, 1990, p. 5, and January 8–11, 1990, pp. 17–18 (closing quotation on p. 18), both "ILGWU GEB Minutes 1989–90" folder, box 2, series 5780/150, ILGWU Papers-Cornell.

57. "Congresswoman Marilyn Lloyd Legislative Update," June 2, 1989, "Floor Statements, Textiles, Trade" folder, box 53, Lloyd Papers; "Imports Blamed for Layoffs at Textile Compa-

nies" (ATMI Press Release), March 22, 1990, "Textile Bill—1990 Clips" folder, box 68, Lloyd Papers (Schrum quotations).

58. Marilyn Lloyd et al. to Carla Hills, June 14, 1990, "Hills Letters" folder, box 68, Lloyd Papers; Marilyn Lloyd to Colleague, July 5, 1990, "Congressional Textile Caucus 1990" folder, box 69, Lloyd Papers.

59. Fawn Evenson to Members of the House Footwear Caucus, March 27, 1990, "Textiles 1989 a and b" folder, box 69, Lloyd Papers; "Textile, Apparel, and Footwear Trade Act of 1990 (Draft)," March 30, 1990, pp. 8–9, "Textile Trade Act 1990" folder, box 69, Lloyd Papers.

60. "Congresswoman Marilyn Lloyd Legislative Update," June 2, 1989, "Floor Statements, Textiles, Trade" folder, box 53, Lloyd Papers (first quotation); "International Ladies Garment Workers Union" (Marilyn Lloyd Speech), pp. 2, 8, April 5, 1989, box 51, Lloyd Papers (other quotations).

61. "Congresswoman Marilyn Lloyd Legislative Update," June 2, 1989, "Floor Statements, Textiles, Trade" folder, box 53, Lloyd Papers; "International Ladies Garment Workers Union" (Marilyn Lloyd Speech), April 5, 1989, pp. 8, 12, box 51, Lloyd Papers (first four quotations); Marilyn Lloyd to Dan Rostenkowski, May 23, 1990, "Letters, Thank Yous and Contacts" folder, box 68, Lloyd Papers (final quotation).

62. Marilyn Lloyd to Colleague, ca. April 1990, "Congressional Textile Caucus 1990" folder, box 69, Lloyd Papers.

63. Marilyn Lloyd et al. to Colleague, June 26, 1990 (first and third quotations), Marilyn Lloyd to Colleague, ca. April 1990 (second quotation), and William Dickinson et al. to Colleague, September 14, 1990 (final quotation), all "Congressional Textile Caucus 1990" folder, box 69, Lloyd Papers; Joyce Barrett, "Textile Bill Passes House, Lacks Veto-Proof Margin," *Daily News Record*, September 19, 1990, p. 2.

64. Congressional Textile Caucus Membership List, ca. 1990, and Marilyn Lloyd to Textile Caucus Colleague, January 9, 1990, both in "Textile Bill—Members 1990" folder, box 68, Lloyd Papers.

65. Marilyn Lloyd to Congressional Textile Caucus Members, July 24, 1990 (first and second quotations), Marilyn Lloyd to Dan Rostenkowski, May 23, 1990 (third quotation), and Orrin G. Hatch to William Kay Daines, April 5, 1990, all "Letters, Thank Yous and Contacts" folder, box 68, Lloyd Papers; H.R. 4496 List of Co-Sponsors, June 8, 1990, "Co-Sponsors for HR 4496" folder, box 69, Lloyd Papers.

66. Frederick D. McClure to The President, July 12, 1990, TA004-13 (Textiles-Apparel-Leather Products-Trade category), White House Office of Records Management Subject File, Bush Library.

67. "Textiles and Apparel: Essential to America's Gross National Product," FFACT Sheet headed "It's Time to Stop Trading Away the U.S.A.," dated May 1, 1990, "1990 Trade Bill" folder, box 13, series 6000/023, UNITE Papers-Cornell; Liz Smith to Jack Sheinkman, June 12, 1990, "It's Time to Stop Trading Away the USA" folder, box 793, ACTWU Papers-Cornell (Smith quotation).

68. ILGWU GEB Minutes, May 8–10, 1990, p. 33 (first quotation), "ILGWU GEB Minutes 1989–90," folder, box 2, series 5780/150, ILGWU Papers; Evelyn Dubrow to Jay Mazur, August 29, 1990 (second quotation), "1990 Trade Bill" folder, box 13, series 6000/023, UNITE Papers-Cornell.

69. ILGWU General Executive Board Minutes, September 24–27, 1990, p. 3 (quotation), "ILGWU GEB Minutes, 1989–90" folder, box 2, series 5780/150, ILGWU Papers-Cornell; "All-out Union Effort on Textile Bill Leads to Overwhelming Victory in House," *Labor Unity*, October 1990, p. 3.

70. "All-out Union Effort on Textile Bill Leads to Overwhelming Victory in House," *Labor Unity*, October 1990, p. 3; Donna Lee McGee to Marilyn Lloyd, September 19, 1990, "Letters, Thanks Yous, and Contacts" folder, box 68, Lloyd Papers (McGee quotation); "Extremely important" quotation in Roger B. Porter to the President, September 17, 1990, TA004-13, White House Office of Records Management Subject File, Bush Library; Last two quotations in George Bush to Tom Foley, September 17, 1990, TA004-13, White House Office of Records Management Subject File, Bush Library.

71. Kyle (?) Lee to Congressman Lloyd, September 25, 1990, and Pat Parsons to Ms. Lloyd, September 26, 1990, both "Letters, Thanks Yous, and Contacts" folder, box 68, Lloyd Papers.

72. Marilyn Lloyd to Colleague, ca. 1990 (quotation), and Marilyn Lloyd to Members of the House Textile Caucus, June 4, 1990, both "Congressional Textile Caucus 1990" folder, box 69, Lloyd Papers.

73. "As New England Goes, So May Go the Nation," *New York Times*, August 16, 1990, p. A24.

74. Zieger, *American Workers, American Unions, Second Edition*, p. 194; Elizabeth M. Smith to Representative, n.d., "It's Time to Stop Trading Away the USA" folder, box 793, ACTWU Papers-Cornell. For a representative academic work from this time that focuses heavily on deindustrialization in heavy industries, see Paul D. Staudohar and Holly E. Brown, eds., *Deindustrialization and Plant Closure* (Lexington, MA: D.C. Heath, 1987). My own initial searches in the *New York Times* highlight the imbalance in coverage. I found, for example, 151 stories by searching under "Steel Industry and Plant Closings and Labor" from 1981 to 2006, compared to just forty stories on textiles under "Textile Industry and Plant Closings and Labor" for the same time period. Stories on steel and autos also tended to be longer and more detailed than those on textiles.

75. Roger Milliken to "Marilyn," June 14, 1990 (first three quotations), Douglas W. Bulcao to "Marilyn," May 1, 1990, and Don Trotter to "Marilyn," June 18, 1990 (final two quotations), all "Letters, Thank Yous, and Contacts" folder, box 68, Lloyd Papers.

76. "Report on the Activities of the Elastic Manufacturers Council," September 24–26, 1990, NTA 1990 Annual Meeting files, NTA Papers.

77. ILGWU General Executive Board Minutes, May 8–10, 1990, p. 5 (Mazur quotations), "ILGWU GEB Minutes 1989–90" folder, box 2, series 5780/150, ILGWU Papers-Cornell; ILGWU GEB Minutes, January 15–17, 1991, p. 43 (closing quotation), "ILGWU-GEB Minutes 1991" folder, box 2, series 5780/150, ILGWU Papers; David Hackett, "Trade Bill Won't Get AAMA Vote," *Daily News Record*, April 5, 1990, p. 2.

78. Chazen quoted in Jay Mazur to Jerome Chazen, July 12, 1990, "1990 Trade Bill" folder, box 13, series 6000/023, UNITE Papers-Cornell; Jerry Chazen et al. to All Employees, July 23, 1990, "1990 Trade Bill" folder, box 13, series 6000/023, UNITE Papers-Cornell.

79. "Textiles Standing Tall," *Southern Textile News*, October 22, 1990, p. 4.

80. The Pro-Trade Group to Marilyn Lloyd, August 3, 1990, William Kay Daines to Marilyn Lloyd, April 11, 1990 (first two Daines quotations), William Kay Daines to Marilyn Lloyd, April 25, 1990, and James D. Robinson III to Marilyn Lloyd, September 14, 1990, all "Textile Bill—Letters Against" folder, box 68, Lloyd Papers; Closing quotation from the Business Roundtable website at http://businessroundtable.org/about-us (accessed March 7, 2011).

81. Paul L. Carroll to Marilyn Lloyd, August 30, 1990, "Textile Bill—Letters Against" folder, box 68, Lloyd Papers; "Support Textile Bill," *Congressional Record*, October 1, 1990, H8439, in "Floor Statements, Textiles, Trade" folder, box 53, Lloyd Papers.

82. "U.S. Textile Policy Is No Bargain," *Los Angeles Times*, August 6, 1990 (first two quotations), "The Risks of a Bad Senate Textile Bill," *Chicago Tribune*, July 25, 1990, and "The Textile Bill's Awful Bill," *New York Times*, July 31, 1990, all clippings in "Textile Bill—Letters Against" folder, box 68, Lloyd Papers; Leslie H. Wexner, "Lining the Textile Industry's Pockets," *Newsday*, September 17, 1990, p. 51; Marilyn Lloyd et al. to Colleague, September 28, 1990 (final quotation), "Congressional Textile Caucus 1990" folder, box 69, Lloyd Papers. Wexner was chairman of The Limited, Inc.

83. ILGWU GEB Minutes, September 24–27, 1990, p. 4 (Mazur quotation), "ILGWU GEB Minutes, 1989–90" folder, box 2, ILGWU Papers (5780/150); Kim Moody, *An Injury to All: The Decline of American Unionism* (New York: Verso, 1988), p. 4; Zieger, *American Workers, American Unions, Second Edition*, pp. 193–94.

84. "Filibusters Have Thwarted Labor Law Reform over the Years," *The Paperworker*, September 1994, p. 8. For studies of the impact of permanent replacements on the labor movement and the legislative effort to ban the tactic, see Julius Getman, *The Betrayal of Local 14: Paperworkers, Politics, and Permanent Replacements* (Ithaca: ILR Press, 1998); Timothy

J. Minchin, "Broken Spirits: Permanent Replacements and the Rumford Strike of 1986," *New England Quarterly* LXXIV:1 (March 2001), pp. 5–31. For a brief overview, see Eileen Boris and Nelson Lichtenstein, eds., *Major Problems in the History of American Workers* (Lexington, MA: D.C. Heath, 1991), pp. 581, 598–600.

85. ILGWU General Executive Board Minutes, May 8–10, 1990, p. 6, "ILGWU GEB Minutes 1989–90" folder, box 2, series 5780/150, ILGWU Papers-Cornell.

86. ILGWU General Executive Board Minutes, January 15–17, 1991, pp. 16–17, "ILGWU GEB Minutes 1991" folder, box 2, series 5780/150, ILGWU Papers-Cornell.

87. James A. Baker III to Dante B. Fascell, September 13, 1990, "Textile Bill" folder, Virginia Lampley files, Bush Library; "International Ladies Garment Workers Union" (Marilyn Lloyd Speech), p. 13, April 5, 1989, box 51, Lloyd Papers (first quotation); "Textile One Minute" (Marilyn Lloyd speech), undated, "Floor Statements, Textiles, Trade" folder, box 53, Lloyd Papers (second quotation).

88. Carla A. Hills to Marilyn Lloyd, April 2, 1990, "Textile Bill—1990 Clips," folder, box 68, Lloyd Papers (Hills quotations); Robert A. Mosbacher to Marilyn Lloyd, September 14, 1990, "Textile Bill—Letters Against" folder, box 68, Lloyd Papers; "Statement by Secretary of Agriculture Clayton Yeutter," September 17, 1990, "Administration Position on Textiles" folder, box 68, Lloyd Papers.

89. Victor Mosquera Chaux et al. to Frank Horton, August 3, 1990, "Textile Bill—Letters Against" folder, box 68, Lloyd Papers; Closing quotation in Robert Mosbacher et al. to The President, May 8, 1989, TA004-13, White House Office of Records Management Subject File, Bush Library.

90. Roger B. Porter to the President, April 5, 1989, TA004-13, White House Office of Records Management Subject File, Bush Library; Richard G. Darman to the President, September 28, 1990, TA004-13, White House Office of Records Management Subject File, Bush Library.

91. "Textile, Apparel, and Footwear Trade Act of 1990—Veto Message from the President of the United States," October 5, 1990, in "13 Textile Bill 101st Congress 1990" folder, box 69, Lloyd Papers; Hollings quoted in Hollings, *Making Government Work*, pp. 238–39.

92. ILGWU GEB Minutes, September 24–27, 1990, p. 21 (first quotation), "ILGWU GEB Minutes, 1989–90" folder, box 2, series 5780/150, ILGWU Papers; Marilyn Lloyd to Textile Caucus Members, October 5, 1990, "Congressional Textile Caucus 1990" folder, box 69, Lloyd Papers; "FFACT Chairman Responds to House Failure to Override Presidential Veto of Textile Trade Bill," *Southern Textile News*, October 22, 1990, p. 1 (Frierson quotations).

93. ILGWU GEB Minutes, January 15–17, 1991, p. 29, "ILGWU GEB Minutes, 1991," folder, box 2, series 5780/150, ILGWU Papers.

94. ILGWU General Executive Board Minutes, June 25–27, 1991, p. 4, "ILGWU GEB Minutes 1991" folder, box 2, series 5780/150, ILGWU Papers-Cornell.

95. ILGWU GEB Minutes, June 8–11, 1970, p. 6 (first quotation), "GEB-1970" folder, box 1, series 5780/084, ILGWU Papers; ILGWU GEB Minutes, October 11–13, 1989, p. 4, "ILGWU GEB Minutes 1989–90" folder, box 2, series 5780/150, ILGWU Papers; William Serrin, "After Years of Decline, Sweatshops Are Back," *New York Times*, October 12, 1983 (other quotations), copy in "Sweatshops—News Clippings, 1983–85" folder, box 7, President's Office files, series 5780/154, ILGWU Papers.

96. Cowell quoted in Susan Cowell to Jay Mazur, Evy Dubrow, and James Parrott, June 4, 1990, "Trade" folder, box 7, series 5780/150, ILGWU Papers; William Serrin, "Combating Garment Sweatshops Is an Almost Futile Task," *New York Times*, October 13, 1983 (Feder quotations), copy in "Sweatshops—News Clippings, 1983–85" folder, box 7, President's Office files, series 5780/154, ILGWU Papers.

97. Quotation in ILGWU GEB Minutes, January 29–30, 1987, p. 3, "ILGWU GEB Minutes 1986–89" folder, box 2, series 5780/150, ILGWU Papers; "The People's Right to Know Day: A Call for Corporate Disclosure," National Labor Committee flyer, October 3, 1998, in "Wal-Mart Corporation" folder, box 2, series 6000/021, UNITE Papers-Cornell. For a fine analysis of why sweatshops returned to the United States, see Rosen, *Making Sweatshops*, esp. pp. 1–6.

98. ILGWU GEB Minutes, January 15–17, 1991, p. 15, "ILGWU-GEB Minutes 1991" folder, box 2, series 5780/150, ILGWU Papers.

99. ILGWU GEB Minutes, June 25–27, 1991, pp. 20, 40 ("wipe out" quotation), and October 15–17, 1991, p. 24, both "ILGWU GEB Minutes, 1991" folder, box 2, series 5780/150, ILGWU Papers.

100. Karl Spilhaus to Jerome Chazen, May 30, 1990, NTA 1990 Annual Meeting Files, NTA Papers (Spilhaus quotation); "Arrangements Committee Meeting," minutes, May 20, 1991, NTA 1991 Annual Meeting Minutes, NTA Papers (second quotation); NTA, "Business Plan for NTA Sponsored Export Trading Company," September 27, 1991, NTA 1991 Annual Meeting files, NTA Papers (final quotation).

101. Hollings, *Making Government Work*, pp. 229–30.

## *Chapter Six*

# "Us Is Spelled U.S.": The Crafted with Pride in the USA Campaign

In the 1980s and early 1990s, the American television networks were saturated with messages from the Crafted with Pride in the U.S.A. Council, a textile industry group that urged consumers to buy American-made clothing and thus protect domestic jobs. Part of what the Council termed an "aggressive public relations campaign," its advertisements were aired during prime-time shows; in 1990, for example, it claimed that its messages had been seen by Americans an average of sixteen times each. The Council's advertisements featured a range of high-profile celebrities, including actors Ted Danson, Linda Evans, Eddie Murphy, and Loretta Swit, model Jerry Hall, and entertainer Bob Hope. Support also came from ex-football player O. J. Simpson, who still had considerable popularity at the time, and from "Wonder Woman" Lynda Carter. All endorsed the central message, "Made in the U.S.A. It matters." The Council insisted that the effort had a considerable impact, asserting in 1990 that 90 percent of Americans believed that American-made textiles were of better quality than imports, and that 50 percent of buyers looked for the "Made in the U.S.A." label when they shopped. Operating alongside efforts to pass import restriction legislation, the Crafted with Pride initiative highlights how the deindustrialization of the textile industry became a high-profile issue in these years. This was a national campaign by an industry with national importance and influence.[1]

The Crafted with Pride campaign deserves to be explored because of its size and reach. Launched in 1984, the initial seven-year program cost $100 million. The commercials were slickly produced, and surveys showed that as many as two-thirds of Americans retained an awareness of them. Between 1986 and 1992, the Council was also a major sponsor of the Miss America pageant, which reached more than fifty million viewers, and Miss America became the Council's public face. Overall, the size of the campaign reflected the size of the industry that was behind it. As one early Crafted with Pride advertisement in the *New York Times* put it, "We're 2.2 million Americans strong. And that's a voice that's going to be heard."[2]

The campaign also provides valuable insight into the life and ideas of its founder, Roger Milliken, a textile magnate whose influence on the fight against imports was immense. In 2004, the *Charlotte Observer* called eighty-nine-year-old Milliken "one of America's industrial titans and South Carolina's wealthiest man." At this time, Spartanburg-based Milliken and Co., a manufacturer of synthetic yarns and fabrics, was the only South Carolina corporation to make *Fortune*'s list of the one hundred best American companies. Although few details about the company and its reclusive founder were released, it had prospered by excelling in quality control and by coming up with an innovative system of warehousing. The company also showed how some textile companies, especially those involved in high-tech synthetic or chemical fibers, had managed to survive by investing heavily in labor-saving equipment and new technology, much of it imported from Europe. While employment fell, productivity and sales increased, mirroring broader trends within the manufacturing sector. The firm was home to one of the world's largest textile and chemical research facilities, and it grew to hold over 2,300 patents in the United States alone. Milliken's sprawling headquarters occupied more than six hundred acres and was known for its proliferation of trees, one of its founder's passions. It also included "Milliken University," with an auditorium and classrooms modeled after those of the Harvard Business School. "Roger Milliken," asserted scholar Dana Frank in 1999, "is one of the most powerful people in the United States."[3] When he died in December 2010, manufacturers felt that they had "lost a giant," and many of them termed Milliken "the greatest American textile leader of the 20th century."[4]

Milliken's influence was certainly felt well beyond the industry. Through his involvement in politics, the business owner played a central role in the growth of both the Republican Party in the South and the conservative movement nationally. As a South Carolina delegate, Milliken attended eight national GOP conventions from 1956 to 1984, and his money helped propel the careers of important conservative figures, particularly Strom Thurmond and Jesse Helms, both key sponsors of the textile bills. Thurmond's papers reveal that he corresponded closely with Milliken throughout his long career in the Senate. As early as 1956, for example, Thurmond wrote "Roger" that "you may rest assured that I shall continue to exert every effort in behalf of the textile industry." Milliken also helped talk Barry Goldwater into running for president in 1964, a crucial turning point for the GOP in the South, while a decade later he played a leading role in the establishment of the Heritage Foundation, a prominent conservative think tank. According to the *National Review*, Milliken was "one of the Right's 'funding fathers.'"[5]

In April 1984, the Crafted with Pride in the U.S.A. Council was formed with Milliken as chairman. The industrialist was the driving force behind the foundation of the group, which was located within his company's New York sales headquarters. Milliken saw the Council as a way of uniting American cotton producers and labor unions with the manufacturers of various textile and apparel products. "My personal involvement with the Council is driven by a conviction that these interdependent groups must maintain their market position," he explained at the time. "The severity of the import challenge has caused the different entities to unite for the first time. This economic sector employs 2.2 million people in markets that exceed $100 billion of America's Gross National Product." Building on Milliken's convictions, the Council's official "mission" was to "convince consumers, retailers, and apparel manufacturers of the value of purchasing and promoting U.S. made products." After some members of the Council feared that "America" might be misconstrued to cover Latin America, "U.S.A" was selected for the title instead. The Council also designed its own distinctive logo of a red-and-blue stylized star that was to be used on labels and other promotional items. A central aim was to have the label attached to clothing and other textile items that were purchased by consumers. To avoid misuse, both the slogan and logo were registered with the U.S. Patent and Trademark Office.[6]

Famously private, Milliken came out of his shell and initiated the Council because he feared that one of America's largest manufacturing industries was in jeopardy. Throughout the 1980s and 1990s, he held to this belief, becoming one of the country's most prominent opponents of the North American Free Trade Agreement (NAFTA). In 1992, Milliken gave $2.1 million to outspoken Republican politician Pat Buchanan, and he also subsequently supported prominent NAFTA critic Ross Perot. Milliken's money helped Buchanan run for president on an anti-NAFTA platform, and Milliken became one of Buchanan's closest advisers. Milliken believed that a country's wealth was determined in large part by what it made. "The Spanish, Dutch and British had all neglected their nations' manufacturing bases," he declared. "If we continue sacrificing our manufacturing base on the altar of free and unfettered trade, (we) will go the way of others." Because he had a net worth of over $1 billion, Milliken ensured that the Crafted with Pride campaign did indeed matter, and his wealth also gave him the ability to shape policy decisions. It was Milliken, for example, who insisted on the choice of the word *crafted* over objections that it was insufficiently upscale. "I thought crafted was the right word," he explained, "It means care, and thoroughness, and commitment."[7]

While Milliken was the crucial influence behind the Council, he was not its public face. That role was given to executive director Robert E. Swift, who ably performed the day-to-day running of the group. A native of the textile town of Fall River, Massachusetts, Swift was educated at the University of Lowell and the University of Virginia. He worked in sales for DuPont before switching to head the Council, a position he held for over fifteen years. He proved to be an articulate defender of the Council's message, which consistently relied on patriotism to mobilize support. "It does matter to all of us," he urged in 1992. "Us is spelled U.S.!"[8]

Crucially, the campaign built on earlier efforts to encourage patriotism among consumers and to protect American jobs. As scholar Dana Frank has shown, "Buy American" campaigns date to the very origins of the Republic, as the Boston Tea Party of 1773 was ultimately a demonstration against British imports. In the 1930s, newspaper magnate William Randolph Hearst also coordinated a major movement that sought to lower unemployment by rejecting both foreign goods and immigrant workers. Crafted with Pride was part of a third wave of these campaigns, as in the 1980s and 1990s many Americans responded to high unemployment and deindustrialization by turning on foreign products. Most famously, U.S. autoworkers mobilized against Japanese imports, even destroying some imported cars with sledgehammers in symbolic protests. Business leaders knew that patriotism had a powerful appeal to consumers, especially at times of economic uncertainty. In the late 1980s and early 1990s, for example, General Motors declared that its Chevrolet brand was the "Heartbeat of America," a message that was reinforced by ultrapatriotic commercials that had a lasting cultural impact.[9] In response to rising import levels, the makers of many other products followed suit with similar initiatives. "The nation is awash with 'Buy American' campaigns," declared the *U.S. News and World Report*.[10]

This modern Buy American movement certainly made its mark. In the early 1980s, President Ronald Reagan bowed to domestic pressure and imposed restrictions on Japanese automobile imports. A decade later, President George H. W. Bush traveled to Japan with the Big Three auto chiefs to demand open markets, while at home some companies gave incentives to consumers who bought American. Meanwhile, the nonprofit Buy America Foundation assumed a national profile, distributing its newsletter in all fifty states and citing surveys that showed that 49 percent of American shoppers said they looked for a "Made in the USA" label. "'Buy American' fever burned in many a brow," summarized the *Cleveland Plain Dealer* in 1993. In the early 1990s the media also frequently reported on the battle between the Ford Taurus and Honda Accord to decide which was the best-selling car in the country. In early 1993, the domestically made Taurus broke the Honda's three-year run, a move that many saw as significant.[11]

Polling confirmed that Crafted with Pride reflected legitimate public concerns. In 1983, a nationwide poll by the *Los Angeles Times* questioned 1,395 adults about products made abroad; 66 percent declared that the United States made the best clothing—the highest score by far—and 68 percent said that they favored restricting imports to protect American jobs. Carried out by

D/M/I for the Reagan administration, a 1985 poll found that little had changed. "It is true that the public largely supports measures to restrict the import of foreign products to help protect American jobs," summarized pollster Jan van Lohuizen. "The link between imports and unemployment is not something that needs to be explained."[12] Research by Kitty Dickerson, a faculty member at the University of Missouri's Department of Clothing and Textiles, also highlighted that consumers had a "strong preference" for U.S. goods and were concerned about imports, findings that encouraged industry and labor groups to launch the campaign.[13] An early fact sheet captured the Council's belief in the power of patriotism. "The majority of Americans think U.S. made clothing offers the best quality," it asserted. "Americans would choose American-made products over imports if given a choice."[14]

The impetus for the campaign also came from Washington. In September 1984, following lobbying from the industry, Congress passed a law that specified that all apparel and home fashions that were manufactured domestically had to be clearly labeled as "Made in the U.S.A." The law closed several loopholes in the 1939 Textile Fiber Products Identification Act; it required, for instance, that all textile products had to be labeled in the "most conspicuous place" with their country of origin, even if mail order or catalog outlets sold them. Labels had to be placed on each individual item and could not just be affixed to packaging materials, as had previously been the case.[15] Milliken saw the law as a unique opportunity to publicize the industry's plight. In late November, the Council launched what the *Southern Textile News* called "an assertive long-term ad campaign" that was designed to take advantage of the legislation, which came into effect on December 24. Costing $10 million a year, the ads stressed the quality, style, and value of American-made goods and were based on Milliken's belief that consumers preferred U.S.-made goods if they were "given a choice." Early attention-grabbing headlines included "She'll be looking for US in her blouse" and "He'll be looking for US in his slacks." Thus, from the beginning there was a strong emphasis on trying to influence consumer behavior.[16]

Working through the ATMI and the NTA, both of which endorsed it, the Crafted with Pride campaign quickly picked up support. By August 1985, the Council had 120 members, drawn from across the industry. Gathering momentum from the fight for H.R. 1562, within a year membership had increased to 360 firms, and it continued to rise thereafter. By September 1989, the Council boasted over five hundred members. Dues were graded accorded to a company's size, with a minimum contribution of $1 million a year for small firms. These hefty payments were needed to fund the Council's national advertising campaign. Throughout the late 1980s and early 1990s, the Council's records indicate that it maintained this membership level. Highlighting the industry's economic importance, some members were nontextile firms that relied on the mills. In 1992, for example, Swift wrote that "approximately one-third of our more than 500 individual company members are from the service sectors that do business with this industry, including electric utilities, insurance companies, banks, material suppliers, etc."[17]

In the campaign's early years, major nontextile contributors included Blue Cross/Blue Shield, Duke Power, and Coca-Cola. Between 1985 and 1988, for example, the soft drinks retailer gave the Council $5 million. The money was donated following an embarrassing controversy in which apparel manufacturers found that much of Coca-Cola's line of "all-American" clothing was actually made in Hong Kong and Taiwan. In response, angry industry executives threatened to pull Coca-Cola's vending machines from their plants. To avoid this, the Atlanta-based conglomerate came up with the hefty donation and promised to produce the clothes domestically.[18]

Within the textile industry itself, significant support came from major companies such as Burlington Industries, West Point–Pepperell, Cannon Mills, and J. P. Stevens. As well as giving money, firms threw themselves into promotional efforts. In early 1985, West Point–Pepperell decided to imprint the "Crafted with Pride" logo on all of its packaging and print materials. At Cannon Mills, the company made heavy use of the logo and flew a Crafted with Pride flag outside of its headquarters in Kannapolis, North Carolina. Several companies also imprinted the logo on all of their trucks, which regularly criss-crossed the country. These moves helped the logo to become well recognized. In 1990, a Council poll found that 57 percent of respondents said that they had seen the symbol during the previous three months.[19]

The ATMI strongly supported the campaign, even establishing a Crafted with Pride in U.S.A. Committee to coordinate its activities. The committee undertook several related programs, such as encouraging Fortune 500 firms to buy American, giving "Gold Star Merchants Awards" to retailers who stocked a high proportion of American-made textiles, and backing a "proven" promotional program titled "Make it a Crafted with Pride Christmas." For Christmas 1987, the ATMI sent out over fifty thousand Christmas cards that depicted Santa Claus with a "Made in the U.S.A." label on his cap, and they also used radio, television, and newspaper advertising. In addition, the Washington-based trade association served as an "information source" for news media interested in the campaign, helping to secure a lot of press coverage.[20]

The ILGWU and ACTWU also endorsed the campaign, donating funds and sending their leaders to Council strategy meetings in New York. In many ways, the involvement of organized labor in the campaign was remarkable because Milliken was so antiunion. Throughout his long life he fiercely opposed all organizing efforts at his mills, and he had even notoriously closed a plant in Darlington, South Carolina, rather than recognize the Textile Workers Union of America (a predecessor of the ACTWU). Milliken shut the mill in 1956, but it was not until 1980—just a few years before the Council was set up—that he agreed to give the workers $5 million in back pay. By that time 126 of the original 553 workers were dead, and the example of the group had served its purpose, keeping the unions out of the company's other plants. As *The Nation*'s David Corn concluded, the case was "the longest-contested case in the history of the NLRB. . . . a monument to Milliken's passionate hatred of unions."[21] When the fate of the industry was at stake, however, both sides were willing to work together. By 1992, Milliken was on first-name terms with ILGWU president Jay Mazur, expressing his "appreciation for your confidence from the outset in this effort." According to Butler Derrick, Milliken had been able to work with unions and Democrats in this campaign because he was "goal-oriented."[22]

When it came to the import issue, labor and management had a lot in common. The Council's efforts indeed built on earlier campaigns by unions, especially the ILGWU and ACWA, to protest against imports and use the "Union Label" to encourage patriotic buying habits. In 1951, the ACWA launched a Union Label program that was designed to "appeal to the social consciousness of the consumer," and they quickly spent $2.5 million promoting the effort. The ACWA label declared that garments were "tailored in the USA by American craftsmen," a message that had strong similarities to the Crafted with Pride slogan. In the 1950s, the ILGWU also initiated a Union Label program and aimed it at the "millions of women" that were shopping for garments; later, Crafted with Pride would also target female shoppers. As the import threat increased, the clothing unions pioneered in using advertising to advance their cause. In November 1975, the ILGWU ran a series of sixty-second TV messages in which union members from across the country stressed the importance of buying domestically made clothing so that they could keep their jobs. Every message concluded with the ILGWU song, whose last line reminded viewers, "So always look for the Union Label, it says we're able to make it in the USA." As the *New York Times* noted, the "popular jingle" undoubtedly raised awareness of the ILGWU's campaign.[23]

Some of these early efforts were targeted to Asian workers, although tactics shifted slightly over time. As the biggest single source of imports at the time, Japan provided an obvious focus, and in the early 1960s the ACWA specifically told consumers to avoid buying Japanese-made clothing, claiming that workers were underpaid.[24] A few years later ILGWU posters on the New York City subway system depicted a huge American flag with the text, "MADE IN JAPAN." Below the image, readers were asked, "Has your job been exported to Japan yet? . . . If not, it soon will be unless you buy the products of American workers who buy from you." The message drew a barrage of protests, especially from Asian Americans, although there was also a lot of positive response from other Americans. In reaction to the criticisms, the ILGWU argued that it was defending its members against "sweatshop competition," while a follow-up advertisement stressed the ethnic diversity of the union's membership. While still attacking imports, future union appeals were also careful to list a range of countries where clothing came from, including European ones.[25]

The long-running union campaigns were popular with many members, and there is also evidence that workers were mobilized by the Crafted with Pride effort, especially as it complemented the fight for import controls. As South Carolina worker Glenda M. Armstrong wrote her senator, "'Crafted with *Pride* in *America*' says a lot and well it should." An employee of Burlington Industries, Armstrong urged passage of the 1985 textile bill, which had just been introduced when she composed her handwritten appeal. In August 1985, more than three thousand workers from Cannon Mills also attended a "Buy American" rally in Kannapolis that featured speeches by a range of political leaders, including congressmen Bill Hefner and Alex McMillan, Senator Jesse Helms, and Governor Jim Martin. Supportive congressmen from South Carolina and Georgia also attended a separate event that was sponsored by Coca-Cola, where the campaign's logo was again prominently displayed. At the rally, workers spoke about why Crafted with Pride mattered. "I have seen pride in people turn into helplessness," declared Cannon worker Nelda Furr. 'Textiles has been a sense of security, but these times are gone. . . . We worry about day to day survival. . . . We have to regain our pride and make the government aware of the import problem. We have to support the Crafted with Pride program, so if it doesn't say 'Made In U.S.A.,' don't buy it!" While some workers may have been pressured by their employers, the huge number of letters that they wrote in support of the textile bill shows that many were genuinely mobilized.[26]

**"Textile workers from across the country mobilizing in support of the Crafted With Pride in the USA campaign, ca. mid-1980s." (Photo courtesy of the South Carolina Political Collections, University of South Carolina)**

Significantly, considerable financial support for the Council came from Wal-Mart, and this helped the program to get off the ground. At the ACT-WU's General Executive Board meeting on July 29, 1985, President Murray Finley read out a letter of support for the "Buy American Campaign" from Sam Walton, Wal-Mart's founder. In it, Walton declared that "products 'Crafted with Pride in the USA' can be competitive with products anywhere in the world." Praising manufacturers as "the entrepreneurs that fuel our economy," Walton saw the campaign as a way of reducing the trade deficit. Overall, the powerful CEO pledged that "our entire management and merchandising staff is committed to this 'Buy American' program."[27] Backing up his words, in 1985 Walton cut imports by 20 percent and purchased $197.3 million of merchandise from domestic suppliers. At a retailing convention, he even "waved a flannel shirt in the air like an evangelist pounding his Bible at a tent revival meeting" as he sought converts to the Buy American initiative.[28]

Understandably pleased, Council supporters held up Walton as a role model. In September 1985, the American Association of Apparel Manufacturers and the Council sponsored a dinner in honor of the Arkansan. At the gathering, Walton was praised for his efforts to replace items "that once had been imported" with American-made goods. In 1985, Burlington Industries gave Wal-Mart its "Golden Scissors Award" in recognition of its "outstanding merchandising efforts" on behalf of American mills, while the leaders of the Georgia Textile Manufacturers Association also wrote Walton to express their "very deep gratitude" for his support.[29]

Wal-Mart used the publicity to cement its image as a patriotic retailer who cared about American workers. In 1988, for example, Wal-Mart vice president Nick White told a gathering of textile executives that 75 percent of the goods stocked by his company were American made. Pitching his firm as a role model, White declared that Wal-Mart would source all of its products domestically if they were competitive in price and quality. It was a big "if," and it was clear that Wal-Mart was actually supporting the campaign on its terms. This meant that if domestic products were more expensive than imports, they would not be purchased. White himself explained that 119 American textile companies had recently bid for Wal-Mart contracts, but seventy had been ruled out on price grounds. Ingeniously, however, White insisted that it was mill owners who were not "receptive to the Buy America campaign." In the early 1990s, the huge retailer got even tougher and started to demand annual price cuts from suppliers if they wanted to keep their contracts. Consumers, however, still saw Wal-Mart as patriotic. In one national survey in 1992, 60 percent of respondents declared that they were aware of Wal-Mart's dedication to domestic sourcing, while 71 percent reported that they consequently shopped more often in the company's stores.[30]

The campaign had clearly helped Wal-Mart, and in the 1980s and early 1990s the opening of its stores in textile communities was even celebrated by residents. Thus, when the company unveiled its first store in Concord, North Carolina—located next to Kannapolis—it was given a "huge welcome" by Fieldcrest Cannon, which had bought Cannon Mills. In July 1987, Fieldcrest Cannon CEO Frank Larkin spoke at a ribbon-cutting ceremony of "the close relationship between Wal-Mart and Cannon products." Sam Walton was such a "strong supporter" of "Buy American" efforts that Wal-Mart's arrival was pitched as a way of safeguarding local textile mills. In retrospect, the celebrations appear ironic; in 2003 the Fieldcrest-Cannon plants, now owned by Pillowtex, were forced to close, and five thousand workers lost their jobs. Many blamed Wal-Mart, noting that it now relied heavily on imported textiles. In a further twist, a lot of the displaced Pillowtex workers ended up working at the new Wal-Mart Supercenter, which opened in Concord just as the mills disappeared.[31]

Wal-Mart's support of Crafted with Pride was a major boost to a program that was having quite an impact. The Council repeatedly insisted that public support was behind it, claiming in November 1985 that 70 percent of Americans believed that domestically made clothing was superior to imports. "The consumer recognizes the Made in USA label as a symbol of quality, value and fashion," declared Swift. Four months later, the Council's research found that 72 percent of those who had seen the star-studded ads were more inclined to buy American-made clothing. Highlighting the campaign's reach, two-thirds of those interviewed had seen the ads, which had aired the previous December. According to Milliken, surveys had confirmed "the effectiveness of our 1985 advertising campaign." After a thorough examination, moreover, Stephen A. Greyser of the Harvard Business School concurred that "according to early results, the campaign seemed to have been successful in its first year."[32]

This initial advertising campaign was certainly successful in recruiting high-profile celebrities. These were, moreover, not just commercial endorsements, as the stars accepted only the minimum wage required by Actors Equity, and many donated the money to charity. In December 1985, TV commercials appeared in twenty-four key markets, featuring Bob Hope, Cathy Lee Crosby, Diahann Carroll, and *Miami Vice* star Don Johnson. In addition, O. J. Simpson and his sixteen-year-old son Jason were hired, a move that reflected the former football star's pulling power before his fall from grace. In the commercials—which were arranged around the slogan "it matters to me"—the celebrities told consumers the many reasons for buying American-made clothing.[33] In a subsequent round of advertising, African American entertainer Sammy Davis Jr. headlined televised messages. "It was with pleasure that I participated in this project and I am so pleased with the results," Davis wrote Swift in September 1986, adding that he had received "numerous letters" from executives and workers as a result. Like other celebrities, Davis endorsed the effort primarily because he wanted to help the American economy.[34]

Through its sponsorship of driver Mike Alexander, the Council also got involved in NASCAR, a sport that was enormously popular in the southern textile belt. At the 1985 Miller 500 race in Charlotte, more than fifty thousand black balloons were released to represent lost textile jobs in the Carolinas, and each car carried Crafted with Pride advertising. According to the *Daily News Record*, a "Buy American" rally that was held at the stadium proved popular, as "fans lined up to sign letters urging Congress to take steps to restrict imports." Following the protest, a petition asking President Reagan to sign the textile bill was flown to Washington.[35]

These early efforts produced concrete gains. Reflecting the pressure generated by both the Council and the broader campaign for H.R. 1562, President Reagan designated December 1986 as "Made in America Month," signing a resolution that was passed by both houses of Congress. The resolution was sponsored by Massachusetts Republican Silvio Conte, who spoke of the need to make consumers more aware of "the pride, skill and craftsmanship of the American worker." As the *Southern Textile News* noted, the resolution was "reinforcement" to the Crafted with Pride campaign, which would carry on despite the "disappointments" of the override effort.[36]

In the late 1980s, the industry also stabilized, and the Council could take some of the credit. Imports slowed in 1987, largely because of trade agreements negotiated after industry pressure, although the softness of the dollar was also important. In addition, profitability and volume rose. In the first eleven months of 1987, imports grew by only 3 percent, compared with rates of 18 to 20 percent a few years earlier. Industry restructuring efforts, which the campaign encouraged through its promotion of "Quick Response"—a program that was designed to speed up the delivery process and make manufacturers more responsive to the demands of retailers—were also a cause of the improvement. In 1990, a study by two economists in the *Clothing and Textiles Research Journal* found that support for Crafted with Pride was "correlated with innovative business practices." Thus, the campaign was energizing the industry, and there was also evidence that it was reaching consumers. As the *New York Times*'s Leslie Wayne concluded in 1988, the textile industry's "turnaround" was partly due to the campaign, which had "heightened consumer awareness of domestic textiles."[37] Because it spurred investment in high-tech equipment, Quick Response showed how parts of the textile industry fought back against imports by turning to technology. As was the case in the manufacturing sector as a whole, new equipment raised productivity but also eliminated jobs.[38]

In subsequent years, advertising maintained this connection with consumers. In 1990, separate surveys by the Good Housekeeping Institute and *Time-CNN* found that 80 percent of female respondents saw American-made clothing as top quality. Into the 1990s, the Council repeated its claims that consumers would buy more domestically made clothes if it were clearly labeled and if they were encouraged to do so. In 1993, the Council reported from tracking tests at four stores in Cincinnati and Nashville that sales of U.S.-made items had increased 24 percent during the weeks that the clothing was clearly identified.[39]

The advertising was supported by public relations initiatives. Most importantly, in 1986 the Council became a major sponsor of the Miss America pageant, supplying both the contestants and the eventual winner with American-made clothing. The 1988 winner, Kaye Lani Rae Rafko, spent her year wearing a special collection of outfits supplied by sixty-one American manufacturers, and consumers were able to buy the same outfits in retail stores. As the *Southern Textile News* explained, "Fashion-conscious consumers won't have to be Miss America to dress like her. They will be able to purchase the same styles that Kaye Lani Rae Rafko selects for her wardrobe at their local retailers, identified by a special 'Made in U.S.A.' Miss America hangtag."[40]

Subsequent winners were also sponsored by the Council, which provided their wardrobe and proscribed them from wearing imported clothing. In addition, Miss America made a large number of "personal appearances" on behalf of the group, reiterating its message to consumers, particularly women. In 1989, for example, Miss America Gretchen Carlson made thirty-four appearances for the Council, logging over one hundred thousand miles and visiting almost every state in the process. Industry leaders insisted that these tactics worked. "We are delighted with the results of our four-year association with the Miss America pageant," declared Swift in 1990. "Miss America is the ideal emissary for our message reinforcing American consumers' belief that the quality of U.S.-made apparel and home fashions gives them the best value for money." Miss America, the Council insisted, was saving American jobs.[41]

Interestingly, the Council tightly controlled Miss America's public appearances and ensured that she stayed on message. Touring apparel factories in Pennsylvania's LeHigh Valley, Gretchen Carlson dutifully declared that "it's a beautiful relationship between the manufacturers and Miss America wearing clothes made in America. It's just a natural." Many of Carlson's appearances were stage-managed by the industry; on one occasion, for example, she was presented to textile executives during a lavish production at Milliken's plush Spartanburg headquarters. Carlson descended onto the stage in a mock hot air balloon and gave a polished multimedia presentation about the campaign, before being led off a revolving stage on Milliken's arm. As the pair exited, a small orchestra played the Miss America theme song.[42] Subsequent holders of the crown followed a similar script. In 1992, for instance, Carolyn Sapp became the fifth Miss America to represent the Council. An experienced performer who had entered Miss Hawaii four times before winning, Sapp "worked the crowd like a pro" on a visit to Baltimore. "How many people got up in the morning, looked in your closet and said, 'What do I have that's made in the USA?'" she asked. Revealingly, she was greeted to what the *Baltimore Sun* called "slightly guilty-sounding giggles" from the audience of more than one hundred women, none of whom answered in the affirmative.[43]

The sponsorship of Miss America was indeed problematic. The Council's male strategists failed to ponder whether their effort to appeal to female consumers could be hurt by their involvement with the pageant, which was declining in popularity in these years. After a peak in the early 1960s, the event's TV ratings began a steady slide, reflecting criticisms that it was sexist and racist (the first African American winner, Vanessa Williams, was not crowned until 1984). Like the domestic textile industry, Miss America was on the slide. In addition, press coverage frequently concentrated on what Miss America looked like, rather than where her clothes were made or the message that she brought with her. Thus, on one occasion when she represented the Council, "the petite, 22-year-old, blond-haired" Carlson was described as being "dressed in a black knit skirt, magenta sweater and coordinating print shawl thrown neatly over her left shoulder." Frequently, crowds queued up to catch a glimpse of Carlson, but it was debatable how much of the Council's message they absorbed. The attention certainly helped Carlson, however, who went on to become a successful anchor for Fox News.[44]

The campaign faced other problems. While the Council claimed that its message was reaching consumers, it is questionable how much their buying behavior was really changed, especially if imports were cheaper. Not surprisingly, the U.S. Association of Importers of Textiles and Apparel was particularly critical of the campaign. "The bottom line," asserted executive director Laura Jones, "is that people look for price and quality when they buy, they don't look at the country of origin."[45] After a thorough analysis of the campaign, the *U.S. News and World Report* reached a similar conclusion. "For all the skepticism they encounter, the 'Buy American' people remain convinced that they can strike a patriotic chord," it noted. "In the end, however, results are likely to hinge less on patriotism and more on price and quality."[46] Observers familiar with consumer behavior made similar points, insisting that while shoppers might profess support for American goods, this did not mean that they actually bought them. It was also the case that many consumers bought clothes without even looking at labels. As Miss America 1991, Marjorie Judith Vincent, admitted at the start of her reign, "Honestly, I didn't look before. If I liked something, I just bought it without looking at the label."[47]

Much of the Council's effort was targeted at women because they were the main purchasers of clothing, but again there were problems. The Council's tracking studies, for example, showed that it was difficult to make female shoppers aware of the domestic industry's plight. By 1991, Swift privately acknowledged these difficulties. "The research," he wrote an industry colleague, "revealed deep concern about the U.S. economy, but only a few of the women related it to the loss of higher paying manufacturing jobs generally and particularly in our industry." This trend was most pronounced among young women, boding poorly for the industry's long-term prospects.[48]

Not all of the campaign's problems were related to consumer behavior. While most of the industry backed the initiative, there were some notable exceptions. Most opposition came from apparel firms who had already moved manufacturing facilities offshore, such as Esprit. Between 1979 and 1985, Esprit's sales rose from $120 million to over $700 million, and the firm insisted that its overseas factories were thriving. The opposition of the world's largest apparel maker, Levi Strauss, was particularly damaging. Levi's management consistently supported free trade and argued that the Council's efforts were misguided. "Just putting a tag on a garment doesn't make it the best," declared Peter Phillipes, Levi's counsel. "American industry has to improve productivity, become more innovative and compete in price and quality."[49]

While Esprit and Levi opposed the campaign from the beginning, other firms were initially supportive but later lost faith. In November 1991, a major defection occurred when Greenwood Mills from South Carolina withdrew its support. Insisting that consumers ultimately wanted "quality products at reasonable prices," CEO W. Matt Self questioned whether the Council's expensive television advertising had done any good. Shortly afterward, Springs Industries also dropped out, its managers arguing that they could compete in a global environment by exporting more. These moves were particularly significant because Greenwood and Springs had thirty-three plants in South Carolina, Milliken's heartland. Even in Spartanburg, critics now spoke out. "It has become clearer and clearer that we're fighting the wrong battle with this," declared Terrell Sovey, the chairman of local Texfi Industries. "We need to stop being so protectionist and concentrate on being more competitive."[50]

Clearly piqued, Swift insisted that the industry was being "destroyed" by imports and had to secure more public support. To highlight this, the Council prepared its hardest-hitting TV commercials ever. Produced by Warwick, Baker, and Fiore, a New York advertising agency, the commercials were inspired by the industry's job losses and asserted that the time had come to "take care of our own." In the fall of 1991, ads titled "Line" and "Crate" were aired on national TV. Whereas earlier efforts had been positive and upbeat—featuring celebrities cheerfully showing off their "Made in the USA" logos—the new advertisements were much more gloomy in tone. "Line" depicted a procession of people, male and female, white collar and blue collar, snaking away toward a faraway horizon, to represent the five hundred thousand Americans who had lost their jobs in the textile and apparel industry recently. "So if you think that looking for the Made in U.S.A. label doesn't matter," the narrator added as a bureaucrat shouted "next" from the window of an unemployment office, "it matters." The second ad showed a huge crate that was stamped "IMPORTED" being unloaded onto a dock, casting a huge shadow over a group of worried faces below. "The time to look out for ourselves is now," warned a narrator. "Buy American, and we won't have to throw in the towel." Overall, the Council saw the "tough" commercials as a "turning point," a move toward a stronger focus on the harsh impact of trade policies. As Swift explained, research showed that while the public was aware of the earlier advertisements, they "did not comprehend the magnitude of job losses in the textile and apparel industry."[51]

**"A still from the Crafted With Pride in the USA Council's 'Line' commercial, 1991." (Photo courtesy of the South Carolina Political Collections, University of South Carolina)**

**"A still from the Crafted With Pride in the USA Council's 'Crate' commercial, 1991." (Photo courtesy of the South Carolina Political Collections, University of South Carolina)**

Despite this fight back, the campaign struggled, and more executives lost faith in it. Following their failure to pass import restriction legislation, many industry executives supported the 1993 North American Free Trade Agreement (NAFTA), largely because they reasoned that American yarn and fabric could supply Mexico's burgeoning apparel industry, creating a powerful trading bloc that could compete with Asia. The move highlighted how much of the industry was becoming more accepting of globalization. NAFTA indeed split the industry, and many executives now questioned the Council's approach. As James Casey of New York's Fiber Industries put it, "We are in the midst of negotiating a historic trade agreement with Mexico. And finally, everyone is now globally oriented. Where does the Council stand on these issues?" Both Milliken and the textile and apparel unions were forceful opponents of NAFTA, however, cutting them off from executives who wanted to boost trade with Mexico.[52] NAFTA's supporters claimed that new ideas were needed. Rather than "Crafted with Pride in the U.S.A.," they suggested that the industry's slogan should now be "Crafted with Pride in NAFTA."[53] Although they opposed NAFTA, in the 1990s the unions also became more accepting of globalization. Instead of seeing foreign workers as a threat, they now strove to organize them and improve their conditions, arguing that what was important was not just where goods were made but that the workers who made them were treated decently. As UNITE leader Harris Raynor recalled, as the union became more international in its focus the Crafted with Pride campaign became seen in labor circles as "jingoistic."[54]

Another problem faced by the Council was policing the use of its label, which was only supposed to be used in accordance with strict guidelines. As member companies established plants overseas, however, abuses of the label increased. In 1993, Swift privately wrote Council members that many of them had been "violating our requirement that the mark be used only with U.S.-produced textile products made from U.S. fiber(s)." No penalties or enforcement machinery existed, however, and the Council relied on members' good will to prevent misuse.[55] It was not enough. As the U.S. Customs Service admitted, the textile trade was susceptible to customs breaches, and it was common for "'Made in the U.S.A.' labels to be sewn into foreign-made garments." The difficulties were familiar to the unions, who had previously struggled to control the use of their labels and ensure their authenticity.[56]

There were other problems. While Milliken had enormous influence within the industry, his conservatism undermined relations with the textile industry's congressional supporters, most of whom were Democrats. As Ed Jenkins recalled, the Crafted with Pride campaign was "helpful" to efforts to pass the textile bill, but he knew that Milliken would never support his reelection campaign. Most Democrats remained suspicious of Milliken, dubbing him "Daddy Warbucks" because of the amount of money he gifted to their political opponents. Although Milliken represented a powerful faction within the GOP, as that party passed a range of free trade agreements in the 1980s and 1990s, he was increasingly marginalized.[57]

The campaign also ran into many of the difficulties that derailed the textile bills, especially forceful opposition from retailers, export-oriented industries, and the press. As soon as Crafted with Pride was launched, the national press was hostile. "So What If It's Made in America?" scoffed Herbert London in the *New York Times*. The *U.S. News and World Report* even accused the campaign of being "an abuse of patriotism" because it interfered with consumers' "free choice."[58] In the early 1990s, the Council's hard-hitting advertising drew particular ire from the press, which depended heavily on advertising revenue from retailers.[59] It was clear that these attacks hurt, as Swift spent much of his time writing lengthy responses to editors, many of which were never printed. He insisted that imports were causing thousands of textile workers to lose their jobs, and even when they found new positions in retail or service industries they were usually paid less and had fewer benefits.[60] Internal records carefully documented the barriers that the campaign faced. According to the Council's early research, retailers favored imports because of "higher mark-ups," while most of the media was "hostile/unsympathetic." The industry was also very diverse, and parts of it had already invested in overseas production. The Council reasoned that patriotism would overcome these obstacles, yet in reality this was not the case.[61]

The increasing power of retailers was particularly important. In the 1980s and 1990s, a number of retailers—especially budget-conscious chains such as Target and Wal-Mart—grew enormously. Efforts to keep big stores out of communities were frequently thwarted by the federal courts and by growth-minded politicians. Gaining the upper hand, big box retailers increasingly relied on imports because they were more profitable, generating hostility from textile manufacturers.[62] Wal-Mart epitomized the trend, especially after Sam Walton's death in 1992. Aired in 1993, an NBC *Dateline* episode exposed that the company was selling clothing under the "Made in the USA" label that was actually made in Bangladesh, and some of the factories allegedly employed child laborers. Even when Walton was alive, domestic suppliers had to meet the price offered by overseas competitors—a clause that the company was careful to conceal. Given the huge disparity in wage rates, most American manufacturers found this to be impossible.[63]

Wal-Mart survived the exposure about its phony "Buy American" campaign and thrived. By 2005, the domestic textile industry was on its death bed, yet Wal-Mart was opening 275 supercenters a year. Highlighting its reliance on imports, Wal-Mart alone was now China's sixth largest export market. As writer John Dicker quipped in *The United States of Wal-Mart*, the company had transformed consumer behavior, encouraging shoppers to search for bargains even though suppliers had to outsource and workers got "screwed on wages." As historian Bethany Moreton has recently shown, moreover, Wal-Mart prospered by upholding a patriotic image and supporting the conservative causes in which Milliken also believed. Political commentators came to see regular shopping at Wal-Mart as an even more accurate indicator of conservative voting than steady church attendance, and in 2004 George W. Bush won the votes of 85 percent of frequent Wal-Mart customers. Like the Council, Wal-Mart also identified woman shoppers—or the so-called Wal-Mart Moms—as its key constituency, cleverly sending them the message that it was helping their "families" by saving them money on frequent purchases, including clothing.[64]

In sharp contrast to Wal-Mart, by the late 1990s the Council was a small, struggling organization that could no longer afford TV advertising. After NAFTA, and especially after the 1997 economic collapse devalued Asian currencies by around 40 percent, the industry experienced large job losses rather than the gains that some executives had hoped for, eroding the Council's membership base and shrinking its media presence. By 1997, Swift wrote that the "Made in the U.S.A" label still struck "a chord of recognition with consumers," but he admitted that the Council was now operating in an environment that had seen a "massive shift" of manufacturing to foreign countries. The "equation" had "turned" in favor of offshore manufacturing, and the Council could do little more than "monitor" imports.[65] In the wake of 9/11, the Council did run some print advertisements that tried to capitalize on the upsurge in patriotism. One Council notice in the *New York Times*, for example, asked whether the American military could depend on "foreign factories" during "times of crisis." Because the textile industry was contracting rapidly, however, the Council had lost its industry focus and now expressed concern about deindustrialization as a whole.[66]

Like the industry that supported it, Crafted with Pride went into decline as its opponents gained the upper hand. A visit to any clothing retailer in the United States quickly highlights how the Council has been outgunned, as imports dominate the racks and even consumers that want to buy American are generally unable to do so.[67] In 2007, the Chinese textile sector was the largest industrial employer in that country and its biggest earner of foreign exchange, and Chinese textile and apparel exports were growing at a rate of 20 percent a year. According to Department of Commerce data, by February 2012 China alone accounted for almost 47 percent of apparel imports to the United States, while imports from Latin America took up another sizeable chunk of the market.[68]

In some ways, it is hard to view this level of import penetration as anything other than a defeat for the Council. Most who have looked back on the campaign have reached similar conclusions, even when they were sympathetic to its aims. Crafted with Pride, declared southern journalist John Monk in 2010, was "destined to be a losing cause." According to Butler Derrick, a close friend of Milliken, ultimately consumers "cared more about price" rather than where goods were made. Even if Americans had bought more domestic products, however, it is hard to see how the campaign could have averted the globalization of production in the industry, which was driven by powerful economic forces, including the strong desire of emerging nations for economic development, the phenomenal growth of import-focused retailers, and increasing support for globalization among domestic manufacturers. As a low-wage, labor-intensive industry, textiles and apparel was particularly vulnerable to international competition; in 1993, for example, textile and clothing producers accounted for 9.3 percent of world exports of manufactures. By the late 1990s, the ILO also calculated that there were some thirty million jobs in the global textile, clothing, and footwear industries.[69]

Despite this outcome, Crafted with Pride did have a lasting impact. Through the high-profile campaign, the industry was able to influence outside observers such as Pat Buchanan, the Republican politician who went on to champion many of Milliken's ideas. As an adviser for President Reagan, Buchanan helped to write the message that the president read when he vetoed the 1985 textile bill. As Buchanan later admitted, however, it was Milliken who persuaded him to change his position. "Within half a decade," he acknowledged, "some of us had seen the light and enlisted in Roger's crusade to preserve the manufacturing core of the country that he rightly saw as inextricably tied to the prosperity and the pre-eminence of the United States." Emerging as a vocal critic of NAFTA and trade liberalization, Buchanan secured funding from Milliken and sought the Republican Party's presidential nomination in both 1992 and in 1996, when he won state primaries in New Hampshire, Alaska, Iowa, and Louisiana. The outcome confirmed that the ideas behind Crafted with Pride retained considerable appeal, and after the election Buchanan continued to criticize U.S. trade policies. Milliken also became a supporter of NAFTA critic Ross Perot, who received nearly 19 percent of the popular vote in 1992 when he ran as an independent. It was one of the ironies of Milliken's life, indeed, that most of the Republican Party that he had helped to build came to embrace free trade. According to Jock Nash, Milliken's former counsel, this outcome "broke his heart."[70]

The Council's ideas also gained a renewed relevance in an America racked by deindustrialization. In the first decade of the twenty-first century, the United States lost around five hundred thousand manufacturing jobs every year, and the textile and apparel industry was one of the main contributors to these figures. The scale of the losses caused even supporters of globalization—such as economists C. Fred Bergsten and Jagdish Bhagwati—to backtrack. By August 2008, Bergsten, the head of the Peterson Institute for International Economics and a man dubbed "one of Washington's high priests of free trade and globalization," was calling for a "grand bargain" to address the costs of trade liberalization.[71]

The Council's philosophy was also taken up other groups, particularly the American Manufacturing Trade Action Coalition, a corporate lobby group that operated with funding from Milliken's company. In 2009, AMTAC media director Lloyd Wood stated that the organization had started out as a "textile and apparel only group" but had "morphed" into a bigger movement against the "industrial crisis the United States is facing."[72] A similar philosophy was adopted by the Alliance for American Manufacturing, a joint labor-management initiative that was founded in 2007, with the bulk of funding coming from steel companies. Also operating out of Washington, D.C., the AAM lobbied for tighter import controls and encouraged patriotic consumer behavior. In November 2010, for example, the group urged its supporters to "Buy American-Made This Holiday Season," adding that "together we can keep it made in America."[73] The ongoing popularity of guides to buying American-made products indicated that some citizens continued to respond to these appeals, and advocates insisted that it is import-obsessed retailers that were the real problem.[74]

In other ways, Crafted with Pride should not be seen as a total failure. According to NTA president Karl Spilhaus, the campaign "had influence in the industry" and helped it to unite to fight its problems.[75] As the industry's opponents were fond of pointing out, the textile industry's power meant that the MFA, which was designed to be temporary, was repeatedly renewed, and quota protections remained in place until 2005. Free-traders had wanted them abolished much sooner. When the Council was at its peak, the industry's demise was also slowed, and the textile and apparel industry still employed almost two million people when NAFTA was introduced. Given the threat that low-wage competition posed to American producers—a danger that had worried them for decades—what is remarkable is not that the industry declined but that it lasted as long as it did. Without the fight against imports, more workers surely would have lost their jobs much sooner. The divisions over NAFTA, however, represented a turning point, paving the way for the demise of one of America's biggest manufacturing industries.[76]

## NOTES

1. Crafted with Pride Commercials (CDs), ca. 1990, in box 1, Harmony Grove Mills Papers (a copy of this CD is in the author's possession, and all of the above quotations are contained on it).

2. Chris Burritt, "There She Is, Miss America—All Decked Out in All-American Attire," *Atlanta Journal Constitution*, November 13, 1987, p. C8; Barbara Nachman, "It Matters to Sally Struthers," *USA Today*, July 22, 1987; "Coalition to Debut Commercials Urging Viewers to 'Buy American,'" *Miami Herald*, November 19, 1987, p. 20C; "She's Going to Be Looking for US Everywhere," *New York Times*, November 26, 1984, p. A24 (quotation); "Anti-Import Campaign Loses Two Companies," Spartanburg, South Carolina *Herald-Journal*, December 6, 1991; "Miss America 1990 Will Be Emissary for 'Made in U.S.A. Fashions,'" September 1, 1989 Press Release, folder 22.12, box 22, NTA Papers.

3. John Monk, "He's An Industrial Titan, He's a Tree Lover: Roger Milliken Uses His Power to Beautify, Teach Value of Nature," *Charlotte Observer*, November 15, 2004, p. 3B (first quotation); John Monk, "Roger Milliken: The Last Textile Giant (Part 1)," *The State*, October 7, 2001, p. D1 ("Milliken university" quotation); Frank, *Buy American*, p. 193 (closing quotation).

4. John Monk, "S.C. Business Giant Milliken Dies at 95," *The State*, December 31, 2010 (first quotation by Lewis Gossett of the South Carolina Manufacturers Alliance); Ben Szobody, "Roger Milliken, Textile Titan, Dies," *USA Today*, December 30, 2010 (closing quotation attributed by Szobody to "numerous sources").

5. Linda Conley, "Textile Magnate, Philanthropist Roger Milliken Has Died at Age 95," Spartanburg (SC) *Herald-Journal*, December 30, 2010; Thurmond quotation in Strom Thurmond to Roger Milliken, March 29, 1956, "Legislation: Tariffs-Textiles" folder, box 9, 1956 Subject Correspondence Files, Thurmond Papers; "Roger Milliken's Moral Fiber, Patriotism, a Testament to American Greatness," Augusta (Georgia) *Chronicle*, January 6, 2011, p. A6 ("funding fathers" quotation). For examples of subsequent close cooperation between Thurmond and Milliken, see Roger Milliken to Strom Thurmond, February 10, 1983, and Strom Thurmond to Roger Milliken, February 17, 1983, both folder 248, box 34, CMS Series, Thurmond Papers.

6. "Crafted with Pride Council Initiates Campaign," *Southern Textile News*, December 3, 1984, p. 5 (Milliken quotations); Crafted with Pride in U.S.A. Council, Inc., "Mission Statement," Spring 1984 (third and fourth quotations), "Crafted with Pride in the U.S.A Council" folder, box 9, series 5780/150, ILGWU Papers-Cornell; Kitty G. Dickerson, "U.S. Industry Pridefully Promotes Domestic Products," *Apparel Industry Magazine*, September 1983, p. 40.

7. John Monk, "Roger Milliken: The Last Textile Giant (Part 2)," *The State*, October 7, 2001, p. D1 (quotations); Frank, *Buy American*, p. 195.

8. Robert E. Swift biography, August 1, 1988, folder 22.10, box 22, NTA Papers; Robert E. Swift to Industry Associate, March 10, 1992 (quotation), folder 22.10, box 22, NTA Papers.

9. Frank, *Buy American*, pp. ix–x. For "The Heartbeat of America" campaign, see the many "Heartbeat of America" commercials on YouTube and the many enthusiastic comments they continue to attract from viewers.

10. "'Buy American' Crusade Struggles On," *U.S. News and World Report*, January 27, 1986, p. 52.

11. "Auto-Deception," *The New Republic*, April 4, 1981, p. 5; Jerry Underwood, "Consumers Growing Cool to 'Buy America' Campaign," *Cleveland Plain Dealer*, January 23, 1993, p. 3D.

12. Stephen A. Greyser, with the collaboration of Robert J. Kopp, *Cases in Advertising and Communications Management, Third Edition* (Englewood Cliffs, NJ: Prentice Hall, 1992), p. 8; Jan van Lohuizen to Bill Lacey, September 1, 1985, "Textile/Trade (1)" folder, William B. Lacy files, OA13030, Reagan Library.

13. Kitty G. Dickerson, "U.S. Industry Pridefully Promotes Domestic Products," *Apparel Industry Magazine*, September 1983, pp. 37–42; "Crafted with Pride in the USA, Inc: Summary of Research Findings," n.d., folder 22.9, box 22, NTA Papers.

14. Crafted with Pride in USA Council, Inc., Fact Sheet, ca. 1985, folder 22.12, box 22, NTA Papers.

15. W. Ray Shockley to Ernest F. Hollings, February 9, 1984 (quotation), and "Testimony of Jack Sheinkman on H.R. 5638 to Amend the Textile Fiber Products Identification Act and the Wool Products Labeling Act of 1939," June 28, 1984, both "Labeling Act 1984" folder, box 790, ACTWU Papers-Cornell. For a summary of the law, which passed as a rider to a drug prescription law and was signed by President Reagan on September 24, 1984, see "Textile Law Orders a U.S. Label," *New York Times*, December 29, 1984, p. 1.

16. "Crafted with Pride Council Initiates Campaign," *Southern Textile News*, December 3, 1984, p. 5.

17. "Council Membership Triples in Past Year," *Southern Textile News*, August 11, 1986, p. 11; "Crafted with Pride in USA Council's Campaign Marks Five Years of Success" (Press Release), September 6, 1989, "Crafted with Pride" folder, box 12, Susan Cowell files, UNITE Papers; "Dues Schedule for Fiscal 1990," "Crafted with Pride in U.S.A. Council" folder, box 9,

series 5780/150, ILGWU Papers-Cornell; "Anti-Import Campaign Loses Two Companies," Spartanburg, South Carolina *Herald-Journal*, December 6, 1991; Quotation in Robert E. Swift to Thomas Bray, January 30, 1992, folder 22.10, box 22, NTA Papers.

18. Frank, *Buy American*, p. 189 (quotation); "New Cola Controversy Bubbles Up: Coke's Line of Clothing Irks Firm," *Philadelphia Inquirer*, August 10, 1985, p. D8.

19. Robert E. Swift to Speakers Bureau, September 23, 1985, and "Crafted with Pride in U.S.A. Newsletter," February 1985, both "Crafted with Pride" folder, box 35, series 5619-C-5, ACTWU Papers-Cornell; "New Flag," *Cannon News*, April 1985, p. 1; Phil Clementi to Crafted with Pride in USA Council Member, October 1, 1991, folder 22.10, box 22, NTA Papers.

20. ATMI Spring Board Meeting Minutes, April 8, 1987, item 12, box 20, series 1998/18, Harmony Grove Mills Papers (first three quotations); ATMI Spring Board Meeting Minutes, April 6, 1988, item 9, box 20, series 1998/18, Harmony Grove Mills Papers (fourth quotation); ATMI Fall Board Meeting Minutes, October 25–27, 1987, item 11, box 20, series 1998/18, Harmony Grove Mills Papers (final quotation).

21. Corn quoted in Frank, *Buy American*, p. 197. For details of the Darlington case, see Hodges, *New Deal Labor Policy and the Southern Cotton Textile Industry*, pp. 193–94; Arthur, "The Darlington Mills Case," pp. 40–47.

22. Roger Milliken to Jay Mazur, January 31, 1992, "Crafted with Pride" folder, box 12, Susan Cowell files, UNITE Papers-Cornell; Derrick quotation in Ben Szobody, "Roger Milliken, Textile Titan, Dies," *USA Today*, December 30, 2010.

23. "They Bet a $ Million and Won," *Liberty*, September 1951 (first two quotations); ACWA Press Release, September 23, 1955; "New Label," *AFL-CIO News*, March 8, 1975 (third quotation); "The ILGWU Union Label: Report to the 1959 ILGWU Convention," pp. 94–99 ("women" quotation on p. 99); "How America Got the ILGWU Message" (Report to 1977 ILGWU Convention), pp. 78–81 (penultimate quotation on p. 81), all in "Union Label Pre-1956" folder, box 2, series 6000/036, UNITE Papers-Cornell; Final quotation in Steven Greenhouse, "Its Heart Is Still 7th Avenue; Garment Union Keeps Piece of Past," *New York Times*, December 3, 1995, pp. 1, 49.

24. "Would You Work for 14c Per Hour?" (ACWA Advertisement), "Union Label 1960–1969" folder, box 2, series 6000/036, UNITE Papers-Cornell.

25. Frank, *Buy American*, pp. 138–43, quotations on pp. 139 and 142.

26. Glenda M. Armstrong to Ernest Hollings, May 11, 1985, box 10, Ninety-Ninth Congress files, Hollings Papers; "Cannon, Coke Sponsor Rally," *Southern Textile News*, September 2, 1985, pp. 7, 12.

27. ACTWU General Executive Board Minutes, July 29, 1985, "GEB 7/29–8/2/85 Tarrytown, New York" folder, box 1006, ACTWU Papers-Cornell (quotations). For similar pledges of support for the campaign, see Sam M. Walton to "American Manufacturers and Suppliers," March 14, 1985, "Textile" folder, box 6, series 329-92-138, Jenkins Papers.

28. Unattributed quotation cited in Greyser, *Cases in Advertising and Communications Management*, p. 351.

29. Robert E. Swift to Speakers Bureau, September 23, 1985 (first quotation), and "Crafted with Pride in U.S.A. Newsletter," February 1985 (second and third quotations), both "Crafted with Pride," folder, box 35, series 5619-C-5, ACTWU Papers-Cornell; Closing quotation from J. Henry Walker III to Sam M. Walton, April 15, 1985, "Textile" folder, box 6, series 329-92-138, Jenkins Papers.

30. "Wal-Mart Executive Pushes Buy American Goods Plan," Spartanburg (South Carolina) *Herald-Journal*, October 18, 1988 (quotations); Robert E. Swift to Industry Associate, March 10, 1992, folder 22.10, box 22, NTA Papers.

31. "Wal-Mart Opens Amid Cheers, Sales, Banner," *Fieldcrest Cannon Today*, July 24, 1987, pp. 16–17 (quotations); "Pillowtex: Five Years Later," website at http://independenttribune.net/index.php/pillowtex/article/judy-hatley/ (accessed December 8, 2008); Ruth Crisco interview with author on June 22, 2010, in Concord, North Carolina. The Pillowtex closure in the Kannapolis area is explored in full in chapter 10.

32. David Olmos, "U.S. Clothing Better, 7 of 10 Americans Say," *Charlotte Observer*, November 16, 1985, p. 21A (Swift quotation); David Olmos, "Buy-American Ads Convince 72

Percent of Viewers, Study Shows," *Charlotte Observer*, March 21, 1986, p. 9C (Milliken quotation); Greyser, *Cases in Advertising and Communications Management*, p. 346 (closing quotation).

33. Robert E. Swift to Wilbur Daniels, July 31, 1985, "Crafted with Pride" folder, box 14, series 6000/010, UNITE Papers-Cornell (quotation); Barbara Nachman, "It Matters to Sally Struthers," *USA Today*, July 22, 1987.

34. Sammy Davis to Robert E. Swift, September 29, 1986, "Crafted with Pride" folder, box 14, series 6000/010, UNITE Papers-Cornell.

35. "Racing for Jobs," *Daily News Record*, October 11, 1985.

36. "'Tis the Month to 'Buy American,'" *Fieldcrest Cannon Today*, December 10, 1986, p. 5 (first two quotations); "Happy Holidays!" *Southern Textile News*, December 22, 1986, p. 8.

37. Douglas and Morganosky, "Textile and Apparel Industry Support for the Crafted with Pride Campaign," pp. 37–44 (quotation from article abstract); Leslie Wayne, "U.S. Textile Industry's Turnaround," *New York Times*, February 15, 1988, p. D1 (last two quotations).

38. Gaventa and Smith, "The Deindustrialization of the Textile South," in Leiter et al., eds., *Hanging By a Thread*, p. 183.

39. "Consumers Go American Way," Rocky Mountain (Colorado) News, July 5, 1990, p. 2S; "Made in the U.S.A.," *The Seattle Times*, May 20, 1993, p. D1.

40. "'Made in USA' Fashions Star at the Miss America Pageant," Council Press Release, September 1, 1989, folder 22.12, box 22, NTA Papers; "Crafted with Pride Council Coordinates Miss America Wardrobe," *Southern Textile News*, October 26, 1987, p. 2 (quotation).

41. "A Winning Combination: Miss America and 'Made in USA,'" Council Press Release, September 1, 1989 (first quotation), folder 22.12, box 22, NTA Papers; "Miss America and 'Made in U.S.A.' An Award-Winning Combination," Crafted with Pride Newsletter, July 1989, "Crafted with Pride in the U.S.A. Council" folder, box 9, series 5780/150, ILGWU Papers-Cornell; "Miss America 1991 Making Clear Statement to Public," *Southern Textile News*, October 15, 1990, p. 13 (Swift quotation).

42. "Miss America Gets Lesson in USA Labels," Spartanburg (South Carolina) *Herald-Journal*, September 27, 1988; Carlson quoted in Lauri Rice, "Miss America Visits L.V. Garment Makers," Allentown (Pennsylvania) *Morning Call*, October 29, 1988, p. B4.

43. Sandra Crockett, "Buy American, Says Miss America," *Baltimore Sun*, March 11, 1992, p. 1D.

44. Lauri Rice, "Miss America Visits L.V. Garment Makers," Allentown (Pennsylvania) *Morning Call*, October 29, 1988, p. B4 (quotations); Annette Reynolds, "Miss America Says to Buy American Products," Baton Rouge (Louisiana) *State Times*, July 21, 1989, p. C2.

45. "Crafted with Pride: Is It Time for a Change?" *Women's Wear Daily*, December 2, 1991.

46. "'Buy American' Crusade Struggles On," *U.S. News and World Report*, January 27, 1986, clipping in "Crafted with Pride in the U.S.A. Council" folder, box 9, series 5780/150, ILGWU Papers-Cornell.

47. Rita Mathias letter, ca. 1985, in "Textile and Apparel Trade Enforcement Act: Opposition Letter from Retail Worker" folder, box 789, ACTWU Papers-Cornell; Kathryn Hopper, "Miss America Personifies 'Made in USA' Campaign," Greensboro (North Carolina) *News and Record*, October 8, 1990, p. 3 (Vincent quotation).

48. Robert E. Swift to Industry Associate, November 20, 1991, folder 22.10, box 22, NTA Papers.

49. Laurie Itow, "Proposed Textile Bill Divides the Industry," *San Francisco Examiner*, August 2, 1985; Phillipes quoted in "'Buy American' Crusade Struggles On," *U.S. News and World Report*, January 27, 1986, clipping in "Crafted with Pride in the U.S.A. Council" folder, box 9, series 5780/150, ILGWU Papers-Cornell.

50. "Crafted with Pride: Is It Time for a Change?" *Women's Wear Daily*, December 2, 1991 (Self quotation); "Anti-Import Campaign Loses Two Companies," Spartanburg (South Carolina) *Herald-Journal*, December 6, 1991 (Sovey quotation).

51. Robert E. Swift, "Crafted with Pride in U.S.A. Council Message: Buying 'Made In U.S.A.' Saves U.S. Jobs," *Southern Textile News*, January 28, 1991, p. 14 (closing quotation); Other quotations in "Buy More 'Made in USA' or Lose More Jobs Is Clear Thrust of Powerful

New Commercials," Campaign Press Release, November 1991, folder 22.9, box 22, NTA Papers; Rick Brooks, "Trade Group Targets Imports in Series of TV Commercials," Greensboro (North Carolina) *News and Record*, December 9, 1991, p. 3.

52. "Crafted with Pride: Is It Time for a Change?" *Women's Wear Daily*, December 2, 1991.

53. Chip Wilson, "For Many, Questions Still Surround NAFTA," *Charlotte Observer*, October 17, 1993, p. 1 (quotation from Jim Conner of the American Yarn Spinners Association); Don Johnson interview with author on June 23, 2010, in Athens, Georgia. The industry's reaction to NAFTA is explored in further detail in chapter 7.

54. Charles Kernaghan to Neil Kearney, December 9, 1997, "Nicaragua Organizing Project" folder, box 34, series 6000/027, UNITE Papers-Cornell; Harris Raynor interview with author on June 18, 2010, in Union City, Georgia. The shift in the attitude of the textile and apparel unions to globalization, and their efforts to organize workers in Central America, is discussed further in chapter 8.

55. Larry Pantages, "Why 'Made in USA Doesn't Mean Much,'" Akron (Ohio) *Beacon Journal*, April 9, 1990, p. D4; Robert E. Swift to Member of the Crafted with Pride in USA Council, June 9, 1993, folder 22.9, box 22, NTA Papers (quotation).

56. U.S. Customs Service, "Textile Fraud Initiatives," January 1986, "Textile/Trade (5)" folder, William B. Lacy files, Reagan Library (quotation); Testimony of Robert M. Tobias, March 6, 1985, p. 133, U.S. Congress, House, Government Operations Committee, *Federal Enforcement of Textile and Apparel Import Quotas (Part 2)*, 99th Congress, 1st Session, 1985.

57. Ed Jenkins interview with author on June 25, 2010, in Jasper, Georgia; Closing quotation in John Monk, "S.C. Business Giant Milliken Dies at 95," *The State*, December 31, 2010.

58. Herbert London, "So What If It's Made in America?" *New York Times*, undated clipping in "Imports, 1986–90" folder, box 19, series 6000/010, UNITE Papers-Cornell (quotation); Harold Evans, "An Abuse of Patriotism," *U.S. News and World Report*, February 3, 1986, p. 86. See also Peter Engardio, "Textile Imports Are Swamping Even the Best Companies," *Business Week*, September 16, 1985, p. 50.

59. See, for example, James Bovard, "High Cost of Textile Protection," *Journal of Commerce*, December 10, 1991, p. 12A.

60. Robert E. Swift to the Editor, *Business Week*, November 24, 1993, Robert E. Swift to *U.S. News and World Report*, November 3, 1994, Robert E. Swift to Joseph Lelyveld, November 15, 1994, and Robert E. Swift, "US Textiles Still a Big Business," *Journal of Commerce*, May 21, 1993, all in folder 22.9, box 22, NTA Papers.

61. "The Fiber, Textile and Apparel Coalition," Burson-Marsteller Presentation, March 8, 1983, folder 22.13, box 22, NTA Papers.

62. "Time to Stand Up and Fight," *Southern Textile News*, 26 August 1985, p. 4. For a good overview of the rise of big-box retailers, see Nelson Lichtenstein, *The Retail Revolution: How Wal-Mart Created a Brave New World of Business* (New York: Metropolitan Books, 2009), esp. pp. 234–37.

63. John Dicker, *The United States of Wal-Mart* (New York: Penguin, 2005), pp. 109–11.

64. Dicker, *The United States of Wal-Mart*, p. 15; Bethany Moreton, *To Serve God and Wal-Mart: The Making of Christian Free Enterprise* (Cambridge, MA: Harvard University Press, 2009), p. 1 and unpaginated photograph caption immediately before p. 145. The quotations are on this later page, in the photograph caption.

65. Robert E. Swift, "Made in U.S.A.: A Label for a Stronger Economy," *Southern Textile News*, December 8, 1997, p. 6 (quotations); Robert E. Swift, "At the Crossroads of Main Street and Wall Street," *Southern Textile News*, December 9, 1996.

66. "Can American Soldiers Depend on Foreign Factories?" *New York Times*, November 11, 2001, p. WK13. For other examples of post-9/11 advertising by the Council, see "Is Trade a 'Jobs' Issue?" (Crafted with Pride in USA #17 Advertisement), *New York Times*, February 10, 2002, p. C15; "Is More Federal Aid the Answer?" (Crafted with Pride in USA #20 Advertisement), *New York Times*, February 24, 2002, p. D13.

67. For a good illustration of these points, see Leigh Dyer and Crystal Dempsey, "In Search of the Elusive 'Made in the U.S.A.' Tag," *Charlotte Observer*, March 2, 2002, p. 1F.

68. Import data from the Office of Textiles and Apparel, International Trade Administration, U.S. Commerce Department, at http://otexa.ita.doc.gov/msrcty/a5700.htm (accessed April 30, 2012).

69. First quotation in John Monk, "S.C. Business Giant Milliken Dies at 95," *The State*, December 31, 2010; Ben Szobody, "Roger Milliken, Textile Titan, Dies," *USA Today*, December 30, 2010 (Derrick quotation); John Singleton, *The World Textile Industry* (London and New York: Routledge, 1997), p. 1; Rosen, *Making Sweatshops*, p. 3.

70. Buchanan quoted in Patrick Buchanan, "Requiem for a Patriot," available on Patrick Buchanan's website at http://buchanan.org/blog/requiem-for-a-patriot-4589 (accessed January 7, 2011, copy of printout in author's possession); "Pat Buchanan," profile, available at http://en.wikipedia.org/wiki/Pat_Buchanan (accessed January 10, 2011). A hard copy of Buchanan's "Requiem" is also available in "Pat Buchanan," Gaffney (South Carolina) *Ledger*, January 5, 2011; Brinkley, *American History*, p. 915; Ben Szobody, "Roger Milliken, Textile Titan, Dies," *USA Today*, December 30, 2010 (Nash quotation).

71. *AAM Update*, January 14, 2011; Tony Walker, "Give and Take of Globalisation," *Australian Financial Review*, August 21, 2008, p. 76.

72. Lloyd Wood interview with author on June 18, 2009, in Washington, D.C.

73. Scott Paul interview with author on June 19, 2009, in Washington, D.C. (first quotation); "Buy American-Made at this Holiday Season," *AAM Update*, November 24, 2010 (other quotations). Copies of all *AAM Updates*, which were supplied to the author by the Alliance for American Manufacturing, are in the author's possession.

74. Roger Simmermaker, *How Americans Can Buy American: The Power of Consumer Patriotism, Third Edition* (Orlando: Consumer Patriotism Corporation, 2008), pp. 7–10 (quotation on p. 7), p. 61.

75. Karl Spilhaus interview with author on April 26, 2011, in Boston, Massachusetts.

76. Cynthia Mitchell, "Textile, Apparel Industries Now Favor Free Trade," *Atlanta Constitution*, October 1, 1992, p. D1.

*Chapter Seven*

# Looking Beyond Our Borders: The Industry in the Era of NAFTA and GATT

On November 17, 1993, the U.S. House of Representatives passed the North American Free Trade Agreement by a vote of 234 to 200, largely because of the overwhelming backing of Republicans. In a hotly contested and emotional vote, the critics of globalization, led by organized labor and environmental groups, were overcome by NAFTA's supporters, principally corporate lobbyists and the Clinton administration. The effort that both sides put into the vote indicated that a lot was at stake, as NAFTA was of enormous importance to the U.S. economy as a whole and the textile industry in particular. It aimed to create the world's largest free trade bloc, one with a population of 370 million and a combined GDP of $6.5 trillion. By eliminating tariffs and other trade barriers between the United States, Canada, and Mexico, NAFTA gave companies in the United States and Canada free access to a burgeoning Mexican market of ninety million consumers, half of whom were under the age of twenty. It also promised to provide Mexico with much-needed foreign investment. Opponents, however, declared that NAFTA would cause job losses in the United States as companies moved south of the border or as cheaper Mexican imports replaced American-made products. Low-wage, labor-intensive industries such as apparel stood to lose the most.[1]

There was no doubt that the passage of NAFTA was a turning point for the U.S. textile and apparel industry, which had traditionally used its political clout to try to contain job losses. Although the textile bills of the 1970s and 1980s had failed, the industry's political influence had slowed the pace of decline and staved off disaster. In 1992—as the agreement was being debated—the U.S. textile and apparel industry still employed 1.9 million workers, eight hundred thousand of them in the southern states. This meant that the industry had lost just over half a million jobs since the early 1970s, when imports had begun to make major inroads. While this was a significant drop, it paled in comparison to what followed. In the decade after NAFTA, employment in the industry halved and many of the largest companies went out of business. Seventeen years after NAFTA's passage, fewer than five hundred thousand workers remained in American mills, many of which were empty and abandoned. While some of these losses were not caused by NAFTA, many were, especially in apparel.[2]

In the wake of NAFTA, the industry's decline was particularly noticeable in the South, where it had the most to lose. Within nine years of the agreement's passage, North Carolina had lost half of its textile and apparel jobs, and the situation was similar in neighboring Virginia and South Carolina. For those on the ground, NAFTA was the obvious cause of the hemorrhaging, and the impact was greatest in small towns that lost apparel factories. In Martinsville, Virginia, which had once proclaimed itself as the "Sweatshirt Capital of the World," officials claimed that the treaty was responsible for the loss of 9,500 local manufacturing jobs in seven years, leaving the area with double-digit unemployment. "You have found the poster child for NAFTA," declared Tom Harned, Martinsville's economic development director. "We're losing jobs by the thousands and replacing them by the hundreds." Among those displaced was Margaret Blankenship, who had sewn together 21,565,440 pairs of sweatpants during a thirty-six year career at Vanity Fair's Martinsville plant. "Dreams? Ambitions? Goals?" she asked. "It's funny, but I've never thought about them. I always figured I'd be sewing."[3]

The textile and apparel industry was at the heart of the divisive debate about NAFTA's impact. "Throughout its duration," summarized economists Gary Clyde Hufbauer and Jeffrey J. Schott in 2007, "NAFTA has been hailed by some and derided by others."[4] Led by organized labor and environmental groups, critics blamed the treaty for heavy job losses, and they often cited the textile and apparel industry as a prime example. In 2003, the Economic Policy Institute—a think tank that represented low- and middle-income Americans—insisted that NAFTA had cost the United States at least five hundred thousand jobs. Placing more emphasis on service and retail industries, business groups and retailers saw the situation differently. According to them, NAFTA had opened markets for exporters and lowered prices for consumers. "NAFTA has 'locked in' trade gains to the benefit of U.S. exporters," asserted the Business Roundtable in one detailed report. "On balance the 'winners' outweighed the 'losers.'"[5]

NAFTA's impact was certainly variegated, and various parts of the textile-apparel complex were affected differently by it. The agreement hurt labor-intensive apparel plants the most, yet some textile companies were able to sell more fabrics and yarn to Mexican garment makers, at least in the short term. According to Carlos Moore of the ATMI—which had backed NAFTA—the real problem was cheap Asian imports. Unlike Mexico, many Asian countries imposed high-import tariffs, making it almost impossible for American goods to penetrate their markets. After the 1997 economic collapse devalued Asian currencies by around 40 percent, Far Eastern garment manufacturers had a decisive advantage. "When the Asian economic downturn came in the late '90s, accompanied by a currency devaluation, resulting in incredibly low textile and apparel import prices, the handwriting was on the wall," summarized the *Daily News Record*. Indeed, by the turn-of-the-century textile executives complained more about unfair competition from Asia, and especially from China, rather than about NAFTA. "China is the 800-pound gorilla," declared industry lobbyist Jock Nash. "I don't know anybody who can compete with them—not in textiles, not in electronics, not in anything." China's rapid emergence stymied U.S. mill owners' hopes of using NAFTA to stem domestic job losses. As some executives later admitted, things had not worked out as they had hoped.[6]

NAFTA originated during the administration of George H. W. Bush, and it reflected the forty-first president's determination to expand free trade, especially within the Americas. Mexican president Carlos Salinas de Gortari, who was important in spearheading the agreement, shared this goal, as did conservative Canadian prime minister Brian Mulroney, who had signed a free trade agreement with the United States in 1988. Salinas's role was particularly decisive. On a 1991 trip to his alma mater of Harvard University, the Mexican leader told the press of his commitment to a North American trade pact: "A free-trade agreement would establish the conditions needed to afford increased certainty and predictability in the future, and would enable us all to take future advantage of our natural complementarity. More jobs will mean higher wages in Mexico, and this in turn will mean fewer migrants to the United States and Canada."[7]

Like its predecessors, the Bush administration promoted a free trade agenda with great enthusiasm, drawing strength from both the domestic economic recovery and from world events. Thus, Bush saw the collapse of Communism in Eastern Europe and the end of the Cold War as positive signs. "Freedom has made great gains," he declared in June 1990, "not just in Eastern Europe—but right here, in the Americas." Free trade policies were thus seen as a way of advancing democracy and opening new markets. "Our aim in the Uruguay Round," he explained in 1990, "is free and fair trade. . . . We must build on the trend we see toward free markets—and make our ultimate aim a free trade system that links all of the Americas—North, Central and South." Through NAFTA, Bush sought to create a free-trade zone that stretched from the Arctic Circle to the southern tip of Mexico, or from the Yukon to the Yucatan. According to the administration, NAFTA would boost the U.S. economy and enhance its global competitiveness.[8]

Early on, the opposition of the domestic textile industry loomed as a major obstacle to Bush's plans. In March 1991, when the president asked Congress for permission to negotiate NAFTA, textile groups were among his most formidable opponents. "The AFL-CIO and the textile industry have put together a coalition that includes some environmental groups and farm interests," warned the *Washington Post*. A "massive lobbying battle" lay ahead, and the textile and apparel industry would be at the heart of it.[9]

The industry's failure to override Bush's veto, however, undermined its willingness to take on the administration again. Thus, in the summer of 1992 the industry's main trade association announced its support for NAFTA. "We as an industry are prepared to back the North American Free Trade Agreement," declared ATMI vice president Carlos Moore. As Cynthia Mitchell pondered in the *Atlanta Constitution*, at first glance the support of the "notoriously protectionist" ATMI for a free trade agreement was puzzling. A closer examination, however, revealed a number of reasons for the shift. Hopes of boosting exports were important, especially for apparel makers. As a Sara Lee spokeswoman put it, "There's 83 million people down there [in Mexico] we'd like to see in Hanes underwear." The move was also linked to the failure of the import bills. "Since the 1980s," explained Mitchell, "the industry failed three times to override vetoes of bills pushing higher trade barriers. It was forced to figure a way to survive." With low-paying sewing jobs already leaving the United States, the industry reasoned that it was better to try to ensure that these jobs went to Mexico, where under NAFTA manufacturers could use American-made fabric and yarn. This would allow the basic textile industry to stay in the United States, while apparel companies could retain distribution centers and white-collar jobs. According to Burlington Industries executive James C. Leonard III, much of the industry realized that it had to take part in the global economy in order to "survive." Finally, the Bush administration clinched the industry's support by promising that Mexico and Canada would not be used as a platform to ship duty-free goods into the United States from other countries.[10]

For NAFTA's supporters in the industry, the rule of origin provision was crucial. The rule declared that the three basic steps of yarn spinning, fabric weaving or knitting, and apparel assembly must all be done in Canada, the United States, or Mexico in order to receive quota-free and duty-free treatment in cross-border trade. Some items not produced in any of the three countries, however, were exempt from the provision.[11] With this rule in place, NAFTA was also endorsed by the NTA, which still represented over one hundred textile companies. At its 1992 annual meeting, the northern group agreed that it would support NAFTA as long as "rule of origin" stipulations protected production within the NAFTA zone.[12] Rather than fighting government policy, the NTA insisted that "partnership" was the way forward. "Consistent with the partnership theme, we would like to explore the potential for our members to develop business opportunities with our new Mexican 'partners,'" wrote NTA president Karl Spilhaus in August 1993.[13]

While some textile executives had broadened their thinking, the industry's decision to work with the government over NAFTA primarily reflected its recognition that it was unlikely to get far by opposing federal policy. The defeat of the three textile bills had forced a change in thinking. In 1994, the *Southern Textile News* spelled out these grim realities in an editorial, with Mason "Chip" Smith reflecting that "the American textile industry has learned a very valuable lesson in the past few years. We have fought tooth and nail to get trade legislation passed that would help level the field with the flood of imports into our market. We have come up empty on each and every attempt. We were fighting our government officials and not trying to work with them." Smith recognized that working with the government might not produce the "level playing field" that the industry desired, but ultimately there was no alternative. "We have lost when we have gone head to head against the political structure," he acknowledged. Rather than trying to change federal trade policies, a declining industry was now trying to soften their impact.[14]

By entering a free trade bloc with Mexico and Canada, supporters reasoned that they had identified a strategy to ensure the industry's survival. The U.S. textile industry, they argued, was much larger and more efficient than its Mexican or Canadian counterparts, and it could build on an expanding export trade with its smaller neighbors. As the ATMI's Charles Bremer put it, "With Mexico and Canada, trade is a two-way street and we're the biggest kid on the block." NAFTA, explained another industry supporter, "creates a preferential trading area that gives preference to North American companies and not to Asia and Europe."[15]

This argument carried a considerable amount of weight within the industry. Vocal members of the ATMI, such as Guilford Mills chairman Charles A. Hayes, enthusiastically embraced the agreement. Hayes was closely involved in the negotiations to devise NAFTA's complex textile provisions, and he assured the administration of the industry's support. In an August 1993 letter to U.S. trade representative Michael Kantor, Hayes went as far as to predict that NAFTA would be "a renaissance for the textile industry," creating jobs as U.S. companies gained access to a lucrative new market.[16] Forthright support also came from the management of Springs Industries, a midsized textile firm that was headquartered in Fort Mill, South Carolina. Writing House Majority leader Richard Gephardt—a prominent NAFTA opponent—Springs CEO Walter Elisha predicted that lean textile firms would "prosper under NAFTA," which would establish a trading bloc "that is the ideal counterpoint to the EC and to the alliances forming in the Far East." Other textile makers agreed. "I feel that NAFTA will be good for our business," declared Peter Frank of Malden Mills in Lawrence, Massachusetts. "It can only help us export goods to Mexico."[17]

Some apparel firms also backed NAFTA, largely because they had already established factories in Mexico. In 1963, Item 807 of the U.S. Tariff Schedule gave incentives to U.S. companies who wanted to move manufacturing abroad. Under Item 807, American apparel makers would cut the cloth needed for garments in the United States and then export it to an overseas factory where the clothing was assembled. Finally, the U.S. apparel company would import the finished garment, paying tariffs only on the value added, or the cost of the labor required, to assemble the garment. Because apparel production was labor intensive, the tariff provision encouraged a shifting of manufacturing capacity to Mexico. By the end of 1991, there were 1925 *maquiladoras* plants on the Mexican side of the border, and they employed half a million workers, mostly in labor-intensive industries. An agreement between the two countries also allowed foreign companies—mainly American transnationals—partial or complete ownership of the *maquiladoras*. NAFTA was thus a significant step in what sociologist Ellen Israel Rosen has termed "the globalization of the U.S. apparel industry," encouraging a further shifting of capacity to Mexico, where workers toiled in poor conditions. Because U.S. textile makers could supply the Mexican facilities with cloth and yarn, many also embraced NAFTA.[18]

The industry's support for NAFTA clearly helped the agreement to pass, especially as it influenced many of the 102 House Democrats who broke with organized labor and voted for it. In an unprecedented move, some representatives from textile districts now backed a free trade agreement. One of them was Georgia congressman Don Johnson, who remembered being lobbied heavily by the ATMI: "ATMI supported NAFTA back in 1993 . . . when we voted on it, because they felt that it was the only way that the fabric manufacturers could survive." Johnson recalled that he was influenced by the ATMI's arguments that American textile makers could supply apparel companies in Mexico. The vote clearly helped Johnson's career, as he went on to become the Clinton administration's adviser on textile issues and an ambassador in the U.S. trade representative's office. He stood by NAFTA, insisting in 2010 that it had been "a plus overall."[19]

Not all executives swallowed these arguments, however, and NAFTA caused damaging divisions that hurt the industry and became a cause of its decline. As the *Washington Post* noted, NAFTA generated "wrenching" splits in the "textile-apparel coalition," which had been a formidable political force. According to the *Post* , "the unraveling of the textile lobby" was a significant boost to the agreement's supporters. The divisions were apparent within the NTA's membership, even though President Karl Spilhaus tried hard to sell the agreement. "U.S. textile manufacturers," he wrote in July 1993, "can expect to capitalize on partnership opportunities afforded by this new international agreement." When NAFTA was discussed at the group's annual meeting a few months later, a "lively question and answer session" ensued. As Spilhaus admitted in a letter to an economist, many of his members worried about "perceived negatives in the agreement for the textile and apparel industry."[20] While the NTA managed to present a united front in public, others aired their differences. On the eve of the congressional vote over NAFTA, Milliken lobbyist Jock Nash traded verbal blows with the ATMI's Charlie Bremer at a forum in Spartanburg, South Carolina. The *Herald-Journal*'s headline—"NAFTA Splitting Textile Industry"—summarized the situation well. Even Spilhaus later admitted that the divisions had been destructive. NAFTA, he recalled, had "split the industry. . . . It just was a mess, and that, combined with the diminution of the industry, just destroyed our political clout."[21]

Opponents of the agreement spoke out because they felt betrayed by their colleagues. As the U.S.'s chief textile negotiator admitted, parts of the industry had done a "flip-flop," yet many others had not shifted. In particular, Roger Milliken fiercely opposed NAFTA, which he insisted would cause "great damage to employment in the United States." As the *Southern Textile News* reported on the eve of the crucial congressional vote, Milliken had "been against NAFTA the entire time. He has taken his stand and has not wavered." Opposition also came from the National Knitwear and Sportswear Association, which saw the pact as flawed because it linked two economies with very different wage rates. Aware that displaced textile workers had usually struggled to find comparable jobs, NKSA director Seth Bodner doubted President Bush's promise to retrain those who lost their positions. "Even if [U.S. officials] meant it, what are these workers going to do?" he asked. "They are not going to be bankers and engineers."[22]

In Congress, many of the industry's traditional allies lambasted the agreement. According to Senator Hollings, NAFTA would be a "real loss" for working people. Hollings emphasized the industry's role in providing decent jobs to unskilled Americans. "Right to the point," he wrote one opponent, "we have 40,000 sewing plant workers in South Carolina. There are over 150,000 in downtown LA, 100,000 in New York and a million good jobs that this country can't afford to lose. While daddy grows tobacco there in Hartsville, mama is working in the sewing plant and together they are trying to send that boy to Clemson. NAFTA would ruin this." In November 1993, the self-proclaimed "textile boy in the Senate" predicted that the domestic industry would lose a million jobs under NAFTA, a prophesy that turned out to be accurate. At the time, however, most executives laughed off Hollings's claims. According to Springs Industries spokesman Robert L. Thompson, they were "ludicrous."[23]

In the House, strong opposition came from long-standing industry supporters, including Butler Derrick and Frank Pallone Jr. (D-NJ), while House majority whip David E. Bonior (D-MI) threatened to use the resources of his office against NAFTA. Ignoring appeals from pact supporters, Congressman Derrick was particularly outspoken. "The textile and apparel industry," he wrote one opponent, "has continually acted as the punching bag for one administration after another, and I believe that NAFTA would be another series of blows to an otherwise vibrant industry."[24] The industry was at the heart of the emotive debate about NAFTA's predicted impact. As National Public Radio show host David Molpus summarized, NAFTA aroused "particularly strong" passions within the textiles and apparel industry, where opponents worried that the agreement would be the last straw for their struggling sector.[25]

Most of these politicians were responding to their constituents' fears that NAFTA would cause massive job losses. Derrick's papers, for example, document the depth of grassroots opposition that existed in the southern textile belt. "I am writing this letter in regards to the North American Free Trade Agreement (NAFTA)," declared Eddie G. Fullbright from Laurens. "I am strongly opposed to NAFTA and everything about it. The only thing I can see resulting from this is a lot of people in this state and many other states losing their jobs." From Central, South Carolina, textile worker Phil Moore was "greatly concerned" about NAFTA. "For years," he explained, "the textile industry has been at the mercy of foreign countries, specifically those countries who employ cheap labor. Since Mexico falls in this category and given its close proximity to the United States, I feel this agreement will be disastrous for the textile industry as a whole and *MY* job in particular." In the old textile states of the North, too, opinion ran strongly against NAFTA. "People are overwhelmingly against it," declared Richard Swett, a Democratic congressman from New Hampshire, in September. "On all the radio talk shows, I got no positive calls." Because of the intensity of this grassroots backlash, some press reports predicted that Congress would reject NAFTA. The situation changed, however, once President Clinton and cabinet officials began campaigning for the agreement in the period immediately before the vote.[26]

Because many textile executives endorsed NAFTA, it exacerbated tensions with the unions, who had wanted to take a more oppositional line with both the Reagan and Bush administrations. Union leaders felt betrayed and refused to participate in the FFACT, which gradually fell into disuse. Private union records throw light on the damaging splits. In October 1991, the ILGWU's General Executive Board expressed frustration with mill owners that supported the Republican Party, which was pushing NAFTA. "The Republicans accept their campaign contributions," noted the union, "but the dominant philosophy within the administration is that the U.S. should be willing to give the apparel industry away." These tensions had also been present during the 1988 presidential election, when many manufacturers had supported the GOP while the unions backed the Democrats.[27]

Unlike the industry, the unions unequivocally opposed NAFTA from the start. "The ILGWU's policy on the North American Free Trade Agreement," noted the union as early as October 1991, "is that, rather than create markets for U.S.-made products, NAFTA will lead to the continued export of U.S. jobs to Latin American countries, enhancing corporate profits through cheaper labor." In the years that followed, this position failed to change significantly. Because both the ILGWU and the ACTWU had lost many members over the previous twenty years, however, they were at a disadvantage as they took on the Bush and Clinton administrations. Between 1970 and 1994, the ILGWU lost over two-thirds of its dues-payers, while the ACTWU's membership fell from four hundred thousand in 1976 to about two hundred thousand when NAFTA was debated. These falls pushed the two unions to join together and create UNITE, but this merger was not formalized until after NAFTA had passed Congress. The fate of the textile unions was symptomatic of a labor movement that was "under siege" even as it launched a major legislative fight. In the 1950s, 35 percent of American workers had belonged to unions, but by the time NAFTA was voted on this figure had slumped to just 15 percent.[28]

Privately, there had also been a shift in the thinking of union leaders. Three unsuccessful legislative campaigns had taken their toll, and labor strategists turned away from economic nationalism and looked for fresh ideas. As ILGWU vice president Susan Cowell summarized in a key memo to Jay Mazur in 1992, "We need a new strategy for trade, adjusting our legislative goals, our tactics, and our rhetoric to fit the new political situation." Trying to oppose free trade agreements was no longer viable. "A purely protectionist argument for apparel quotas is, I think, unwinnable," admitted Cowell, who predicted that NAFTA would pass "in some form." As the way forward, Cowell suggested that the answer lay in "linking trade with labor rights, labor standards and environmental protections." Like the industry, the unions now tried to amend trade agreements so that they were as palatable as possible rather than trying to stop them. Cowell's memo foreshadowed new union campaigns in which overseas workers were seen as partners rather than threats. In the wake of NAFTA, the ILGWU and UNITE tried to forge alliances with foreign workers around universal issues of labor rights and environmental justice. According to the union, textile and apparel workers across the globe faced common challenges and needed to work together.[29]

NAFTA's opponents realized that they were fighting an uphill battle, especially as President Bush threw the full weight of his office behind the agreement. As he promoted NAFTA, Bush admitted that some jobs would be lost, yet he insisted that the economy as a whole would benefit. In October 1992, the Bush administration used figures from the Institute for International Economics to claim that NAFTA would cost 150,000 jobs, but 325,000 positions would be created. The lost jobs would be concentrated in manufacturing industries, especially low-wage ones, whereas service and retail industries were predicted to grow. Such calculations were of little comfort to anxious mill workers. As Dennis Julian of the North Carolina Textiles Manufacturers Association put it, "There's no consolation to say to someone: You got bit, but other parts of the economy will benefit."[30] Hopes that the new Democratic administration might sponsor different trade policies quickly evaporated. The day before he was inaugurated as president, Clinton declared that the speedy conclusion of NAFTA was "a top trade-related priority." Pitching the agreement's benefits to exporters, Clinton made no mention of domestic industries that were likely to be hurt by imports, instead stressing that NAFTA would be "a positive force for creating American jobs."[31]

Once in office, Clinton's aides repeated many of the arguments of their Republican predecessors. On the eve of the congressional vote on NAFTA, White House Press Secretary Dee Dee Myers was asked by a reporter what she would advise a textile worker whose job was threatened. According to the questioner, these workers were "fueling the calls and letters to Congress." Myers replied that while there would be "some dislocations" under NAFTA, the "vast majority" of Americans would benefit. The administration would also help to retrain those who lost their jobs. Listening to these comments, textile leaders worried that their sector was being traded away by policy makers who failed to appreciate its economic importance, especially to small-town America. As ILGWU leader Gus Tyler wrote in his memoirs, many politicians "believed that America was really not a fit place for textile and apparel manufacture. They maintained that workers dispossessed in the textile and apparel trades would find better-paying jobs."[32]

In many ways, it was not surprising that policy makers acted in the interests of other sectors of the economy, particularly service industries and agriculture. Broad economic shifts, particularly deindustrialization and the growth of the service sector, meant that manufacturing industries no longer had a dominant influence over trade policy. Although it remained powerful, the textile lobby was no match for its opponents. In 1999, for example, USTR Charlene Barshefsky estimated that the service sector accounted for 70 percent of the U.S. economy and about a seventh of the global economy.[33] Export lobbies were also very influential. In 1998, the United States was the largest exporter of agricultural goods in the world, with annual agricultural exports of around $49 billion, or about one-quarter of total U.S. agricultural production.[34] As Ellen Rosen has shown, lobbying from the "well-funded and highly organized" retail industry was also crucial in promoting NAFTA and other free trade initiatives. The retail industry continued to work through RITAC, a very significant group. In March 1992, Bush's Chief of Staff, Samuel K. Skinner, wrote RITAC head Leslie H. Wexner that "you and other members of the Retail Industry Trade Action Coalition have been excellent supporters of ours and we really appreciate your continued involvement." Responding to lobbying from Wexner, Skinner added that the administration was "determined to have a successful outcome both to the Uruguay Round and NAFTA, for we know how much that means to the country and to dynamic industries such as yours."[35]

When the NAFTA vote came up, therefore, its supporters had decisive advantages. The well-funded export and retail lobbies bombarded representatives with material and were able to overpower their opponents, who mounted a sizeable effort of their own. Congresswoman Marilyn Lloyd, for example, received slick dossiers from groups such as the U.S. Chamber of Commerce, which argued in a thirty-two-page document that NAFTA would "create more U.S. jobs, lower prices for consumer goods, and strengthen competitiveness for American firms at home and abroad."[36] In frenzied activity prior to the congressional vote, President Clinton also leaned heavily on his Democratic colleagues. In mid-September 1993, for example, Clinton wrote Butler Derrick and urged him to change his mind. "NAFTA," he declared, "opens the Mexican market, already a strong market for U.S. exports in textiles and apparel, to even further growth." While Derrick withstood the pressure, many of his colleagues did not, causing crucial last-minute defections. In order to placate members who were concerned about the lack of enforceable labor rights and environmental protections in the treaty, Clinton appended side agreements that were designed to monitor implementation of national laws relating to labor and the environment and to establish forums for consultation and dispute resolution. In reality, however, the side letters were difficult to enforce and weak. Between 1995 and 2000, over twenty complaints were filed under the labor side agreement, citing the failure to protect the right to organize and strike. Although hearings concluded that serious violations had occurred, nothing happened, largely because trade sanctions for failing to comply with the letter were missing. This outcome undermined UNITE's new strategy of trying to organize Mexican workers.[37]

The same economic forces pushed Clinton to promote other free trade initiatives. Soon after he came into office, the president declared that he was determined to complete the GATT talks, where negotiations begun in Punta del Este, Uruguay, had languished for many years. "A successful Uruguay Round would lower tariff and nontariff barriers to manufactured products," he declared, "thereby increasing cumulative world output by more than $5 trillion and cumulative U.S. output by more than $1 trillion over the next 10 years." Exports accounted for nearly one-sixth of the employment in the domestic manufacturing and agricultural sectors, and the administration therefore privileged export-oriented industries over import-sensitive ones. Six months later, Treasury Secretary Lloyd Bentsen confirmed the administration's commitment to "expanding trade." "We want to wrap up the Uruguay Round and do it quickly," he added, as the United States headed into a G-7 meeting in Tokyo.[38]

The mood was shared by Congress, which voted in July to renew the president's fast track authority to complete the round. Strengthened by this mandate, Clinton declared that he wanted to secure an agreement by the end of his first year in office, insisting that the "world's leading exporter" would "benefit significantly" from it. Still, he recognized that the talks—which involved more than one hundred nations and had been in progress for seven years—would not be easily resolved. Along with agriculture, textiles and apparel was one of the most sensitive areas. The ATMI and NTA continued to lobby for government assistance, but they faced some powerful opponents.[39]

Initially sponsored by the Bush administration, the proposal to replace the MFA with global quotas drew howls of protest from the textile lobby, especially as the quotas would be removed within ten years. As early as June 1990, thirty-four members of the Congressional Textile Caucus had warned USTR Carla Hills that "a virtually unlimited flood of foreign imports" would hit American shores if the proposal were adopted. The Caucus instead pressed for a "strengthened MFA with stronger bilateral agreements," as this would ensure that imports were not allowed to increase by more than 1 percent a year, the key goal of the 1990 textile bill. According to the Caucus, the industry was being used as a "bargaining chip" to win concessions for other areas of the economy, particularly services and banking.[40] Initially, industry leaders also spoke out. In February 1991, ATMI president Donald R. Hughes called the proposal "a fraud" that would not deliver the access to foreign markets that domestic industries had been promised. Rather, it would "systematically surrender the U.S. textile market to imports over the next 10 years." Pulling no punches, Hughes termed the agreement a "total disaster" and a "lousy deal" for his industry. "A factory is being traded for a credit card," he declared.[41]

Determined to get a deal, the Clinton administration reached out to domestic textile leaders and gradually neutralized their opposition. In July 1993, USTR Mickey Kantor announced that the new administration recognized the industry's importance. "There are great numbers of Americans employed in the textile and apparel industries," he explained. "We believe that the combination of the phase-out of the multifiber arrangement over a 10-year period and textile cuts as proposed by the previous administration would not have been helpful to that industry." In contrast, Kantor claimed to have secured market access as a precondition for the MFA phase out, as well as a more gradual elimination of tariff cuts and tighter language to prevent "certain countries" from getting around the quotas.[42]

Still, the Clinton administration was unable to bring the Uruguay Round to a speedy conclusion, and disagreement over the textile and apparel provisions was a central reason for the delay. At the end of 1993, no deal had been struck, partly because Clinton had promised the Congressional Textile Caucus that he would seek a fifteen-year extension. This was strongly opposed by developing nations, who wanted a quicker phase out. According to Don Johnson, the Clinton administration's chief textile negotiator, the industry was "very important" to these emerging economies, and it was impossible to shield American producers from their demands. While Clinton tried to appease the textile lobby, the power of competing domestic economic interests was also reflected in his actions. Thus, the president claimed at the end of the year that the Uruguay Round agreement held out "important benefits for U.S. industry, services, and agriculture." Keen to deliver these benefits, the Clinton administration eventually agreed to a ten-year phase out, disappointing textile industry leaders. The Uruguay Round was completed in April 1994, although its provisions did not take effect until the following January.[43] It was a clear victory for industry opponents such as RITAC and the American Association of Exporters and Importers, who had been pushing for the MFA's abolition for decades.[44]

The GATT treaty confirmed that the textile industry now operated from a position of weakness, rather than strength, in its dealings with the federal government. In early 1995, ATMI President William J. Armfield IV explained that the industry had "mixed feelings" about the abolition of quotas but felt that it did not have the strength to push the issue to the wall. "Every other business group in this country favored the GATT and passage was inevitable," he declared. "So we tried to make the best deal we could and make change work for us." By working with the government, Armfield argued that the ATMI had won greater access to foreign markets, and he urged his members to take advantage of it. "Let's prove those wrong who look at ours as a sunset industry," he declared. Despite these brave words, few mill owners believed that better days lay ahead.[45]

The industry's political power was certainly on the wane, and even traditional allies could no longer be relied on. At the end of 1994, for example, Maine's William Cohen announced that he would vote for GATT. This was a surprise, as earlier Cohen had opposed the treaty on the grounds that it was "trading off textiles for gains in services, intellectual property and agriculture." Since entering the Senate in 1978, Cohen had been an established champion of his state's ailing shoe and textile manufacturers, but these industries had steadily lost jobs and political influence. Maine's economy was changing, and the senator was now lobbied heavily by export-oriented firms, many of them in the retail or service industries. In announcing his support for GATT, Cohen explained that "hundreds of Maine businessmen and women are succeeding in the world economy. Many of them represent small firms that, to take full advantage of export opportunities, need the help that GATT will provide." Cohen's stance also reflected pressure from the local press, which urged political leaders to vote for the state's future rather than its past. "A vote for GATT is a vote for Maine," asserted the *Portland Press Herald*, the state's largest circulation newspaper. What had occurred in the Pine Tree State was illustrative. In the winter of 1994, pressure from the national press and the business community helped to ensure that Congress ratified the GATT agreement.[46]

When the vote took place, other key industry supporters were no longer in office. In particular, several influential southern Democrats had been undermined by the rise of the Republican Party in the region. In January 1993, Ed Jenkins gave up his seat after eight terms, largely as a response to the increasing dominance of conservatives in Georgia. "The entire state really has become very conservative, and Republican," he explained later. As the industry crumbled, so did the political base of its most ardent supporters. In 1994, after twenty years in Congress, Butler Derrick also stood down and was replaced by Republican Lindsey Graham. Derrick's assertion that "it was time to do something else" was undoubtedly influenced by his failure to buck the Clinton White House over NAFTA. Also under threat in an increasingly conservative district, Marilyn Lloyd decided not to seek an eleventh term. After retiring from politics in 1994, Lloyd worked in her yard, went to church, and advocated for elderly Americans. Republican Zach Wamp replaced her.[47]

In his relations with the textile industry, President Clinton was clearly in the driving seat, and he duly pressed ahead with his free trade agenda. "The overriding commitment of this Administration in trade policy has been to open markets and expand trade," he declared. Clinton also promised to stem unfair trade practices by importers, but few executives believed that he would do so.[48] The Clinton White House saw NAFTA and GATT as significant accomplishments, including both on internal documents that summarized the administration's main achievements. Reflecting on the landmark agreements, as well as the accession of China to the WTO and the expansion of trade preferences for Caribbean Basin countries, the administration boasted in 2000 that it had "an unequalled record for opening foreign markets to U.S. exports and expanding prosperity through free trade."[49]

During Clinton's second term, an economic boom boosted the administration's confidence and encouraged Americans to overlook the desperate plight of the domestic textile and apparel industry. As the President's Council of Economic Advisers boasted in 1999, the United States had "never been more prosperous" or "as integrated into the world economy." The Council was in no doubt that the two things were linked. "America benefits from market liberalization," it confidently declared. Much of the press was also optimistic about what the *U.S. News and World Report* called the "sizzling economy."

Any jobs that were being lost were in "sunset industries," claimed economists, and they were being replaced by a greater number of "sunrise jobs." The recovery influenced U.S. policy to China and underpinned some important changes that occurred during the second term, especially as it was China's rapid growth that devastated the domestic textile industry.[50]

In these years Clinton followed a policy of "engagement" with China that was sharply at odds with the position taken by domestic textile leaders, especially the unions. In 1997 the administration renewed most-favored-nation trading status for the Asian power, chiefly on the grounds that this was the best way of integrating China into the international community. In October 2000, Clinton also signed historic legislation that granted China Permanent Normal Trade Relations status, and this followed presidential certification of the terms of China's accession to the WTO. The administration pitched China's accession to the WTO, which replaced GATT as an international organization, as a way of boosting American exports and promoting reform within China. Signed in November 1999, the U.S.-China bilateral WTO Agreement trumpeted improved market access for America's service sector, especially banks and telecommunication companies. In a recognition that the agreement would also allow for increased imports from China, it included a textile safeguard provision that was to remain in effect until December 31, 2008.[51]

The practice of transhipping—or the false relabeling of goods—also continued to fuel China's growth. It was widespread in Hong Kong, where Chinese apparel was unloaded and taken to local factories for finishing and relabeling. In other instances, phony labels such as "Made in Fiji" and "Made in Macao" were sewn into garments even before they left the Chinese factories. There was no way of knowing exactly how many clothes were transhipped, but it was clearly a vast industry. In 1996, the Clinton administration's annual report on foreign trade barriers found that China's illegal shipments were a major problem. Furthermore, the U.S. Customs Service estimated in a "painstaking study" that China's textile exports totaled $13 billion, yet the world's countries reported importing over $23 billion worth of textiles from the Asian nation. According to one U.S. official, China "would clothe most of the world if we let it." American policy makers made only half-hearted efforts to tackle the problem; illegal textile exports were not a high priority for the U.S. Customs Service, which was more interested in fighting drug trafficking and money laundering, and the State Department was reluctant to openly criticize China, especially when it was striving to join the WTO. American officials were also afraid of threatening lucrative exports to China, particularly from the agricultural sector.[52]

Much of the Chinese textile industry's expansion was legitimate, however, and the industry grew at a remarkable pace. As was the case in other developing countries, China's politicians promoted the industry because of its labor-intensive nature and its ability to generate valuable export revenue. In 1988, the state-run industry was China's biggest foreign exchange earner. By 2000, China's garment exports were worth $36.1 billion, fifty times more than in 1978. Chinese mills employed an amazing eighteen million workers, more than double the entire population of North Carolina, America's largest textile state.[53] Rather than Manchester, New Hampshire, the eastern Chinese city of Shengze was now home to a mill that measured more than a mile in length. Between 1999 and 2004, the number of mills in Shengze tripled. The industry dominated the economy of the small city, employing eighty thousand people and accounting for 90 percent of its tax revenue. Like their early American counterparts, moreover, most Chinese mill workers were rural migrants who relied on their employers for housing and subsidized recreational facilities. In another similarity with the industry's development in the United States, the Chinese workers were also predominantly young women.[54]

The difficulties of competing with this vast, low-paid workforce were immense. In 2002, the average wage of manufacturing production workers in China was fifty-seven cents an hour, or about 3 percent of the amount earned by their American counterparts. Rather than just relying on this cheap workforce, the Chinese industry was also modernizing. In the late 1990s, the number of workers fell as Chinese companies automated jobs to improve productivity, sharpening the industry's technological edge. Cuts were also driven by the privatization of China's manufacturing sector and by fierce global competition, but they were only temporary. According to the BLS, after 2002 the number of manufacturing workers in China increased by as much as 25 percent a year. In addition, China's manufacturing wages remained a "small fraction" of those paid to workers in "developed and newly industrialized Asian economies."[55]

In the United States, the industry's decline was accelerated by China's accession to the WTO, which was formally approved in 2001 after lengthy negotiations. Pointing to China's "violations of human rights," the AFL–CIO mounted an intensive campaign against admission. Although UNITE played a central role in the effort, the powerful free trade lobby again prevailed. Reassuring many doubters, the Clinton administration helped to secure the deal. "China's accession to the World Trade Organization will help promote reform, accountability, and openness in China," promised the president's press secretary in 2000. Determined critics responded that China had a poor record of living up to its international obligations, and the Asian power's increasing dominance of global textile production certainly allowed it to brush off Western criticisms of its labor practices and human rights record.[56]

Combined with the 1994 peso crisis in Mexico, which encouraged the shifting of low-wage manufacturing jobs to that country, the rapid emergence of China had a devastating effect on the U.S. textile and apparel industry.

Several years after the passage of NAFTA, the ATMI's leaders were still selling its benefits, yet a constant tide of plant closings was undermining their claims. In 1996, President James M. Fitzgibbons reiterated that NAFTA allowed U.S. companies to become major yarn and fabric exporters. Summing up the way that most of the industry had now rejected economic nationalism, Fitzgibbons declared that "the time has come for us to look beyond our borders. We have a lot to offer the rest of the world."[57]

At the grassroots level, however, people saw the situation very differently. Residents of affected communities again wrote to express their heartfelt frustration and pain. "I just wanted to let you know how much the NAFTA Treaty has hurt SC," explained Greenwood resident Georgeann M. Nickles to Senator Hollings in 2001. "All the textile plants around us are closing and I for the life of me cannot understand why our country is getting so dependent on other countries. What is going to happen to us?" In Roanoke Rapids, North Carolina, displaced WestPoint Stevens worker Polly Gibson also lashed out at the agreement. "I think NAFTA is one of the worst things that's happened to a lot of people," she declared in 2003. "It makes you ill."[58]

Press accounts of plant closings related similar views. In St. Pauls, North Carolina, where the first textile mill had been built before the town was even incorporated, local people blamed NAFTA for a string of plant closures. What had occurred in the little-known town on the Virginia and Coastal Railroad was replicated across the southern textile belt. "NAFTA is killing textiles in small towns just like it killed the steel plants in the North," summarized St. Pauls mayor Gordon Westbrook. In the North, where decline had been occurring for longer, some residents were more restrained. In eastern Pennsylvania, the industry had once employed tens of thousands of workers, but by the turn of the century only a handful remained. "All NAFTA did was hasten the outcome," thought Bill Schneider, the president of the Pennsylvania Apparel and Textile Association.[59]

On the ground, however, feelings also ran strong in the Keystone State, which lost 150,000 manufacturing jobs in the decade after NAFTA's passage. When Beaufab Mills closed its fabric mill in Stroudsburg in 1996, owner David Turk candidly identified the main culprit. "The North American Free Trade Agreement has hurt," he acknowledged. "We felt we wouldn't be vulnerable because we have state-of-the-art equipment. But we can't compete with the cheap labor in Mexico." Not surprisingly, local union president Beth Ann Berger endorsed these comments. "I'm with Mr. Turk," she explained. "NAFTA killed us." At the national level, textile union leaders remained fierce critics of the agreement. "NAFTA was extremely destructive to the manufacturing base in this country, particularly the apparel and textile industries," asserted Mark Levinson, UNITE's chief economist.[60]

Pennsylvania's Lehigh Valley illustrated how NAFTA and GATT finished off an industry that had been struggling for some time. As the *New*

*York Times*'s Michael Janofsky noted in a special feature, between 1972 and 1990 the region lost almost 54 percent of its apparel jobs, as companies tried to cope with increasing international competition and the high cost of doing business in the North. Further mill closures followed. Watching the passage of NAFTA and GATT, most workers were apprehensive. "It seems like a dying industry," commented thirty-seven-year-old mother of three Tammy Impechiate. "Used to be, there was a blouse mill on every corner. Even when I started out of high school 19 years ago, mills were everywhere. Now, it's scary." Worried that she was not qualified for other jobs, Impechiate was typical of the workforce as a whole. They were "men and women of modest means from modest towns," thought Janofsky, and they had "no idea what they could do" if the mills closed down. Many women relied on the industry's day shift, which allowed them to leave work before their children finished school. It was difficult to replicate this arrangement in the service sector. Like their counterparts in the South, some Lehigh workers were angry. "I blame Clinton," explained cutting room worker Ronnie Smith. "He lied like hell. . . . Everybody here's losing their job." Still, others managed to retain a black sense of humor. "Textiles are gone," declared Nancy Shoemaker, fifty-four, a single mother who had used her sewing job to raise three children. "We ought to have a Boston Tea Party for textiles, bomb the ships as they bring in the jobs. . . . I'm going to be on welfare, if the Republicans don't do away with it."[61]

In other parts of the North, the wave of closures eradicated what was left of a once-vast industry. Decades after the industry had begun to decline in Massachusetts, workers at Anglo Fabrics in Worcester lost their jobs in an import-related closure. Although not a surprise, the 1998 shutdown still hurt workers economically and psychologically. "There are a lot of families where both paychecks come from Anglo," explained Craig Provost, a loom technician. "They're getting burned badly." Kathy Dupont reflected on the experience of working in the plant as it gradually ground to a halt. "It's sad and depressing," she declared. "It's like being locked in a room for a month-long wake." Pointing to manufacturing's role in creating related jobs and in stimulating technological developments, some New Englanders insisted that the industry's demise had broader meaning. "Without manufacturing," wrote Howard N. Stewart from Manchester, New Hampshire, "a society is doomed to decline."[62]

Even some of the industry's most respected names fell victim to NAFTA. In 1996, Oregon-based Pendleton Woolen Mills, the makers of the iconic plaid shirt popularized by the Beach Boys, eliminated 235 production jobs in its home state. In the previous year, the company had closed two U.S. plants and moved production to Mexico. It blamed the outcome on NAFTA, which it had opposed. "We were one of the last recognizable brands to do this," explained human resources manager Gary Benson. "We didn't want to do this. But if everybody else goes to a less expensive labor area, what can we do?" Apparel workers in Mexico, Benson explained, received 11 percent of what the company paid its Oregon workforce, a huge disadvantage given that few consumers were willing to pay more for their clothing. The move was a significant shift for Pendleton, which had operated in Oregon since 1863. Global competition now threatened to remove the one small American factory that the company had left.[63]

Over time, more and more executives defied the ATMI and openly blamed NAFTA for plant closures. In Rutherford County, North Carolina, for example, Mastercraft Fabrics went through a series of layoffs and plant closures in the decade after the treaty was signed. The firm had once employed 3,500 people, but by 2005 only a couple of hundred remained, and they were mainly white-collar or administrative staff. "NAFTA has hurt us all," admitted Carol Cooper, the company's human resources administrator. "I don't care what the President says. NAFTA has destroyed the manufacturing production area of the United States." By 2003, former industry executive Jim Leonard had become Deputy Assistant Secretary of Commerce over textiles, and he acknowledged that things had not turned out as planned. "Early in NAFTA," he explained, "we had a positive trade balance with Mexico and were shipping a lot of raw materials there, but more American industries moved their operations to Mexico than anyone thought would."[64]

As the rate of plant closings increased, even ATMI leaders were forced to backtrack. By the tenth anniversary of NAFTA, Chuck Hayes's prediction that the agreement would lead to "the renaissance of the textile industry" had clearly not come true. As the *Dallas Morning News* commented, "Today, on the eve of NAFTA's 10th anniversary, that rebirth has yet to arrive. Instead, one round after another of mill closures, bankruptcies and job losses battered the industry." Although many executives blamed Chinese imports—rather than NAFTA—for their woes, some admitted that they had put too much faith in the agreement. "NAFTA didn't live up to anybody's expectations," acknowledged Allen Gant Jr. of Glen Raven Mills. A key problem was that the agreement's promised advantages fell victim to factors beyond its control. In particular, the 1997 Asian currency devaluations handed Far Eastern imports a significant price advantage in the U.S. market. Four years later Asian currencies were still valued at only 35 to 70 percent of their precrash levels, creating cheaper imports. In addition, the subsequent granting of tariff preferences to Caribbean countries enticed apparel makers away from Mexico. In the new millennium, both managers and union leaders watched as the industry disappeared. "The industry is doomed," declared Wayne Hill, Vanity Fair's vice president of textiles. "We used to compete against the mill down the street. Now we're up against the world." UNITE official Anthony Coles agreed. "I think we are seeing the end of the textile industry as we know it," he thought. For those who had depended on the industry for decades, this end came quickly, and the effects were painful and dramatic.[65]

## NOTES

1. Zieger, *American Workers, American Unions, Second Edition*, p. 203; Karl Kahler, "Dissolving the Borders on Trade," San Jose *Mercury News*, October 3, 1993, p. 20A; Cynthia Mitchell, "Textile, Apparel Industries Now Favor Free Trade," *Atlanta Constitution*, October 1, 1992, p. D1.

2. Cynthia Mitchell, "Textile, Apparel Industries Now Favor Free Trade," *Atlanta Journal-Constitution*, October 1, 1992, p. D1; Katherine Yung, "Industry's Boost from Trade Pact Didn't Last; China Seen as Spoiler," *Dallas Morning News*, September 28, 2003, p. 1D.

3. Ariel Hart, "North Carolina: A Case Against Free Trade," *New York Times*, October 18, 2003; "America's Textile Industry Is in Deep Crisis," Charleston (West Virginia) *Daily Mail*, January 5, 2002, p. 5C ("poster child" quotation); Jeffrey Gettleman, "Hitting a Snag: Globalization Putting New Wrinkles in Textile Industry," *Seattle Times*, March 12, 2002, p. A3 (Blankenship quotations). For another example of local officials and workers blaming NAFTA for textile and apparel plant closings, see: David Sinclair, "Whisper Knits Blames Closing on Free Trade," Fayetteville (North Carolina) *Observer*, September 29, 1998.

4. Gary Clyde Hufbauer and Jeffrey J. Schott, "NAFTA Revisited," p. 1, Peterson Institute for International Economics study available at http://www.iie.com/publications/papers/print.cfm?researchid=898&doc=pub (accessed November 29, 2010, copy in author's possession).

5. Jeff Faux, "Viewpoints: NAFTA at 10," EPI document available at http://www.epi.org/content.cfm/webfeatures_viewpoints_nafta_legacy_at10 (accessed April 24, 2008, copy in author's possession); "NAFTA: A Decade of Growth," p. 24, Business Roundtable Publication available at http://www.businessroundtable.org/publications (accessed April 28, 2008, copy in author's possession).

6. Dave Baity, "Cause of Lost Jobs Is Bigger Than NAFTA," *Charlotte Observer*, December 2, 2001, p. 1L; S. Gray Maycumber, "110 Years of Textiles; A Once-Booming Industry Now Faces Brutal Competition from Abroad," *Daily News Record*, December 31, 1991; Nash quoted in Jim Nesbitt, "Textile Trouble: Imports Will Cut U.S. Jobs, Close Plants, Experts Say," Augusta (Georgia) *Chronicle*, August 10, 2003, p. D1.

7. "Address by the President of Mexico, Carlos Salinas de Gortari, during the annual meeting of the American Society of Newspaper Editors" (at Harvard University), April 10, 1991, quotation on p. 12, "Trade-US-Mexico FTA and Fast Track Extension Parts 1 and 2" folder, box 33, Lloyd Papers.

8. "Text of Remarks by the President on the Enterprise for Americas Address," June 27, 1990 (Bush quotations), "GATT" folder, box 8, series 5780/150, ILGWU Papers-Cornell; Stuart Auerbach, "Farm, Textile and Labor Groups Oppose Goals of Bush, Big Business," *Washington Post*, March 2, 1991, p. A8.

9. Stuart Auerbach, "Farm, Textile and Labor Groups Oppose Goals of Bush, Big Business," *Washington Post*, March 2, 1991, p. A8.

10. Lawrence H. Kaufman, "US Textile Export Outlook Brightens, Gains May Help Cut Trade Deficit," *Journal of Commerce*, March 1, 1993, p. 3A (Leonard quotation); Cynthia

Mitchell, "Textile, Apparel Industries Now Favor Free Trade," *Atlanta Constitution*, October 1, 1992, p. D1 (other quotations).

11. "Textiles and Apparel in the North American Free Trade Agreement: A Summary," "GEB Meeting, New York, September 14–16, 1992" folder, box 1023, ACTWU Papers-Cornell.

12. NTA Press Release, September 20–22, 1992, 1992 NTA Annual Meeting Files, NTA Papers.

13. Karl Spilhaus to Bill Reed, August 6, 1993, 1993 NTA Annual Meeting Files, NTA Papers.

14. "Time to Compete, Not Retreat," *Southern Textile News*, April 25, 1994, p. 4.

15. Joan Lowy, "These Industries Would Be Winners under NAFTA," *Scripps Howard News Service*, October 30, 1993 (Bremer quotation); "Pact Puts Hollings, Textile Industry at Odds," *The State*, November 4, 1993, p. 6B (second quotation by Robert L. Thompson of Springs Industries).

16. Charles A. Hayes to Michael Kantor, August 4, 1993, 1993 Annual Meeting files, NTA Papers.

17. Walter Y. Elisha to Richard Gephardt, September 29, 1992, box 38, Butler Derrick Papers; Frank quoted in "Textile, Apparel, Retail Leaders' NAFTA Plans," *Daily News Record*, November 18, 1993, p. 5.

18. Rosen, *Making Sweatshops*, pp. 137–38, 154–56 (quotation in title); Michelle Haberland, "Women's Work: The Apparel Industry in the United States South, 1937–1980" (PhD dissertation, Tulane University, 2001), pp. 154–55; "Textile, Apparel, Retail Leaders' NAFTA Plans," *Daily News Record*, November 18, 1993, p. 5.

19. Don Johnson interview with author on June 23, 2010, in Athens, Georgia.

20. Stuart Auerbach, "Mexican Trade Pact Unravels the Once-Durable Textile Lobby," *Washington Post*, May 12, 1991, p. H1 (first three quotations); Karl Spilhaus to Jennifer Hillman, July 26, 1993 (first two Spilhaus quotations), "Theme of Partnership Evident throughout Northern Textile Association's 139th Annual Meeting," NTA Press Release, October 18, 1993 (penultimate quotation), and Karl Spilhaus to Ms. Thea Lee, September 8, 1993 (closing quotation), all 1993 NTA Annual Meeting Files, NTA Papers.

21. "NAFTA Splitting Textile Industry; Lobbyists Defend Opposing Stands," Spartanburg (South Carolina) *Herald-Journal*, November 5, 1993; Karl Spilhaus interview with author on April 26, 2011, in Boston, Massachusetts.

22. Cynthia Mitchell, "Textile, Apparel Industries Now Favor Free Trade," *Atlanta Constitution*, October 1, 1992, p. D1 (first quotation); Roger Milliken to Butler Derrick, July 7, 1993, box 41, Derrick Papers (Milliken quotation); "The Time Has Come," *Southern Textile News*, November 15, 1993, p. 4 (third quotation); John Maggs, "Knitwear Manufacturers Plan to Oppose NAFTA," *Journal of Commerce*, August 21, 1992, p. 3A (closing quotation).

23. Bill Hughes, "Free-Trade Agreement May Cost Jobs in S.C." *The State*, August 13, 1992, p. 1A (first Hollings quotation); Ernest F. Hollings to Edward E. Saleeby, November 18, 1993, box 9, 103rd Congress files, Hollings Papers (second and third Hollings quotations); "Pact Puts Hollings, Textile Industry at Odds," *The State*, November 4, 1993, p. 6B (last two quotations).

24. Keith Bradsher, "House Whip Relents on Using Office to Fight NAFTA," *New York Times*, September 11, 1993; Sander Levin et al. to Mickey Kantor, April 21, 1993, box 41, Derrick Papers; Butler Derrick to Tench P. Owens, October 5, 1993, box 41, Derrick Papers (Derrick quotations).

25. "NAFTA Controversy Continues in Textile Industry," NPR *Weekend Edition*, October 9, 1993 (transcript in author's possession). This transcript contains the *Wall Street Journal* quotation cited above.

26. Eddie G. Fullbright to Butler C. Derrick Jr., August 19, 1993, box 41, Derrick Papers; Phil Moore to Butler Derrick, September 9, 1993, box 41, Derrick Papers. For another similar example, this time from a mill owner, see John Hamrick to Ernest F. Hollings, November 24, 1993, box 9, 103rd Congress files, Hollings Papers. The Swett quotation is in "Grass Roots Choking Trade Agreement," Riverside (California) *Press-Enterprise*, September 12, 1993, p. A1.

27. ILGWU General Executive Board Minutes, October 15–17, 1991, p. 25, "ILGWU GEB Minutes 1991" folder, box 2, series 5780/150, ILGWU Papers-Cornell.

28. ILGWU GEB Minutes, October 15–17, 1991, p. 24, "ILGWU GEB Minutes, 1991" folder, box 2, series 5780/150, ILGWU Papers-Cornell; "The 2 Big Apparel Unions to Outline a Merger Today," *New York Times*, February 20, 1995, p. D1; "Siege" quotation in Frank Swoboda, "Labor's Day in Martinsville: In an Old Mill Town, Textile Workers Find a Rare Union Success," *Washington Post*, September 5, 1994, pp. 1, 16; E. J. Dionne Jr., "In a Changed Economy, Labor Tries New Tactics," *New York Times*, October 26, 1987, p. A15.

29. Susan Cowell to Jay Mazur, November 12, 1992, "LAC for Trade Negotiations, 1988–92" folder, box 21, series 6000/010, UNITE Papers-Cornell. These organizing campaigns are detailed further in chapter 8.

30. Laurel Kenner, "Free Trade: Who Wins?" Torrance (California) *Daily Breeze*, October 25, 1992, p. B2; Paul Nowell, "Trade Pact's Impact on U.S. Textile Industry Unclear," *Charlotte Observer*, August 26, 1992, p. 4 (Julian quotation).

31. Clinton quoted in White House Press Release, January 19, 1993, available from the William J. Clinton Presidential Library at http://clinton6.nara.gov/1993/01/1993-01-19-president-clinton-proclaims-world-trade-week.html (accessed August 29, 2010). For a good illustration of the Clinton administration's commitment to free trade, see also "Press Briefing by Secretary of the Treasury Lloyd Bensten," July 1, 1993, available at http://clinton6.nara.gov/1993/07/1993-07-01-briefing-by-sec-bensten.html (accessed August 29, 2010). Copies of all documents from the Clinton Library website are in the author's possession.

32. "Press Briefing by Dee Dee Myers," November 8, 1993, available at http://clinton6.nara.gov/1993/11/1993-11-08-dee-dee-myers-daily-briefing.html (accessed August 29, 2010); Gus Tyler, *Look for the Union Label: A History of the International Ladies' Garment Workers' Union* (Armonk, NY: M. E. Sharp, 1985), p. 270.

33. The White House, "Press Briefing by National Economic Adviser Gene Sperling and U.S. Trade Representative Charlene Barshefsky," November 24, 1999, p. 5, available at http://clinton4.nara.gov/WH/New/WTO-Conf-1999/briefings/19991124-1245.html (accessed August 29, 2010).

34. "The Clinton Administration Agenda for Seattle WTO: Expanding Opportunities for American Agriculture," December 1, 1999, available at http://clinton3.nara.gov/WH/New/WTO-Conf-1999/factsheets/fs-009.html (accessed August 29, 2010).

35. Rosen, *Making Sweatshops*, pp. 192–94, quotation on p. 194; Skinner quotations in Samuel K. Skinner to Leslie H. Wexner, March 5, 1992, TA004-13, White House Office of Records Management Subject File, Bush Library.

36. U.S. Chamber of Commerce, "North American Free Trade Agreement: Implications for U.S. Business," September 1991, p. i, "NAFTA B" folder, box 33, Lloyd Papers.

37. Bill Clinton to Butler Derrick, September 13, 1993, box 41, Derrick Papers (Clinton quotations); Gary Clyde Hufbauer and Jeffrey J. Schott, "NAFTA Revisited," p. 3, Peterson Institute for International Economics study available at http://www.iie.com/publications/papers/print.cfm?researchid=898&doc=pub (accessed November 29, 2010); Robert H. Zieger and Gilbert J. Gall. *American Workers, American Unions, Third Edition* (Baltimore: The Johns Hopkins University Press, 2002), pp. 263–64.

38. Clinton quoted in White House Press Release, January 19, 1993, available from the William J. Clinton Presidential Library at http://clinton6.nara.gov/1993/01/1993-01-19-president-clinton-proclaims-world-trade-week.html (accessed August 29, 2010); "Press Briefing by Secretary of the Treasury Lloyd Bensten," July 1, 1993 (Bensten quotations), available at http://clinton6.nara.gov/1993/07/1993-07-01-briefing-by-sec-bensten.html (accessed August 29, 2010). For a useful summary of the Uruguay Round from the website of the World Trade Organization, see http://www.wto.org/english/thewto_e/whatis__e/tif_e/fact5_e.htm (accessed January 12, 2011, copy in author's possession).

39. "Statement by the President," July 3, 1993, available at http://clinton6.nara.gov/1993/07/1993-07-02-uruguay-release.html (accessed August 29, 2010).

40. Marilyn Lloyd et al. to Carla Hills, June 14, 1990, "Hills Letters" folder, box 68, Lloyd Papers.

41. "ATMI President Calls Uruguay Round Agreement 'A Fraud on U.S. Industry,'" *Southern Textile News*, February 25, 1991, p. 1.

42. "Press Briefing by U.S. Trade Representative Ambassador Mickey Kantor," July 7, 1993, available at http://clinton6.nara.gov/1993/07/1993-07-07-press-briefing-by-mickey-kantor-japan.html (accessed August 29, 2010).

43. Don Johnson interview with author on June 23, 2010, in Athens, Georgia; "Press Briefing by Mickey Kantor, U.S. Trade Representative," December 10, 1993, available at http://clinton6.nara.gov/1993/12/1993-12-10-press-briefing-by-mickey-kantor-us-trade-representative.text.html (accessed August 29, 2010); Clinton quoted in "Statement of the President in Response to Rep. Gephardt's Decision to Support the Uruguay Round Implementing Legislation," December 21, 1993, available at http://clinton6.nara.gov/1993/12/1993-12-21-presidents-statement-on-gephardt-support-of-gatt.html (accessed August 29, 2010).

44. Rosen, *Making Sweatshops*, pp. 192–94.

45. "ATMI President Urges U.S. Textile Industry to Focus on Global Marketplace," *Southern Textile News*, April 3, 1995, pp. 1, 11.

46. First Cohen quotation in William S. Cohen, American Textile Institute Speech, February 26, 1991, "Trade-1985-95" folder, box 11, MS106.3.4.6, Cohen Papers; Second Cohen quotation in Senator William Cohen Press Release, December 1, 1994, "December 1994," folder, box 9, MS106.3.4.2, Cohen Papers; Betty Mills, "Cohen Joins in Bipartisan GATT Support," Brunswick (Maine) *Times Record*, December 2, 1994, clipping in "Summary of News Coverage" folder, box 52, MS106.3.4.5, Cohen Papers; "Will Sen. Cohen Vote for a Brighter Future?" Portland (Maine) *Press Herald*, December 1, 1994, clipping in "Summary of News Coverage," folder, box 52, MS106.3.4.5, Cohen Papers (closing quotation).

47. Ed Jenkins interview with author on June 25, 2010, in Jasper, Georgia (Jenkins quotations); Lacrisha Butler, "Jenkins Prepares to Leave Congress—With $300,000," *USA Today*, September 11, 1992; "Derrick's Retirement Loss to S.C., Congress," *The State*, February 18, 1994, p. 12A (closing quotation); Beverly Majors, "Lloyd Back on Campaign Trail," *The Oak Ridger*, April 29, 2010.

48. "Statement of the President in Response to Rep. Gephardt's Decision to Support the Uruguay Round Implementing Legislation," December 21, 1993, available at http://clinton6.nara.gov/1993/12/1993-12-21-presidents-statement-on-gephardt-support-of-gatt.html (accessed August 29, 2010).

49. "Keeping Faith with America: A Look at President Clinton's Accomplishments during the First Two Years," undated but ca. 1995, available at http://clinton1.nara.gov/White_House/Accomplishments/html/accomp-plain.html (accessed August 29, 2010); "A Nation Transformed: Clinton-Gore Administration Accomplishments, 1993–1999," undated, available at http://clinton3.nara.gov/WH/Accomplishments/foreign.html (accessed August 29, 2010); Quotation in "Opening Global Markets and Expanding Prosperity," undated but ca. 2000, available at http://clinton5.nara.gov/WH/EOP/NSC/html/nsc-19.html (accessed August 29, 2010).

50. "America's Interest in the World Trade Organization: An Economic Assessment" (A Report by the Council of Economic Advisers), November 16, 1999, p. 1 (first three quotations), available at http://clinton5.nara.gov/media/pdf/WTO-Final.pdf (accessed August 29, 2010); Amy Saltzman, "Making It in a Sizzling Economy," *U.S. News and World Report*, June 23, 1997, p. 50; William J. Holstein, "The New Economy," *U.S. News and World Report*, May 26, 1997, p. 42 ("sunset" and "sunrise" quotations).

51. Quotation in "Press Briefing by National Security Advisor Sandy Berger and USTR Ambassador Charlene Barshefsky," May 19, 1997, available at http://clinton2.nara.gov/New/Remarks/Mon/19970519-8419.html (accessed August 29, 2010); The White House, "Engaging China to Promote and Protect American Interests," October 2000, available at http://clinton5.nara.gov/WH/EOP/NSC/html/nsc-03.html (accessed August 29, 2010); The White House, "Summary of U.S.-China Bilateral WTO Agreement," November 16, 1999, available at http://clinton4.nara.gov/WH/New/WTO-Conf-1999/factsheets/fs-006.html (accessed August 29, 2010).

52. Raymond Bonner, "Altering Labels, Not Clothes, China Sidesteps Trade Limits," *New York Times*, April 1, 1997, p. A4.

53. P. T. Bangsberg, "China Urged to Boost Investment to Stay in Global Textile Race," *Journal of Commerce*, January 12, 1988, p. 4A; "China-Made Garments Said to Account for One-Fifth of Global Market," *Xinhua News Agency*, April 30, 2001, in "Trade: China WTO-107th Congress" folder, box 16, series 6000/007, UNITE Papers-Cornell; Stella M. Hopkins, "Tough Times Ahead for Home Textiles," *The Charlotte Observer*, December 12, 2004, p. 1D; "Chinese Premier Praises 1999 Textile Industry Profits," *BBC Monitoring International Reports*, January 25, 2000. This last item is based on a report from the Xinhua News Agency.

54. Stella M. Hopkins, "Textile Jobs: Goodbye U.S., Hello China," *Charlotte Observer*, November 21, 2004, p. 1A; Dublin, *Women at Work*, pp. 23–57; Pun Ngai, *Made in China: Women Factory Workers in a Global Workplace* (Durham: Duke University Press, 2005), pp. 1–6.

55. Judith Banister, "Manufacturing Earnings and Compensation in China," *Monthly Labor Review*, August 2005, p. 22; "Testimony of NCTO President Cass Johnson," U.S.-China Economic and Security Review Commission Public Hearing, January 2005, available at http://www.ncto.org/tradejobs/index.asp (accessed August 20, 2009); Erin Lett and Judith Banister, "China's Manufacturing Employment and Compensation Costs: 2002–06," *Monthly Labor Review* 132:4 (April 2009), pp. 31, 37 (quotations).

56. John J. Sweeney to Senator, March 14, 2000 (first quotation), and "The U.S.-China WTO Agreement Will Help Promote Reform, Accountability, and Openness in China," White House Press Release, March 8, 2000 (second quotation), both folder 2, box 11, series 6000/010, UNITE Papers-Cornell.

57. "ATMI President Urges U.S. Textile Industry to Look beyond Its Borders," *Southern Textile News*, November 4, 1996, p. 1.

58. Georgeann M. Nickles to Ernest Hollings, June 22, 2001, box 9, 107th Congress files, Hollings Papers; Gibson quoted in Katherine Yung, "Trade Deal Hurts U.S. Textiles," *Dallas Morning News*, October 19, 2003, p. F1.

59. Venita Jenkins, "Historic Ties Unravel," *Fayetteville Observer*, September 2, 2001 (Westbrook quotation); Mariella Savidge, "Textiles in Transition: Eastern PA. Keeps Losing Textile Jobs, and Deals Like NAFTA Are Only Part of the Reason," Allentown (Pennsylvania) *Morning Call*, April 18, 1999, p. D1 (Schneider quotation).

60. "Research Center Finds Reason Not to Cheer NAFTA," Erie (Pennsylvania) *Times-News*, December 21, 2003, p. 1; Dan Shope, "Beaufab Mills to Close, 80 Workers to Lose Jobs," Allentown (Pennsylvania) *Morning Call*, May 18, 1996, p. B24 (Turk and Berger quotations); Levinson quoted in Michael Davis, "NAFTA Ten Years Later: Jury Still Out over Impact on Virginia, Rest of Nation," Norfolk (Virginia) *Virginian-Pilot*, January 11, 2004, p. D1.

61. Michael Janofsky, "Trade Pact Casts Shadow for Garment Workers," *New York Times*, December 12, 1994, p. A14.

62. John Dignam, "Anglo Nears End of Era: Workers Cope with Closing," Worcester (Massachusetts) *Telegram and Gazette*, March 16, 1998, p. B1; Stewart quoted in "Loss of Manufacturing a Serious Blow for U.S." Kennebec (Maine) *Journal*, November 26, 2005, p. 5A.

63. "Pendleton Woolen Mills' Future in US Not Sewn Up," *Journal of Commerce*, December 23, 1996, p. 4A (Benson quotations); Nick Freeth, *Made in America: From Levi's to Barbie to Google* (St. Paul: MBI Publishing Company, 2005), p. 214.

64. Jean Gordon, "Mastercraft Cuts 115 Jobs at Oakland Plant," Forest City (North Carolina) *Daily Courier*, July 19, 2005 (Cooper quotations); Leonard quoted in Steven Stiefel, "Trade Impacts Local Jobs," Fort Payne (Alabama) *Times-Journal*, September 26, 2003. For other similar examples of plant closures blamed on NAFTA, see Chris Gautreau, "A Disappearing Industry: Textile Jobs in Louisiana, Southeast Continuing to Suffer from GATT, NAFTA trade agreements," Baton Rouge (Louisiana) *Advocate*, February 10, 2002, p. 1L; Al Greenwood, "Jobless Seek Employment," Fayetteville (North Carolina) *Observer*, August 19, 2001.

65. Charles A. Hayes to Michael Kantor, August 4, 1993, 1993 Annual Meeting files, NTA Papers (Hayes quotation); "U.S. Textile Makers Cut Jobs, Close Mills as NAFTA Hopes Fray," *Dallas Morning News*, September 28, 2003, p. 1D (Gant and Coles quotations); Fran Daniel, "Textile Industry Steps Up Efforts to Level Playing Field with Asia, Keep Jobs in U.S."

Winston-Salem (North Carolina) *Journal*, June 14, 2001, p. 1A; Jeffrey Gettleman, "Hitting a Snag: Globalization Putting New Wrinkles in Textile Industry," *Seattle Times*, March 12, 2002, p. A3 (Hill quotation).

## *Chapter Eight*

# A Tidal Wave: The Collapse of the Industry in the New Millennium

In the first decade of the twenty-first century, the U.S. textile and apparel industry collapsed at a dramatic and unprecedented pace. Between January 2001 and January 2005, for example, the BLS reported that the industry lost a remarkable 373,800 jobs, or 35.7 percent of its total capacity.[1] On January 1, 2005, moreover, all global textile and apparel quotas were lifted, a move that paved the way for massive domestic job losses. From 2000 to 2010, employment in the industry plummeted from over one million workers to around four hundred thousand, and this latter figure is still falling. If job losses continue at their current pace, an industry that has existed in the American Republic since its foundation will soon be virtually extinct.[2]

The industry's demise was widespread, and it had national consequences. As the *Southern Textile News* noted in 2004, the downfall of this "once-vibrant manufacturing sector" had caused "premature gray hair from Woonsocket to Westpoint."[3] Because the bulk of the northern industry had been lost before the turn of the century, however, the post-2000 decline was felt most acutely in the South. Between 2000 and 2007, half of all textile and apparel jobs in the Carolinas—the industry's heartland—were lost. "The states, once reliant on textiles as an economic backbone," wrote *Charlotte Observer* reporter Tony Mecia, "now employ just 116,000 people in the industry out of a total workforce of about 6 million."[4]

The pace of the decline surprised even seasoned observers. Among those most affected was Harris Raynor, a straight-talking New Yorker who had worked as UNITE's southern director since the mid-1990s. In an interview conducted in 2010, Raynor admitted that he was "shocked" by the way the industry had "left so quickly," causing devastation for workers across the region. He added, "As far as the union is concerned this was an absolute tidal wave, and it was what drove this union to . . . shrink in size."[5] In 2002, respected North Carolina think tank MDC similarly compared the industry's decline to a "tsunami."[6] While the industry's problems had been evident for decades, the speed of its demise also surprised professional economists. In 1997, BLS economist Mark Mittelhauser had predicted in the *Monthly Labor Review* that the industry could adjust to increased competition and would still provide more than 1.3 million jobs in 2005. According to Mittelhauser, the industry was showing "tenacity" and would not disappear rapidly. In fact, at the start of 2005 only 673,400 jobs—about half the number predicted—remained. As late as 2004, the BLS forecast that textiles and apparel would still provide 449,800 positions in 2012, a target that also proved unrealistic.[7]

In these years, moreover, textile and apparel workers continued to symbolize both the broader decline of the manufacturing sector and the central role that trade played in causing job losses. Between 1994 and 2001, over one million American workers were certified as eligible for Trade Adjustment Assistance (TAA) or NAFTA–TAA, an extension of the program that was designed to assist those hurt by NAFTA. Of these one million, 35 percent were textile and apparel workers.[8] The first decade of the new century was a terrible time for American manufacturing, which lost over five million jobs. As was the case in textiles, many of these losses were inextricably linked to the rise of China. In April 2010, the Alliance for American Manufacturing estimated that the trade gap with China had cost the United States 2.4 million jobs over the previous decade. Asked to explain the textile industry's recent collapse, Harris Raynor replied succinctly, "Competition with China."[9]

The TAA figures highlight that the textile and apparel industry had been hit hard by imports, as the Department of Labor would not certify workers unless there was a compelling case that they had lost their jobs because of foreign competition. By the new millennium, even free-traders admitted that imports were increasing faster than they had anticipated. In 2004, the Harvard Center for Textile and Apparel Research, which tended to support trade liberalization, estimated in a careful study that textile and clothing imports had doubled in volume over the previous eight years. Inevitably, the ending of quotas would only make the situation worse.[10]

Quota abolition was a defining event. Under the WTO's Agreement on Textile and Clothing (ATC), all volume quotas on textile and apparel goods were phased out over a ten-year period between January 1, 1995, and January 1, 2005. These quotas had been in force since the Short-Term Agreement of 1961, which had regulated the textile trade through product-specific, bilateral agreements. The ATC was the product of seven years of negotiations under the Uruguay Round (1988 to 1994), and its goal was to bring the MFA quota system to an end. Quotas were removed in three stages, lasting three, four, and three years respectively. At each stage, a defined minimum volume percentage of a country's imports in 1990 were to be placed off quota. For the United States, for example, 16 percent of its clothing and textile imports would be removed from quota protection during phase 1 (1995 to 1997), with the Americans able to choose which would be selected. The ATC represented a dramatic change, especially as it covered the vast majority of imports. In 2002, for instance, 93 percent of textile and apparel goods entering the United States came from WTO members. Furthermore, the ATC's scope was much more extensive than earlier agreements because it applied to all products regardless of whether they had been covered by restrictions during the MFA period. As the Harvard Center for Textile and Apparel Research put it, the abolition of quotas represented a "monumental liberalization of international trade."[11]

The ATC also included a special "safeguard" that allowed countries, during the transition period, to apply member-by-member quantitative quotas for up to three years if the receiving nation had experienced "serious damage" to its domestic industry. In the United States, it was up to the Commerce Department's Committee for the Implementation of Textile Agreements (CITA) to decide if safeguard relief was appropriate. If the committee approved an industry petition, a consultation process was begun with the importing country. If no agreement was forthcoming, the United States could impose its own restrictions, although the WTO's Textiles Monitoring Body could review these. Restrictions could be no lower than the level of imports in that category in the year before the petition was filed.[12] Overall, the safeguard provisions were only of limited help, especially as they failed to roll back imports or link them to the growth of the domestic market. As a result, textile executives did not look forward to the new millennium. As the *Southern Textile News* reported in 1999, the industry was racked by "closings, layoffs, consolidations and mergers," and the companies that remained were "hanging on for dear life." As quotas were removed, the *News* knew that there would be further closures. "The prospects are frightening," it acknowledged.[13]

The early years of the new century duly delivered a litany of negative news. In the closing days of the Clinton administration, Congress passed the U.S.-Caribbean Basin Trade Enhancement Act, which was often referred to as the Caribbean Basin Initiative. Designed to boost American fabric sales to Caribbean apparel makers, the Act allowed twenty-four Caribbean nations to import apparel products quota-free and duty-free if they were made from U.S. fabric. While the idea attracted some support from the ATMI, once again there were divisions. Opponents pointed out that the Act encouraged foreign-owned firms to set up knitting mills in the Caribbean, adding to global oversupply and putting more pressure on domestic manufacturers. Less than a year after its passage, moreover, even ATMI leaders were complaining that their government was not enforcing regulations that the fabric and yarn needed to be "wholly formed" in the United States in order to benefit from the law. Around the same time as the Caribbean Basin Initiative was implemented, similar provisions were extended to forty-eight nations in sub-Saharan Africa, worrying many in the industry. Keen to get the laws on the books before he left office, President Clinton promoted them heavily.[14]

If 2001 was a turning point for the United States, the textile and apparel industry was again a barometer of broader trends. As the *Southern Textile News* admitted, it was a "dreadful year." In the course of the twelve months, the industry lost a staggering $356 million, laid off 148,000 workers, and closed more than one hundred plants. The downturn caused by 9/11 added to the industry's problems, and textile stocks became almost worthless. For an industry that depended heavily on consumer confidence, 9/11 was especially damaging. "Consumer demand for textile products and apparel fell sharply after Sept. 11," summarized the Greensboro *News and Record.*[15]

While most closures occurred in the South, other parts of the country were also affected. Shutting a mill was a painful process for many executives, especially when they lived in communities dependent on their factories. Ultimately, the emotions that managers experienced were very similar right across the country. In December 2001, for example, Seville Dyeing Company announced that it was closing its operations in Woonsocket, Rhode Island. Vice President Nicholas Picciotti, who had helped to found the company with his brother, wrote President Bush to describe his feelings. "It breaks my heart to have to make that announcement," he explained. "I have had many loyal and dedicated workers in my employ for many years. I feel I have betrayed them." In a seven-page letter, Picciotti blamed federal trade policies for his company's demise, which had left him and many of his workers in tears. There was no record of a reply from Bush, although in general the president expressed sympathy for textile workers but insisted that his policies were creating jobs.[16] In the same year, when plant supervisor Leonard Huffstetler informed workers that Doran Mills in Shelby, North Carolina, was closing, he also found it a traumatic experience. Like many of the employees, Huffstetler had worked at the plant since high school. "I stayed up all night," he recalled. "I sat at the table and drank coffee. I knew a lot of people were going to be hurt."[17]

In 2001, a key trade vote accelerated the industry's demise. At the end of the year, the administration won a House vote to secure Trade Promotion Authority (TPA) by just one vote (215–214) after putting pressure on southern Republicans to toe the line. As the *Southern Textile News* reported, the textile industry took "center stage" in the debate, as the administration promised Republicans from textile districts several concessions, including greater access to export markets. The vote meant that the new president had the authority to "fast track" trade deals, with the Senate and House allowed only up or down votes on the agreements. Because Bush was committed to trade liberalization, the vote had important ramifications.[18]

In order to win the vote, Bush also promised to help textile workers. Appealing for support, the president visited struggling textile communities in North Carolina's Eight District, including Kannapolis, Concord, Laurinburg, and Rockingham. Bush insisted that the textile industry would remain "a cornerstone of U.S. manufacturing," while Commerce Secretary Donald Evans toured a mill and pledged a "level playing field" for American manufacturers. Once again, employer groups were willing to trust a Republican administration. According to the *Southern Textile News*, Bush was "a man of his word," and executives should "have confidence in this administration." In contrast, the unions criticized Bush and Republican members from textile districts who had voted for Fast Track. Led by UNITE, organized labor targeted many of these officials and pressured them to do more to help the manufacturing sector.[19]

Even as the industry hemorrhaged thousands of jobs, many employers were reluctant to criticize Bush, especially in the South. In 2002, the *Southern Textile News* admitted that these were "times of despair," but editor Mason "Chip" Smith continued to believe that the administration would help. "But you have to hand it to Evans and the rest of the Bush administration," he declared. "They are making an effort to reach out to this battered industry, hear its concerns and commit to doing something about the problems it is encountering. As we have said in this publication, that's more than was done by a previous administration." Even as frustration mounted within the industry—especially in the North—the *News* called for caution. "We ask that you be patient," wrote Smith in March 2002, "at least until the industry sees solid results."[20] In 2002, however, the industry's plight worsened. Early in the year, ATMI president Chuck Hayes declared that the industry was experiencing "the worst economic period" in its history. By February, five major textile firms were in bankruptcy, including Pillowtex, Burlington Industries, Guilford Mills, and Malden Mills. Imports and the poor environment in retail continued to be the major problems. The CEO of Guilford Mills, Hayes tried to juggle the leadership of his embattled company with the massive task of heading the ATMI. At a time when the industry association desperately needed strong leadership, the presidency was rotated among practicing executives, a further weakness.[21]

The industry's decline did produce some political response, especially in the South. In the spring of 2002, for example, the Democratic governors of Virginia, North Carolina, South Carolina, and Georgia convened a "textiles summit" to discuss ways to address the industry's "collapse." The gathering was held in Gaston County, North Carolina, a struggling area west of Charlotte that *The State* described as "ground zero when it comes to displaced textile workers." As well as the governors, around three hundred local politicians and industry representatives attended. Out of the summit came a range of recommendations to preserve the industry, including proposed penalties for countries that devalued their currency. "The major reason for textile layoffs is the currency devaluations in Asia since 1997," explained Hayes. "When the dollar is so strong, the imports come in here. . . . They can make a profit by bringing [in] that cheap crap." A large, forthright man, Hayes echoed the findings of "Crisis in U.S. Textiles," an ATMI study that blamed the industry's decline on "illegal Asian imports and weak Asian currencies." Revealingly, the report tried to downplay NAFTA's role in causing the crisis.[22] Many of the summit's recommendations were clearly aimed at the Bush administration, and several attendees accused the president of not keeping his promises. On the whole, Bush continued to champion free trade, and it was revealing that while the summit was being held the president was visiting Mexico to promote further trade links.[23]

While the U.S. economy picked up in 2003, the textile industry's downward plight continued. In July, Pillowtex went out of business, taking 7,650 employees with it. As the *Southern Textile News* noted, the fall of the one-hundred-year-old company "sent huge shock waves through the industry and the Southeast," and as such it is a closure that warrants detailed exploration.[24] The shutdown was clearly related to the abolition of quotas, which caused a loss of confidence in the domestic industry. In the aftermath of the Pillowtex announcement, UNITE-led efforts to find a buyer willing to take over the plants got nowhere. "The answer we got back is how can we invest in this industry knowing what's going to happen in 2005," recalled Harris Raynor.[25] In September, Cone Mills also collapsed. Founded in 1891, Cone grew to become one of the largest denim producers in the country, but in the 1980s and 1990s it lost most of its market to Asian imports. The move highlighted how the textile and apparel industries were inextricably linked, as Cone's announcement came just days after Levi Strauss announced the closing of its last four manufacturing and finishing plants in North America. For ninety years, Levi's had been Cone's largest customer, but now the apparel firm had completed its shift away from owned-and-operated manufacturing.[26]

The high-profile closures at Cone and Pillowtex also helped to spur political action. In November 2003, 165 members of Congress signed letters to Bush urging him to invoke the safeguard provision against China, while other representatives wrote individually with the same demands. The letters served as a reminder that the industry still had lobbying power, even in the North. "Recently, there have been announcements of major plant closings in Massachusetts and Maine," explained William Giblin, the chairman of the Northern Textile Association. "The crisis in the textile and apparel industry isn't regional, it's national. That's why members of Congress from California to Maine have signed letters released today." A key lobby group with strong textile links, the American Manufacturing Trade Action Coalition (AMTAC) claimed that it had coordinated the transmission of about thirty thousand emails and letters to Washington, D.C., and all contained the same demands. The effort paid off, as at the end of November the Commerce Department granted safeguard relief on three textile products imported from China—knit fabrics, brassieres, and dressing gowns. Now, negotiations began with the Chinese to limit the influx of these items, and the Americans could take unilateral action if no agreement was reached. Still, the vast majority of imports were unaffected. As mill owner Steve Dobbins admitted, "We won a little skirmish, but we haven't begun to win the battle." Some executives were less conciliatory. "Everybody knows the answer," fumed North Carolina mill owner Gerald Cauthen. "They don't have the guts to step up and turn the ships back to China."[27]

Responding to anger in the industry—especially in the politically important South—Bush made another visit to struggling textile communities in North Carolina. During his November trip to the Winston-Salem area, it was no accident that the president talked with Scott Hiner, a former mill supervisor who was using the TAA program to retrain for a career in biotechnology. Like many conservatives, Bush argued that retraining was the main solution to the industry's problems, and he liked to stress individual success. "In other words," he commented, "things are beginning to brighten up for people looking for work, which is positive. And, therefore, we must make sure that people are trained for jobs that exist."[28]

Occurring in the final days of 2003, the shutdown of Levi Strauss's last factories in the United States was another significant marker in the industry's decline. Although some plants still performed contract work, almost all of the company's jeans would now be made in Asia and the Caribbean. The move was important because Levi's jeans were so well known. As the *San Francisco Chronicle* noted, the company's pants were "an American classic" and "the very fabric of America." By the time of the closures more than 3.5 billion pairs of the riveted, red-tag jeans had been made in the United States, and virtually every American had pulled on a pair at some time. They had been popularized by high-profile celebrities such as Madonna and James Dean and had featured prominently on Bruce Springsteen's backside on *Born in the U.S.A*, his best-selling album. With some justification, the company claimed that its jeans were "the consummate American icon." Along with products such as Coca-Cola, Wrigley's gum, and John Deere tractors, Levi's regularly made lists of "all-American products," one of the only textile and apparel products to do so. "It's the end of an era," commented sociologist Patricia Leavy, as the last plants in San Antonio fell silent.[29]

This feeling was shared by workers at the factories, who reacted with a mixture of anger and sadness at the news. "I make $12 an hour," commented Tonie Ann from San Antonio. "The people who'll be doing the work, they get paid $12 a week. They'll be saving money but using out-of-the-country manufacturers, and I don't think the quality will be as good." Disputing this assertion, Levi's managers stressed that the company was moving away from manufacturing and becoming "marketing and product-driven." The final closures came after several previous layoffs, which were linked to competition from retailers such as Old Navy, JCPenney, and Wal-Mart. These stores sold cheaper jeans that were made for them overseas. Levi Strauss had once operated sixty-three manufacturing plants in the United States, but closures in 1997, 1999, and 2002 reduced this number. Most of Levi's plants had been unionized, and even production jobs provided decent pay and benefits to a workforce that included many black and Hispanic women. In San Antonio, where the labor force was 75 percent female and 95 percent Latino, most employees had been at the plant for at least twenty years, and they earned $10 to $12 an hour even when their knowledge of English was limited. Now, they wondered where they could get another job that paid as well. "They have to go back to the beginning," summarized worker Alma Martinez.[30]

In 2004, there were divergent reactions as the industry and its opponents prepared for the abolition of quotas. Insisting that mill owners had been overprotected for decades, free-traders eagerly anticipated the move. "The end of textile quotas presents a textbook opportunity to realize the benefits of free trade," declared the *New York Times*. "Gone are the days when President John Kennedy, seeking to coddle New England knitting mills in Fall River, Woonsocket and New Bedford, first introduced the world to the quota program that has severely limited American imports of clothing from other countries." In a similar vein, the *New Republic* agreed that it was time to end the industry's "protectionist regime." Keenly awaiting the change, the United States Association of Importers of Textiles and Apparel even put a clock on its website that counted down the time left until the quotas expired. In contrast, most mill owners were apprehensive, especially as they realized that they would have to compete head-on with China. "The prospect is frightening," wrote the *Southern Textile News* on the eve of quota abolition, "unless you're an importer champing at the bit to aid and abet a country that undervalues its currency, engages in intellectual property theft, tranships its goods, closes its markets, et al."[31]

The industry's fears were understandable. In December 2004, *Charlotte Observer* writer Stella M. Hopkins traveled to China in order to complete a special series on the ending of quotas. She concluded that China would be "the big winner" when the final restrictions were lifted. To back this up, she showed what had happened in categories where quotas had already been removed. In 2002, for example, blankets lost import protection, and as a result China's share of the American market increased from less than 7 percent to over 25 percent in just one year. Hopkins noted, moreover, that after January 1 more than forty countries would be free to ship unlimited amounts of textile goods to American stores. "That is devastating new competition for business that belonged to the Carolinas for a century," concluded Hopkins.[32] Still, the industry got little sympathy from supporters of globalization, who accused it of hypocrisy. "Low-wage (non-union) southern U.S. states once were happy to lure jobs away from New England and New York City," wrote Greg Rushford in the *Far Eastern Economic Review*, which tended to promote the interests of Asian textile producers. "Now they cry foul when economic logic dictates that such employment can be performed more efficiently by low-wage (non-union) Asian countries."[33]

As the deadline approached, the textile industry ramped up its campaign for public support. In October 2004, industry groups launched a grassroots campaign that was designed to highlight America's "broken" trade policy before the presidential election. In North Carolina, they erected forty-eight billboards in at least thirty-two communities. All declared "Stop Sending Jobs Overseas: Fix Trade Policy Now." In addition to the boards, textile companies used the same slogan on bumper stickers and yard signs, many of which were displayed by workers and concerned citizens. In South Carolina, AMTAC erected billboards that were personal and hard-hitting. "Lost Your Job To 'Free Trade' and Offshoring Yet?" they asked. Although the campaign was nonpartisan, it was clearly designed to put pressure on the Bush administration.[34]

Bush countered with his own offensive. On the eve of the 2004 election, the president visited Charlotte and met with displaced textile workers. He also took part in a town hall forum that featured three local women, including a laid-off mill worker. "I know what it's like here with the textile industry," he declared, "It's been hit hard." The president discussed the industry's plight in detail and promised to take a tough stance against China and other foreign competitors. "What I'm saying to other nations is, 'You treat us the way we treat you.' If you want to trade with us and you treat us fairly, Americans can compete with anybody, anytime, anywhere." The key question was whether these pledges meant anything, and even some Republicans doubted that they did. Nevertheless, Bush's visit clearly helped to shore up support for the GOP in the textile belt.[35]

Although many passing motorists noticed the billboards, they failed to have a decisive impact on voting behavior. In the presidential election, Bush still won a second term, although the result was close and the winner was not determined until the day after the vote. Clearly, however, many workers—and industry executives—stuck with the GOP despite their misgivings about its trade policies. In the insecure post-9/11 environment, the party was perceived as a stronger defender of national security, a key advantage. In addition, many voters felt that the Republicans were more supportive of gun ownership and more opposed to abortion, important issues in the Bible Belt. Even in North Carolina's textile-dominated eighth district, Republican congressman Robin Hayes—who had come under fire for supporting fast track at the last moment in 2001—was easily reelected. A native of Kannapolis and the grandson of textile magnate Charles Cannon, Hayes was seen as a traitor by some mill workers, but this was not enough to unseat him. Hayes's district also included conservative suburbs in eastern Charlotte, and this helped him to win.[36]

The ongoing support of the industry's main publication also helped Bush. In late 2004, for example, the *Southern Textile News* praised Jim Leonard, the deputy assistant secretary of commerce who had previously worked for Burlington Industries. "Leonard understands the pain the industry is enduring," it declared.[37] On the eve of election, the *News* still backed Bush rather than John Kerry, declaring that the president was a stronger defender of national security. "Traditionally, at least in the South, most folks with manufacturing interests lean Republican," it explained. Only later would the *News* criticize the administration, and even then it did so in muted terms.[38]

A few weeks after the election, the final quotas were abolished. As predicted, the move triggered a surge in imports from China and other low-wage countries, something that even free-traders were forced to acknowledge. The *New York Times* used trade figures from the Chinese government to show that textile and apparel imports from China jumped 75 percent in the first month after quotas were lifted. Its headline, "Free of Quota, China Textiles Flood the U.S," summarized developments well.[39] In the ensuing months, the trend continued. In December 2005, an analysis by the Harvard Center for Textile and Apparel Research acknowledged that "imports from China have surged since the elimination of quotas on January 1, 2005." Using data collected from the Department of Commerce's Office of Textiles and Apparel, the Center found that apparel imports from China jumped 85 percent in the first eight months of 2005 compared to the previous year's levels. In the high-volume cotton shirt category, they grew by over 250 percent. Still, the Center insisted that domestic firms could compete, especially as they were closer to the consumer market.[40]

The Bush administration responded to these developments. Following industry complaints, in May the administration got thirty-four "sensitive" textile items put back under quota as part of a four-year bilateral agreement with China. Ardent free-traders were not impressed with the administration's moves to placate the industry. "What they're doing is just delaying the inevitable," declared Heritage Foundation economist Aaron Schavey. Despite this effort, the Chinese continued to make inroads. By 2008, the industry claimed that China had a 39.6 percent share of the U.S. textile and apparel import market, up from 24.5 percent in 2004. On January 1, 2009, the bilateral agreement expired, and the United States could not reimpose the restrictions, allowing China to make further gains.[41]

In both the North and South, many plant closures were linked to the lifting of quotas. For struggling firms in the North, the move was often the final nail in the coffin. In December 2004, for example, Hoffman Mills announced that it would be shutting a mill in Shippensburg, Pennsylvania, that had been weaving fabric for over sixty years. Around 330 people in the small community lost their jobs. In a statement, the company blamed "the faltering nature of our business here within the United States and increased competition with China" for the move. With all quotas about to be removed, the company concluded that its situation was "dire and hopeless."[42]

Some northern mills that had been doing much better, however, were also eliminated at this time. In Fall River, Massachusetts, quota abolition had a devastating impact upon Quaker Fabric Corporation. As recently as 2003, the fabric maker had employed 2,500 people, but the situation changed quickly once quotas were removed. In 2007, the company laid off its last nine hundred workers, with chief executive Larry A. Liebenow blaming "fierce competition from imported Chinese fabrics" for the outcome. The move devastated Fall River, an historic mill town with a weak economy. In 2009, the *Boston Globe* reported that the city's unemployment rate was 16 percent, twice the state average. The local "career center" was one of the busiest places in town. "We're used to fighting for survival every day," explained resident Kenneth Fiola Jr., "even in the good times, because we've lost so many manufacturing jobs." Other northern mill centers had a similar experience. In Biddeford, Maine, Chinese competition claimed the local blanket mill, which had operated for 159 years. Many workers cried when they heard the news. "It's the end of a fine, fine era," declared George "Pete" Lamontagne, a city councilor who had worked in the plant for thirty-seven years.[43]

In the South, the quota shakeup also claimed plenty of casualties. In early 2005, for example, WestPoint Stevens claimed that "lower-cost textile imports" had forced it to slash jobs in the Carolinas and Virginia and file for bankruptcy.[44] Other notable closures occurred just as quotas were lifted. In South Carolina, Springs Industries announced that it would be shutting two plants, wiping out 540 jobs, because retailers were increasingly turning to overseas suppliers. "What's happening is that there are more and more products that we can't manufacture competitively here in the United States," admitted CEO Crandall Bowles.[45]

By 2005, retailers were in the driving seat with the industry. As Bethany Moreton has shown in a prize-winning study, the dominant role was played by Wal-Mart, the biggest company on the planet. "If it were the independent Republic of Wal-Mart," Moreton wrote in 2009, "it would be China's sixth largest export market and its economy would rank thirtieth in the world, right behind Saudi Arabia's."[46] In interviews, both industry and union leaders agreed that Wal-Mart had played a decisive role in the textile industry's collapse. AMTAC's Lloyd Wood cited the retailer's practice of forcing domestic suppliers to match the low prices offered by foreign producers. "The number of companies that have gone under trying to sell to Wal-Mart are enormous," he asserted. Wal-Mart, thought Harris Raynor, was "the greatest customer of China."[47] Industry frustrations with Wal-Mart—the former darling of the Crafted with Pride campaign—occasionally boiled over. In one press conference, Guilford Mills CEO John Emrich claimed that Wal-Mart had "done more to put people out of work" in American factories than any other entity. In response, a Wal-Mart spokesman stressed that many of the company's consumable products were sourced domestically. It was a different story in the textile sector, where Wal-Mart opposed the industry's campaign to maintain quotas.[48]

In the lucrative home textiles sector, Wal-Mart's influence was particularly important because large producers such as Pillowtex, WestPoint Stevens, Burlington Industries, and Springs Industries relied on retailers to sell their sheets, towels, and pillowcases. When these stores began to buy from abroad, the industry died. During her investigations, Stella Hopkins found that "retailers' profit-pinching" was a central problem. "Creating the price cuts hyped by Wal-Mart's yellow smiley-face 'Rollback Man' means wringing every penny from every deal—or going to another supplier," she explained. "To compete, other retailers followed suit." Between 1990 and 2004, the number of workers employed by Springs Industries in the Carolinas fell from 15,000 to 5,300, while Stevens and Pillowtex suffered even greater declines and were forced into bankruptcy. A Springs spokesman told Hopkins that for the previous ten years Wal-Mart had demanded price cuts of 2 to 3 percent a year, while in 2004 they had insisted on drops of 11 percent on certain products. After quotas were removed, Springs lost much of its retail business. As a result, within a few years Crandall Bowles announced the "sad" news that the firm was closing its last American plants. It was the end of an era for Springs, which had been making sheets in the United States for over 120 years.[49]

Wal-Mart's dominance also accelerated the decline of the domestic apparel industry. In 2004, a *New York Times* investigation found that the company had numerous contracts with Chinese apparel makers. Apart from offering much lower labor costs, Chinese firms had cornered the market by producing huge quantities of specific items in certain cities. As reporter David Barboza put it, there was "one city for each drawer in your bureau." The booming metropolis of Datang in coastal China, for example, produced nine billion pairs of socks each year, yet twenty-five years earlier it had been a rice farming village with a population of just one thousand. Local entrepreneur Hai Yun Shi epitomized the industry's rapid growth. "I started out making socks by hand when I was 18," he explained. "In '96 we founded this company. Now, we have a contract with Wal-Mart."[50]

Wal-Mart's rise also hurt archrival K-Mart, which in turn harmed domestic textile makers. In 1990 K-Mart had more stores and employees than Wal-Mart, but within a decade the situation had been dramatically reversed. Wal-Mart's obsession with low costs was a central reason for the turnaround, and it forced competitors to copy the tactic or perish. It was an effect that the media dubbed "'Wal-Martization.'" Rapidly losing market share, K-Mart filed for bankruptcy in 2002. The retailer's demise hurt companies such as Dan River, Inc., which had supplied it with a wide variety of textile products. As a result of the move, Dan River had to increase its bad debt reserve, precipitating its own bankruptcy. It was a sad end for a firm that had once employed fourteen thousand workers in Danville, Virginia, a mill town that was devastated by the shutdown. Also hurt by K-Mart's downfall was Russell Corporation, as the retailer accounted for 3 percent of Russell's annual sales, or around $12 million. Under cost pressure, Russell switched production overseas and laid off most of the workforce in Alexander City, Alabama, a small city that was heavily dependent on the mills.[51]

Ironically, Wal-Mart often built its stores in the empty spaces created by the collapse of textile mills. In scores of southern communities, Wal-Mart facilities sprung up, relying on the major highways that had previously linked the region's mills together. In Cleveland County, North Carolina, where the unemployment rate was one of the highest in the region, Wal-Mart built a sprawling distribution center that employed up to six hundred people. Even those that got the jobs, however, found that they were no panacea. As the *Charlotte Observer* concluded, former textile workers were struggling. "While service-sector jobs, such as retail clerks, are plentiful," noted journalist Sharon E. White, "those typically pay less than sought-after textile and manufacturing jobs."[52] Industry figures also stressed that service jobs were not a true replacement for manufacturing ones. Some spoke to the broader consequences of this shift. "We're exporting our middle-class jobs," charged mill owner Roger Chastain in 2005, "the American dream for the next generation."[53]

Individual examples illustrate these broader trends. In 2003, the president of National Spinning Company in Washington, North Carolina, related the case of an employee he had laid off as his company shrank. The story highlighted how service jobs were easily available but were no substitute for industrial jobs, especially as they lacked comparable benefits. "I saw one of our former employees preparing food for guests at a local Hampton Inn last week," explained Jim Chesnutt in an interview. "She told me she wanted to come back to her family at National Spinning Co., Inc. She starts at 4 a.m. every day, leaves at 10.30 a.m., goes to Wal-Mart for a second job and works as many hours as allowed. Her total pay is less than that at National, with no health-care, no vacation, no retirement and no future. So much for the service economy!"[54] Others had an even harder time, especially when they confined their job searches to their local area. In 2001, Deborah Powers lost her job at Alamac Knits in Lumberton, North Carolina, after twenty-nine years with the firm. Three months later, she and many of her co-workers were still searching for new posts. "A few people I know have been able to locate full-time employment, but the vast majority is still looking," she declared. Powers acknowledged that many of her colleagues were reluctant to move out of Robeson County, a depressed textile area. Workers' attachments to their jobs and communities—which had been so important as they endured the hardships of mill life—now made it harder for them to find opportunities. These workers failed to fulfill economists' predictions of a new, mobile workforce who would rationally relocate to find new jobs. As one worker from the struggling mill town of Eden, North Carolina, put it, "I don't really care about driving in heavy traffic. And if you talk about moving to a big city, you've got drugs—not to say we've not got drugs here—and you've got crime."[55]

Quantitative research confirmed that textile workers were hit hard by the industry's demise. In 2003, one study by the Organization for Economic Cooperation and Development (OECD) found that two-thirds of reemployed textile and apparel workers earned less on their new jobs than they had previously, while one-quarter experienced losses greater than 30 percent. Although textile jobs paid poorly by manufacturing standards, they still exceeded those in the retail and service sectors, and they came with a range of fringe benefits, including employer-sponsored health care, which service jobs often lacked. In 2007, data collected by the industry found that textile workers earned 136 percent more than retail store workers, and they also received health care and pension benefits.[56]

The fate of textile workers was illustrative of the problems experienced by displaced workers in general. Many economists have found that when laid-off workers locate new jobs, they usually earn less. In one study of BLS data, Robert W. Fairlie and Lori G. Kletzer concluded that "for many workers, adjusting to permanent job loss can be difficult, with low probabilities of reemployment, long durations of joblessness, and sizable earnings losses." In 1994 and 1996, the Bureau's data showed that displaced workers earned 15 percent less in their new jobs, many of which were part time. In 2001, another detailed BLS study found that workers without formal educational qualifications fared worst when they lost their jobs.[57]

Deindustrialization is also a major cause of America's health care crisis. In 1993, BLS figures showed that about half the workers in private service industries took part in a health plan that was at least partially paid for by their employer, whereas in manufacturing four-fifths of workers received health insurance from their jobs. As the National Coalition on Health Care put it, "The service sector offers less access to health insurance than its manufacturing counterparts." As manufacturing declined, the number of Americans without health care rose steadily, even when workers were gaining new jobs in service industries. In 2007, federal data indicated that forty-six million Americans, or about 18 percent of the population under the age of sixty-five, were without health insurance. Between 2000 and 2007, moreover, the number of uninsured Americans increased by almost eight million, and the figure continued to inch up as the global financial crisis generated a new wave of layoffs, especially in manufacturing.[58]

The demise of the textile sector was an important cause of this increase, as most mill workers depended heavily on employer-sponsored health care. In 1993, over 81 percent of workers in the basic textile industry were covered by an employer health plan, a rate that was only exceeded by industries that were much better paid. As the *Philadelphia Inquirer* summarized in a story on the industry's decline, "For many workers, losing health insurance is worse than losing paychecks." In particular, workers on prescription medication now struggled to pay bills that had been met, at least partially, by company plans. Some even had to sell their cars and other assets in order to meet their medical expenses. As Harris Raynor recalled, the loss of health care benefits represented an "absolute disaster" for displaced workers and their families.[59]

Events in Virginia illustrated how textile and apparel workers desperately needed employer-provided health care. Following a series of plant closings in the late 1990s, especially in its main center of Martinsville, Henry County had an unemployment rate of nearly 20 percent, the highest in the state. In December 1999, for example, more than two thousand workers lost their jobs when Tultex, one of the country's leading manufacturers of sweat suits and athletic wear, suddenly went into bankruptcy. The closure was a major blow to UNITE, which had organized the plant five years earlier after a massive campaign. Following the shutdown, displaced workers insisted that the loss of health insurance was their main worry, and they implored local lawmakers to help them. "I don't know what to do," admitted unemployed worker Jeanette Gravely. "I know there are people who are worse off than me. But I'm between a rock and a hard spot." Gravely needed surgery on a damaged nerve but could not afford the operation. Others had even more urgent needs. "NAFTA took my job and it very well may take my life if someone does not come up with a plan where I fit into a slot," added Katy Burnette, a worker with heart disease who was about to lose her health insurance. Five years earlier, Burnette's open heart surgery had cost $80,000, and without insurance she could not afford another operation.[60]

After traveling to Henry County to meet with laid-off mill workers, a group of Democratic state legislators came up with a plan. Led by Ward L. Armstrong (D-Henry), they introduced the Textile Workers Relief Act, which promised to offer at least two years of health insurance to workers who had lost their jobs because of NAFTA. It also raised weekly unemployment benefits by 43 percent for people living in areas with high unemployment. Armstrong justified the costs as a way of mitigating the harsh impact of mill closures on small communities. "With 7,000 people unemployed," he commented, "I'm losing the shoe store, the gas station, and the grocery store." The bill was strongly opposed, however, by Republican governor Jim Gilmore, who argued that it penalized jobless Virginians who lived in more prosperous areas. After twice traveling to Richmond to ask for the governor's support, displaced textile workers were in tears. "This kind of shoots everything out that I thought was good about this state," noted former Tultex worker Kern Law. "I thought the governor would be for us." The bill's political sponsors were also unimpressed. "Marie Antoinette had more of a social conscience," declared Clifton "Chip" Woodrum (D-Roanoke).[61]

Stung by accusations that he was insensitive, Gilmore responded with his own plan. Although it promised economic development grants and higher unemployment benefits in depressed areas, critics noted that it failed to provide health insurance. "The money from benefits is important," admitted former Tultex worker Robin Hairston, a mother of two, "but it's not as important as having health insurance. We're skating on thin ice. We don't have money for insurance or the money to pay for it. You just pray nothing happens." Agreeing with these sentiments, state legislators rejected Gilmore's proposal. "They should not have to decide between health insurance and economic development," explained Armstrong. "It's like choosing between food and water."[62] In Martinsville, there was no doubt that workers' health care needs were immense. In 1999, a group of local doctors and nurses began volunteering their services at a weekly health clinic that operated out of a disused textile mill. Soon the clinic was treating over three thousand patients a year, and many patients would line up for hours to try to improve their chances of seeing a doctor.[63]

Because the situation in Martinsville was not unusual, the Bush administration was also pushed to act. After 2002, workers who lost manufacturing jobs to foreign competition became eligible for a federal health insurance subsidy that reduced medical costs considerably. The Health Coverage Tax Credit covered about 260,000 jobless workers across the country, with textile workers one of the most affected groups. Introduced ahead of the 2002 congressional elections, the program received most publicity when Pillowtex went bankrupt. Recipients got a tax credit equal to 65 percent of their health insurance premium and were also eligible for extended unemployment benefits, career counseling, basic educational help, and retraining. Many workers insisted, however, that they could not afford to pay the 35 percent share, while others failed to claim the benefit because they were not aware of it. Because local unions spread news of the scheme, organized workers were more likely to apply, yet the vast majority of textile workers were not union members.[64]

The tax credit initiative never overcame these problems. In early 2004, the *New York Times* reported that the program had "gotten off to a slow, sputtering start," largely because workers were required to spend a significant amount of money in order to claim the credit. Under the scheme, the premiums required to cover former textile worker Gloria J. Craven and her husband varied from $1,700 to $5,400 a month, with their share being between $595 and $1,890. The couple, which had a range of health problems, drew just $416 a month in unemployment after Mrs. Craven lost her job at a mill in Eden, North Carolina. "The tax credit would help if the insurance rates were affordable, but the rates were so high that I couldn't afford it," she explained. This case was representative. At the end of 2003, the Bush administration admitted that just 8,374 workers were receiving tax credits for health insurance under the scheme, a tiny fraction of those eligible.[65]

Health coverage remained an issue even for those who did find new jobs. As the economy changed, most of the jobs that were created were part time, and they frequently came without health insurance. Many former textile workers now found themselves in these positions. According to a study by the Employee Benefit Research Institute, in 2003 some 19 percent of the nation's twenty-five million part-time workers had employee health benefits, while a further 37 percent were covered as dependents of other family members. This meant that 44 percent of all part-timers—eleven million people—were not covered by any employer. "When something goes wrong, I go immediately to my pharmacist at Walgreen's; that's my health coverage," commented part-time employee A. J. Catanzaro. Because he had no insurance, Catanzaro had suffered a brain aneurysm after he ignored painful headaches.[66]

In the South, the industry's demise also had wider economic ramifications. It certainly contributed to the yawning gap between rural and urban areas, a disparity that troubled liberal southerners. As early as 1986, regional think tank MDC had carefully documented the emergence of "two Souths, one metropolitan and prosperous, the other rural and facing serious trouble," linking the phenomenon to a "simultaneous decline in agriculture and manufacturing." Over the next two decades, the persistent gap remained a central concern of the group.[67] Because most textile and apparel plants were located in nonmetropolitan areas, the industry's demise was a major cause of the problem. As MDC found, between 1978 and 2000 metropolitan areas accounted for fifteen million of the 17.7 million jobs that the region had gained. Over the same period, however, nearly half of the region's losses in manufacturing occurred in rural counties. As industry groups had pointed out for years, textile mills were a vital source of decent jobs for small-town residents.[68]

As the industry's demise accelerated, the economic gap between rural and urban areas widened. In 2002, an MDC report on the rural Carolinas concluded that "the sort of job loss that rural communities are suffering essentially destroys the middle class. Those who can't find comparable opportunities either have to move out or accept lower-paying jobs."[69] In the same year, MDC's *State of the South* saw the collapse of the textile industry as a major cause of rural poverty. "For decades," it noted, "manufacturing provided the economic base of the South's small towns." In 2001, a third of all layoffs in North Carolina were in textiles, and 69 percent of these occurred in rural counties. As the report concluded, "The people who held these jobs—predominantly older workers with low education levels, including many women—have few or no options for alternative employment." Although the South had a reputation for economic growth, in 2002 the region was home to 44 percent of the country's nonmetropolitan population but 51 percent of its nonmetropolitan poor. Harris Raynor had witnessed these changes firsthand. "Basically the rural South has been destroyed," he asserted later.[70]

The industry's collapse also had a harsh impact on southern blacks, especially when they lived in nonmetropolitan areas. Both executives and union leaders had frequently warned that blacks would be hard hit by mill closures, predictions that were now borne out. As the *State of the South* summarized in 2000, black men were especially vulnerable because they were "overrepresented" in semiskilled factory work. The industry's demise contributed to the wider failure of African Americans to close the economic gap with whites, a key shortcoming of the post–Civil Rights era. MDC found that the median net worth of southern white families—which it defined as the "total value of a family's material and financial assets minus its liabilities"—far outpaced that of black families in the region. In 1994 the figure for whites was $68,660, but for blacks it was just $18,800. As these statistics highlighted, racial minorities could not afford to lose their jobs because they had few outside assets, such as equity in property or ownership of stocks and bonds, to fall back on.[71] In the 1990s, Latino migrants also broke into industrial jobs, and by 2002 they represented almost 16 percent of workers in the basic textile industry, up from 7 percent in 1990. Many lost mill jobs only a short time after they were hired, and because of language barriers they were often unable to retrain. Unsuccessful in their search for work, they often left decaying textile towns, although some stayed because of the cheap housing available.[72]

Using BLS data, labor economists have documented that African Americans fared particularly badly when they lost manufacturing jobs. Between 1984 and 1992, black men experienced rates of job displacement that were some 30 percent higher than white men, and their reemployment rates were also 30 percent lower. By 2003—the year that many large mills closed—unemployment among blacks was rising twice as fast as it was for whites, and most of the jobs being lost were in manufacturing, where the pay for African Americans has historically been higher than in other fields.[73]

"The number of jobs and the types of jobs that have been lost have severely diminished the standing of many blacks in the middle class," declared William Lucy, the president of the Coalition of Black Trade Unionists. In 2004, a study by the BLS itself found that black workers who lost their jobs saw their earnings decline by almost twice as much as their white counterparts. In 2009, the national unemployment rate was almost twice as high for blacks as it was for whites.[74]

Individual examples illustrate the importance of the industry to African Americans, especially women. In Lancaster, South Carolina, Springs Industries dominated the local economy, and the main plant billed itself as the "world's largest textile mill" under one roof. For decades, however, production jobs were reserved for whites. In the 1960s, after civil rights laws pushed manufacturers to hire blacks, residents such as Esterlean McGriff went from caring for the children of white mill workers to working alongside them. "It was a better job for us," she recalled, adding that her three children had followed her into the mill. For McLean, as for many other African Americans, the industry's decline was devastating. By 2003, Lancaster County's unemployment rate was over 10 percent, and McLean spent her days volunteering at the local senior center. She worried that Lancaster, a small community built by the mill companies, would become a "ghost town."[75]

As McLean's comment implies, the industry's economic dominance increased the impact of its downfall. In the South, textiles had been the main employer for decades, and it was responsible for the existence of scores of small towns, especially in the Piedmont. They were communities such as Fort Mill, South Carolina, where residents recalled how tufts of cotton had often floated through the air and how traffic had backed up through town when shift changes at the mill took place. As the *New York Times*'s William E. Schmidt had written in 1984, "The mills, with their aging brick factories, remain the dominant life force in many small towns, the source not only of paychecks but civic energy, fielding softball leagues as well as the labor and sometimes the cash to help rebuild churches and repair school gymnasiums." The decline of such a large employer had enormous cultural and psychological ramifications.[76] As journalist Katherine Yung summarized in the *Dallas Morning News* in 2003, the industry was "in tatters" and the social consequences were massive. "Without trade protections from the government or a whole new strategy," she asserted, "a way of life in the South for more than a century faces extinction."[77]

Because most workers had only ever worked in mills, they found it hard to imagine life without them. Despite many warnings and layoffs, few were prepared for plant closures. In 2002, when Martinsville's Mary Lou Ramey lost her sewing job, her reaction was representative. "It's like all we've ever known is textiles; it's all we've ever done," she declared. "I do not have a clue as to where I'm gonna go and what I'm gonna do." For both workers and managers, job loss was very painful. When Burlington Industries closed its plants in Halifax and Clarksville, Virginia, workers reacted with "tears" and "blank stares." As plant manager Lott Rogers explained, "It's devastating to me because this is my family. It's very hard to stand in front of those people and tell them their job is going away."[78]

As plants closed, the same kinds of reactions were frequently reported. When Burlington shut its plant in Mooresville, North Carolina, in July 1999, the community no longer depended on the mill, but most employees still found the shutdown "traumatic." They were proud of their jobs, which had provided a stable living to generations of local people. Although they were aware of the industry's problems, most reasoned that their jobs were safe. "I thought Mooresville Mills would be there forever," commented fifty-five-year-old George Abernathy. "The mill meant a whole lot to me. If it re-opened tomorrow, I'd go back to work there."[79] After closures, workers mourned for an industry that had been a central part of their lives, and some also used the family metaphor. "That silent mill down there is like a death in the family," summarized a resident of Ware Shoals, South Carolina, one of many communities left with an empty mill in its midst. "You used to hear the mill whistle blow and the clackety-clack of the machinery. But it's silent now." While some of these recollections glossed over the harsh aspects of mill village life, there was no doubting that the psychological and cultural impact of the industry's demise was immense.[80]

It was not just employees who were affected. Because mills were usually built in small towns, their disappearance weakened the local tax base and forced cuts in municipal services. In Ware Shoals, the loss of the main employer meant that the town was unable to fix its antiquated water filter plant, which had originally been provided by the mill. Instead, it had to buy water from the Greenwood Commission of Public Works, causing residents' bills to rise by up to 20 percent.[81] In 1999, the closure of Stonecutter Mills in Spindale, North Carolina, a town of less than four thousand residents, led the community to lose 42 percent of its property tax base. Although it was a larger community, Martinsville was also wounded by the shutdown of the large Vanity Fair plant, which forced the board of education to close four schools. Even in Spartanburg County, South Carolina, which was often held up as a classic Sunbelt area, mill closures forced cuts in the education and fire budgets.[82] All of these cases were representative. In 2001, more than a dozen Piedmont textile towns hired a lobbyist to try to recoup funds that had been lost because of mill closures. "The impact from the undoing of this once-vibrant industry will be more far-reaching than the empty pay envelopes of workers, the demolition of plants and the changes in landscape seen in most mill villages," summarized one local journalist.[83]

The industry's demise also had symbolic consequences. Scores of southern communities had originated as mill towns, and the factories had often been constructed before the communities around them even existed. When the industry disappeared, civic leaders had to find new sources of identity. For the town of St. Pauls, North Carolina, the closure of five mills even dictated a modification of the municipal seal, which depicted a cone of yarn with the motto "The Textile Center of Robeson County." As Mayor Gordon Westbrook admitted, "We will have to change the seal because it's misleading." By 2000, the outsourcing of denim production similarly meant that the small town of Erwin, North Carolina, could no longer boast that it was the "World's Denim Capital"; a new slogan was required.[84]

Another revealing episode occurred in 2006, when the South Carolina–based Piedmont Blood Center reported that it was facing a "critically low supply of blood" because collection drives had usually been held at local mills. "With textiles all going away, it's difficult to find a place to go and collect large quantities," explained office manager Regina Lambert. It was important to find a new venue because the PBC was the sole provider of blood for hospitals in three South Carolina counties. In a sign of the changing times, the PBC decided to hold its drives at Wal-Mart stores.[85] Many mills had also supported charities and philanthropic foundations, and these were similarly affected as the industry died. The case of apparel maker Outer Banks—which closed its factory in Lumberton, North Carolina, in 2006—was representative. "That's really going to hurt us," declared local United Way director Sandra Oliver, explaining that the firm's employees had donated $35,000 over the previous year.[86]

For many residents of the southern textile belt, another wrenching consequence of the industry's demise was the physical destruction of mill buildings. After 2000, the region's landscape was transformed as scores of empty mills were razed. If mills were located close to growing urban areas, developers and municipal leaders wanted to knock them down so that the land could be reused. The industry's rapid collapse also meant that there was a massive oversupply of empty mills, and it was costly to convert them to other uses. In late 2003, for example, city officials in Lowell, North Carolina, located just west of Charlotte, oversaw the demolition of two unwanted Pharr Yarn plants. In a 124-year-old manufacturing town that was named after Lowell, Massachusetts, many saw the demolition as "symbolic of change," as the *Charlotte Observer* put it. Former workers certainly found the demolitions painful. "They can tear them down," declared eighty-seven-year-old Gladys Parker, who had worked at one of the mills for nearly fifty years, "but I'll never forget."[87]

In 2005, the demolition of the Pillowtex complex in Kannapolis and the Burlington Industries headquarters in Greensboro were notable markers in the industry's demise. Starting life as Burlington Mills and Cannon Mills, these two companies had been built from the ground up by Spencer Love and Charles Cannon, respectively. Love had died in 1962 and Cannon in 1971, and they left behind two of the industry's biggest and best-known firms. According to the *Southern Textile News*, both men were "spinning in their graves" as their corporate headquarters were destroyed. Carried out rapidly, the demolitions were a tangible sign that the industry was gone for good. "To see actual physical destruction of icons of an industry that shaped the history of the South for more than 100 years is certainly disheartening," concluded the *News*.[88]

Watching the explosions, many spectators agreed. Thousands witnessed the destruction of Burlington's landmark headquarters in Greensboro, a community described by a reporter as "a layoff-battered city in the buckle of the textile belt." As the *Greensboro News and Record* reported, the crowd saw a 430,000 square foot building taken down "in seconds." Immediately afterward, "Eye rubbing commenced, but not all was dust related." Although many local people recognized the building's importance, it was demolished because it contained a lot of asbestos and because there was little demand for office space in Greensboro. Revealingly, retailers redeveloped most of the site.[89]

The demolition represented quite a change in fortunes for the giant firm. Just seven years earlier, Burlington Industries had celebrated its seventy-fifth anniversary with much fanfare. Then, the *Southern Textile News* had run a special sixteen-page issue on the company, which it proclaimed as a "Leader in its Field." The cover featured a photograph of Burlington's "unique corporate offices," in Greensboro, which were seen as a symbol of its innovation and success. "Although the structure is completely functional and provides modern office space for 1,000 Burlington employees, it is truly a work of art," declared the *News*. Apparently one of the strongest companies in the industry, Burlington had embraced globalization, expanding its exports and establishing joint ventures overseas. Overall, the company was well placed to survive for many decades.[90]

With the dramatic rise of China, however, Burlington found that it had to slash its operations, especially in the import-sensitive apparel and home furnishings sectors. Between 1998 and 2003, the company shut scores of plants, most of them in small towns where the mill was the main employer. Even large, innovative firms were not spared as the industry collapsed, and the empire that the fiery and indefatigable Love had taken decades to nurture was gone in the space of a few years. At its peak, Burlington had eighty thousand employees, 149 plants, and a high-rise sales office in New York City. Perhaps the most recognizable of all textile companies, Burlington even sponsored the *Ed Sullivan Show*. By the time of the bankruptcy, however, only fifteen thousand workers and twenty plants remained, and even they were unsustainable for a company whose stock had been booted off the New

York Stock Exchange.[91] Although financier Wilbur Ross bought both Burlington and Cone Mills in 2003, he was soon slashing jobs and encouraging outsourcing, and he also showed little interest in keeping the Burlington headquarters. Moreover, the two firms no longer technically existed but were subsumed within the anonymously named International Textile Group (ITG), part of a new textile industry that aggressively shifted manufacturing overseas and only maintained marketing and distribution centers in the United States.[92]

The industry's demise also hurt its professional associations, especially the ATMI. Between 1998 and 2001, the industry's main trade association lost at least 40 percent of its revenue, forcing cuts in staff levels. Some of the decline was caused by corporate liquidations, while firms that stayed in business often decided that they could no longer afford to pay dues. "Bankruptcies, consolidations and plant closings due to unfairly priced Asian imports and the recent economic slowdown have taken a toll on us," admitted president Chuck Hayes. Among those let go were "high-level" personnel that worked on trade policy, a move that reduced the ATMI's lobbying power in Washington. "If ATMI were a choir," explained the *Southern Textile News* in 2002, "it would soon sing a more subdued tune. . . . The organization is being forced to pink-slip a quartet of its top executives." The cuts hurt, and three years later the ATMI went out of business. The move came after some members resigned and joined AMTAC, the Milliken-funded group that opposed further trade liberalization. The ATMI, they insisted, was not representing the industry effectively. "Essentially, it [the ATMI] went bankrupt," declared Lloyd Wood, AMTAC's director of media relations. After the ATMI's downfall, its remaining supporters established the National Council of Textile Organizations (NCTO), which sought to work with the Bush administration and persuade it to give the industry a fair deal.[93]

The industry's demise also took its toll on state-level textile associations, most of which were folded into broader business organizations. In 2002, the 101-year-old Alabama Textile Manufacturers Association merged with the Alabama Chemical Association and the Alabama Industry and Manufacturers Association to create Manufacture Alabama, Inc. While treasurer and mill owner Hollis Mann Jr. tried to put a positive spin on the move, it meant that the declining textile sector had to fight for attention with export-oriented industries such as chemicals. In a similar fashion, the South Carolina Textile Manufacturers Association became part of the South Carolina Manufacturers Alliance, a group that was more focused on attracting new industries rather than protecting "old" ones. In 2003, 60 percent of the SCMA's members were "nontextile" firms. The same fate befell the Georgia Textile Manufacturers Association and North Carolina Textile Manufacturers Association, both of which had wielded considerable power in their heyday. Industry publications fared no better; in 2008, for example, the *Daily News Record*, once the key journal for the men's apparel business, went out of business after 118 years in print.[94]

By the early twenty-first century, most of the industry's strongest political allies had also dropped out of public life, partly because their textile constituencies had eroded so much. The industry's loss of political power was illustrated well in 2005, when Fritz Hollings gave up the Senate seat he had held for almost forty years rather than seek reelection in an increasingly conservative South Carolina. His successor, Republican Jim DeMint, was an avid free-trader who regarded textile jobs as expendable. During the campaign, DeMint's office declared that "we don't want to go back to having textile mills in the South. There are good-paying, high-tech jobs we would rather have." DeMint's hostility forced textile executives to break ranks with the GOP and support Democrat Inez Tenebaum. Despite the industry's efforts, DeMint won office quite easily.[95]

As their political power shrank, beleaguered mill owners needed to stick together, yet the split between the ATMI and AMTAC highlighted that this was unlikely. The ATMI had supported NAFTA, which many executives now blamed for their problems, and the NCTO similarly argued that the industry could only survive by embracing globalization. In 2005, divisions resurfaced when the NCTO endorsed the Dominican Republic–Central American Free Trade Agreement. According to the NCTO, increased trade within the Central American "hemisphere" was "part of a strategy for remaining competitive against China." Designed to create an expanded free trade area throughout Central America, DR–CAFTA was a priority for the Bush administration, and the president used his trade promotion authority to push it through. Once again, Republican-leaning industry executives were won over or neutralized by presidential promises of good will. In letters written on May 3 and 4, for example, administration officials pledged to hire more customs staff and agreed to meet the industry's rule of origin concerns. The NCTO's endorsement split it from AMTAC and the NTA, who opposed the agreement. AMTAC pulled no punches, calling CAFTA "a job killer for U.S. manufacturing and the textile industry in particular." The split was the last thing a struggling industry needed. "One thing is certain," noted a *Southern Textile News* editorial, "By splintering from its brethren on the DR–CAFTA issue, the industry is back to its old ways of sending mixed messages to Congress. . . . Whoever's right, our only hope is that the industry isn't one day in the company of worms, dead and buried."[96]

The CAFTA episode also reflected how much of the industry had started to give up on domestic production. By 2000, fabric makers Cone Mills, Galey & Lord, and Burlington Industries had all established garment factories in Mexico, and that nation's denim-production capacity had tripled in the space of a few years. Executives from these firms argued that outsourcing was inevitable. "Given the present trade and consumer environment," declared Cone CEO John Bakane, "either we play the game by looking at the most cost-effective way of production, or we go out of business." Significant parts of the home textiles industry had also moved overseas. In 2002, West-Point Stevens opened an office in Shanghai to work with suppliers, and similar operations in India and Pakistan were planned. The company also had factories in Mexico and had formed a partnership with a Brazilian towel manufacturer. Well before CAFTA, many apparel companies had also set up operations in Central American countries such as Guatemala, Honduras, and El Salvador, as well as in the Caribbean. In all of these locations, firms took advantage of the concessions available in special free trade zones created by an expansion of Item 807 of the U.S. Tariff Schedule. By the turn of the century, the International Labour Organization calculated that there were approximately thirty million jobs in the global textile, apparel, and footwear industries, the bulk of them held by women.[97]

Reacting to this shift in production, the U.S. unions tried to organize textile and apparel workers in Central America, clashing with employers who were keen to keep labor costs as low as possible so that they could compete with China. UNITE's files detail organizing campaigns in Honduras (1994 to 1995), Guatemala (1996 to 1997), Nicaragua (1997 to 1998), and El Salvador (1997).[98] In every campaign, organizers tried to expose the poor conditions that existed in the Central American free trade zones. In Nicaragua, for instance, the union claimed that female garment workers received just eleven cents for making a pair of jeans that JCPenney sold in the United States for $14.99.[99] All of the union's efforts were strongly opposed by the American companies or their overseas subsidiaries, and gains were minimal. In February 1995, organizer Bruce Fieldman reported from Honduras that a small group of five local unions represented "the only organized workers in the maquila for the entire Central America and Caribbean region with long standing viable collective bargaining agreements." Even in Honduras, there was significant resistance to new organizing, and one grassroots labor leader was fired for wearing lipstick.[100] This incident was typical, as organizers constantly complained that union supporters were harassed or dismissed. As staffer Alan Howard reported, employers also undermined the campaign by telling their workers that the American unions were "stirring up trouble in order to persuade multinational companies to return to the U.S." Howard's report highlighted how the alliance between employers and organized labor had largely collapsed. Overall, indeed, the union was strongly opposed to the industry's "long-range strategy" of using the Caribbean and Latin America to create a "huge base of low-wage labor . . . to compete against Asian producers."[101]

The offshore factories did not impress Roger Milliken, who had traditionally destroyed his old textile machinery rather than see it shipped to other countries, particularly China. In 2000, Milliken left the ATMI and urged others to follow.[102] Two years later, the tireless eighty-six-year-old announced the formation of the American Textile Trade Action Caucus (ATTAC). Promising a hard-line stance against trade liberalization, ATTAC leaders lashed out at the ATMI and its allies. "This industry is going into the tank, probably because of a whole bunch of trade associations that haven't done their jobs," charged Milliken counsel Jock Nash. In response, Chuck Hayes insisted that the industry would get nowhere by opposing the administration, as the events of the 1980s had proved. He also appealed for unity. When ATTAC's policy program was announced in May, however, it differed sharply from that of the ATMI. "Clearly, the U.S. textile industry is an industry worth saving," explained Milliken. "The United States must change its trade policy now."[103]

Significantly, the new group was co-led by Milliken and UNITE president Bruce Raynor. Nash defended the move, claiming that it was necessary to increase the industry's lobbying power. "All of the political power that was ever put together by our industry was always in connection with the unions," he explained, "the same way that the steel industry could not have accomplished what it has accomplished without the steel union." In an about-turn, however, ten months later ATTAC split with UNITE. Now renamed as AMTAC, the new group was an industry-only operation whose members included nontextile companies. Although Milliken downplayed the rift with Raynor, both men were forthright characters who found it hard to work with others. The outcome was another illustration of how difficult it was to form lasting alliances between management and labor, even when the two sides needed one other. As Nash's comments implied, the loss of labor support also weakened AMTAC.[104] The union never came back, and efforts to recruit nontextile companies also had little success. In 2009, Lloyd Wood refused to identify AMTAC's corporate sponsors but admitted that the "bulk" of them were textile and apparel firms. AMTAC remained closely allied with Milliken, and no merger with the NCTO had occurred. The NCTO indeed criticized Milliken for establishing some facilities abroad, a move that he defended as necessary to ensure the survival of his business. Butler Derrick also pointed out that Milliken only established these plants when it became "absolutely clear" that efforts to protect the industry were not going to work.[105]

After the abolition of quotas, however, the severity of the industry's problems did enable AMTAC and the NCTO to work together on key issues. One of these was America's mounting trade deficit; by 2007, for example, the textile and apparel trade deficit with China was a record $31.8 billion. The industry thus provided a focus for those who wanted harsher action taken against China, including measures to increase the value of the yuan.[106] Both groups joined the Global Alliance for Fair Textile Trade, a coalition of ninety-six trade groups from fifty-four countries that were united in their opposition to China's "monopolization" of the textile trade. Formed in 2004,

GAFTT attracted some of the poorest nations in the world, who needed the textile industry to generate export revenue. China, however, retained the support of several powerful nations, particularly India and Russia, and it was thus able to foil GAFTT's efforts to restrict its textile exports.[107]

Despite the efforts of both AMTAC and the NCTO, the U.S. textile industry continued to shrink, and news stories about the industry constantly mentioned its decline, even when it was tangential to the topic. When Crystal Lee Sutton died in September 2009, for example, her obituaries were influenced by the industry's desperate plight. In the early 1970s, it was Sutton's stand for union rights that had helped to publicize poor working conditions in southern mills. Fed up with low pay and meager benefits, Sutton had joined the TWUA, and she became the inspiration for the eponymous lead character in *Norma Rae*. Fired for talking about the union on the job, Sutton had responded by writing "UNION" on a piece of cardboard, climbing onto a table in the middle of the factory floor, and silently raising her sign in front of her co-workers. Reenacted in the film, the episode became "one of the most memorable scenes in cinematic history," according to the *Los Angeles Times*. By 2009, however, most of the mills—including the Roanoke Rapids factory where Sutton had once folded towels for $2.65 an hour—no longer existed. "She got involved in the labor movement in textiles just as North Carolina's stature as a manufacturing giant was about to decline," noted the *Charlotte Observer*. "What with many companies having moved abroad in search of lower-cost labor," added the *Raleigh News and Observer*, "the industry isn't what it used to be in North Carolina (an understatement)." Crystal Lee, however, would "always be part of its history."[108]

As Sutton was laid to rest, the demise of the industry that she had toiled in also seemed complete. In the same year, the union that she had fought to establish represented just 3,500 mill workers in the entire South. "Part of my job is still to protect them," reflected Harris Raynor, "even though I have real questions about their future." Raynor acknowledged that the union could only survive by organizing workers in service industries because their jobs were more secure. In 2009, however, a damaging split within UNITE HERE—formed five years earlier when UNITE merged with the Hotel Employees and Restaurant Employees Union—led to Bruce Raynor suing his HERE counterpart and then leaving the union. As the industry died, what was left of its union destroyed itself in a bitter civil war.[109] Also in 2009, the *Southern Textile News* ceased publication after sixty-four years and 2,453 issues. It was a fitting endnote for the South's "first industry," now robbed of a voice in print. With the industry on its back, advertisers were no longer willing to buy space in the *News*. "How do you know an industry is shutting down or ceases to exist?" pondered editor and publisher Mason "Chip" Smith III. "When you quit writing about it. . . . We've held on to support the industry, but it's just no longer economically feasible to publish."[110]

# NOTES

1. "Post-Quotas," *Southern Textile News*, March 14, 2005, p. 4. All post-2001 issues of the *Southern Textile News* were accessed electronically from the *News*'s website at www.textilenews.com/archives. The *News* went out of business in 2009, and all page numbers from the post-2001 issues cited here refer to the pages of the author's hard copy printouts.

2. BLS employment data at http://www.bls.gov/iag/tgs/iag_index_alpha.htm (accessed January 13, 2011); National Council of Textile Organizations, "U.S.-China Textile and Apparel Trade Fact Sheet," September 30, 2008, available at http://www.ncto.org/newsroom/index.asp (accessed August 20, 2009). Copies of these documents are in the author's possession.

3. "Choppy Seas Foretell Storm of Century," *Southern Textile News*, September 27, 2004, p. 15.

4. Tony Mecia, "Textile Graduates Find It's Key to Stretch," *Charlotte Observer*, January 3, 2007, p. 1D.

5. Harris Raynor interview with author in June 18, 2010, in Union City, Georgia.

6. MDC, *The State of the South 2002: Shadows in the Sunbelt Revisited* (Chapel Hill: MDC, Inc., 2002), p. 15. Copies of this report are available from the MDC website at http://www.mdcinc.org/ (accessed August 9, 2009). For more on the history of MDC, which originated as a spin-off of the North Carolina Fund and was earlier known as the Manpower Development Corporation, see Robert R. Korstad and James L. Leloudis, *To Right These Wrongs: The North Carolina Fund and the Battle to End Poverty and Inequality in 1960s America* (Chapel Hill: University of North Carolina Press, 2010), p. 354.

7. Mittelhauser, "Employment Trends in Textiles and Apparel," pp. 24, 28, 30, 33 (quotation); "Post-Quotas," *Southern Textile News*, March 14, 2005, p. 4; Jeffrey Sparshott, "An Industry Unraveling," *Washington Times*, December 26, 2004, p. A1.

8. Bruce Raynor to Senator, September 20, 2001, "Trade Adjustment Assistance" folder, box 46, series 6000/007, UNITE Papers-Cornell. For more information on the TAA program, as well as other federal programs to help displaced textile and apparel workers, see U.S. Department of Labor, *The Past, Present and Future of Employment in the Textile and Apparel Industries: An Overview* (Washington, DC: U.S. Government Printing Office, 2004), pp. 11–18, 29–32.

9. *AAM Update*, January 27, 2010, and April 13, 2010; Raynor interview with author (closing quotation).

10. Clare Chiron, "The Influence of Quotas, Tariffs and Bilateral Trade Agreement on Post 2005 Apparel Trade," June 18, 2004, p. 1, Harvard Center for Textile and Apparel Research paper summarized at http://www.hctar.org/pages/pub-textileappretail.html (accessed October 25, 2009). Copies of all of the Harvard Center reports cited below are in the author's possession.

11. Clare Chiron, "The Influence of Quotas, Tariffs and Bilateral Trade Agreement on Post 2005 Apparel Trade," June 18, 2004, pp. 1–3, Harvard Center for Textile and Apparel Research paper, available at http://www.hctar.org/pages/pub-textileappretail.html (accessed October 25, 2009); Frederick H. Abernathy, Anthony Volpe, and David Weil, "The Future of the Apparel and Textile Industries: Prospects and Choices for Public and Private Actors," December 22, 2005, p. 2 (quotation), Harvard Center for Textile and Apparel Research paper, available at http://www.hctar.org/pages/pub-textileappretail.html (accessed October 25, 2009).

12. Chiron, "Influence of Quotas," p. 2 (quotations); WTO Uruguay Round Agreement, "Agreement on Textiles and Clothing," 1994, text available from the WTO's official website at www.wto.org/english/docs_e/legal_e/ursum_e.htm#cagreement (accessed August 24, 2010). A full, printed copy of this agreement is in the author's possession.

13. "Textiles' Bridge to 21st Century Quickly Eroding," *Southern Textile News*, December 6, 1999, p. 4.

14. Chris Burritt, "Seven Years into NAFTA, Textile Makers Seek Payoff in Mexico," *Atlanta Journal Constitution*, December 17, 2000, p. Q1; Jeanne Bonner, "Textile Organization Releases Industry Report," Anderson (South Carolina) *Independent-Mail*, August 24, 2001 (quotation); "Trade Measure Passes Senate," *Southern Textile News*, November 8, 1999, p. 1;

Eric Schmitt, "Senate Passes Trade Bills for Caribbean and Africa," *New York Times*, November 4, 1999, p. A11.

15. "A Fool in a China Shop," *Southern Textile News*, January 7, 2002, p. 8 ("dreadful year" quotation); "Don't Let the Doomsayers Win," *Southern Textile News*, February 4, 2002, p. 22; "Tough Times in the Triad," Greensboro (North Carolina) *News and Record*, December 30, 2001, p. E1 (closing quotation).

16. "Where's the Vision?: Industry Leader Shares View," *Southern Textile News*, January 28, 2002, pp. 15–21, Picciotti quotations on p. 15.

17. Ken Moritsugu, "Jobs Vanishing in the Textile Industry," *Philadelphia Inquirer*, September 8, 2001, p. C1.

18. Devin Steele, "TPA Passes House: Textile-District Lawmakers Help Seal Deal," *Southern Textile News*, December 17, 2001, pp. 1–2 ("center stage" quotation on p. 1).

19. "Concessions Reassuring," *Southern Textile News*, December 24, 2001, p. 10 (quotations); Robert Neal interview with author on June 22, 2010, in Concord, North Carolina.

20. "Wounded But Roaring, Industry Stays in Hunt," *Southern Textile News*, January 21, 2002, p. 1 (first quotation); "Don't Let the Doomsayers Win," *Southern Textile News*, February 4, 2002, pp. 22–23 (second and third quotations on p. 23); "TPA Swing Voters Paddle-Weary," *Southern Textile News*, March 4, 2002, pp. 14–15, closing quotation on p. 15.

21. "Chuck's Challenges," *Southern Textile News*, March 18, 2002, pp. 1–7, quotation on p. 2; "Scaled-Back Pak Package Still 'Will Hurt,'" *Southern Textile News*, February 18, 2002, p. 5; "Bankruptcy Bug Bites G & L," *Southern Textile News*, February 25, 2002, p. 5.

22. "Textile Industry Topic of Summit," *The State*, March 21, 2002, p. B6 (first three quotations); Hayes quoted in David Rice, "3 Governors Call for U.S. Aid for Ailing Textile Industry," Winston-Salem (North Carolina) *Journal*, March 23, 2002, p. 1; Jeanne Bonner, "Textile Organization Releases Industry Report," Anderson (South Carolina) *Independent-Mail*, August 24, 2001 (last two quotations). Virginia governor Mark Warner had planned to attend the summit but ended up missing it due to severe flooding in southwest Virginia.

23. David Rice, "3 Governors Call for U.S. Aid for Ailing Textile Industry," Winston-Salem (North Carolina) *Journal*, March 23, 2002, p. 1.

24. "Pillowtex Throws in Towel," *Southern Textile News*, August 3, 2003, p. 1. The important Pillowtex closure is examined in detail as a case study in chapter 10.

25. Raynor quoted in Doug Palmer, "No Future for Textiles in 'City of Looms,'" *The Neil Rogers Show*, December 29, 2004 (South Florida radio show), available at http://www.neilrogers.com/news/articles/2004122905.html (accessed December 15, 2008). A hard copy of this document is in the author's possession.

26. "Cone Files Ch. 11; Accepts Ross Offer," *Southern Textile News*, September 29, 2003, pp. 2–3.

27. Marilyn Geewax, "Textile Makers Press Bush," *Atlanta Journal Constitution*, November 16, 2003, p. H1; "Bipartisan Support Shown for China Safeguard," *Southern Textile News*, November 11, 2003, p. 4 (Giblin quotation); "China Safeguards in Three Categories Invoked by CITA," *Southern Textile News*, November 24, 2003, pp. 1–3 (Dobbins quotation on p. 1); Cauthen quoted in Julia Oliver, "Too Little, Too Late?" Fayetteville (North Carolina) *Observer*, December 10, 2003.

28. Rob Christensen, "Bush Upbeat on Economy," The Raleigh (North Carolina) *News and Observer*, November 8, 2003, p. A1 (Bush quotations).

29. "The Very Fabric of America," *San Francisco Chronicle*, July 4, 1987, p. 11 (first two quotations); Lynn Downey, Jill Novack Lynch, and Kathleen McDonough, *This Is a Pair of Levi's Jeans: The Official History of the Levi's Brand* (San Francisco: Levi Strauss and Company, 1995), p. 7 ("icon" quotation); "All-American" quotation on the front cover of Freeth, *Made in America*; "Faded Glory: An American Icon Is about to Become an Overseas Import," Watertown (New York) *Daily Times*, December 21, 2003, p. E1 (other quotations).

30. "Faded Glory: An American Icon Is about to Become an Overseas Import" (Ann quotation and second quotation, by Levi's spokeswoman Katie Otto); Elizabeth Allen, "S.A. Loses an American Institution: Levi's No Longer Made in U.S.A.," San Antonio *Express-News*, January 9, 2004, p. 1A (Martinez quotation). For earlier layoffs at Levi's, see Frank Swoboda, "Levi Strauss to Cut a Third of North American Jobs," *Washington Post*, November

4, 1997, p. C3; Frank Swoboda, "An American Emblem's Presence Fades: Levi Strauss to Close 10 Factories in U.S., Send Nearly 6,000 Jobs Overseas," *Washington Post*, February 23, 1999, p. A1; Jenny Strasburg, "Levi Closing 6 Plants: Firm to Cut Most U.S. Production, Ax 3,300," *San Francisco Chronicle*, April 8, 2002, p. A1.

31. "A New World Order," *New York Times*, December 17, 2004, p. A34; Franklin Foer, "Fabric Softener: The Textile Lobby v. The War on Terrorism," *New Republic*, March 4 and 11, 2002, pp. 19–21, quotation on p. 21; "Quota Clock's a-Runnin'" *Southern Textile News*, December 6, 2004, p. 16.

32. Stella M. Hopkins, "Tough Times Ahead for Home Textiles," *Charlotte Observer*, December 12, 2004, p. 1D.

33. Greg Rushford, "America's Dirty War on Chinese Clothing," *Far Eastern Economic Review*, December 2004, pp. 31–36, quotations on pp. 31–32.

34. Devin Steele, "Industry Steps Up Pressure, Launches Billboard Campaign," *Southern Textile News*, October 11, 2004, pp. 1–3, quotations on p. 1.

35. "Chesnutt Rebuts with Zeal, Skill," *Southern Textile News*, October 25, 2004, pp. 18–19 (Bush quotations); Devin Steele, "Textile-District Lawmakers Help Seal Deal," *Southern Textile News*, December 17, 2001, p. 2.

36. "Elections: A Ball of Confusion," *Southern Textile News*, October 11, 2004, p. 14.

37. "Chesnutt Rebuts with Zeal, Skill," *Southern Textile News*, October 25, 2004, p. 18.

38. "Elections: A Ball of Confusion," *Southern Textile News*, October 11, 2004, p. 14. For an example of subsequent indirect criticism of the administration, see Devin Steele, "Should CAFTA Menu Include Poo-Poo Platter," *Southern Textile News* (editorial), March 14, 2005, p. 16.

39. David Barboza and Elizabeth Becker, "Free of Quota, China Textiles Flood the U.S.," *New York Times*, March 10, 2005, p. A1.

40. Chiron, "The Influence of Quotas," p. 3; Abernathy, Volpe, and Weil, "The Future of the Apparel and Textile Industries".

41. "Sensitive" quotation in "U.S.-China Textile and Apparel Trade Fact Sheet," (NCTO Document), September 30, 2008, available at http://www.ncto.org/newsroom/index.asp (accessed August 20, 2009, copy in author's possession); "73 Members of Congress and U.S. Textile Industry Urge U.S. Govt. to Expand Textile Monitoring Program to Imports from China," NCTO et al. Press Release, September 30, 2008, available at http://www.ncto.org/newsroom/index.asp (accessed August 20, 2009, copy in the author's possession); Tony Mecia, "Governors to be Voice of Textiles," *Charlotte Observer*, March 22, 2002, p. 1D (Schavey quotation).

42. Elizabeth Becker, "Textile Quotas to End Soon, Punishing Carolina Mill Towns," *New York Times*, November 2, 2004, p. C1; Tom Dochat, "Shippensburg to Lose Textile Mill, Chinese Imports Blamed for Closing," *Harrisburg Patriot-News*, December 15, 2004, p. C1 (quotations).

43. Robert Gavin, "Quaker Fabric Expected to Close," *Boston Globe*, July 4, 2007, p. 1C (Liebenow quotation); Erin Ailworth, "Life on the Brink: Waves of Shutdowns, Layoffs Overwhelm Fall River," *Boston Globe*, March 18, 2009, p. 1 (Fiola quotation); Noel K. Gallagher, "Biddeford Mill Closing in Sad Day at WestPoint Home, 121 Jobs Will Be Lost," Portland (Maine) *Press Herald*, April 4, 2009, p. A1 (Lamontagne quotation).

44. James D. McWilliams, "Upstate Braces for More Job Losses," *The State*, January 12, 2005, p. E1.

45. Stella M. Hopkins, "Tough Times Ahead for Home Textiles," *Charlotte Observer*, December 12, 2004, p. 1D.

46. Moreton, *To Serve God and Wal-Mart*, p. 6.

47. Lloyd Wood interview with author on June 18, 2009, in Washington, D.C.; Harris Raynor interview with author on June 18, 2010, in Union City, Georgia.

48. Paul B. Johnson, "Textile Leader Rips Wal-Mart," *Knight-Ridder/Tribune Business News*, August 12, 2003 (Emrich quotation); Franklin Foer, "Fabric Softener: The Textile Lobby v. The War on Terrorism," *New Republic*, March 4 and 11, 2002, p. 19.

49. Stella M. Hopkins, "Tough Times Ahead for Home Textiles," *Charlotte Observer*, December 12, 2004, p. 1D (first three quotations); Stella M. Hopkins, "Springs' Slashed Work

Force in S.C., Will Now Be without Any Plants; 120 Years of Manufacturing Fades Away," *Charlotte Observer*, June 28, 2007, p. 1D (closing quotation).

50. David Barboza, "In Roaring China, Sweaters Are West of Socks City," *New York Times*, December 24, 2004, p. A1.

51. Vance H. Trimble, *Sam Walton: The Inside Story of America's Richest Man* (New York: Dutton, 1990), pp. 291–92; Quotation in Richard Craver, "10 Years of NAFTA: New Free-Trade Policies Show Effects of Treaty," Winston-Salem (North Carolina) *Journal*, January 1, 2004, p. A1; "Suppliers Respond to Kmart Filing," *Southern Textile News*, January 28, 2002, p. 25; "Russell to Increase Bad Debt Reserve," *Southern Textile News*, February 4, 2002, p. 20; Malcolm A. Cross, *Dan River Runs Deep: An Informal History of a Major Textile Company, 1950–1981* (New York: The Total Book, 1982), p. 1.

52. Sharon E. White, "Jobs Available, But Seekers May Face a Pay Cut," *Charlotte Observer*, June 6, 2001, p. 1L (quotation); Peter T. Kilborn, "Jobs Are Scarce in the Newest Economy," *New York Times*, October 9, 2001.

53. Lloyd Wood interview with author on June 18, 2009, in Washington, D.C.; Chastain quoted in Woody White, "Textile Industry Looking to Regain Quotas, But Will It Really Help?" Greenville (South Carolina) *News*, April 10, 2005, p. 1.

54. "AYSA, Chesnutt Keep Pressure on Washington," *Southern Textile News*, September 1, 2003, p. 6.

55. Al Greenwood, "Jobless Seek Employment," Fayetteville (North Carolina) *Observer*, August 19, 2001; Closing quotation from Alma Jean Biggs in "Hanging On in Textile Country," *New York Times*, June 7, 1991, p. D1.

56. OECD study summarized in Jeffrey Sparshott, "An Industry Unraveling: U.S. Textiles Threatened as Quotas Expire," *Washington Times*, December 26, 2004, p. A1; 2007 data in "Imports of Chinese Apparel Soar After Safeguards Removed," NCTO press release, March 16, 2009, available at http://www.ncto.org/newsroom/index.asp (accessed August 20, 2009).

57. Robert W. Fairlie and Lori G. Kletzer, "Race and the Shifting Burden of Job Displacement: 1982–93," *Monthly Labor Review*, September 1996, pp. 13–23, quotation on p. 19; Steven Hipple, "Worker Displacement in the Mid-1990s," *Monthly Labor Review*, July 1999, pp. 16, 23–24; Ryan T. Helwig, "Worker Displacement in a Strong Labor Market," *Monthly Labor Review*, June 2001, p. 14.

58. Meisenheimer, "The Services Industry in the 'Good' Versus 'Bad' Jobs Debate," p. 30; Lori G. Kletzer, *Job Loss from Imports: Measuring the Costs* (Washington, DC: Peterson Institute for International Economics, 2001); Quotation in "Facts About Health Care—Health Insurance Coverage," available from the National Coalition on Health Care website at http://www.nchc.org/facts/coverage.shtml (accessed January 22, 2009). A copy of this document is in the author's possession. For an update on these figures, according to the U.S. Census Bureau in 2008 forty-seven million Americans, or 20 percent of the population under the age of sixty-five, were without health insurance. See http://www.nchc.org/facts-resources/fact-sheet-coverage (accessed January 17, 2011, copy in author's possession).

59. Harris Raynor interview with author on June 18, 2010, in Union City, Georgia; Ken Moritsugu, "Jobs Vanishing in the Textile Industry," *Philadelphia Inquirer*, September 8, 2001, p. C1; Meisenheimer, "The Services Industry in the 'Good' Versus 'Bad' Jobs Debate," p. 30.

60. Frank Swoboda, "Labor's Day in Martinsville: In an Old Mill Town, Textile Workers Find a Rare Union Success," *Washington Post*, September 5, 1994, pp. 1, 16; Jamie C. Ruff, "Laid-Off Workers Seek Health Benefits, Other Aid," *Richmond Times-Dispatch*, January 23, 2000, p. C1 (quotations).

61. Christina Nuckols, "Vote Near on Relief for Textile Workers," Roanoke (Virginia) *Times*, February 7, 2000, p. A1 (Armstrong quotation); Christina Nuckols, "Pilgrimage Fruitless for Textile Workers," Roanoke (Virginia) *Times*, February 10, 2000, p. A1 (other quotations).

62. Pamela Stallsmith and Michael Hardy, "Gilmore Offers Bill to Increase Benefits for Laid-Off Workers," Richmond (Virginia) *Times-Dispatch*, February 23, 2000, p. A1 (Hairston quotation); Pamela Stallsmith, "Virginia Legislature Rebuffs Governor's Proposal for Econom-

ic Development," *Knight Ridder/Tribune Business News*, April 20, 2000 (Armstrong quotation).

63. Kirstin Downey, "Health Care Subsidy Helps Some Jobless," *Washington Post,* December 31, 2003, p. E1.

64. Kristin Downey, "Health Care Subsidy Helps Some Jobless," *Washington Post*, December 31, 2003.

65. Robert Pear, "Sluggish Start for Offer of Tax Credit for Insurance," *New York Times*, January 25, 2004, p. N16 (Craven quotation). The Health Coverage Tax Credit will be explored in more detail in the Pillowtex case study in chapter 10.

66. David Koeppel, "When 'Job' Means Part Time, Life Becomes Very Different," *New York Times*, October 10, 2004, p. W1 (Cantanzaro quotation); Erik Eckholm, "Health Benefits Found to Deter Switches in Jobs," *New York Times*, September 26, 1991, p. A1.

67. MDC, *The State of the South 2002: Shadows in the Sunbelt Revisited*, p. 5 (first quotation), p. 6 (second quotation).

68. MDC, *The State of the South 2000*, (Chapel Hill: MDC, Inc., 2000), pp. 39, 46.

69. MDC, *Strengthening the Rural Carolinas: A Conceptual Framework for the Program for the Rural Carolinas* (Chapel Hill: MDC, Inc., 2002), pp. 3–4.

70. MDC, *The State of the South 2002*, pp. 14, 15 (first quotation), p. 16 (second quotation); Harris Raynor interview with author on June 18, 2010, in Union City, Georgia.

71. MDC, *The State of the South 2000*, p. 60 (first quotation); MDC, *Income and Wealth in the South: A State of the South Interim Report* (Chapel Hill: MDC, Inc., 1998), p. 8 (second quotation). For further detail on the way that the persistent economic gap between the races was the key failure of the ongoing black freedom struggle, see Timothy J. Minchin and John A. Salmond, *After the Dream: Black and White Southerners since 1965* (Lexington: University Press of Kentucky, 2011), esp. pp. 6–7.

72. U.S. Department of Labor, *The Past, Present and Future*, pp. 71–72; Ruth Crisco interview with author on June 22, 2010, in Concord, North Carolina.

73. Robert W. Fairlie and Lori G. Kletzer, "Jobs Lost, Jobs Regained: An Analysis of Black/White Differences in Job Displacement in the 1980s," *Industrial Relations* 37:4 (October 1998), pp. 460–77 (statistics on p. 460); Louis Uchitelle, "Blacks Lose Better Jobs Faster as Middle-Class Work Drops," *New York Times*, July 12, 2003. For similar findings, see also Francis W. Horvath, "The Pulse of Economic Change: Displaced Workers of 1981–85," *Monthly Labor Review* 110:6 (June 1987), pp. 3–12; Diane E. Herz, "Worker Displacement in a Period of Rapid Job Expansion," *Monthly Labor Review*, 113:5 (May 1990), pp. 21–33, esp. p. 23.

74. Uchitelle, "Blacks Lose Better Jobs Faster As Middle-Class Work Drops" (Lucy quotation); Ryan Helwig, "Worker Displacement in 1999–2000," *Monthly Labor Review*, June 2004, pp. 66–67; Sylvia Allegretto and Devon Lynch, "The Composition of the Unemployed and Long-Term Unemployed in Tough Labor Markets," *Monthly Labor Review* 133:10 (October 2010), p. 8.

75. Jim Davenport, "As Mills Close, Lancaster Faces End of Era," *The State*, September 8, 2003 (quotations); Jim Davenport, "Textile-Plant Closings Reshaping Life in South," *San Jose Mercury News*, September 22, 2003, p. 6E.

76. Cory Engle et al., "Counties Brace for Closure," *Charlotte Observer*, July 11, 2003, p. 1Y; William E. Schmidt, "Future of 2 Southern Industries Raises Concern," *New York Times*, December 9, 1984, p. 46.

77. Katherine Yung, "Industry's Boost from Trade Pact Didn't Last; China Seen as Spoiler," *Dallas Morning News*, September 28, 2003, p. 1D (quotations).

78. "America's Textile Industry Is in Deep Crisis," Charleston (West Virginia) *Daily Mail*, January 5, 2002, p. 5C (Ramey quotation); Jamie C. Ruff, "Textile Firm Sets Job Cuts: Two Burlington Plants Will Close," Richmond (Virginia) *Times-Dispatch*, January 11, 2002, p. A1 (other quotations).

79. "Mill's Ex-Workers Weave New Life," *Charlotte Observer*, November 21, 1999, p. 4I.

80. Chris Burritt, "Like a Death in the Family," *Atlanta Journal Constitution*, April 14, 1991, p. A1.

81. Burritt, "Like a Death in the Family."

82. MDC, *The State of the South 2002*, p. 16; "America's Textile Industry Is in Deep Crisis," Charleston (West Virginia) *Daily Mail*, January 5, 2002, p. 5C; Jeffrey McMurray, "Southern Lawmakers Struggle to Get Help for Textile Industry," Anderson (South Carolina) *Independent-Mail*, January 14, 2002.

83. Dave Baity, "Cause of Lost Jobs Is Bigger Than NAFTA," *Charlotte Observer*, December 2, 2001, p. 1L; Gary Henderson, "Closings Take Jobs, Tax Dollars from County," Spartanburg (South Carolina) *Herald-Journal*, January 28, 2002, p. A6 (quotation).

84. Venita Jenkins, "Historic Ties Unravel," Fayetteville (North Carolina) *Observer*, September 2, 2001 (St. Pauls quotations); Chris Burritt, "Seven Years into NAFTA, Textile Makers Seek Payoff in Mexico," *Atlanta Journal and Atlanta Constitution*, December 17, 2000, p. Q1 (Erwin quotation).

85. Scott Baughman, "Piedmont Blood Center Faces Critical Drain on Local Supply," Gaffney (South Carolina) *Ledger*, April 12, 2006.

86. Roxana Ross, "Closings Leave 1,300 Textile Jobs," *The Robesonian* (Lumberton, North Carolina), September 17, 2006, p. A1.

87. Joe Depriest, "Bricks May Fall but Memories Last," *Charlotte Observer*, November 23, 2003, p. 1L.

88. "What Goes Up?" *Southern Textile News*, February 14, 2005, pp. 20–21. The Pillowtex demolition is discussed further in chapter 10.

89. Chris Burritt, "Seven Years into NAFTA, Textile Makers Seek Payoff in Mexico," *Atlanta Journal Constitution*, December 17, 2000 ("buckle" quotation); Jim Schlosser, "The Countdown, The Boom, The Collapse," Greensboro (North Carolina) *News and Record*, May 24, 2005, p. A1 (other two quotations); "Starmount Plans to Redevelop Burlington Industries' HQ Site into Mixed-Use Area," *The Business Journal of the Greater Triad Area*, March 8, 2004.

90. "Leader in Its Field," *Southern Textile News*, August 17, 1998, pp. 1–16, quotations on pp. 1, 2.

91. Jim Schlosser, "Burlington Files for Bankruptcy: Founder Spencer Love 'Spinning in His Grave,'" Greensboro (North Carolina) *News and Record*, November 16, 2001, p. A1; Hall et al., *Like A Family*, pp. 238–48; Paul Nowell, "Burlington to Slash 4,000 Jobs," *Durham Herald-Sun*, January 11, 2002, p. B8; Eric Heisler, "NYSE Boots Burlington: Textile Company Searches for Trading Market," Greensboro (North Carolina) *News and Record*, November 20, 2001, p. B11. For examples of press accounts that detail the company's plant closures prior to bankruptcy, see Stella M. Hopkins, "2420 Carolinas Textile Jobs Cut," *Charlotte Observer*, January 27, 1999, p. 1A; Andrew Shain, "Burlington Lops 1,600 Jobs," *Charlotte Observer*, September 15, 2000, p. 1D.

92. Katherine Yung, "Trade Deal Hurts U.S. Textiles," *Dallas Morning News* column, reprinted in *The State,* October 19, 2003, p. F1; "Asset Firm Agrees to Purchase Burlington Industries," *New York Times*, July 29, 2003.

93. "ATMI to Cut Four Positions," and "Industry's Voice to Grow Quieter," *Southern Textile News*, January 21, 2002, p. 3 (first and second quotations), p. 13 (third and fourth quotations); Lloyd Wood interview with author on June 18, 2009, in Washington, D.C. (final quotation).

94. "Mann: Merger, Sans Honeymoon, Working," *Southern Textile News*, May 12, 2003, pp. 1–6; "SCMA: Fertilizing Mfg. Ground Group's Goal," *Southern Textile News*, May 12, 2003, pp. 8–11 ("nontextile" quotation on p. 10); Devin Steele, "McCall: NCMA Work Continues," *Southern Textile News*, October 25, 2004, pp. 1–3; "Trade Association Annual Meeting," *Southern Textile News*, September 27, 2004, p. 5. For information on the demise of the *Daily News Record*, see http://www.thenewmagazinecity.com/daily-news-record.html (accessed February 11, 2011, copy in author's possession).

95. "SC Senate Race," *Southern Textile News*, September 27, 2004, p. 12.

96. NCTO quotations in "2007 Proves to Be a Transitional Year for U.S. Industry," NCTO Press Release, February 15, 2008, available at http://www.ncto.org/newsroom/index08.asp (accessed August 20, 2009, hard copy in author's possession); Devin Steele, "NCTO Members Vote to Endorse DR–CAFTA," *Southern Textile News*, May 9, 2005, pp. 1–3 (AMTAC quota-

tion on p. 2); "As the Worms Turn," *Southern Textile News*, May 23, 2005, p. 20 (Smith quotations).

97. Chris Burritt, "Seven Years into NAFTA, Textile Makers Seek Payoff in Mexico," *Atlanta Journal Constitution*, December 17, 2000, p. Q1 (Bakane quotation); Stella M. Hopkins, "Tough Times Ahead for Home Textiles," *Charlotte Observer*, December 12, 2004, p. 1D; Rosen, *Making Sweatshops*, pp. 3, 150–52.

98. These campaigns are all detailed in box 34, UNITE Papers-Cornell (6000/027). For a representative overview of these efforts, see Rhett Doumitt, "Nicaragua Situation Update," January 12, 1997, "Nicaragua Organizing Project" folder, box 34, series 6000/027, UNITE Papers-Cornell.

99. "Anatomy of Exploitation: JCPenney 'Arizona' Jeans Produced at Chentex," November 12, 1997, "Nicaragua Organizing Project" folder, box 34, series 6000/027, UNITE Papers-Cornell.

100. Bruce Fieldman to Jay Mazur et al., February 3, 1995 (Fieldman quotation); Bruce Fieldman to Jeff Hermanson, December 11, 1995, both "Honduras Organizing Project" folder, box 34, series 6000/027, UNITE Papers-Cornell.

101. Bruce Fieldman Activity Report, October 1–December 31, 1994; Alan Howard to Jay Mazur, May 19, 1994 (first Howard quotation); Other Howard quotations in Alan Howard to Jay Mazur, November 24, 1995, all "Honduras Organizing Project" folder, box 34, series 6000/027, UNITE Papers-Cornell.

102. "Industry's Voice to Grow Quieter," *Southern Textile News*, January 21, 2002, pp. 13–14; Pietra Rivoli, *The Travels of a T-Shirt in the Global Economy: An Economist Examines the Markets, Power, and Politics of World Trade, Second Edition* (Hoboken, NJ: John Wiley, 2009), p. 189.

103. Devin Steele, "Goal of New Coalition: To Save Jobs," *Southern Textile News*, April 1, 2002, pp. 8–10 (Nash quotation on p. 93); "Lobbying Coalition Launches," *Southern Textile News*, May 27, 2002, pp. 2–4 (Milliken quotations on p. 3).

104. Devin Steele, "Goal of New Coalition: To Save Jobs," *Southern Textile News*, April 1, 2002, p. 10 (Nash quotations); "Milliken Alliance Realigns," *Southern Textile News*, March 17, 2003, pp. 1–2; Lloyd Wood interview with author on June 18, 2009, in Washington, D.C.

105. Lloyd Wood interview with author on June 18, 2009, in Washington, D.C; Ben Szobody, "Roger Milliken, Textile Titan, Dies," *USA Today*, December 30, 2010; Butler Derrick interview with author on April 13, 2011, in Easley, South Carolina.

106. See, for example, "Currency Legislation Urgent as Trade Deficit with China Soars in 2007," NCTO Press Release, February 14, 2008, available at http://www.ncto.org/newsroom/index08.asp (accessed August 20, 2009). A copy of this document is in the author's possession.

107. Quotation in "Global Alliance Presses Governments and WTO to Halt Chinese Monopolization of Global Trade in Textiles and Clothing," GAFTT Press Release, January 26, 2005, available at http://www.fairtextiletrade.org/ (accessed August 2, 2009). A copy of this document is in the author's possession. Many other documents giving further insights into GAFTT's work are available from this website. In this discussion, I particularly drew on "Textile and Clothing Trade Associations Endorsing the Istanbul Declaration as of October 5, 2005," available at http://www.fairtextiletrade.org/istanbul/ids.html and "96 Trade Groups from 54 Countries Supporting the Principles of the Istanbul Declaration," November 30, 2004, available at http://www.fairtextiletrade.org/newsroom/pr200406.html (both accessed August 2, 2009, copies in author's possession).

108. Elaine Woo, "Crystal Lee Sutton, 1940–2009: Union Organizer Inspired Film 'Norma Rae,'" *Los Angeles Times*, September 20, 2009, p. A44; Martha Quillin, "Activist Who Inspired 'Norma Rae' Dies," *Charlotte Observer*, September 15, 2009 ("stature" quotation); "Symbol for Fairness," *Raleigh News and Observer*, September 17, 2009, p. A10 (two final quotations).

109. Harris Raynor interview with author on June 18, 2010, in Union City, Georgia (Harris Raynor quotations); Steven Greenhouse, "Unions Focus Attention on Workers in Service Industries," *New York Times*, June 16, 2006, p. C1; Sam Hananel, "Merged Union's President Quits as Battle for Control Escalates," *Washington Post*, May 30, 2009, p. A15. For more information on this split, which largely resolved around tensions between Bruce Raynor and

HERE president John Wilhelm, see: Steven Greenhouse, "Two Unions in Marriage Now Face Divorce Talks," *New York Times*, February 8, 2009, p. A18.

110. Henry P. Leiferman, "Trouble in the South's First Industry: The Unions Are Coming," *The New York Times Magazine*, August 5, 1973, p. 10 (first quotation); Tony Mecia, "Textile Paper Writes Its Own Obituary," *Charlotte Observer*, August 15, 2009, pg. 10.

*Chapter Nine*

# Fighting Back: Lowell, Massachusetts, and the Long Battle against Deindustrialization in the North

In 2010, the Oscar-winning movie *The Fighter* vividly recounted the true story of "Irish" Micky Ward, a struggling boxer from Lowell, Massachusetts, who overcame adversity to win the world welterweight title. Filmed almost entirely in the old mill town, *The Fighter* shows Ward battling both self-doubt and the control of his half-brother and trainer Dicky Eklund, a wayward crack addict who spends much of the film in jail. With the help of new girlfriend, Charlene, Ward is able to turn his career around after a series of defeats and secure the title. In many ways, the film is also a metaphor for Ward's hometown, which has had to deal with a great deal of adversity following the demise of the textile industry. For decades after the mills closed, Lowell fought high unemployment and economic decline, but in recent years it has managed to find new success as a cultural heritage site and film location. Richard P. Howe Jr., a local resident and the city's Register of Deeds, has commented on the analogy between the struggles of the city and those of one of its most famous sons. "*The Fighter*'s almost like a metaphor for the city," he reflected in 2011. "Lowell . . . it never gave up, it always was fighting back. It's such a struggle to succeed, as an urban community in America, that many just kind of throw in the towel, but Lowell always is coming up with a way to reinvent itself."[1]

Lowell's importance as a case study is clear, as it is hard to think of a more significant center of textile production. The city illustrates well how the textile industry was the first American industry, and how its decline deserves to be at the heart of the story of deindustrialization. According to Paul Tsongas, a local resident who became a U.S. senator and presidential candidate, at its peak Lowell was "the textile capital of the world." The "Spindle City" played a central role in the textile industry's early development and in the industrialization of the United States as a whole. Although integrated machine production of cotton cloth had been achieved in Waltham, Massachusetts, in 1815, the limited waterpower provided by the shallow Charles River restricted it. Fueled by the vast waterpower potential of the Merrimack River, which dropped thirty-two feet in one mile, it was in Lowell that the first large-scale output of staple cotton goods was achieved. Prior to the Civil War, Lowell became the leading textile center in the country; no other city produced more textiles, employed more people in the industry, or had more capital invested in mills. "Lowell," declares social historian Mary Blewett, "has always meant the mass production of cotton textiles." Although this system of mass manufacturing spread across the country, it originated in Lowell. As local industry executive John Rogers Flather put it, "The beginning of industry in the United States really started in Lowell."[2]

Lowell's textile mills, however, started to close in the 1920s, and the pace of decline accelerated after World War II. Between 1940 and 1974, the number of textile workers in the city fell from ten thousand to under four thousand.[3] Like many New England mill towns, Lowell suffered greatly in the 1950s, a time when the rest of the economy was booming. In fact, the decade brought the closure of Boott Mills and Merrimack Manufacturing Company, two of the city's oldest and largest mills. The shutdowns devastated Lowell, which suffered from high unemployment and economic malaise for years afterward. By the early 1980s, when the term *deindustrialization* was coined, Lowell had already experienced many decades of industrial decline. Overall, therefore, Lowell's importance as a pioneer of both industrialization and deindustrialization is clear. As historian Cathy Stanton has put it, "One of the earliest American places to become industrialized, Lowell was also among the first to experience the shock of deindustrialization."[4]

A great deal of scholarship has focused on Lowell in the early nineteenth century, but much less consideration has been given to the city's more recent history, especially events after World War II. As historian Laurence F. Gross has noted, histories of the Lowell mills have "generally ended" at the Civil War, with much more being written on the industry's development rather than its decline. The recruitment of thousands of young women into the first mills has received particularly close attention, and it was Lowell's mills that helped to establish the industry's reliance on female labor.[5] Carefully examining the events that led to the Boot closure in 1955, Gross's *The Course of Industrial Decline* helps to redress this chronological imbalance, yet it fails to explore the impact of the shutdown, especially on workers, or to look at Lowell's broader experience. Since the publication of this book in 1993, more valuable work on Lowell has been completed, especially on the establishment of the National Park in 1978, but this important turning point has served as an ending for most studies rather than a beginning.[6]

It is especially important to bring the story forward, so that Lowell's extended battle with deindustrialization can provide lessons for many other American communities, including southern textile towns that declined much later.[7] In many ways, Lowell could be seen as a model success story, yet its road to recovery was long and uneven, and at the time of writing uncertainty about the city's vitality remains. While Lowell has fared better than many other New England mill towns, its experience still highlights just how hard it is for textile communities, and especially for displaced workers, to recover from the industry's disappearance. Above all, the upturn took a long time to occur; it was not until the late 1970s, with the establishment of the National Park, that Lowell began to put the pain of the Boott and Merrimack closures behind it. Even after this, the city suffered setbacks. In the early 1990s, the bankruptcy of Wang Laboratories, a computer maker that had become the area's largest employer, led to a return of high unemployment and a painful, fruitless search for a new economic anchor. During the recession that began in 2007, Lowell continued to suffer from above-average unemployment; in April 2010, for example, the city's jobless rate was 11.4 percent, above the rates for the state (9.1 percent) and nation (9.9 percent).[8]

This case study will focus chiefly on the Boott and Merrimack closures.[9] These two shutdowns throw light on the demise of the New England textile industry in the period immediately after World War II, a crucial decade. Between 1947 and 1957, for example, New England witnessed a 50 percent drop in textile employment, an unprecedented rate of decline, and the closures in Lowell were at the heart of this fall.[10] According to David Weltman, whose family had owned the Merrimack, the giant plant was "the lifeblood" of the Spindle City. "It together with the Boott Mills probably were the largest two employers in town," he added. The Merrimack, explained the *Lowell Sun* in 1955, was "Lowell's largest plant and manufacturer of world-famous velveteen and corduroy." The maker of the well-known "Drywell" and "Wipe-Dry" towels, and the holder of numerous patents and trademarks, Boott Mills was another plant with enormous economic and psychological significance to the city. As mill director J. R. Flather boasted in 1954, "The Boott Mills name has had a top-notch reputation for 120 years." Occurring within three years of one another, the loss of these two defining plants signaled the industry's demise for good in Lowell. While the Boott closure was related to southern competition, the loss of the Merrimack was largely due to imports. As a result, the two shutdowns illustrate the central reasons for the broader decline of the northern textile industry and the way that imports gradually replaced domestic competition as the chief culprit.[11]

By the 1940s, the Boott and the Merrimack were especially important to Lowell's economy because most other original mills had already closed. In the early twentieth century, the growth of the southern industry led to shutdowns in Lowell, often by firms who moved to take advantage of cheaper wages. Between 1912 and 1918 the Middlesex and Bigelow Manufacturing companies left town, while in 1926 the Hamilton, Suffolk, and Tremont Mills all suspended their operations. By 1930 the Massachusetts Manufacturing Corporation had also closed, along with the Lowell Machine Shop and the Appleton Company. What occurred in Lowell was part of a broader trend; between 1923 and 1927, $100 million of New England mill capital moved to the South. Compounded by the Great Depression, these closures caused tremendous suffering in Lowell, which was visited by writer Louis Adamic in 1931. "In Lowell," he wrote in *Harper's Magazine*, "I saw shabby men leaning against walls and lamp-posts and standing on street corners singly or in twos or threes; pathetic, silent, middle-aged men in torn, frayed overcoats or even without overcoats, broken shoes on their feet, slumped in postures of hopeless discontent." For years after Adamic's visit, life in the Spindle City remained grim, and as late as 1938 some 40 percent of the city's population was still on government relief.[12]

Despite the industry's problems, it retained a major presence in Lowell and was revived by the wartime boom. Boott Mills became the largest supplier of Twill Uniform Cloth for the U.S. Navy, winning several government awards in the process. The Boott was the first cotton mill in New England to receive the Army-Navy "E" pennant, and the only textile plant in the nation to receive five stars on its pennant. "Only a good mill could have won this recognition," director J. R. Flather wrote later.[13] Born in 1938, Flather's son Newell grew up in Lowell in the wartime era and remembered that the mills still dominated life in the town. "I was just a boy," he recalled, "but I certainly was aware that in one way or another most everybody deferred to my father, and my grandfather, to the family name . . . I remember driving downtown with my mother and the police always seemed to, when they spotted her and her car they seemed to hold up traffic and allow her to drive by. Textiles were a principal employer."[14]

Even after World War II Lowell had a heavy dependence on the textile industry, and it was this that made the loss of mill jobs so painful. In 1952, when Newell was fourteen, 44.7 percent of Lowell's manufacturing employees worked in textiles, while nine years later the industry remained the biggest employer within the manufacturing sector. As late as 1973, textiles retained this position as the largest manufacturing employer in the city. Two of the better-known textile firms, New Knit Manufacturing Company and Wannalancit Textile Company, did not close until 1977 and 1980 respectively. Between 1950 and 1966, seven medium-sized mills had also shut, while between 1960 and 1972 twenty-seven smaller textile firms closed, wiping out the mills that many former Boott and Merrimack workers had moved to. The post–World War II era, then, was when Lowell felt the full force of deindustrialization. For the first time, most unemployed textile workers were forced to leave the industry if they wanted to find work.[15]

The Boott and Merrimack closures illustrate Lowell's dependence on the textile industry particularly well, especially as they occurred so close together. First to go was the Boott. Built between 1835 and 1900, the company was one of Lowell's oldest, occupying an impressive site on the banks of the Merrimack River. The main complex was made up of nine mill buildings that comprised seven hundred thousand square feet of interconnected industrial space.[16] With its imposing clock tower and huge inner courtyard, the mill was a landmark in Lowell, yet its age and size became a liability, especially once the wartime boom was over. In March 1945, J. R. Flather told the Appellate Tax Board that the company was finding it increasingly difficult to operate the oldest surviving cotton mill in the North. "Since April 1929 the weak, unstable, narrow, unadaptable aggregation of curiously shaped buildings have increasingly become more and more valueless than they were then," he declared, "because of wear, tear, obsolescence, and constantly increasing adverse economic factors." The old buildings meant that the company could not run one fabric steadily but had to change frequently, necessitating costly loom adjustments. Newer mills in the South did not face this problem. "We have no intention of going out of business," wrote Flather, "but it is problematic how long we can hold this business in Lowell."[17]

In his papers, Flather complained that the Boott could not compete with southern mills that did not pay their workers as much. Most of these mills were nonunion, yet the Boott had been organized since 1942, when wartime production demands had influenced its decision to reluctantly recognize the TWUA. By the early 1950s, the company estimated that 94 to 96 percent of toweling—its main product—was made in the South. The company's case illustrated how the wage differential undermined the northern industry, and how the textile industry in general was vulnerable to competition from mills with cheaper labor.[18]

In the early 1950s, the situation came to a head. In April 1951, the Boott's managers went along with other New England mills and agreed to a 7.5 percent wage raise. They were subsequently very concerned when a general strike in the South failed to secure a comparable increase. By early 1953, when its contract was due for renewal, Boott executives insisted on being exempted from the New England pattern and sought a wage cut of some twenty-four cents an hour, at a time when the average wage in the plant was $1.34 an hour. According to the company's figures, this reduction represented the wage and benefit differential between the Boott Mill and its southern competitors, especially Cannon Mills, which was nonunion. In March 1953, F. and J. R. Flather explained to workers that cuts were inevitable because the company was in the red. "The reason we are losing money," the father and son directors wrote, "is that we must, in order to get orders, meet the low prices of our Southern competitors, although our wages are higher than Southern mills. You know that a company that continually loses money cannot stay in business, so our objective must be to stop these losses."[19]

The union saw the situation very differently. Worried that the reduction would undermine its New England pattern, labor leaders argued that the company could ride out the crisis by drawing on its financial reserves. As Gross has detailed, relations between the two sides had been poisoned by a lengthy strike in 1947 to 1948. Then, the company had annoyed the union by arguing that wages could only increase if workloads got much heavier. By the early 1950s, J.R. Flather could not understand the union's position, complaining that its "iron resistance" to change was dooming the mill.[20] On another occasion he elaborated that "the union policy of forcing wage advances on us, and then this very same Union's failure to win equality of wages in the South, is slowly but surely killing off New England textile jobs."[21]

The Boott closure illustrated well how deindustrialization caused a horrible dilemma for union leaders, whose job was to deliver improved wages and conditions for their members. Thus the union's institutional survival was threatened by requests to be exempted from the northern wage pattern. Writing members in August 1953, local union president John J. Duff encapsulated the TWUA's stance: "The position of the Union has not changed one iota; we feel very strongly that Boott workers are just as good as any other textile worker." The job of the union was "to bring about a better life for its members and their families," and this would be impossible if wages were falling, especially at a time when other American workers were winning pay increases.[22]

With neither side willing to give ground, the situation became serious, especially as the ending of the Korean War in July 1953 led to an economic downturn across the textile industry. On March 3, 1954, J. R. Flather warned the union that he would "run out and close down the entire mill" if the wage cut was not agreed to within a week. No agreement was reached, but the mill struggled on. In an apparent effort to break the impasse, the company then pressed for an increase in workloads, but the union resisted. According to TWUA regional leader M. Michael Botelho, the company wanted "revolutionary changes" in workloads, and the union would only agree if its members' wages were protected while the new assignments were tried out.[23] The Flathers disagreed, calling the union's conditions "crippling and nullifying." Clearly out of patience, they decided to liquidate the mill. By September 1954, two-thirds of the plant was idle, and the rest of the mill would soon follow.[24]

Despite the alienation that existed between management and labor, most of which J.R. Flather directed at the union leadership, his papers reveal that he worried about the welfare of his workers, especially older employees who had been with the company for decades. He saw the mill as a local family business, and as the shutdown started to bite his anxiety increased. "People in Lowell know that we had on our payroll hundreds of middle age and older men, and hundreds of middle age and older women, and that when they are laid off most of them cannot get work elsewhere," he wrote in 1954. Flather knew that job loss would be devastating for these workers, especially as their "lifetime skill and experience" would no longer be recognized. He predicted that most of them would end up on relief or in lower paying jobs; "only a very few" would land better posts.[25] Aware of how much Lowell still depended on the textile industry, Flather also knew that replacing the mills would be very difficult. "We hear much about new industries," noted a company document, "but it is indeed doubtful if the new industries which might replace Boott cotton manufacturing would ever prove as stable to employees throughout good times and bad as Boott has for 120 years."[26] Based on interviews with more than two hundred displaced Lowell textile workers that were conducted just as the Boott Mill was closing, a study by Northeastern University economist William H. Miernyk confirmed Flather's fears. In *Inter-Industry Mobility* (1955), Miernyk documented that most of the interviewees suffered long periods of unemployment or found jobs in other textile mills. Moreover, younger workers were "best able" to land posts outside the industry. "It is clear that in Lowell at least the displaced textile worker does not readily transfer to one of the growth industries," he concluded.[27]

While Flather was justifiably proud of his company's long history, Boott Mills' neighbor on the Merrimack River was even older. Lowell's first mill, the Merrimack Manufacturing Company, was founded in 1822, and it helped Lowell to become one of the best-known industrial cities in the country. In February 1822, the new company had paid $15,000 to the Boston Manufacturing Company in order to "use any machinery now in use at Waltham" by that firm. As a result, the Waltham system of mass production was introduced to Lowell, where land was more plentiful and the supply of waterpower much greater. At the new site, the thirty-foot drop in the Merrimack River could power ninety mills the size of Waltham's.[28] The company also ordered a large number of timber joists that were, according to their supplier, "sound and perfectly square." Used in early construction, they supported a six-story building that was a prime example of the big mills that made Lowell famous. As the mill's first superintendent, Kirk Boott played a leading role in the life of early Lowell, a city that was not founded until four years after Merrimack Manufacturing Company shipped its first cloth to Great Britain.[29]

After the Civil War, the Merrimack Manufacturing Company remained a mainstay of the local economy. In 1900 the company established a plant in Huntsville, Alabama, and this foothold in the South helped the firm to survive the textile depression of the 1920s better than most northern textile firms. Even in 1937—when most mills were still struggling—the Merrimack's large complex in Lowell employed over one thousand people. During the wartime boom, employment rose significantly and more women were hired, some of whom were retained after the war.[30] By the post–World War II period, the Merrimack remained Lowell's largest plant and was, as the *Lowell Sun* put it, "in the forefront of the nation's textile industry." The company advertised nationally and was also known for its New York fashion shows. Unlike the Boott, the Merrimack had a history of "labor-management cooperation," and the TWUA never succeeded in organizing it. Rather, in 1950 an Independent Union was certified at the plant. A few years later, the company boasted that it made the "World's Finest Corduroy" and that it offered its workers decent wages, "steady employment," and "liberal benefits."[31]

After World War II, however, corduroy and velveteen began to be manufactured in large quantities by other countries, especially Japan. The shutdown was a classic illustration of wider themes, especially the rise of foreign competition and the commitment of federal officials to free trade. The company's fate came to a head in 1957, when the Japanese promised to restrict their textile exports to the United States. In particular, the Asian power agreed to hold its velveteen exports to 2.5 million yards annually while Italy—another important competitor—agreed to reduce its exports by a half a million square yards. When these agreements were announced, the Merrimack received new orders, reemployed nine hundred workers, and went back into full production. Subsequently, however, the company's managers complained that the Japanese had not adhered to the cuts, and they petitioned President Eisenhower to take action. Swayed by a desire to extend free trade and to build a better diplomatic relationship with Japan, Eisenhower refused to intervene. The mill's fate had been decided. "The company," declared the *Lowell Sun* in December 1957, "has been a victim of the government's failure to create and maintain adequate protective tariffs."[32]

In oral history interviews, key Merrimack managers agreed that the closure had been caused by imports. "Our selling office kept hounding us, telling us that [foreign] competition was beating us," recalled former plant superintendent Robert Brassil. Malcolm Chace, whose family co-owned the Merrimack Company when it closed, confirmed Brassil's account. "The great problem," he elaborated, "was that the Japanese could ship velveteen to the east coast, and undercut the price by 60 or 70 percent. . . . It . . . became a question of the cheap velveteen coming in. It couldn't compete." According to former co-owner Phil Lehner, the situation came to a head when Merrimack's managers were unable to persuade the Eisenhower administration to put antidumping duties on Japanese velveteen. Then, executives felt that they had no choice but to liquidate the mill. Officials in Washington, thought

Lehner, saw textiles as an industry that belonged "outside the United States."[33]

Former workers also linked the closure to imports. "The Merrimack was one of the last ones [to close]," recalled experienced velvet cutter Raymond Ryan, "but I mean they were feeling the pinch with imports, like everybody else." Once the mill's payroll clerk, Robert Cooper concurred: "It was obvious in 1956–57 that things weren't getting any better, and the competition was getting more fierce from outside the United States, as well as the people that moved to the South, that Merrimack made the decision in 1958 that they were going to call it a day." Reasoning that textiles had no future, Cooper left the mill before the closure was announced and took a job in an electronics plant.[34]

The twin closures really hurt, especially as both mills had declined quite quickly. In 1944 the Boott mill had employed 2,500 workers, but once the war ended the situation changed quickly. By June 1952, employment had dropped to 604 employees, while three years later just thirty-two people remained on the books. In 1953 to 1954, unemployment claims in Lowell spiked by over 36 percent, largely because of the mass layoffs at the Boott Mills.[35] The Merrimack closure was equally devastating; it threw over one thousand people out of work, and many of them were heads of families. "The loss of the Merrimack will have a negative effect upon the city's economy," admitted the *Lowell Sun*, which called for greater efforts to attract new industry. As recently as July 1955, the Merrimack had employed over 1,600 people.[36]

Lowell struggled to recover from the double whammy. According to Louis Vergados, a former union organizer who had also worked at the Merrimack, in the wake of the closures Lowell was an "empty, desolate" place. "Nobody has any work," recalled the Greek American. "You walked down, you saw people, proud people, hunchback, no money, no work. Depressed." Feeling that "something had to be done," Vergados felt that the closures spurred early efforts by municipal leaders to attract new industries. Things did not get better quickly, however. According to one summary compiled by the Center for Lowell History, "By the late 1950s, Lowell consisted of millions of square feet of empty five- and six–story brick mill buildings, a active but slowly decaying business district, and high unemployment."[37]

In oral histories collected by the Center, former workers and managers agreed that the Merrimack shutdown had a particularly severe economic impact. The closure, recalled mill superintendent Robert Brassil, was "devastating as far as the average worker is concerned." As Brassil explained, many of these workers had earned good wages on piecework. A relatively young man at the time, John Kadir got another job quite easily, but older workers were not so fortunate. "The older people, you know, they didn't have no other place to go," he declared. "They felt it." Local employment security data confirms that veteran workers were disproportionately affected as the Merrimack collapsed. In 1961, for example, 49 percent of Lowell's male unemployment claimants were aged fifty-five or older, compared to just 37 percent nationally.[38] The impact of the Merrimack closure was accentuated by the fact that even younger workers had a lot of seniority, as it was usual to start in the mill at an early age and stay there. A lifelong Lowellian with a Polish and Lithuanian background, William Wyskoczka began in the mill in the late 1930s, when he was still at high school, and was later offered a permanent post as a dyer. "Most of the people that worked there," he recalled, "at that time if you had a job you stayed. You didn't move around you know?" When the mill shut, Wyskoczka "felt terrible," although his knowledge of chemicals allowed him to eventually land positions with Raytheon and then Polaroid. Like most former Merrimack workers, Wyskoczka expressed pride in the work that he had done at the mill. "Our quality was the best," he declared.[39]

Even when workers found new jobs, these positions rarely offered the wages or job security that the mills had. Over time, many former Boott and Merrimack workers did secure assembly-line jobs in light industries, especially in electronics plants. One of the country's leading electronics firms and an important defense supplier, Raytheon arrived in Lowell in 1952 and hired many former mill workers, but most toiled in low-level jobs. In her thesis on Lowell's economy after the mill closures, Maura Doherty carefully documented that most of the new industries that located in the city actually paid less than either high-tech growth industries or traditional manufacturing, causing wages to drop and pushing more women into the workforce to supplement their partners' wages. By 1970, 47 percent of Lowell's working-age women were in the labor force compared to 41 percent nationally, while among minority women the participation rate was even higher. "The postindustrial economy," concluded Doherty, "had not replaced the old jobs with higher-paying new ones."[40]

The experience of individual workers highlights that new industries were not always an improvement, and many of those laid off found jobs within the industry. Harry Dickenson, for example, went to work at the Merrimack when the Boott closed. When the Merrimack went under, he found work in a radio assembly plant, working there until it also shut. His pay was $1 an hour, much less than the $1.75 he had earned in textiles. After losing his job at the Merrimack, loom fixer Albert Cote similarly worked in either textile mills or electronics plants. "Mostly all the mills I worked in are all shut down today," he reflected in retirement, adding that he had "adjusted" to the various closings and layoffs as they had occurred. Skilled male mechanics were one of the few groups who were able to avoid this shift into assembly-line work. As former Merrimack spinner Jean Rouses explained, "After the mills closed, the mechanics got mechanics' jobs, and most of the women went into stitching." Many women indeed got jobs in small apparel and shoe shops, but because these businesses were vulnerable to import competition, workers lacked job security.[41]

As J. R. Flather had predicted, the mill closures also had a significant psychological impact upon workers. While acknowledging that life in the mill had been very hard, former employees often expressed regret about the demise of the town's main industry. "Nobody wanted the mills to go," declared Ruth Ann Sharpe, an African American woman who worked at the Merrimack for fifteen years before it closed. Following the shutdown, Sharpe changed jobs frequently, spending most of her time in ailing shoe and textile shops, and she looked back on her mill days with some fondness. "We were friendly, the women and the men," recalled Sharpe, who had overcome resentment from a few individuals who were not used to interacting with blacks. In fact, when the plant closed the migrant from Georgia had been its only African American worker. Although she held an office job for more than twenty years after the closure, Jean Rouses also "missed" working on spinning frames. "I used to be ashamed to say I worked in the mill," she reflected, "but then I wasn't because it was a job that you did and you had pride in it." White-collar employees shared these feelings. Robert Cooper, for example, felt that it was "sad" when the company closed. "It was the heritage of the city that was gone," he reflected. "It's like losing a parent."[42]

Because it was difficult to find jobs that paid as well as the mills, many displaced textile workers now had to travel for work. Expanding car ownership played an important role in mitigating the effects of deindustrialization, although it also undermined the close-knit ethnic neighborhoods that had defined prewar Lowell. What occurred in the Spindle City was representative of broader social trends; between 1950 and 1980 the American population doubled but the number of cars on the road quadrupled, and the vast interstate network was being completed as the Boott and Merrimack shut.[43] As former worker Leo Paradis recalled, when the mills closed "loads of people commuted." In the past, added Raymond Ryan, mill workers had walked or taken a bus, but after the closures many began to travel "fifty-sixty miles on a job." Another former Merrimack worker, James Ellis, agreed that car ownership helped to soften the blow of the shutdowns. Before the war, he recalled, "Nobody could afford a car. So if you lost your job in Lowell you couldn't go to Arlington. You couldn't go to Medford for a job. But after the war you could do that. Companies started building along the Route 3 of Boston, and people were able to go twenty miles, they had to commute back and forth." Data backs up these recollections. In 1971, for example, the metropolitan Lowell area had the highest rate of out-commuting in the state, as more than 50 percent of the workforce held jobs outside the area.[44]

While workers drove to other towns, Lowell's mill district languished, its deteriorating buildings one of the most obvious signs of the industry's decline. As former Boott worker Valentine Chartrand put it, "First thing you know they were all empty here, one after the other. . . . A lot of people out of work then. . . . There was nothing here." With so many mills standing vacant, civic leaders argued that the best option was to demolish them, and Lowell became affected by the push for "urban renewal," which favored the destruction of unused industrial buildings to make way for new factories, housing, and roads. In November 1959, for example, the owners of the Merrimack mill announced that the entire complex would be bulldozed, a move that was defended by the *Lowell Sun*. "The demolition of the Merrimack should not cause any alarm," it wrote in an editorial. "It might, on the other hand, be considered an advance toward progress." Overall, the urban renewal program was "a wise program of revitalization" that should bring "Modern Manufacturing" to the city. In reality, however, the Merrimack Mill was replaced with a high-density housing project and a parking lot.[45]

The Merrimack demolition reflected the belief that empty mills were a liability rather than an asset, the same type of thinking that was dominant in the South after the plant closures of the 1990s and 2000s. As Malcolm Chace explained later, his family had knocked down the factory partly because they "didn't want the obligation of a bunch of empty mill buildings for people to wander through." Phil Lehner, who had co-owned the mill with the Chaces when it closed, stressed that the demolition was also designed to reduce the Merrimack's tax bill of $70,000 a year, which the city had refused to cut. Lehner admitted, however, that several of the old stone buildings "would have been handsome structures today."[46]

Others who were connected to the mill also regretted its disappearance. One-time plant manager Frank Maria, who had left Lowell by the time of the closure, bemoaned the destruction of the "historic" complex. The nephew of former Merrimack owner Jacob Ziskind, David Weltman went as far as to term the demolition "a very low point in Lowell's history." A talented local entrepreneur, Ziskind died prematurely in 1950, and many workers felt that the mill had struggled to recover. Occurring a few years later, the demolition of former company-owned row houses on Dutton Street was also widely lamented. "For the history of Lowell it's a shame they got torn down," declared Margaret Simon, a former secretary at the Merrimack. The destruction of the houses proved to be a turning point, however, invigorating efforts to preserve Lowell's unique textile landscape before it was too late.[47]

In contrast to the Merrimack, the Boott Mill survived as rental space for a wide variety of enterprises, and J. R. Flather's efforts were now devoted to trying to find tenants. By January 1956, the mill's occupants included a retail store, a cafeteria, a couple of small sewing shops, and various other enterprises. It was also used for storage. Conducting an "aggressive drive for tenants," Flather worked tirelessly to try to fill the vast mill.[48] The Spindle City clearly suffered from an image problem, however, as Flather had to combat a "fear" that staff would not be willing to relocate, especially from Boston. Lowell had many advantages, he continued in one letter to a skeptical Bostonian, including "surplus labor" and good road links that made it easy to commute. Revealingly, he also sold the mill's riverside location to industrial clients. "We are still on the banks of the Merrimack River," he declared, "so that you will have no water or waste disposal problems. You will find our location handy for your workers as well as for yourself."[49]

Although Flather tried hard to market the mill, his task was not easy. Complaining that the Boott buildings were cold and leaky, tenants pushed for lower rents, and Flather found it difficult to rebuff them. "It is true that the roof occasionally leaks," he admitted to one renter, "but we repair it as a leak appears." Well into the 1970s, it was difficult to persuade companies to move into Lowell's empty mills. In 1973, staff from the locally based Human Services Corporation interviewed fifty-four firms that were now located in old mill buildings. Tenants praised the cheap space that the factories provided but complained about the lack of parking and the fact that most of their premises were not on the ground floor. In the battle with the new suburban business parks, Lowell was clearly at a disadvantage. In addition, the survey's authors also interviewed prospective employers, finding that many were dissuaded by Lowell's high level of unemployment and the fact that few of the jobless were skilled. Overall, both the mills and their workers were struggling to find a new path. When the survey was conducted, for example, Lowell had 1,922,000 square feet of vacant industrial space, most of it in old textile buildings, but even at sixty cents a foot it was unable to find takers. According to industrial realtor Bill McInerney, who was pictured in the *Lowell Sun* standing in the vast spaces of an empty mill, the city had a number of handicaps, including high property taxes and a plethora of old plants that needed "domestic surgery." In addition, new industries that did not secure a ground floor site in the mills had to install rigging equipment and shore up the floors, both of which were expensive.[50]

In an effort to meet some of these objections, Lowell's public officials also tried to develop new industrial sites. In the 1950s, one of the first tasks of the Lowell Development and Industrial Commission was the establishment of the suburban Industrial Park. Designed to stabilize the city's "long-wobbly economy," as the *Lowell Sun* put it, the Park had some success. By the time of the Merrimack closure, it had attracted three companies—CBS-Hytron, Cambridge Corporation, and Reiss Associates—and they employed around 1,400 people, including some former mill workers. The Park illustrated well how Lowell's leaders had not given up the fight to revive their troubled city.[51]

Despite these efforts, Lowell remained wedded to manufacturing just as it was starting to decline. Even most of the companies that located in the Industrial Park were manufacturers. As late as 1971, 37 percent of Lowell's jobs were in the manufacturing sector, compared to only 25 percent of jobs nationally. Manufacturing employed more people than the service sector, and both textiles and apparel were included in the list of the five leading manufacturing industries. "The economy of Lowell," concluded one study in the files of the Human Services Corporation, "has suffered greatly due to the trend of its Manufacturing Sector, and at the same time still depends significantly upon it." Over the course of the 1970s, little changed. By 1980 some 41.6 percent of Lowell's labor force was still employed in manufacturing, even though the proportion of Americans employed in this sector was falling all the time.[52]

Because most mills were located near the center of Lowell, the downtown also suffered once they went out of business. While the demise of urban downtown areas was a broader phenomenon that was linked to suburbanization and increasing car ownership, there is little doubt that in Lowell it was compounded by the decline of the textile industry. Between 1948 and 1963, for example, the number of retail establishments in Lowell fell from 1201 to 882, and the figure dropped further after the Burlington Mall opened in 1965. When he became mayor in 1970, Richard P. Howe Sr. remembered that two-thirds of stores in the city were vacant, while most of the others were hanging on for dear life. During four terms in office, Howe worked hard to try to turn this situation around, but it took time.[53]

Lowell's long struggle to recover from the mill closures was illustrated well in 1975, when the *Sun* ran a detailed series of articles on the local economy. A downcast air infused the reports, reflecting the reality of life in a struggling city with a "bleak" downtown. "One wonders if the mills will ever be full again," declared reporter Alberta Cook. "Lowell," she elaborated, had "more to overcome than the average city," including high unemployment, a patchy record in attracting new businesses, and an "unfortunate image." Many in the city, including Howe, saw demolition of the mill buildings as the only answer, arguing that it would provide a clean break with the burdens of the past. Despite this wish, the city lacked the resources to carry out extensive redevelopment, and most mills were left to rot. On a closing note, however, Cook saw hope in a proposal to establish the country's first urban national park. Rather than being a liability, Cook predicted that the empty mills could actually "help the city develop a uniqueness necessary in fostering an urban park theme."[54]

Consistently higher than state or national averages, the unemployment rate was perhaps the most telling marker of Lowell's long fight with the consequences of deindustrialization. In 1958—the year that the Merrimack closed—unemployment in Lowell stood at 11.3 percent, much higher than the national rate of 6.6 percent. Seven years later, Lowell's official jobless rate of 8.2 percent was almost double the national average, while actual unemployment was even higher. Arriving in 1965, historian Mary Blewett remembered that the city "bore the scars of decades of industrial decline" and was crippled by high unemployment. In 1966, the Department of Labor ranked Lowell as one of its areas of "substantial unemployment," not the first time that the city made this unenviable list. By 1971, Lowell's unemployment rate had jumped to 12.1 percent, compared to a national average of 5.9 percent, while four years later further mill closings had pushed it to almost 13 percent. What was even more striking was that unemployment had remained high despite steady out-migration. Between 1940 and 1970, thirty thousand people left Lowell, reducing the city's population to ninety-four thousand. "The higher a person's standing academically at Lowell High School, the less likely it was that person would later live in the city," recalled Paul Tsongas.[55]

Tsongas was one of the most notable exceptions to this trend, and the rising political star would play a key role in helping Lowell to finally turn its economic prospects around. Born in 1941, Tsongas was raised in the city as it struggled to cope with the Boott and Merrimack closures, and the experience had a lasting effect on him. "Growing up in Lowell, I learned firsthand about decline," he wrote later. "It is pervasive, it eats away at everyone and everything." The economic climate affected Tsongas's family, as his father—a small businessman—worked hard but was "robbed . . . of financial success" by the city's plight. Tsongas, however, considered the old mill town home, and he always retained a house in the city. "Lowell was where people cared about us—my title notwithstanding," he explained. As a result, he was determined to change Lowell's fortunes, and especially to end the in-fighting between the municipal government and the private sector that had plagued the city during the 1950s and 1960s. Elected to the city council in 1969, to the U.S. Congress in 1974, and then to the U.S. Senate in 1978, Tsongas consistently worked to transform the fortunes of his hometown. His dream was to make Lowell the best midsized city in America.[56]

Two key developments helped Lowell to turn the corner, and Tsongas was integrally involved in both. In 1978, Congress established the Lowell National Historical Park on the site of the vast Boott Mills, with a mandate to interpret the Industrial Revolution in the U.S. Recognition of Lowell's central role in the industrialization of America, the move also highlighted how local officials had started to see that the mills could be used to promote economic development through tourism and historical preservation. As the Greater Lowell Area Planning Commission now boasted, Lowell was a "monument to the Industrial Revolution." The Park came to fruition by uniting a broad coalition of business groups, public officials, and educators, who included both "economic and educational dimensions" in its programs. Surpassing the initial urge to demolish the mills, they were now recognized as a valuable economic and cultural asset. The Park also built on the ideas of Patrick J. Mogan, the local school superintendent, whose concept of the "educative city" envisioned using the entire community as a "learning laboratory." A determined leader, Mogan was centrally involved in the 1971 foundation of the Human Services Corporation, a private nonprofit corporation that was dedicated to enhancing the quality of life in Lowell. Throughout the 1970s, the HSC helped to build support for the National Park proposal, and it was subsequently involved in many other programs to revive Lowell.[57]

A talented congressman, Tsongas played an important role in lobbying for the Park in Washington. In March 1977, for example, he wrote President Carter's chief domestic policy adviser, Stuart Eizenstat, in order to solicit the administration's support. The public and private sectors, he explained, had already sunk $26 million into "Park-related projects" in Lowell. "However," he continued, "these efforts will not succeed without federal recognition of the city's historical and cultural contribution to America and a commitment to protect these resources for the benefit of present and future generations." In a warm reply to his fellow Democrat, Eizenstat agreed that the proposal offered "an unprecedented opportunity to preserve an important aspect of the industrial revolution."[58] The following month, Congressman Tsongas introduced the legislation that led to the Park's foundation. In May 1978, when H.R. 11662 was approved, Tsongas was delighted, describing the outcome as "the culmination of ten years of work by the people of Lowell." The idea indeed dated to the late 1960s, when City Councilor Tsongas had helped to forge the coalition that sponsored the proposal. With the establishment of the one-hundred-acre park, Lowell received much-needed federal funds, as H.R. 11662 declared that $21.5 million would be spent on the implementation of the park preservation plan while a further $18.5 million was set aside for the "acquisition and development" of properties by the Secretary of the Interior.[59]

Lobbyists had succeeded partly because they had cleverly turned Lowell's economic stagnation to their advantage. In 1972, for example, a resolution by the Lowell City Council claimed that the Park was needed because the community was "currently experiencing economic problems which have affected the City adversely." Combined with the city's historic importance—which supporters constantly stressed—these were compelling arguments.[60] The establishment of the Park was a turning point, as Tsongas and his allies were now able to argue that Lowell had "the potential to be a national model of how a city can revitalize itself." To fulfill this vision, in 1979 Tsongas and city manager Joseph Tully established the Lowell Plan, which encouraged public and private sector leaders to develop economic development goals. The Plan worked in tandem with the Lowell Development and Financial Corporation, which provided loans and incentive financing to carry out various revitalization projects, including the expansion of the Lowell Regional Transit Authority and the funding of a feasibility study for a minor league baseball team.[61]

As a result of these initiatives, Lowell began to attract positive media attention, the first it had received for decades. When the Park was established, popular syndicated columnist Neil Pierce wrote that "a town widely depicted a few years ago as a blighted remnant of the Industrial Revolution, plagued by outmigration and high unemployment, has quite suddenly turned a corner." The mills were at the heart of the turnaround; rather than vacant liabilities, they were now "seen as the architectural gems they are." By 1983, the Park was bringing 437,000 visitors to Lowell each year, and Tsongas wrote that it had also been "the catalyst for private investment in the project area."[62] Lowell soon came to epitomize how obsolete industries could be given a "second life" as heritage, providing a model for other federally designated heritage areas. As scholar Cathy Stanton has shown, just as the original "Lowell experiment" of a planned industry city provided a blueprint for communities as they industrialized, the city's imaginative efforts to promote its industrial past came to influence projects in both the United States and abroad.[63]

Despite the Park's success, in terms of employment it was no substitute for the mills. The mills had been Lowell's economic anchor, and Boott Mills alone had once employed two thousand people. As pictures from the late nineteenth century indicate, it was a workforce big enough to fill its huge inner courtyard, yet the Park's staff of fifty or so looked lost when they were pictured in the same vast space many years later. Tsongas understood the need for more jobs, and he constantly pushed for more federal support. Pitching the city as a test case in the fight against industrial decline, he promised citizens that he could turn around Lowell's fortunes. "If Lowell fails, if it can't come back," he declared in 1979, "then it can be argued that no city can come back."[64]

Just as Kannapolis would later receive federal help, in the 1970s government programs eased Lowell's economic pain. Between 1970 and 1978, the Department of Defense awarded nearly $777.5 million to local defense contractors, the largest of which was Raytheon. A large contingent of former Boott and Merrimack workers got hired at Raytheon, and although most held low-paid positions, they were still glad to be in work. By the early 1970s, indeed, Raytheon was Lowell's biggest employer. Also between 1970 and 1978, the Department of Health, Education and Welfare spent over $244 million on the city, including social security payments for those unable to find jobs.[65]

Perhaps Tsongas's greatest victory came in 1977, when he convinced Dr. An Wang, a Chinese immigrant who headed Wang Laboratories, to make Lowell his company's world headquarters and principal manufacturing center. In 1951, Wang had left the Harvard Computation Laboratory to establish a small computer manufacturing company, and the growth of his firm was part of the wider emergence of high-tech industries in the Boston area. Like

Wang Laboratories, many of these companies originated in the city's high-quality educational institutions and subsequently moved out in search of manufacturing space. In 1957, for example, Digital Equipment Company was established in an old wool plant in Waltham after founder Ken Olsen quit the MIT-affiliated Lincoln Lab. Observing the emergence of these high-tech companies, free-traders insisted that New England had recovered from the demise of the textile industry. After testing these claims, an exhaustive academic study reached a very different conclusion. In 1982, Bennett Harrison, the coauthor of the classic *The Deindustrialization of America*, found that New England's reinvention as a high-tech center had bypassed former textile communities. In an MIT/Harvard study, Harrison looked at the 674,000 workers who left the textile industry between 1958 and 1975, finding that just twenty thousand of them got jobs in high tech during this time.[66]

Still, Wang's arrival was welcome in Lowell, where the company gave jobs to a wide variety of local residents, including new immigrants and the children of textile workers. For a decade, Wang helped to revitalize Lowell, and the city's unemployment rate dropped below 3 percent. More than ten thousand people worked for the company at its peak, and it seemed like the "Massachusetts Miracle" really did exist. In 1981, *Newsweek* declared that Lowell had been "reborn" partly because of Wang, while the *U.S. News and World Report* credited "High Tech" with ending "a Long Slump in an Old Mill Town." Lowell, declared Stephen Solomon in *Science Digest*, had become a "computer boom town." By 1984, the local Chamber of Commerce was able to boast that the revitalization of the greater Lowell area was "incredible."[67]

The good times were short lived, however, as Wang soon fell victim to intense competition in the home computer market. Failing to keep up with the rapid pace of technological innovation, Wang was surpassed by IBM, Apple Macintosh, and Hewlett-Packard. By the late 1980s Wang was in serious trouble, and in 1992 it filed for bankruptcy. The experience highlighted that even high-tech jobs did not bring the economic security that the mills had provided. An Wang died in 1990, and his company's buildings in Lowell, which totalled 1.5 million square feet of space and included a six-story downtown complex, were sold at auction for 1 percent of their cost. After coming out of bankruptcy in 1993, Wang ran down its manufacturing facilities and instead concentrated on marketing and consulting. By 1994, the firm had lost 80 percent of its workforce.[68]

At the time of the bankruptcy, Wang provided employment for around 10 percent of workers in Greater Lowell, so the economic impact of its collapse was enormous. It was compounded by the national recession of the early 1990s. According to Richard P. Howe Sr., who was mayor at the time, Wang's demise "was a haymaker . . . it knocked everybody out."[69] Workers who had counted on their jobs to finance new houses and cars were certainly stunned. "I'm surprised nobody's snapped," commented one anonymous employee after the announcement. In the wake of Wang's failure, Lowell's unemployment rate jumped to 10.7 percent, and three local banks went out of business. John Marsh, the last large department store, left the downtown, and smaller stores soon followed. In a 1992 feature, the *Boston Globe* found that Lowell was "reeling" from Wang's collapse. "Empty storefronts mark Merrimack Street like missing teeth," it added. "Abandoned houses pock historic neighborhoods, the boards in the window signs of drug raids or unpaid mortgages."[70]

As its economy faltered, Lowell suffered from social problems that were common in postindustrial cities, including widespread drug use and elevated levels of petty and violent crime. In 1995, the HBO documentary *High on Crack Street: Lost Lives in Lowell* was filmed in the city and helped to publicize these problems, much to the annoyance of civic leaders, who tried to block the film's release. Featuring the lives of three crack addicts, including the real-life Dicky Eklund, the documentary took place against a backdrop of high unemployment, most of it the result of Wang's collapse. It graphically highlighted how the cultural renaissance spearheaded by the National Park and the Lowell Folk Festival had done nothing to improve the lives of many ordinary citizens. City leaders, however, argued that the film was overly negative; the crime rate was dropping, they insisted, and the economy was on the mend.[71]

These claims had some validity. In the wake of Wang's collapse, most local people refused to get despondent. Lowellians, they insisted, were used to hard times and could endure this latest blow. As the *Boston Globe*'s Maggie Farley and Katherine Yung summarized, "While Lowell residents acknowledge Wang's troubles are a new twist of the knife, they insist it is not fatal—they have survived recessions before." City manager Richard Johnson epitomized residents' resilience. "There still remains a light in the city," he declared. "As the economy starts to turn around, Lowell will start to turn around. I think Lowell will bounce right back." Importantly, the National Park continued to give Lowell an advantage over other postindustrial towns. At the time of the Wang bankruptcy, the Park was attracting over half a million tourists a year, and it was also securing positive publicity. According to *Historic Preservation*, Lowell was the "premier rehabilitation model for gritty cities worldwide."[72]

Using the National Park as a platform, the Spindle City was indeed able to turn its prospects around in the decade or so after Wang's demise. Thus, by 2007 the *Globe* could declare that Lowell was "vibrant again."[73] Several factors help to explain the city's revival. An agency of the U.S. Department of the Interior that was established by the same statute that created the Lowell National Historical Park, the Lowell Historic Preservation Commission was able to use federal and private funding to restore much of the city's historic streetscape. Among its major achievements were the reconstruction of an old mill workers' boarding house as the Patrick J. Mogan Cultural Center, the development of the Park's historic replica trolley system, and the completion of a network of canalside walkways. Overall, between 1975 and 1995 more than 250 historic buildings were restored with the Commission's support. "Today rehabilitation has overtaken decay," it declared in 1995. These efforts laid the groundwork that allowed Lowell's leaders to promote their city and its cultural vitality. Thus by 2007 visitors were encouraged to stroll along the canalside paths and take rides on the restored trolley. Tourism efforts were also spearheaded by the largest free folk festival in the country, as well as by various programs that sought to market Lowell's connection with the writer Jack Kerouac, who grew up in the West Centralville district of the city. Kerouac's first novel, *The Town and the City* (1950), was heavily autobiographical. In particular, the book's fictional mill town, Galloway, bore a close resemblance to Lowell.[74]

The Park sparked other programs to revitalize Lowell. Starting in 1996, a community improvement organization called "Lowell: The Flowering City" oversaw efforts to clean up the canals and plant roadside gardens. Overall, the group worked to fulfill an ambitious twenty-five-year plan that was designed to "beautify" Lowell. The group believed in the city, and their programs impressed many observers, including former governor Michael Dukakis. An important ally for the city, the longest-serving governor in Massachusetts history declared that he had Lowell "in his veins" when he helped the group celebrate its tenth anniversary. "You have a plan and people," he added, "a concept of what you want your city to look like."[75]

The turnaround was helped by other factors. Importantly, efforts to diversify the local economy bore fruit, especially when high-tech firm Getronics moved in and took over some of Wang's buildings. By 2000, the Dutch company employed over one thousand people in Greater Lowell. One clear sign of the recovery occurred in 1998, when the former Wang headquarters in downtown Lowell—which had been auctioned off for just $525,000 at the height of the downturn—sold for $103 million. By this time the 1.1 million square foot building had thirty-one tenants and was almost full. Because the building was widely seen as a symbol of Lowell's fortunes, its revitalization was important. Although no one firm was able to replace Wang, service sector jobs helped to fill the void, while the state government also became an important employer. In 1991, the University of Lowell was integrated into the UMass system, opening the way for considerable expansion. Twenty years later, a report by the Lowell Plan and the university found that the educational institution had 640 staff and fourteen thousand students, and they had the potential to spend $10 million a year in local businesses. As UMass Lowell Chancellor Marty Meehan commented, "The university has a significant positive impact on downtown Lowell." By acquiring Wang's downtown training center and relocating there, Middlesex Community College also helped to revitalize the downtown.[76]

Arriving in 1996 after years of lobbying by municipal leaders, a minor league baseball team also boosted the city's economic and cultural vitality. As the *Boston Herald* noted, the Lowell Spinners quickly became "one of the greatest success stories in all of minor league baseball." Between 1999 and 2006, the team's home fixtures sold out for an unprecedented 252 games. Much of the Spinners' success was credited to its affiliation with the well-liked Boston Red Sox, although affordable ticket prices and the attractiveness of LeLacheur Park also played their part. By 2006, the team was so popular that fans faced a five- to ten-year waiting list for season tickets, while some who secured them traveled from Boston to attend games. According to four-time mayor Richard Howe Sr., overall the Spinners were a "big plus" for Lowell.[77]

The film industry also had a positive economic impact upon the city. In the new millennium a number of films, including *Monkey Dance* (2004), *The Busker* (2006), *The Invention of Lying* (2009), *Four Single Fathers* (2009), *The Edge of Darkness* (2010), and *The Fighter* (2010), were all shot in Lowell. Film-tax laws that earned Massachusetts the nickname "Hollywood East" were crucial in attracting movie makers. Under the 2006 legislation, companies that filmed in the Bay State received a 25 percent tax credit on all payroll and production expenses, and they were also exempt from sales tax on most purchases. For so long considered a liability, Lowell's industrial streetscapes now lured producers who needed distinctive sets. Five years after the passage of the legislation, movies shot in the Bay State had generated $36.3 million in tax revenues and created nearly two thousand jobs, although the state had also handed out $260 million in tax breaks. For Lowellians, however, the benefits were obvious. According to Representative Tom Golden, a Lowell Democrat, *The Invention of Lying* and *The Fighter* were a "major boost" to the local economy, especially downtown businesses. The movies also brought positive exposure, a fact highlighted when actor Christian Bale (Dicky Eklund in *The Fighter*) thanked "everybody in Lowell" during his Oscar acceptance speech. "That stuff is priceless," exclaimed Golden.[78]

A large influx of immigrants from Southeast Asia also revitalized Lowell, especially as they helped to end the city's long period of population decline. In the early 1980s, Asian migration to the city was facilitated by the federal government's policy of dispersing refugees throughout the country, as well as by "refugee-friendly" state government policies and the presence of a Buddhist temple in North Chelmsford. When the Wang-led IT boom took off, Cambodian immigrants were also attracted to Lowell by the availability of entry-level industrial jobs and affordable housing. According to "Ethnicity in Lowell," a special report commissioned by the National Park Service, by

2000 approximately twenty thousand Southeast Asians lived in Lowell, and they represented about one-fifth of the city's population. About 90 percent of these migrants were Cambodians, while the rest were predominantly Vietnamese or Laotians. Overall, Lowell was home to the second largest population of Cambodians in the United States, outdone only by the much larger city of Long Beach, California.[79]

These immigrants have clearly contributed to the city's recovery. By 1997, more than one hundred new businesses had opened in the Lower Highlands neighborhood that were either run by Cambodians or served the new community. Between 1997 and 2002, moreover, the number of Asian-owned businesses in Lowell grew 150 percent, compared to 24 percent nationally. In Lowell's Asian community, rates of home ownership and political participation also rose, and Cambodian American Rithy Uong was elected to the city council in 1999, 2001, and 2003.[80] The new arrivals clearly felt a sense of belonging in the Spindle City, which had a long history of accepting immigrants. As Cambodian-born Sovann-Thida Loeung put it, she felt "very secure" when she moved to Lowell as a twenty-year-old. "Lowell gives the opportunity for individual ethnic group to enjoy, to celebrate, to hold on to their heritage," she added. "I think that's a good thing about Lowell for me."[81] Just as they had turned their industrial heritage into an asset, Lowell's leaders began to sell their city's cultural diversity, promoting the range of ethnic cuisines available and offering walking tours of immigrant neighborhoods. They also started the Southeast Asian Water Festival, which honored Lowell's Cambodian, Thai, Vietnamese, and Laotian communities and attracted over sixty thousand visitors each year. In 2011, they also initiated moves to create a "Little Cambodia" district within the Lower Highlands neighborhood.[82]

While Lowell clearly recovered from the Wang bankruptcy, it still had plenty of problems, and it is important to keep its revival in perspective. Above all, there was no direct replacement for the mills, and the new "cultural economy" did not create a large number of jobs. As Newell Flather commented in 2011, the city still lacked a "major employer."[83] Because it did not start until the late 1970s—more than two decades after the Boott and Merrimack closures—Lowell's revival was also of little help to those who lost their jobs in these shutdowns, many of whom had retired or died by this time. This was especially true of the older workers that Newell's father had worried about. The National Park was also disconnected from many Lowellians, especially newer arrivals. As the "Ethnicity in Lowell" report acknowledged, many immigrants were "unaware" of the National Park, and this could only be changed through extensive "outreach." Some residents also complained that much of Lowell's revival was not aimed at local people. "Lowell has clearly come a long way, and it is for many people who live and work here a much nicer place than it used to be, say 20, even 10 years ago," acknowledged community activist Laura Buxbaum in 2005. "But I am very concerned about the direction that Lowell is continuing to head in. The focus of the revitalization is much too heavily on people of means, bringing people of means into the city both to live and as visitors." Lowell's economic weaknesses were graphically highlighted during the recession that began in 2007, when the jobless rate soared. In January 2010, for example, Lowell's unemployment rate of 13.1 percent was well above state and national norms.[84]

Apart from ongoing economic weaknesses, there were other problems, especially in the heart of the city. Despite the much-heralded revival of the downtown, it was difficult for visitors to stay there. When UMass Lowell turned the last downtown hotel into student dormitories, most tourists had to lodge out of town. Concerned about the quality of public education in the city, wealthier residents moved permanently to the suburbs or other towns. This flight was not just restricted to the white population, as some successful Asian immigrants also moved away. In addition, the police in Lowell had an ongoing struggle with gang violence, much of it generated by small Cambodian gangs who generally targeted other Asians. After 1997, when Paul Tsongas died from cancer at the age of just fifty-five, there was no one leader who could focus efforts to tackle these issues. As the *Lowell Sun* acknowledged in 2007, Tsongas was "a giant whose shoes have yet to be filled." More than a decade after Tsongas's death, those with long memories acknowledged that life in Lowell had improved greatly, but they also pointed out that many of the city's historic buildings had only survived because things had been so bad for so long. As Newell Flather put it, "Lowell, in that period, was so down on itself it didn't even make an effort to dissemble the city, to do urban renewal, so when the idea of the Park, of the first national park, came along, almost everything was there, and had been preserved."[85]

Despite these problems, overall it was clear that Lowell had fared better than other mill towns in Massachusetts, at one time the country's leading textile state. Between 1985 and 1997, manufacturing employment in New Bedford fell by more than 53 percent, and the unemployment rate tipped 20 percent. According to the *Boston Globe*, the town became "one of the nation's poorest and most depressed communities." By 1997, unemployment in New Bedford was more than double the Massachusetts average, and the town fought with neighboring Fall River to try to secure a proposed casino development. In the end, however, neither won the prize. Across the Bay State, former mill communities consistently struggled to prosper even during good times. In 1998—when Massachusetts boasted the lowest unemployment rate in a decade—New Bedford, Fall River, Holyoke, and Lawrence all suffered from jobless rates that were more than twice the state average.[86]

There were certainly plenty of problems in Holyoke, a former mill town on the Connecticut River about ninety miles west of Boston. The city was plagued by crime and unemployment, and in 2002 its per-capita income of

$18,296 was the lowest in the entire state.[87] It was a similar story in other former mill towns. Located just a few miles from Lowell, the former wool center of Lawrence fared much worse than its neighbor, inviting comparisons between the two. Lowell certainly possessed natural advantages; its larger land size allowed it to retain the tax base of middle-class neighborhoods, while its city manager system of local government was more efficient than Lawrence's, which required most mayoral decisions to be subject to council approval. Above all, however, Lowell had imperceptible fighting qualities, and this made a difference. As the *Boston Globe*'s John Powers put it, "Much of what Lowell has and Lawrence lacks is intangible—a sense of purpose, of resilience, of bustle."[88]

Elsewhere in New England, former textile centers struggled to match Lowell's recovery. Over the state line in Rhode Island, Pawtucket and Woonsocket experienced economic malaise for decades after the mills left. "Poor Pawtucket," lamented journalist Sacha Pfeiffer in 2007. The city was home to America's first permanent spinning mill, but it had "yet to fully recover from the collapse of the textile industry that once anchored its economy." Although it was trying to ape Lowell's success in attracting tourists and artists, Pawtucket was lumbered with vacant stores, and most of its mills had "fallen into decrepitude."[89]

During the economic recession that began in 2007, Massachusetts' old mill towns again suffered heavily. In February 2009, the jobless rate in New Bedford was 15.2 percent, nearly double the state average of 8.3 percent. Things were even worse in Fall River, where unemployment topped 18 percent. "It's not hard to find people here who have lost hope," wrote *Boston Globe* reporters Noah Bierman and Johnny Diaz. "This former manufacturing city, once home to humming factories, has for years been pummeled by one economic blow after another." Although Lowell was also hurt by the downturn, it was doing better than its counterparts. In particular, its mills were not empty and neglected but had been put to a wide variety of uses. In April 2011, the *Lowell Sun* reported that 95 percent of the "once-decaying" mills had been renovated, and there were plans to deal with the remaining 5 percent. The landmark Boott Mills was now home to upmarket apartments, many offering views over the cleaned-up river. The mill also housed the successful National Park museum and a variety of small businesses. Several other mills had been turned into artists' studios, their high ceilings and large windows proving perfect for this purpose. At the Appleton Company and the Hamilton Company, qualified artists who rented or purchased live-work units received reduced rents or mortgage rates, concessions that proved popular.[90]

Lowell's example is especially relevant for Kannapolis, North Carolina, and for other southern mill towns that are now confronted with the long fight to recover from the loss of their main employer. Overall, the lesson seems to be that recovery will be painful and slow and may not occur at all, but there is hope for communities that have effective and determined leadership. While Lowell was one of the first towns in the country to experience deindustrialization, fifty years later Kannapolis went through the same painful experience when the industry moved offshore in search of cheaper labor. There were many similarities between the two stories, especially as both cities tried to replace textiles with high-tech jobs, with limited success. The two case studies are directly linked because it was Cannon's towels, made by cheaper, nonunion workers in the South, which helped to put the Boott Mills out of business.[91]

There were also personal connections, especially as many Lowellians responded to the decline of the textile industry by moving to the South. As Newell Flather recalled, when he was growing up it had been "the norm" for his friends to sell up and leave the city. "You could follow the industry south, or find new employment in other cities," he explained. After losing his job as the superintendent of the Merrimack Manufacturing Company, Robert Brassil moved to the Charlotte area and got a position with a local textile firm that involved visiting other companies' facilities. Brassil was able to spend the rest of his career in the Queen City area, and as he did so he witnessed the closure of many local mills. It was the large Pillowtex shutdown that really stuck in his mind, however. "That was a huge operation in Kannapolis, North Carolina," he recalled. "I did an awful lot of work at that plant. They recently closed and that was the largest single closing of any textile plant in the South." Overall, Brassil felt that it was "amazing" to see the industry go through another wave of decline some fifty years after its demise in the North. Just like the Merrimack, moreover, Pillowtex and numerous other southern mills had fallen victim to imports. "They just can't compete," he reflected.[92]

## NOTES

1. "'Fighter' Star Christian Bale Tours Lowell for Film Locations," *Lowell Sun*, May 12, 2009; Chris Camire, "'Fighter' Prize Called 'Priceless' for MA Economy," *Lowell Sun*, March 1, 2011; Richard P. Howe Jr. interview with author on April 28, 2011, in Lowell, Massachusetts (quotations). This summary of *The Fighter* is also based on the author's viewing of the film.

2. Paul Tsongas, *The Road from Here: Liberalism and Realities in the 1980s* (New York: Alfred A. Knopf, 1981), p. 18 (first quotation); Dublin, *Women at Work*, pp. 9, 11, 21, 133; Norton et al., *A People and a Nation,* pp. 234, 259–60; Blewett, *The Last Generation*, p. 3 (Blewett quotations); Closing quotation in J. R. Flather to L. S. Bryant, May 28, 1951, "Correspondence 1944–1957" folder, box 27, Flather/Boott Mills Papers, 1836–1979, held at the Center for Lowell History, University of Massachusetts Lowell, hereafter cited as "CLH."

3. Marc Miller, "Who Won the War?" in Robert Weible, ed., *The Continuing Revolution: A History of Lowell, Massachusetts* (Lowell: Lowell Historical Society, 1991), p. 314.

4. Cathy Stanton, *The Lowell Experiment: Public History in a Postindustrial City* (Amherst: University of Massachusetts Press, 2006), p. 4.

5. The scholarly concentration on early Lowell is emphasized in Gross, *The Course of Industrial Decline*, pp. xiii–xiv, 41 (quotation). For important work on the industry's development in Lowell, including the recruitment of women workers, see: Caroline F. Ware, *The Early New England Cotton Manufacture: A Study in Industrial Beginnings* (Boston: Houghton Mifflin, 1931); Dublin, *Women at Work*; Robert F. Dalzell Jr., *Enterprising Elite: The Boston Associates and the World They Made* (Cambridge, MA: Harvard University Press, 1987). The essays in Arthur L. Eno Jr., ed., *Cotton Was King: A History of Lowell, Massachusetts* (Somersworth, NH: New Hampshire Publishing Company, 1976) also focus largely on Lowell before the Civil War. Another collection of essays on Lowell, Mary H. Blewett, ed., *Surviving Hard Times: The Working People of Lowell* (Lowell, Massachusetts: Lowell Museum, 1982), concentrates largely on labor radicalism in the city in the late nineteenth and early twentieth centuries. Another influential work on Lowell, with some coverage of the industry's problems before World War II, is that by geographer Margaret Terrell Parker, *Lowell: A Study of Industrial Development* (New York: The Macmillan Company, 1940). The Center for Lowell History also holds a rich body of material on the early industry, including hundreds of letters written by mill girls to their families, many of which are now available on the Center's website. See, for example, Sarah Hodgson to Mary Hodgson, n.d., "Lowell Mill Girl Letters" collection, letter transcribed by the CLH, available at http://library.uml.edu.clh/All/hod01.htm; Rebecca P. Hardy to Mary J. Hardy, September 13, 1854, letter transcribed by the CLH, available at http://library.uml.edu/clh/All/har.htm (both accessed March 11, 2011, copies in author's possession).

6. In Gross, *The Course of Industrial Decline*, the narrative ends with the 1955 closure of the mill (pp. 230–49). For two helpful theses on Lowell that do explore deindustrialization but conclude with the establishment of the National Park in 1978, see Maura Doherty, "Spindle City Blues: The Impact of the Maturing Industrial Economy on the City of Lowell, Massachusetts, 1947–1978," (PhD dissertation, New York University, 1998), and Mehmed Ali, "To Save a City: From Urban Renewal to Historic Preservation in Lowell, Massachusetts, 1920 to 1978" (PhD dissertation, University of Connecticut, 2006). The origins of the Lowell National Park are also explored in detail in Loretta Anne Ryan, "Lowell in Transition: The Uses of History in Urban Change" (PhD dissertation, Columbia University, 1987). For a detailed published study of the National Park and the public historians that work for it, see Stanton, *The Lowell Experiment*.

7. Scholarly work that deals exclusively with deindustrialization in Lowell is limited. Apart from the theses by Doherty and Ali, whose coverage terminates in 1978, other work on deindustrialization in Lowell includes the oral histories in Blewett's *The Last Generation*, a collection of interviews that were carried out in the 1970s and 1980s. The interviews focus on workers' life stories in general but do give some coverage to the industry's decline. Deindustrialization in Lowell is also covered to some extent in several of the essays in Weible, ed., *The Continuing Revolution*, especially Lawrence D. Gall, "The Heritage Factor in Lowell's Revitalization," (pp. 397–405), Miller, "Who Won the War?" (pp. 301–21), and Loretta A. Ryan, "The Remaking of Lowell and Its Histories" (pp. 377–95). Again, however, the bulk of the essays in *The Continuing Revolution*, which was published in 1991 by the Lowell Historical Society, focus on the city's history before World War II. A comparative study of Lowell and Manchester, New Hampshire, Brian O'Donnell's "The Spindles Stop: Lowell, Massachusetts and Manchester, New Hampshire Respond to the Collapse of the New England Textile Industry" (Ph.D. dissertation, Massachusetts Institute of Technology, 1995), focuses on the period from the industry's development in the nineteenth century through to the 1970s. None of the above studies covers the effects of the Wang Bankruptcy or the post-1992 period in general.

8. David Perry, "Job Market Limps toward Recovery," *Lowell Sun*, June 3, 2010.

9. In the discussion that follows, these companies will frequently be referred to as "the Boott" and "the Merrimack," titles that were widely used locally and which convey the mills' importance to the city.

10. Hartford, *Where Is Our Responsibility?* p. 151.

11. First two quotations in David Weltman interview with Jim Beauchesne on October 22, 1997, in Boston, p. 4, "Closing of the Merrimack Mills" series, CLH; "Merrimack Manufacturing Grants Workers Pay Boost," *Lowell Sun*, July 25, 1955, p. 1; Flather quoted in "Estimated

Value of Assets: Boott Mills," November 2, 1954, "Correspondence with Werner Textile Consultants, June 3, 1954–December 10, 1954" folder, box 65, Flather/Boott Mills Papers.

12. Gross, *The Course of Industrial Decline*, p. 165; Adamic quoted in David Pevear, "Today's Pain Has Nothing on Misery of 1920s and '30s," *Lowell Sun*, March 13, 2009; Closing statistic in Stanton, *The Lowell Experiment*, p. 103.

13. J. R. Flather, "1953 Summary," January 8, 1954, p. 7, "Working Files 1953–54 Labor" folder, box 63, Flather/Boott Mills Papers.

14. Newell Flather interview with author on April 27, 2011, in Boston, Massachusetts.

15. Doherty, "Spindle City Blues," pp. 101–02, 113–14; David Sylvester, "New Knit Textile Closes Its Doors," *Lowell Sun*, November 4, 1977, p. 1; Peter Anderson, "Lack of Mechanics Dooms a Mill," *Boston Globe*, October 9, 1980, p. 1.

16. "Boott Mills Estimated Value of Assets," November 2, 1954, "Correspondence with Werner Textile Consultants, June 3 1954–December 10, 1954" folder, box 65, Flather/Boott Mills Papers.

17. Testimony before Appellate Tax Board by J. R. Flather, February 28 and March 1, 1945, "Working File 1966" folder, box 27, Flather/Boott Mills Papers (quotations on the cover page and p. 6).

18. Gross, *The Course of Industrial Decline*, p. 198; J. R. Flather to S. Leonard Arnold, February 16, 1954, "Working Files 1953–54 Labor" folder, box 63, Flather/Boott Mills Papers.

19. Minchin, *What Do We Need a Union For?* pp. 154–59; "Supplement for Directors," May 5, 1951, "1951" folder, box 38, Flather/Boott Mills Papers; "1953 Summary," January 8, 1954, "Working Files, 1953–54 Labor" folder, box 63, Flather/Boott Mills Papers; Closing quotations in J. R. and F. Flather Jr. to "Our Fellow Workers," March 9, 1953, "Working Files, 1953–54 Labor" folder, box 63, Flather/Boott Mills Papers.

20. "Summary of Union Contract Negotiations," May 20, 1953, "Working Files, 1953–54 Labor" folder, box 63, Flather/Boott Mills Papers; Gross, *The Course of Industrial Decline*, pp. 216–21, 228; J. R. Flather Memo, July 26, 1954, "Closing 1954" folder, box 66, Flather/Boott Mills Papers (quotation).

21. "Appeal to the CIO and Boott Mill Workers to Join with the Company in Trying to Save the Mill from Closing," November 4, 1953, "Working Files, 1953–54 Labor" folder, box 63, Flather/Boott Mills Papers.

22. John J. Duff to TWUA Local 538 Members, August 4, 1953, Untitled folder, box 70, Flather/Boott Mills Papers.

23. J. R. Flather to Victor J. Canzano, March 3, 1954 (first quotation), and M. Michael Botelho to Frederick A. Flather, March 22, 1954 (Botelho quotation), both "Working Files 1953–54 Labor" folder, box 63, both Flather/Boott Mills Papers.

24. "Labor," May 21, 1954, "November 1954–July 1955" folder, box 71 (quotation); J. R. Flather to Francis E. Barrett, September 4, 1954, "November 1954–July 1955" folder, box 71; Henry H. Newell to J. R. Flather, December 13, 1954, "Memos and Correspondence on Closing of Mill, Part Business, Part Personal" folder, box 72, all Flather/Boott Mills Papers.

25. J. R. Flather Report, December 7, 1954, pp. 3, 4, "Working Files 1953–54 Labor" folder, box 63, Flather/Boott Mills Papers (quotations); J. R. Flather to William H. Miernyk, March 16, 1954, ibid.

26. "Appeal to the CIO and Boott Mill Workers to Join with the Company in Trying to Save the Mill from Closing," November 4, 1953, "Working Files, 1953–54 Labor" folder, box 63, Flather/Boott Mills Papers.

27. Miernyk, *Inter-Industry Labor Mobility,* pp. 37–44 (first quotation on p. 44, second quotation on p. 42). Although the Boott Mill was not identified by name, Miernyk's Lowell chapter was apparently based on the mill's case, which is discussed explicitly on pp. 34–36.

28. Quotation in "Agreement for Purchase of Patent Rights between Merrimack Manufacturing Co. and Boston Manufacturing Co.," February 28, 1822, Merrimack Manufacturing Company Business Records (MS1111.522), held at the American Textile History Museum, Lowell, Massachusetts, hereafter cited as "Merrimack Manufacturing Company Records"; Gross, *The Course of Industrial Decline*, p. 4.

29. "Isaac Riddle and Sons Contract for Kirk Boott," January 9, 1822, Merrimack Manufacturing Company Records; "Merrimack Mills Plan to Expand Operations," *Lowell Sun*, December 28, 1952, p. 1.

30. O'Donnell, "The Spindles Stop," p. 130; "Presenting Merrimack Manufacturing Company, Huntsville, Alabama," pp. 1, 29, company brochure held at the American Textile History Museum, Lowell, Massachusetts; Marc Scott Miller, *The Irony of Victory: World War II and Lowell, Massachusetts* (Urbana: University of Illinois Press, 1988), pp. 51, 70.

31. "Merrimack Mills Plan to Expand Operations," *Lowell Sun*, December 28, 1952, p. 1 (first quotation); "Merrimack Manufacturing Grants Workers Pay Boost," *Lowell Sun*, July 25, 1955 (second quotation); "The Grass Is Greener!!" (Merrimack Manufacturing Company Advertisement), *Lowell Sun*, October 30, 1955, p. 30 (final three quotations).

32. "Merrimack Mfg. to Close Plant within Six Months," *Lowell Sun*, December 10, 1957, p. 1; "Leading the Fight," *Lowell Sun*, December 26, 1956; "900 to Get Jobs Back at Merrimack Manufacturing," *Lowell Sun*, February 1, 1957; Closing quotations in "The Merrimack Closes," *Lowell Sun*, December 11, 1957.

33. Robert Brassil interview with Gray Fitzsimons on October 19, 2004 in Lowell, Massachusetts, p. 23, "Closing of the Merrimack Mills" series, CLH; Malcolm Chace interview with Mehmed Ali on December 21, 1998, pp. 4, 5, "Ethnic Solidarity" series, CLH; Phil Lehner interview with Mehmed Ali on February 8, 1999, pp. 2, 5 (quotation), "Ethnic Solidarity" series, CLH. The transcripts of the Chace and Lehner interviews do not specify where the interviews took place; interview locations are provided here whenever they are available from the transcripts held at the Center for Lowell History.

34. Raymond Ryan interview with Jim Beauchesne on January 5, 1998, in Dracut, Massachusetts, p. 20, "Closing of the Merrimack Mills" series, CLH; Robert Cooper interview with Mehmed Ali on September 12, 1998, in Lowell, Massachusetts, p. 9, "Ethnic Solidarity" series, CLH. For other interviewees who link the closure of the Merrimack mill to imports, see John Goodwin interview with Jim Beauchesne on October 8, 1997, in Chelmsford, Massachusetts, p. 6, and David Weltman interview with Jim Beauchesne on October 22, 1997, in Boston, p. 18, both in the "Closing of the Merrimack Mills" series, CLH.

35. "Boott Mills—Number of Employees," June 30, 1955, "Plant Closing Working File March 1955–1956," folder, box 72, Flather/Boott Mills Papers; Miller, *The Irony of Victory*, p. 116; Doherty, "Spindle City Blues," p. 101.

36. "The Merrimack Closes," *Lowell Sun*, December 11, 1957 (quotation); "Business," *Lowell Sun*, July 31, 1955, p. 38.

37. Louis Vergados interview with Mehmed Ali, August 15, 1997, p. 1, "Ethnic Solidarity" series, CLH; Closing quotation in "Merrimack Manufacturing Company Demolition 1960," CLH summary available at http://library.uml.edu/clh/Lophoto/Mill/mmd.htm (accessed March 24, 2011, copy in author's possession).

38. Robert Brassil interview with Gray Fitzsimons on October 19, 2004, in Lowell, Massachusetts, p. 27, "Closing of the Merrimack Mills" series, CLH; John Kadir interview with Maryrose Lane on April 29, 1994, in Lowell, Massachusetts, p. 6, "Closing of the Merrimack Mills" series, CLH; Doherty, "Spindle City Blues," p. 144.

39. William Wyskoczka interview with Mehmed Ali on July 1, 1999, in Lowell, Massachusetts, pp. 2, 15 (first, second, and last quotations), p. 16 ("terrible" quotation), "After the Last Generation I" series, CLH.

40. Blewett, *The Last Generation*, p. 158; William J. Farrell, "7000 New Jobs Here Since Development Unit Formed," *Lowell Sun*, December 21, 1958, p. 38; "Electronics Industry Area's Biggest Employer," *Lowell Sun*, November 17, 1972, p. E7; Doherty, "Spindle City Blues," pp. 143–57, closing quotation on p. 148.

41. Blewett, *The Last Generation*, p. 139 (Rouses quotation), pp. 158, 164, 192 (Albert Cote quotations).

42. Ruth Ann Sharpe interview with Maryrose Lane on April 14, 1994, in Lowell, Massachusetts, pp. 2, 9, "Closing of the Merrimack Mills" series, CLH; Blewett, *The Last Generation*, p. 139 (Rouses quotations); Robert Cooper interview with Mehmed Ali on September 12, 1998, in Lowell, Massachusetts, p. 14, "Ethnic Solidarity" series, CLH.

43. Brinkley, *American History*, p. 810.

44. Leo Paradis interview with Gray Fitzsimons on September 9, 1999, in Lowell, Massachusetts, p. 39, "After the Last Generation 1" series, CLH; Raymond Ryan interview with Jim Beauchesne on January 5, 1998, in Dracut, Massachusetts, p. 25, "Closing of the Merrimack Mills" series, CLH; James Ellis interview with Mehmed Ali on July 30, 1999, in Lowell, Massachusetts, p. 10, "After the Last Generation 1" series, CLH; Closing data in Mark Raymond Shanahan, "Housing and the Urban Crisis: Selected Community Responses in Eastern Massachusetts" (PhD dissertation, Case Western Reserve University, 1983), p. 330.

45. Valentine Chartrand interview with Diane Novelli on October 8, 1994, in Lowell, Massachusetts, p. 44, "Mill Workers of Lowell" series, CLH; "Merrimack Revisited," *Lowell Sun*, November 19, 1959 (*Sun* quotations).

46. Malcolm Chace interview with Mehmed Ali on December 21, 1998, p. 8, "Ethnic Solidarity" series, CLH; Phil Lehner interview with Mehmed Ali on February 8, 1999, p. 2, "Ethnic Solidarity" series, CLH.

47. Frank Maria interview with Jim Beauchesne on October 16, 1997, in Warner, New Hampshire, p. 16, "Closing of the Merrimack Mills" series, CLH; David Weltman interview with Jim Beauchesne on October 22, 1997, in Boston, p. 13, "Closing of the Merrimack Mills" series, CLH; "Business," *Lowell Sun*, October 22, 1950, p. 61; Blewett, *The Last Generation*, p. 139; Margaret Simon interview with Jim Beauchesne on December 30, 1997 in Nashua, New Hampshire, p. 29, "Closing of the Merrimack Mills" series, CLH.

48. "Boott Tenants," January 23, 1956, "Mill Plans" folder, box 68, Flather/Boott Mills Papers; Quotation in Rogers Flather to L. Richmond, November 25, 1955, "Boott Mills-Tenants" folder, box 68, Flather/Boott Mills Papers.

49. Rogers Flather to Ben Feinberg, January 4, 1956 (first and second quotations), and Rogers Flather Brochure Notes, n.d., both "Richard N. Stone Business Notes and Documents 1955" folder, box 69, Flather/Boott Mills Papers (other quotations).

50. J. R. Flather to Joshua Morrison, March 16, 1955, "Closing File 1955" folder, box 72, Flather/Boott Mills Papers (first two quotations); "Industrial Survey: Preliminary Report on Determinants of Business Migration and Satisfaction in Lowell and the SMSA," April 30, 1973, folder 14, box 19, Human Services Corporation Papers, CLH; McInerney quotation in "Much Industrial Space Now Available for Development Here," *Lowell Sun*, November 12, 1972, p. E20.

51. Fred E. Day, "Building Lowell," *Lowell Sun*, November 29, 1956 (quotation); William J. Farrell, "7000 New Jobs Here Since Development Unit Formed," *Lowell Sun*, December 21, 1958, p. 38.

52. "Area Manpower Profile," ca. 1971, in folder 7, box 44, Human Services Corporation Papers, CLH; Quotations in David M. Luce to Gary Jefferson, August 3, 1972, p. 6, folder 7, box 44, Human Services Corporation Papers, CLH; Robert Forrant and Christoph Strobel, "Ethnicity in Lowell: Lowell National Historical Park Ethnographic Overview and Assessment," Report prepared by the National Park Service's Ethnography Program, Northeast Region, March 2011 (copy in author's possession), pp. 113–14.

53. Doherty, "Spindle City Blues," p. 130; Richard P. Howe Sr. interview with author on April 28, 2011, in Lowell, Massachusetts.

54. Alberta Cook, "Trying Times," *Lowell Sun*, February 2, 1975, p. 2 (first two quotations); Alberta Cook, "Even When Economy Good—Lowell in Trouble," *Lowell Sun*, February 3, 1975, backpage (third, fourth, and fifth quotations); Alberta Cook, "Attitude Key to Lowell Revitalization," *Lowell Sun*, February 5, 1975, back page (final quotation).

55. Doherty, "Spindle City Blues," p. 119; Blewett, *The Last Generation,* p. xv (Blewett quotation); Stanton, *The Lowell Experiment*, p. 103; "Jobs Awaiting," *Lowell Sun*, October 22, 1966, p. 4 ("unemployment" quotation); Tsongas, *The Road from Here,* pp. 18–19, closing quotation on p. 18.

56. Tsongas quoted in O'Donnell, "The Spindles Stop," p. 215 (first two quotations); Paul Tsongas, *Heading Home* (New York: Vintage Books, 1984), p. 33 (third quotation), pp. 41–42 (fourth quotation).

57. Ryan, "Lowell in Transition," pp. xv, 87–88 ("monument" quotation), 356 ("dimensions" quotation); "Origins of the Park," n.d., folder 11, box 4, Human Services Corporation Papers, CLH (final two quotations).

58. Paul E. Tsongas to Stu Eizenstat, March 31, 1977, and Stuart E. Eizenstat to Paul E. Tsongas, April 8, 1977, both "PA3 1/20/77–7/20/77" folder, box PA3, White House Central Files, Carter Library.

59. Paul E. Tsongas to Frank Moore, May 23, 1978, "PA3 7/21/77–5/31/78" folder, PA3 box, White House Central Files, Carter Library (first quotation); Stu Eizenstat and Bill Deller to The President, June 5, 1978, "PA 6/1/78–11/30/78" folder, box PA3, White House Central Files, Carter Library (other quotation).

60. Lowell City Council Resolution, October 31, 1972, folder 6, box 28, Human Services Corporation Papers, CLH.

61. Quotation in B. Joseph Tully, Paul E. Tsongas, and James Shannon to Friend, July 27, 1979, "108A-1 Washington" folder, box 108A, Paul E. Tsongas Congressional Papers, CLH, hereafter cited as "Tsongas Congressional Papers"; Prudence Brighton, "The Lowell Plan: Helping to Transform the City for 30 Years," *Lowell Sun*, September 27, 2009; Tsongas, *The Road from Here*, p. 20.

62. Neal R. Pierce, "New Life in 'Spindle City,'" December 18, 1977, newspaper column in "New Life in Spindle City" folder, box 2, Human Services Corporation Papers.

63. Stanton, *The Lowell Experiment*, pp. 4–6 ("second life" quotation by scholar Barbara Kirshenblatt-Gimblett on p. 5).

64. Paul E. Tsongas to Mark O. Hatfield, June 4, 1984, "108C-3 Washington" folder, box 108C, Tsongas Congressional Papers; Stanton, *The Lowell Experiment*, pp. 51, 111, 113–14 (Tsongas quotation on p. 114).

65. Ryan, "Lowell in Transition," pp. 24–25; Blewett, *The Last Generation*, pp. 114, 139, 207, 228, 312–13.

66. O'Donnell, "The Spindles Stop," pp. 201–04; Bennett Harrison, *Rationalization, Restructuring, and Industrial Reorganization in Older Regions: The Economic Transformation of New England since World War II* (Cambridge, MA: Joint Center for Urban Studies of MIT and Harvard University, 1982), p. 89.

67. "Lowell: A Town Is Reborn," *Newsweek*, September 28, 1981, p. 38; "'High Tech' Ends a Long Slump in an Old Mill Town," *U.S. News and World Report*, April 6, 1981, p. 65; Stephen Solomon, "Computer Boom Town," *Science Digest*, March 1983, p. 108; Closing quotation in "Greater Lowell's Revitalization—It's Incredible" (Greater Lowell Chamber of Commerce Document), January 1984, "108A-1 Washington" folder, box 108A, Tsongas Congressional Papers.

68. Stanton, *The Lowell Experiment*, pp. 117–19, 126, 272; Richard Kindleberger, "Wang Towers Plans Detailed," *Boston Globe*, February 18, 1994, p. 73.

69. Richard P. Howe Sr. interview with author on April 28, 2011 in Lowell, Massachusetts.

70. Opening quotation in Jeffrey Krasner, "Wang Labs: The Next Chapter—Fear Tempers Workers' Relief," *Boston Herald*, August 19, 1992, p. 27; Other quotations in Maggie Farley and Katherine Yung, "Boom to Bust: Wang Bankruptcy Leaves Lowell Sagging under the Weight of Recession," *Boston Globe*, August 25, 1992, p. A37; Michael E. Knell, "Wang Labs: The Next Chapter: 5000 Losing Jobs in Wang Bankruptcy," *Boston Herald*, August 19, 1992, p. 1.

71. Russo and Linkon, "The Social Costs of Deindustrialization," pp. 187–95; Richard Chacon, "Depiction in Film Grates on Lowell," *Boston Globe*, July 26, 1995, p. 17; Michael Blowen, "It's America, not Lowell, that HBO Puts to Shame," *Boston Globe*, August 4, 1995, p. 49.

72. Maggie Farley and Katherine Yung, "Boom to Bust: Wang Bankruptcy Leaves Lowell Sagging under the Weight of Recession," *Boston Globe*, August 25, 1992, p. 37 (first three quotations); *Historic Preservation* quotation in Peter Stamas to President Jimmy Carter, June 24, 1991, folder 2, box 16, Human Services Corporation Papers.

73. Sacha Pfeiffer, "Vital Signs—This Once-Industrial City Now Has a Hipper, Younger Feel," *Boston Globe*, January 31, 2007, p. E8.

74. Charles Parrott and Gretchen Sanders Joy, *Lowell Then and Now: Restoring the Legacy of a Mill City* (Lowell: Lowell Historic Preservation Commission, 1995), p. vi (quotation); Jack Kerouac, *The Town and the City* (London: Quartet Books, 1973), esp. pp. 3–7. Kerouac's first

novel, *The Town and the City* has been through many editions and was originally published in the United States by Harcourt Brace Jovanovich in 1950.

75. "Lowell: The Flowering City," A Report from the Project Anthopolis Charrette, April 21, 1996, folder 37, box 3, Human Services Corporation Papers ("beautify" quotation); Kirk Boutselis, "Flowering City Celebrates 10 Years, Sets New Goals," *Lowell Sun*, November 6, 2006, p. 1 (Dukakis quotations).

76. "Getronics to Replace Last Signs of Wang," *Boston Globe*, March 5, 2000, p. 9; Richard P. Howe Jr. interview with author on April 28, 2011, in Lowell, Massachusetts; David Bushnell, "Lowell Is Making the Transition to a 'Destination City,'" *Boston Globe*, February 14, 1998, p. E9; Lyle Moran, "UML Vital in Downtown Economy," *Lowell Sun*, January 19, 2011 (Meehan quotation).

77. Maureen Mullen, "More Than a Minor Success; In Their 10th Anniversary Season, the Lowell Spinners Are Still Setting the Standard for Fan Fervor, Friendliness, and Fun," *Boston Herald*, July 30, 2006, p. B14; Richard P. Howe Sr. interview with author on April 28, 2011, in Lowell, Massachusetts.

78. Rachel R. Briere, "Welcome to Hollywood East (aka Massachusetts)," *Lowell Sun*, July 6, 2009 (first quotation); Chris Camire, "'Fighter' Prize Called 'Priceless' for MA Economy," *Lowell Sun*, March 1, 2011 (Golden and Bale quotations).

79. Forrant and Strobel, "Ethnicity in Lowell," pp. 115, 141, 146–47 (quotation on p. 147).

80. Brian MacQuarrie, "For Cambodians in Lowell, Killing Fields' Scars Linger," *Boston Globe*, December 22, 1997, p. B1; Richard P. Howe Sr. interview with author on April 28, 2011, in Lowell, Massachusetts; Forrant and Strobel, "Ethnicity in Lowell," p. 159; Alexander Reid, "Leading Lowell's Asian Boom; Cambodian Entrepreneurs Finding Success, Trying New Ventures in the City," *Boston Globe*, September 3, 2006, p. 1.

81. Sovann-Thida Loeung interview with Mehmed Ali on January 22, 2006, in Lowell, Massachusetts, pp. 19, 24, "Khmer [Cambodians] II" series, CLH. For similar reflections, see Narin Sao interview with Suzette Jefferson, May 17, 1986, pp. 17–18, "Southeast Asians" Series, CLH.

82. Sacha Pfeiffer, "Vital Signs—This Once-Industrial City Now Has a Hipper, Younger Feel," *Boston Globe*, January 31, 2007, p. E8; Ike DeLorenzo, "A Melding of Ethnicities, Flavors; Lowell Is Home to a World of Restaurants," *Boston Globe*, April 28, 2010, p. G16; Lyle Moran, "Lowell to Create 'Little Cambodia' District," *Lowell Sun*, April 7, 2011. For details of the water festival, see www.lowellwaterfestival.org/ (accessed May 18, 2011, copy in author's possession).

83. Newell Flather interview with author on April 27, 2011, in Boston, Massachusetts. The "cultural economy" quotation is drawn from the author's interview with Richard P. Howe Jr. on April 28, 2011, in Lowell, Massachusetts, although this phrase is also used quite widely to describe Lowell's new economy.

84. Forrant and Strobel, "Ethnicity in Lowell," pp. 190–91, first two quotations on p. 191; Buxbaum quoted in Michael LaFleur, "Lowell Leaders, Residents Field Question: Is City on Right Track?" *Lowell Sun*, October 23, 2005, p. 1; David Perry, "Job Market Limps toward Recovery," *Lowell Sun*, June 3, 2010.

85. Jordana Hart, "Lowell Takes on Cambodian Gangs," *Boston Globe*, October 29, 1991, p. 21; "Many Come to Say Goodbye to Paul Tsongas," Quincy (Massachusetts) *Patriot Ledger*, January 22, 1997, p. 29; David Perry, "A Giant Whose Shoes Have Yet to be Filled," *Lowell Sun*, January 18, 2007, p. 1 ("giant" quotation); Newell Flather interview with author on April 27, 2011, in Boston, Massachusetts.

86. Diane E. Lewis, "Jobless Rate High in S.E. Mass. Report: Region Isn't Benefiting from Boom," *Boston Globe*, May 11, 1999, p. D1; Quotation in "A Better Deal for New Bedford," *Boston Globe*, July 28, 1996, p. F6; Don Aucoin, "Job-Hungry Fall River, New Bedford Face Off in a High-Stakes Casino Game," *Boston Globe*, March 31, 1997, p. A1; Thomas Grillo, "Jobless Rate Still High in Some Cities," *Boston Herald*, September 17, 1998, p. 39.

87. Thomas Grillo, "Once-Proud Holyoke Aims to Reverse Its Decline," *Boston Globe*, August 17, 2002, p. D10.

88. John Powers, "Of Mills and Momentum," *Boston Globe*, May 11, 1997, p. 14 (quotation); David Pevear, "Lawrence, like Lowell Decades Ago, Moving Forward," *Lowell Sun*,

March 15, 2009; Sarah Schweitzer, "Hope Recedes in Lawrence, Where Unemployment Is Highest in Mass." *Boston Globe*, July 22, 2009, p. B6.

89. Sacha Pfeiffer, "On a Comeback; The Once-Proud Industrial Town Is Making a Cultural Rebound," *Boston Globe*, February 7, 2007, p. E8.

90. Laura Crimaldi, "Recovery Road: New Bedford Sees Whale of a Future," *Boston Herald*, April 5, 2009, p. 4; Noah Bierman and Johnny Diaz, "Rising Tide of Opportunity Falters in Fall River; Relentless Economic Woes Sap City's Hope," *Boston Globe*, December 18, 2010, p. A1 (quotations); "Quietly, Mills Have Marked Rebirth of Mill City," *Lowell Sun*, April 9, 2011.

91. Doherty, "Spindle City Blues," p. 242; Gross, *The Course of Industrial Decline*, p. 225.

92. Newell Flather interview with author on April 27, 2011, in Boston, Massachusetts; Robert Brassil interview with Gray Fitzsimons on October 19, 2004, in Lowell, Massachusetts, pp. 32, 33, "Closing of the Merrimack Mills" series, CLH.

*Chapter Ten*

# "It Knocked This City to Its Knees": A Case Study of Deindustrialization in Kannapolis, North Carolina

In July 2003, textile firm Pillowtex announced that it was closing all sixteen of its U.S. plants, filing for bankruptcy for the second time in three years, and laying off virtually all of its 7,650 workers. Around 4,800 of these jobs were in Kannapolis, North Carolina, and the mass layoff was the largest in the state's history. The scale of the shutdown stunned economic and political leaders, especially as it eliminated textile production from one of the nation's most historic mill communities. The lost jobs also represented one-sixth of Kannapolis's entire population. "It's a tragedy," declared Charles Bremer, a vice president of the ATMI. "We've never seen a day like this." U.S. Senator John Edwards agreed, adding that "an economic shock wave has hit North Carolina." In Kannapolis, residents were stunned by the demise of the mills, which had operated for almost 120 years. "It knocked this city to its knees," explained Kannapolis mayor Ray Moss later. "When a hurricane hits, it takes away homes. What happened here is a catastrophe that took away jobs and left houses. They own homes they can't pay for because they have no jobs."[1]

While it was unusual for so many workers to lose their jobs in one day, Pillowtex's closure was representative of broader trends. In fact, the company was one of several large textile firms that went bankrupt in the early twenty-first century, and it epitomized the industry's post-NAFTA collapse. As the *Southern Textile News* put it, the loss of Pillowtex represented the demise of "another grand dame of the U.S. textile industry."[2] The closure of the Kannapolis plants, which had dominated life in the town since its foundation, also illustrated the harsh social and economic impact of deindustrialization, especially in the small communities that the industry was concentrated in. "When a textile mill closes," summarized the National Council of Textile Organizations, "the entire community feels the ramifications, with local businesses, churches and government being hurt."[3] Finally, Kannapolis was a major textile center in North Carolina, a state that was deeply affected by the industry's collapse. Between 1993 and 2003, North Carolina lost an average of fifteen thousand textile and apparel jobs a year, or more than forty jobs each day, and critics of NAFTA frequently cited the state's experience to bolster their case. Between 2004 and 2006, following the closure of numerous textile mills, along with the shutting of many tobacco and furniture-making plants, the Tar Heel state even led the nation in trade-impacted layoffs. The fate of the Kannapolis workers graphically highlighted how plant closings were devastating southern towns just as they had the more familiar communities in the northeast and Midwest. As former Pillowtex worker James Mellons declared in 2004, "This is Dodge City right now."[4]

Press observers certainly viewed the Pillowtex closure as very significant, a reminder of how deindustrialization was recasting the economic landscape right across the country. As CNN writer Leslie Haggin Geary noted, "If Smokestack America has a geographic center, it may be Kannapolis, N.C. That's where locals used to produce sheets, towels and other linens at the Pillowtex manufacturing plant." The fate of the Kannapolis workers, added Patrik Jonsson in the *Christian Science Monitor*, "became a rallying cry for critics of global outsourcing." As Jonsson pointed out, the Kannapolis workforce was given just two hours to vacate a plant where most had spent their entire working lives. Some employees even had to disassemble the company's looms and get them ready for shipment to Pakistan, where newly hired workers would now make sheets and towels for the massive American market. In 2004, when independent filmmaker Greg Spotts made *American Jobs*, a documentary about the impact of low-wage foreign competition on communities across the country, he visited Kannapolis and interviewed both workers and community leaders. The town, he asserted, allowed viewers to see "the damage" caused by deindustrialization with their own eyes.[5]

Because of these criticisms, some federal and state officials also tried to view Kannapolis as an example of how the economy could recover from job losses in the manufacturing sector. In 2007, Federal Reserve Bank Chairman Ben S. Bernanke picked out the former mill town as a symbol of the broader changes that were transforming the U.S. economy. He praised the subsequent redevelopment of the mill site as a biotech research campus, insisting that this would create many new jobs. Speaking in Charlotte, Bernanke was upbeat about the future. "What happened to the former Pillowtex site itself is a good metaphor for the transformation under way in the region," he declared. "Though the loss of manufacturing jobs is painful, the ongoing development of the Pillowtex site as the North Carolina Research Campus illustrates this region's ability to shift resources from industries that are shrinking to those that are expanding." Many in the local business community, who were keen to move forward and try to attract new jobs, enthusiastically received Bernanke's words. They argued that growth-minded southern communities could lure new businesses and easily recover from the decline of manufacturing.[6]

Like Bernanke, advocates of globalization and free trade emphasized the overall strength of the American economy and asserted that displaced manufacturing workers could simply find work in new areas, particularly the growing service and biotech sectors. This viewpoint was expressed well by the Business Roundtable, a politically conservative group of CEOs from leading U.S. corporations. In the wake of the Pillowtex closure, the Roundtable argued that laid-off textile and apparel workers were rehired "as quickly as workers in other industries, and were generally paid higher wages in their new jobs." Like many corporate groups, the Roundtable also insisted that the benefits of free trade outweighed the costs, especially as it lowered prices for consumers and created new markets for exporters. "Import competition has cost some U.S. jobs and challenged some U.S. industries," admitted one Roundtable publication, "but exports have boosted the economy and job growth."[7] While more cognizant of the costs of globalization, similar arguments were espoused by C. Fred Bergsten, the head of the powerful Peterson Institute for International Economics, and by leading economists such as Jagdish Bhagwati, who wrote in his pioneering *In Defense of Globalization* that globalization was "generally a benign force." The experience of the former Pillowtex workers in Kannapolis, however, allows us to test these claims and ultimately highlights that they downplayed the difficulties that former manufacturing workers faced in finding comparable jobs. Like Lowell's workers fifty years earlier, those who lost their jobs in Kannapolis struggled to find positions that paid as well, with older workers being the hardest hit of all. With the advent of the global financial crisis, moreover, it became even harder to land good jobs, a shift that pushed advocates of globalization onto the defensive. Seven years after the closure, the American economy was mired in a deep recession, and interviews with former Pillowtex workers revealed that most were still struggling financially.[8]

When the mills closed, Pillowtex had owned the Kannapolis site for six years, but the mills there had a much longer history. As was the case across the southern textile belt, local industrialists had built the Kannapolis mills because they were keen to develop the economic strength of the region after the Civil War.[9] In 1887, local businessman James W. Cannon had started the Cannon Manufacturing Company, and the main mill in Kannapolis began operations in 1908. After his death in 1921, James handed over control of the company to his son Charles, and he proceeded to expand operations, especially into the manufacture of sheets. By 1971, when Charles died, Cannon Mills' sales exceeded $305 million, and the company controlled over half of the country's towel business and over 20 percent of its sheet business. At 5.9 million square feet, Cannon's factory in Kannapolis covered 158 acres and was larger than Sears Tower or the Pentagon. It was, declared the *New York Times*, "the nation's largest textile plant." The mills manufactured products that most Americans were familiar with; as journalist Patrik Jonsson later wrote, "This was the mill that made the sheets that America slept on and the towels that hung in her bathrooms."[10]

Cannon Mills controlled life in Kannapolis, providing workers with not just jobs but also houses and municipal services. "Almost every street, every home, even the fire stations and grocery stores were owned by Cannon," wrote historian Barbara Griffith in an important study. "The mayor, the police chief, and the ministers were all part of the Cannon 'family,' as were, of course, the workers." By 1960, 34,647 people lived in Kannapolis, making it the largest unincorporated city in the world, and every resident either worked in the mills or had a close relative that did. Managers took a close interest in workers' lives, and they resisted high-profile union drives in 1946 and 1974, earning the firm considerable notoriety in labor circles. As the TWUA's main historian has written, Cannon Mills was "a company that symbolized the seeming immutability of antiunionism in the southern textile industry perhaps more than any other."[11]

Many workers saw the company as a provider and were reluctant to oppose the wishes of "Uncle Charlie." After the closure, some still expressed feelings of gratitude to the company for looking after them. "Charlie's the one who built up the mill and gave us jobs and houses," declared Audrey Beaver, who felt that the town should erect a statute of Cannon on the mill site rather than one of the NASCAR driver Dale Earnhardt Sr., who was another famous native.[12] Many others, however, emphasized workers' lack of autonomy during the Cannon years. According to former union organizer and long-time Kannapolis resident Robert Freeman, "Cannon Mills built this town and everything in it was owned by Cannon Mills, everything from the sheriff's department to county commissioners to state legislators . . . They controlled them, so they didn't think that anyone could ever destroy their empire."[13]

By the 1980s, however, a lot had changed. In 1982, real estate tycoon David Murdock bought Cannon Mills and 660 acres of surrounding real estate from the Cannon family, including the downtown business district and 1,600 houses. Under Murdock, the old corporate paternalism broke down; Kannapolis was incorporated, many houses were sold, and those that remained were rented out at a much higher rate of return. When he sold Cannon Mills to Fieldcrest in 1985, Murdock terminated the Cannon pension plan and took with him the interest that it had earned to date. Following considerable controversy, Murdock only settled the issue after being sued by the ACTWU. The case helped generate support for the union, which narrowly lost an NLRB election at the site in 1991. After the Pillowtex takeover of Fieldcrest, the union continued its organizing efforts, and in June 1999 it finally won representation rights at the site. The vote reflected workers' desire for increased pay and benefits, as well as more autonomy on the job. Given the company's importance within the largely nonunion textile industry, the victory carried enormous symbolic significance. "I think it puts the lie to the notion that Southern workers are anti-union," asserted UNITE leader Bruce Raynor. "Southern employers are anti-union."[14]

Despite the celebrations, UNITE had organized a company with serious financial problems. When they bought Fieldcrest Cannon in 1997, Pillowtex executives agreed to assume all of Fieldcrest's debt, a decision that would subsequently haunt them, especially as Fieldcrest was a bigger firm than Pillowtex. Fieldcrest-Cannon's long-term prospects were also poor; the firm was heavily reliant on selling its products to budget stores such as K-Mart and Wal-Mart, and these retailers were increasingly stocking their shelves with cheap textiles made by low-wage workers in Asia and Latin America.[15] This was not the only costly acquisition that Pillowtex had made. Between 1970 and 2000, the Dallas-based company had bought sixteen companies, and in the process it acquired what *Homes Textiles Today* called "a mountain of debt." In 1995, for example, Pillowtex had paid $171 million for Beacon Manufacturing Company, while five years later the firm purchased terry producer Leshner Mills for $80 million. In making these commitments, Pillowtex's managers had counted on an expanding domestic market, but as conditions worsened their debts only increased. In the third quarter of 2000 Pillowtex paid $27 million in interest costs—more than six times its cash flow—and by the end of the year the firm was in bankruptcy. In early 2001, the company closed four plants, including one in Kannapolis itself, in a vain effort to reduce its debts. Although it emerged from bankruptcy in June 2002, Pillowtex lost $27 million over the next ten months, paving the way for the closure of the remaining Kannapolis operations.[16]

In an open letter to employees written on July 30, 2003, Pillowtex CEO Michael Gannaway blamed foreign competition for the closure of the historic plants. "Cheap imports are flooding the U.S. market and driving down prices," he wrote, "while global sourcing has created a new business model for textile companies that we are unable to replicate without substantial investments."[17] Although managers were quick to pass the buck, they must also bear some responsibility for the shutdown, especially as they had burdened the company with a huge amount of debt at a time when the industry was contracting. As the *Charlotte Observer* concluded, "While Pillowtex blamed competition from low-cost imports, an *Observer* investigation found that management mistakes also played a significant role." Probing the true reasons for the closure, the *Baltimore Sun*'s Lauren Weber reached a similar conclusion. Even the probusiness *Charlotte Business Journal* pondered why workers had to "suffer the consequences" of the shutdown when the company had given $4 million in golden parachutes to several departing executives the previous year. In contrast, many of the workers who lost their jobs had been working reduced hours for several months and were owed vacation pay and other benefits.[18]

Despite all the negative signs, many residents were not prepared for the closure. This was partly because they could not accept that such a large and long-standing company could ever shut completely. Even when Pillowtex entered bankruptcy, most remained upbeat. "I don't think they're going to go under," claimed one worker in late 2000. "I think they'll reorganize and go on." Most locals identified strongly with the mill and found it impossible to accept the possibility of closure. As Louise Davey put it, "For so many people, the mill has been their total life, and it still is." Less than two months before the layoff was announced, workers were still insisting that the mills would keep operating regardless of what happened to Pillowtex. "Nobody really seen this coming," admitted one of the laid-off workers later.[19]

The news of the shutdown consequently left inhabitants reeling. "When the word came," recalled local minister Joe Crawford, "it was like everyone in Kannapolis got a punch in the stomach. It was like your favorite uncle died." Because of their strong degree of identification with their jobs, many workers found it hard to move on, especially psychologically. Like textile workers elsewhere, they assumed that they had jobs for life and had made no plans for retirement or new careers. "I thought I would be there for a long, long time as a forklift operator in plant 1," recalled one worker. "It's such a shame for the people that only knew the mill as their work."[20]

In the immediate aftermath of the closure, UNITE representatives tried to find a buyer that could take over and operate the mills, but their efforts came up short, largely because of the depressed outlook for U.S. textile makers. Referring to the impending abolition of all textile quotas, a change that most mill owners opposed, Harris Raynor explained that "the answer we got back is how can we invest in this industry knowing what's going to happen in 2005."[21] Observing these events, some onlookers tried to associate the union with the mill's shutdown. In the wake of the closure, the John Locke Foundation, a right-wing group based in North Carolina, blamed the union for scuttling a deal that Pillowtex had made with Springs Industries that could have salvaged some of the jobs in Kannapolis. Union officials, however, opposed the pact because they asserted that it did not include the retention of the Kannapolis-area operations. Writing on behalf of the conservative Hudson Institute, Diana Furchtgott-Roth even linked the closure to the union's election victory, suggesting that it was common for firms to close plants after union wins. "Instead of offering workers promised benefits," she wrote, "unions can be blamed for lost jobs and benefits." In Kannapolis itself, some antiunion workers also insisted that UNITE was to blame for the mills' closure, yet it is important to recognize that scores of unorganized textile firms also closed in these years. In 2003, the Department of Labor reported that just 6.5 percent of U.S. textile and apparel workers belonged to unions, yet this did nothing to prevent the industry's collapse.[22]

The composition of the Pillowtex workforce increased the impact of the mill's closure. When the plant shut, the average Pillowtex worker was forty-six-years old and had worked in the plant for seventeen years. In addition, 59 percent of workers were women and 45.7 percent of all employees did not have a high school diploma or a GED.[23] These characteristics were typical of the textile workforce as a whole, which contained disproportionate numbers of racial minorities as well. In 2002, U.S. Census data showed that blacks held 19.9 percent of all textile jobs, compared with 9.6 percent of manufacturing posts as a whole. At the same time, women held 45.5 percent of textile positions compared to 30.7 percent of all manufacturing jobs. The average age of the textile workforce was 42.6 years, again above average for the factory sector. Because racial minorities and women faced discrimination in hiring, the mill shutdowns hurt them badly. The proportion of textile workers who did not have a high school diploma was also more than double the figure for manufacturing employees in general, and these workers found that their options were very limited once they lost their jobs. In 2008, however, school leaders in the Kannapolis area complained that too many students were still dropping out of high school and looking for jobs in the mills. "Parents have the mentality that there's textile jobs here," explained student services director Tim Smith, "but there's not."[24]

For most of the Pillowtex group, finding new work, particularly in the service sector, was not easy. The impact of the closure was immediately reflected in Cabarrus County's unemployment rate, which spiked to 10.9 percent in the late summer of 2003 after averaging 5.5 percent in 2002 and 4.7 percent in 2001.[25] Testimony confirms that workers lost economically when the mills closed. Commenting on the shutdown, Robert Freeman noted in August that "I have friends who have lost their job and are now dealing with foreclosures, having their cars taken away, and telling their kids they can't pay for college this fall."[26]

Released in 2004, a detailed study of the Pillowtex closure by three economists from the University of North Carolina confirmed that the immediate impact of the shutdown had been catastrophic. By the first week of August 2003, 43 percent of the Pillowtex workers were behind in their rent or mortgage payments, while over 10 percent had received eviction or foreclosure notices. Despite their pressing needs, many workers found it difficult to "confront reality," while those that did often possessed "little or no computer skills, rendering them ineffective in a job search." Six months later, little had changed, as 3,115 former Pillowtex workers were receiving weekly income support payments. A year after the closure, a detailed investigation by the

*USA Today*'s Barbara Hagenbaugh concluded that of the 4,800 people who had lost their jobs, 500 had retired, 1,600 were in school, and 1,100 had found jobs. This meant that around 1,600 workers—one-third of the total—were still looking for work a year later. Most found it a deeply frustrating process. "We hear everyday, 'Pillowtex was a good job, I want to go back there,'" explained Linda Burton, whose office put workers in touch with employment counselors. "I don't think any job will take the place of Pillowtex." Interviewed in early 2004, former supervisor Robert Brawley illustrated these broader trends well. Brawley's income had fallen dramatically, and he had also suffered psychologically. "Really, my whole life has just went totally downhill in the last six months, in the last eight months," he commented. "My mental status right now, sometimes I feel like I've just plumb lost it, really. I mean, it's just a mess, it really is, a mess."[27]

Federal programs did try to help. In the wake of the closure, the Pillowtex workers received the usual twenty-six weeks of unemployment benefits plus an additional twenty-six weeks of government payments under the Trade Adjustment Assistance program, which was designed to help workers who had lost their jobs at least partly because of the pressures of foreign trade. Under the TAA, which dated back to the Trade Act of 1974, workers who stayed in school could get another year of benefits, with their schooling paid for. Certifying the Pillowtex workers on September 9, 2003, U.S. Secretary of Labor Elaine L. Chao trumpeted the Bush administration's plan of action: "This Administration is committed to getting help as quickly as possible to the workers who worked at Pillowtex. On top of the $20.6 million that has already been given in national emergency grants, this certification means up to two years of training, up to 104 weeks of weekly income support, job search and relocation benefits, and a health coverage tax credit that covers up to 65 percent of monthly health premiums for workers and their families." The administration's prompt response reflected the publicity that the Pillowtex layoff had generated, as well as pressure from a range of state political leaders, including senators Elizabeth Dole and John Edwards and Governor Michael F. Easley. Chao's Labor Department later boasted that the administration's efforts had been very effective and that the Pillowtex case had provided "a blueprint for how federal programs can be used to assist transitioning workers, not just in textile and apparel, but in other industries as well."[28]

While federal officials insisted that their programs were sufficient to mitigate the effects of the closure, most workers saw the situation differently. Although many did take up the opportunity to retrain, they admitted that it was difficult to start again after a long career in the mills. Even former managers such as Ken Geathers, who had an undergraduate degree, found it a challenge to return to the classroom. "Here I am, a 60-year-old guy, trying to write a research paper and studying at night," he declared in July 2004. "It's worse than working." If they completed the training, workers also found it difficult to secure suitable positions, and they stressed that it was costly to move to areas where jobs were available. Many were also deeply attached to Kannapolis and were reluctant to relocate. In early 2005, former Pillowtex worker Brenda Miller related that many of her classmates had found it difficult to complete retraining, and only a small number had landed new jobs. "A friend of mine quit school," explained the community college student. "She just said, 'I'm too old for this.' These people lost their jobs, and they just weren't ready to go back to school." As *Spiegel* journalist Alexander Osang reported from the town in 2005, moreover, some workers had undertaken retraining primarily to get the extra year of unemployment pay. "There isn't much else to do in Kannapolis," he explained.[29]

State officials admitted that there were problems. In 2005 Linda Burton, who had worked for the North Carolina Employment Security Commission (ESC) for over thirty years, acknowledged that the scale of the shutdown was testing the TAA program's effectiveness. "Never have we had so many who had worked for so long at one place lose their jobs," she declared. While trying to trumpet the success of the retraining program, even H. Martin Lancaster, the president of the North Carolina Community College system, acknowledged that many of the Pillowtex group were finding it hard to secure appropriate positions after they finished their courses. "There is evidence of continued unemployment and under-employment," he confessed.[30]

Using wage data, the ESC carefully tracked workers' careers and documented these problems. In 2007, the Commission reported that the proportion of former Pillowtex workers who had found other jobs in the state had risen from 27.8 percent in the fourth quarter of 2003 to 60.4 percent in the fourth quarter of 2006. The biggest proportion of these workers had found jobs in other manufacturing industries, however, and just 15.2 percent worked in professional and business services. Many of these service jobs were also very different from the high-tech positions promoted by state leaders. "A substantial amount of growth that is occurring in Professional and Business Services is actually due to the growth within Temporary Help Services," admitted Commission economist Betty McGrath in late 2007. The ESC also found that the median quarterly wage in these new posts was $5,490.50, suggesting that few workers earned more than they had in the mill. When Pillowtex closed, the average hourly wage was $11.60, or about $5,560 a quarter.[31]

Rather, there were plenty of workers who ended up taking sizeable pay cuts after the mills shut. They were people like Delores and Robert Gambrell, who had earned about $75,000 a year between them when Pillowtex was running. It was enough to buy a house, take their children on vacation, and put away some savings for the future. Eighteen months after the shutdown, however, Delores worked nights making ceramic auto parts and Robert toiled at a fencing factory. They had a combined income of $27,000. Like many others, the Gambrells felt angry and betrayed, especially as they had been forced to refinance their mortgage. "I didn't pay 26 years on a house to give it up to someone else," Dolores fumed. "I had but five years left on my mortgage. Now where's my American dream? It's in the garbage. It's a heartbreak when you have to tell your son, 'I'm not going to have enough money to send you to college.'" Leann Harrington, a former Pillowtex worker who had struggled to land a low-paying job as a waitress, was equally downcast. "I think the middle class is pretty much gone here," she told a journalist who visited Kannapolis in 2004. "In one year our receipts in the café have been cut in half. People are starting to lose their unemployment benefits, and then there will be nothing left."[32]

Like many displaced textile and apparel workers, a large contingent of Pillowtex employees went to work for Wal-Mart. As the mills shut, the giant retailer expanded rapidly, and in many ways it symbolized the new economy; jobs were available for both men and women, but they paid poorly and came with few benefits. Many of them were also part time.[33] Searching for cheaper prices, Wal-Mart's suppliers had turned to imported textiles, and it was thus ironic that the Pillowtex employees should end up working there. Like other retailers, Wal-Mart had also lobbied hard for the passage of NAFTA, partly because it wanted access to new markets in Mexico. In Kannapolis, the Wal-Mart Supercenter opened in the summer of 2003, just as Pillowtex collapsed. Among those who made the switch was Judy Hatley, a veteran sheet inspector who got a post in the bakery department. According to Hatley, when the store opened more than half of its staff were laid-off Pillowtex employees. In an interview with the local press, Hatley did not comment on how she felt about her new job but admitted that she missed the mill, which had been "the life of the town." She explained that "people will remember those relationships they had back then."[34]

A few years later, former Pillowtex workers portrayed working at Wal-Mart as a grim necessity. "Quite a few . . . work there, and work at all the Wal-Marts, because they've got to have income," claimed Ruth Crisco in 2010, adding that the pay was much lower than it had been in the mill. In a further irony, the low incomes of displaced textile workers meant that most now shopped in low-cost retailers that relied on imports rather than more upscale stores. It was an irony appreciated by those who understood the connection between their roles as workers and consumers. "We're defeating our purpose," admitted one former mill employee.[35]

For racial minorities, the closure had a particularly severe impact. Like other southern textile companies, Cannon Mills had relied largely on white labor until the late 1960s, when civil rights legislation and pressure from African American workers gradually led to some desegregation.[36] Changes occurred slowly, however; in 1969, for instance, Charles Cannon defended his company's record against charges of discrimination he had received from federal officials. "We have not discriminated," he wrote. "It has been the policy of the Company to comply with Civil Rights laws. We have employed thousands of the minority race and there are several thousand working for us now." Cannon failed to mention that the vast majority of these black workers toiled in low-level positions and that the company still provided segregated housing for its employees. Black workers wanted change, and in 1970 a group of thirteen plaintiffs filed a class action suit under Title VII of the 1964 Civil Rights Act, which prohibited racial discrimination in employment. Led by Donald Ray Hicks, it charged the company with no fewer than thirteen discriminatory practices, including the provision of "inferior" housing for black employees.[37]

The *Hicks* case was not settled until 1982, when Cannon Mills paid out $1.65 million to 3,700 African American workers in order to compensate them for past discrimination. Although many other textile firms were also sued in these years, *Hicks* represented one of the largest settlements of its type. In interviews, African American workers claimed that the agreement had reduced discrimination in the mills but added that there were still some problems.[38] In the 1980s and 1990s, black workers gradually worked their way into the better-paying jobs as whites retired, but they were seeking promotions at a time when the mills were contracting. Immediately after World War II some twenty-four thousand people had toiled at the Kannapolis site, but this number steadily declined to less than five thousand in 2003. Still, after the plant closed workers such as Janet Patterson, who had started as the first black hemmer in the sheet department, were hit hard. "I made good money," she told the *Newshour with Jim Lehrer* in late 2003, "even to the point I used to make enough money, they had to pay me in two checks." Patterson's mill job had supported her and the five grandchildren that she was raising, but this all changed when she was laid off. "It's like they took everything from us," she commented. "At my age, they aren't hiring unless you are young or you got experience in some other trade. And I haven't experienced any other job outside . . . of Pillowtex. It hurts." Bernetha Brown, the African American head of the UNITE local union, added that Patterson's experience was typical, especially for older workers.[39]

Some of the African Americans who had worked at the plant were reluctant to claim that they had been disproportionately affected by the closure. Acutely aware of the suffering experienced by the entire community, they were wary of seeing their experience as exceptional. "It affected all race, the African Americans, the Caucasians, and the Mexicans too," asserted Robert Neal, who had worked at the mill since 1969. Warren Ellis, another veteran black worker, concurred: "It affected everybody, black, white . . . whoever." Some of these interviewees also acknowledged, however, that their familiarity with hardship had helped them to cope. When he started work soon after integration, Robert Neal recalled that blacks had performed the "less appreciated" jobs, and even decades later it was hard for them to become supervisors, a barrier that Neal had been unable to break. These experiences had helped him to stay positive and philosophical. "You've just got to keep hope alive," he declared. An ebullient woman who had started at the mill in 1972, Ruth Crisco remained upbeat even when she described hardships. "I know they wouldn't hire black women, at one time," she related, "and then when they finally hired the black women in the mill they gave them the hardest jobs they could give them." She added that "as blacks we're a little stronger, we wouldn't let it take us to suicide, you know. We was really stronger than that because we are *used* to surviving, you know, with little or nothing." By budgeting and avoiding large purchases, Crisco had adjusted to earning half of what she had in the mill.[40]

There were other nonwhite workers who were also affected by the closure. When the plant shut, it contained five hundred workers who spoke very little English, most of them recent arrivals from Latin America. In the 1990s and early 2000s, thousands of Latinos had moved into the southern states, and most took low-paying jobs in industries such as textiles, food processing, and construction. Because of its large number of industrial jobs, North Carolina soon had a large Hispanic population; over the course of the 1990s the number of Latinos in the state jumped 394 percent, the third fastest rate in the nation.[41] These new migrants were vulnerable when they lost their jobs, especially when they were undocumented. At Pillowtex, a large number of these employees had taken jobs in the cut and sew facilities. In August 2003, at a meeting of Spanish-speaking workers, a state official told the crowd that those present who did not possess legitimate documents should leave. Many did so, and some never returned to Kannapolis.[42]

The closure did not have entirely negative consequences, however, especially for mobile and well-qualified immigrants. While illegal workers were not eligible for employment benefits or other forms of government assistance, legal immigrants stood to benefit a great deal from such programs. As *The Economist* reported from Kannapolis, several hundred immigrants did qualify for training, and in the process they received a free education. Most of these employees had only ever worked as manual laborers, but they were now able to acquire new skills and apply them to a range of jobs. They included Ying Xiong, a thirty-eight-year-old Laotian woman who was learning English and computing skills because she wanted to become a medical secretary.[43]

In addition to its impact on the workers themselves, the Pillowtex closure also hurt the broader community. For a century, the mill had been the main employer in "The City of Looms," and the community's dependence on it was still immense. Most residents were hit hard, especially as almost every local family contained at least one member who had lost his or her job. "They were saying, 'Well, it only affects 4,500 employees,'" recalled former mill worker and City Council member Richard Anderson. "Not true in my mind. When you consider the employee, the spouse and the average family of two children, now you're talking 16, 17 or 18,000 people." As the ESC documented, the closure also meant that local merchants lost customers, the housing market weakened, and the community faced declining tax revenues from which to provide basic public services. Visiting Kannapolis more than a year after the closure, *New York Times* journalist Elizabeth Becker described it as "an economic ghost town" populated by former textile workers who now eked out their livings as best they could. "Dislocation is an understatement for what has happened to the people in this town," she concluded.[44]

As was the case elsewhere, the loss of employer-provided health care also affected the Kannapolis workers and their families enormously, and their experience illustrates this broader problem particularly well. When the plant closed, Pillowtex was self-insured, with a group plan for its workers administered by Blue Cross Blue Shield, a standard arrangement for textile firms. The bankruptcy filing terminated the plan, leaving around $5 million in unpaid claims pending. In the wake of the shutdown, the United Way reported that many workers were unable to meet medical expenses, especially the cost of prescription drugs. A few months later, the UNC study found that 93 percent of workers said that they could not afford or secure health insurance. Mill jobs had been physically demanding, and even younger workers often had medical conditions that required ongoing treatment. Both public and private agencies did try to meet these needs. Opening just four days after the shutdown, the Community Service Center gave grants to help workers meet prescription costs. These awards were desperately needed; in the nine months after the closure, the Center reported spending $30,000 a month on prescriptions alone. Requested by state leaders, a National Emergency Grant also provided funding for health care costs while TAA certification and benefits were pending. Subsequently, the federal government pledged that workers who were in training should be eligible for the Health Coverage Tax Credit of 65 percent of their health care premium.[45]

Despite this, displaced workers complained that the program was of little help because they were still required to spend substantial amounts of money on insurance premiums before they could secure the credit. Because premiums reflected preexisting health conditions, many could not afford to pay the 35 percent, which sometimes exceeded $1,000 a month. Undoubtedly, however, it was workers who were not in the training program who were the worst off. "The most devastating thing to my whole family is the loss of health insurance," explained Robert Neal in 2004. With an unemployment payment that failed to cover his house note, the fifty-year-old struggled to buy medication for his wife, who had diabetes. He also bought his glasses from the dollar store and stopped going to the dentist. Another poignant case was that of Charles Morris, a fifty-six-year-old worker who developed serious health problems soon after the plant shut, including Lou Gehrig's disease and diabetes. With no insurance, Morris and his wife quickly depleted their life savings and were forced to sell their cars. They only held onto their modest home with the help of their children, who scraped together enough money to buy it. Even Pillowtex workers that did find new jobs often had to work without health insurance or only got access to it once they had completed probationary periods.[46]

Only charitable acts stopped the plight of many workers from getting any worse. Particularly notable was the role of Kenny Tokunboh, a Nigerian-born doctor who offered free medical care to Pillowtex employees after the plant closed. Using complimentary samples from pharmaceutical companies, Tokunboh was able to treat Morris and many others. "I did medicine to help," explained the modest director of Kannapolis's Grace Medical Clinic. "You want people to continue to have their dignity." By 2008, Tokunboh estimated that he had seen between 1,500 and 2,000 former Pillowtex employees, and that he had lost count of the number who had broken down in tears in his office. Other doctors helped patients that they knew well. When she lost her job after thirty-three years in the mill, for example, Pat Treece struggled to afford regular prescriptions for Synthroid, a drug that controlled her hypothyroidism. "I go beg my doctor in Concord, if I'm close enough to my Synthroid running out, to give me a couple to do me until I can get some, or a little sample pack," she explained in 2004. Other tried to make do as best they could. "We are seeing a lot of people who are cutting their medications, trying to save them," explained social services director Bruce Jacobs at the time.[47]

Like these doctors, most observers were sympathetic to the Pillowtex workers' plight. Reacting to stories about the closure, some bloggers blamed politicians who had supported free trade agreements, while others pointed out that consumers were also responsible for the shutdown. As "bleedingheart" noted, "All my towels are Fieldcrest and Royal Velvet. I supported them but alas most people want the cheapest brands . . . all made overseas."[48] Some North Carolinians, however, insisted that the decline of the textile industry was inevitable and that mill workers did not deserve much sympathy. "What a bunch of B.S.!!!!" exhorted one Charlotte resident in reaction to a 2005 *Spiegel* story that was broadly sympathetic to the Pillowtex workers. "The area surrounding Charlotte (which includes Kannapolis) is one of the hottest economic regions in the southeast. The city of Charlotte and surrounding satellite towns like Kannapolis are almost unrecognizable due to incredible PROSPERITY for about 30 years. Industries like textiles have been dying for over the same 30 years, and as bad as it is for the people in the article, my God, they have had 30 F**king years to make the transition to another job. . . . I don't enjoy kicking people when they are down, but a segment of the population here refuses to change with the times."[49]

Even in Kannapolis, many residents were aware that the mills would never run again, and efforts to redevelop the sprawling Pillowtex complex began shortly after the shutdown. In 2004, Dole Foods owner David Murdock bought the site, and in the following year he announced that he was going to build the $1.5 billion North Carolina Research Campus on it. Backed by state political and educational leaders, Murdock aimed to bring the best scientific minds in the state to Kannapolis to study nutrition and its role in preventing serious diseases, particularly cancer. In a few years, Murdock hoped to attract over one hundred biotechnology companies to the huge site, which was slated to incorporate corporate, academic, commercial, and residential space.[50]

To realize this ambitious dream, the huge Plant No. 1 was demolished in late 2005, with the remainder of the towel distribution center being imploded in early 2006. The mills, which had taken over a century to build, were thus demolished in just over a year, although crews had to use more dynamite than they had anticipated in order to destroy the central support column. The third largest demolition project in U.S. history, it was carried out by D. H. Griffin Wrecking Company, the firm that had helped clean up Ground Zero after the terrorist attacks of 9/11. Later in 2006, the iconic "Fieldcrest" and "Cannon" smokestacks and the red-and-white-checkered water tower were both toppled, removing the final physical vestiges of Kannapolis's textile heritage from the downtown landscape. Many workers felt sad as they watched the plants disappear, and some even wept as the landmark smokestacks crumbled. "This is like giving up a home," explained ninety-four-year-old Helen Gaddy, who had worked in the plant for fifty-four years. "I learned to know and love a lot of people here. I guess time goes on."[51]

Murdock, however, was unrepentant. "I don't have any compunction about tearing those old buildings down," he explained. "They're tired and empty and would have amounted to little more than six million square feet of rats' nests that someone would eventually demand to have removed. Now we can take that space and build a beautiful, landscaped area with parks and playgrounds and everything you can imagine to provide a wonderful quality of life." True to his word, Murdock pressed on with a vigor that belied his eighty-two years. In September 2007, the entrepreneur gifted $35 million to Duke University to fund a groundbreaking medical study into the treatment of cancer. Two decades earlier Murdock had lost his wife, Gabrielle, to the disease, and he was determined to try to find a cure. "I was very devastated when I lost my wife and I thought I would go to work and I would work on the problems," he explained to local radio.[52]

Despite Murdock's zeal, and his success in attracting commitments from corporations, universities, and the state government, job creation was slow at the campus. In late 2007, the *Charlotte Business Journal* reported that just twenty-two employees had been hired at the site, which was "expected to play a central role in the Cabarrus economy in the future." In October 2008, the North Carolina Research Campus officially opened, but only a small part of it was operational. "The three buildings that are opening represent only a small corner of the 350-acre campus," explained the *Charlotte Observer*'s Adam Bell, "and there's still far to go to fulfill Murdock's dream."[53] The sharp economic downturn that occurred at the end of 2008 cast further uncertainty over the campus, and in February 2009 construction on the main part of the site was suspended. Two years later, with the national economy still in recession, the Campus's website admitted that efforts to fulfill Murdock's "vision" were ongoing. It added that "an experienced team of scientists is working quickly to bring the campus to life." Ten companies were listed as campus tenants, well short of the one hundred that Murdock had aspired to. By April 2012, five buildings had been completed, but the entire campus employed just 130 people, a tiny fraction of those laid off by Pillowtex.[54]

Even before the Campus had opened, informed observers questioned whether it would be much help to displaced manufacturing workers. In April 2008, an investigation by the *Nation* concluded that the biotech research center would only create "up to 300" good jobs, and few of them would go to former mill workers. "A fair number of those jobs," admitted NC State University economist Michael Walden, "will be high-level research and not accessible to these folks." The following month, journalist Jim Tankersley also asserted that many of these positions would be "out of reach for some of the 4,000-plus workers laid off when the Pillowtex mill closed five years ago." Biotech positions, he noted, were more likely to attract highly educated migrants from other states, leaving mill workers on the sidelines. While one local magazine promoted the campus under the headline "From Mill to Millions," this slogan bore little relation to the lives of those who had actually worked in the plants.[55]

Former Pillowtex workers also doubted Murdock's claims that the campus would create hundreds or even thousands of new jobs for them. Many were suspicious of the billionaire entrepreneur, who they linked to the pension scandal of the 1980s. A mill worker for almost three decades, sixty-three-year-old Elvia Tucker commented in the summer of 2008 that the campus "might be real good for the young people who can get lots of higher education, but I don't really know about the older people." While the campus is still in the process of being developed, it seems unlikely that it will ever take the place of Pillowtex or Philip Morris, another major employer that has shut down its local operations. While some believed the boosters' rhetoric, other residents remained skeptical about the entire venture of building a large biotech center in an old textile town. As one blogger wrote in late 2008, "My goodness. How long can David Murdock beat this dead horse? It's Kannapolis people!"[56]

Certainly, evidence from other communities—including old mill towns in New England—suggests that the growth of high-tech industries is only of limited help to unemployed textile workers. In one study of North Carolina's high-tech industries, economist Robert Bowles found that 45 percent of the employees hired by these industries came from service occupations or the retail trade, while just 22 percent relocated from "non-High-Tech manufacturing." Clearly, some former mill workers had landed high-tech posts, but they were only a small minority of those displaced. In general, moreover, high-tech companies needed fewer workers than their manufacturing counterparts.[57] In 2006, a study by social scientists at the University of North Carolina in Charlotte found that workers from labor-intensive industries such as textiles were "not well prepared to be very competitive in the state's efforts to attract more sophisticated, high-technology industries." Many of these employees lacked formal educational qualifications and were poorly equipped to hold down jobs in a new, IT-led economy. "This under-educated labor force," concluded the study, "may be the 'Achilles Heel' of future economic development efforts by the state."[58]

Five years after the shutdown, the *Kannapolis Independent-Tribune* ran a special series of articles that documented the difficult transition that many former Pillowtex workers were still going through. As writer Ben McNeely concluded, while the new Research Campus gave outsiders a positive impression of the town's fortunes, "the stories behind the scenes are not so bright: Former mill workers are struggling to make it in a new, globalized economy that doesn't recognize their skill set." McNeely cited the case of Ruth Crisco, who at forty-seven had returned to school to earn an associate diploma in early childhood development. Still unable to find a job in her new field, Crisco earned less than half what she had at the mill, and regularly worked eighty or ninety hours a week in a variety of jobs to try to make up the difference. "I'm still struggling from the loss of Pillowtex, yes, five years later, I'm still struggling," she admitted. For workers over fifty, the situation was even more bleak; many were unable to find jobs, and they faced an uphill battle to pay medical bills now that they had lost their health coverage. Kannapolis, claimed the wife of one ailing mill worker, was "like a ghost town for the older generation." Aside from monetary considerations, former workers were also struggling to replace the sense of community they had felt in the mill. Many again returned to the family metaphor to describe how they felt. According to Agatha Overcash, who had worked at Pillowtex for over forty years, "It was a family at the mill. Your family worked there and the people you worked with were your family. That was tough to see go."[59]

Two years later, in the summer of 2010, my own interviews with former Pillowtex workers in Kannapolis highlighted that little had changed. Workers were unanimous in viewing the campus as a poor substitute for the mill, and it had made little difference to them. The former mill site remained eerily empty, and the few Research Campus buildings stood as lonely outposts on the vast site. Still searching for a job in childhood development, Crisco related that the financial and emotional costs of the shutdown had been enormous: "A lot of them lost their houses and cars, everything. Some of them lost their sanity; we even had people to be suicidal, they killed theirselves." While it was impossible to document that these suicides were wholly related to the mill closing, former workers believed that this was the case. "It was devastating, people lost, *really* lost," added Joeann Bullard, who had worked in the plant for over twenty years. The director of social services for Cabarrus County, Jim Cook, confirmed that the closure had indeed been responsible for an increase in drug and alcohol abuse and an upsurge in people contemplating suicide. Local agencies, moreover, had not been able to handle the sheer number of patients suffering from these problems.[60]

Crisco and Bullard were keen to point out that they were doing better than many others. Crisco was proud that she had held onto her car, which she had bought just before the mill shut. Revealingly, however, she could only afford to put $10 of fuel in the vehicle each week, severely restricting her mobility. Still, some had truly fared even worse. An experienced production worker, African American Sylvia Glover, had gone from earning $21 an hour at Pillowtex to less than half that at a struggling local mattress maker. In 2010, moreover, she lost this job and had not found another. She vividly recalled the Pillowtex shutdown: "It was just terrible, it was devastating, it was just awful. You have your life based on a certain level, and then all of a sudden it drops that bad, it hurts bad. . . . Me and my husband had to file bankruptcy. . . . With me being out of work and when he can't get work, we're just having it hard. And I have had to sell a lot of my jewelry, to pay my bills, and then the bills keep going up. . . . It's very hard; sometimes it makes you want to cry." Glover, who had had suffered a "nervous breakdown" when the mill closed, linked the shutdown to a rise in physical and mental health problems in the community. She also worried about the future. "The age I am now, I can't just pop up and go get a $20, $30 job any more," she acknowledged.[61]

Interviewees reiterated that it was older workers that had been hardest hit, as most had been unable to get other jobs. These elderly residents also had strong attachments to the mill, as it was the only job that most had ever done. A mill worker for twenty-eight years, Glover distinguished herself from a large cohort that had more than thirty years in the plant. "Some of the older people," she explained, "they just took their life, that was their life! They looked forward to coming to work every day. . . . Some of them started before they got out of school, during the summer, and that's all they knew." Robert Neal agreed. "There was a lot that worked there over thirty years," he recalled, "and they didn't know nothing but textile, and they couldn't get a job nowhere else because all they knew was textiles." Some workers had extraordinary records of loyalty, which they took considerable pride in. Illustrating these points was Jack Thompson, who had been working at the mill for sixty-three years when it closed down. According to the *Southern Textile News*, Thompson should not have been "shown the door" after he had given the company his "heart and soul."[62]

While the closure still hurt, it was also true that after seven years some workers had been able to retrain and even forge new careers. Joeann Bullard went back to college and earned a degree in early childhood education, using it to qualify as a kindergarten teacher. Despite these accomplishments, she had yet to find a job in her new field. More encouraging was the case of Robert Neal, who had endured "bad" days when he had first lost his job and health insurance. Showing considerable strength of character, Neal worked through his problems and used the TAA program to attend Rowan Community College, where he requalified in youth work. He eventually secured a job counseling juvenile offenders. Rationalizing his experience as a "learning block," Neal also offered informal counseling to some of his former co-workers. Although they desperately needed retraining, many older workers found it difficult to follow Neal's example. As Sylvia Glover put it, studying at her age was hard "because your brain don't function like it used to."[63]

Ultimately, the experience of this "quintessential company town" reveals much about the broader transition that the American economy is going through as historic manufacturing jobs disappear and service industries strive to take their place. It also shows how the textile industry deserves to be at the center of this story. Like scores of communities across America, Kannapolis is caught between a manufacturing-based past and an uncertain future. Booster-minded business leaders now want to forget the mills and wipe out any sign of their presence, but most former mill workers cannot move on so easily. "The Kannapolis of yesterday is gone," declared Atlanta-based economic consultant J. Mac Holladay in 2006. "It is physically torn down. What is rising in its place is a new city, a new campus, a new downtown." Holladay, who advised city leaders about the redevelopment of Kannapolis, suggested that the past could be erased easily, but many workers felt differently. At a reunion of former Pillowtex employees held in May 2008, participants recalled meeting lifelong friends and partners in the mills, which most thought would never close. Attending the gathering was Lloyd Bittle, a long-term mill worker who was in the plant until the last day of operation. The veteran explained that he still carried his employee I.D. card with him "in case we start back up one day."[64]

## NOTES

1. Woody White, "Pillowtex Idles Factories; 6450 Textile Jobs Lost," The Greenville (South Carolina) *News*, July 30, 2003 (Bremer and Edwards quotations); Moss quoted in Doug Palmer, "No Future for Textiles in 'City of Looms,'" *The Neil Rogers Show*, December 29, 2004 (South Florida radio show), available at http://www.neilrogers.com/news/articles/2004122905.html (accessed December 15, 2008). A hard copy of this document is in the author's possession.

2. "Shutdown Initially to Cost 6450," *Southern Textile News*, August 3, 2003, p. 1.

3. National Council of Textile Organizations overview statement, undated, available at http://www.ncto.org/ustextiles/index.asp (accessed August 20, 2009). A hard copy of this document is in the author's possession.

4. Testimony of Betty McGrath, Labor Market Information Division, Employment Security Commission of North Carolina, September 6, 2007, available at www.uscc.gov/hearings/2007hearings/transcripts/sept_6/betty_mcgrath.pdf (accessed December 8, 2008, copy in author's possession); Michael L. Walden, "Doing Right by Jobless Textile Workers," Raleigh (North Carolina) *News and Observer*, August 14, 2003, p. A15; Patrik Jonsson, "A Beleaguered Mill Town Struggles toward Reinvention," *Christian Science Monitor*, November 3, 2004 (Mellons quotation).

5. Leslie Haggin Geary, "Vanishing Jobs," January 9, 2004, available at http://money.cnn.com/2003/12/17/pf/q_nomorework/ (accessed December 12, 2008); Patrik Jonsson, "A Beleaguered Mill Town Struggles toward Reinvention," *Christian Science Monitor*, November 3, 2004; Spotts quoted in *American Jobs* (Spottsfilm, 2004, written, produced, and directed by Greg Spotts).

6. Ben S. Bernanke, "At the Presentation of the Citizen of the Carolinas Award," November 29, 2007, available at http://www.federalreserve.gov/newsevents/speech/bernanke20071129a.htm (accessed December 9, 2008). The redevelopment of the mill site as a biotech research campus is detailed in full below.

7. "NAFTA: A Decade of Growth," February 2004, p. 23 (first quotation), p. 24 (Business Roundtable White Paper), and Business Roundtable, "Trade Myths and Realities," June 1, 1997 (second and third quotations), both available at http://www.businessroundtable.org/publications (accessed April 28, 2008). Hard copies of both of these documents are in the author's possession.

8. C. Fred Bergsten, "Fifty Years of the GATT/WTO: Lessons from the Past for Strategies for the Future," April 30, 1998, available at http://www.iie.com/publications/wp/print.cfm?doc=pub&ResearchID=144 (accessed October 20, 2008); Jagdish Bhagwati, *In Defense of Globalization* (New York: Oxford University Press, 2004), p. 6.

9. For key studies of the growth of the southern textile industry in the late nineteenth and early twentieth centuries that illustrate these points well, see Hall et al., *Like a Family*, esp. pp. xi–xx, 44–113; Carlton, *Mill and Town in South Carolina.*

10. Barbara Hagenbaugh, "Lives Unraveled," *USA Today*, July 30, 2004; "A Phoenix Rising from the Ashes," available at the *Kannapolis Independent Tribune*'s "Pillowtex Five Years Later" site at http://independenttribune.net/index.php/pillowtex/article/part_4/ (accessed December 8, 2008); David Firestone, "Union Victory at Plant in South Is Labor Milestone," *New York Times*, June 25, 1999, p. A16 ("textile plant" quotation); Patrik Jonsson, "A Beleaguered Mill Town Struggles toward Reinvention," *Christian Science Monitor*, November 3, 2004 (closing quotation).

11. Griffith, *The Crisis of American Labor,* p. 46; "Collection Overview: Records of Cannon Mills, 1836–1983," held at Perkins Library, Duke University, available at http://library.duke.edu/digitalcollections/rbmscl/cannon/inv (accessed December 12, 2008); Ben McNeely, Josh Lanier, and Eric C. Deines, "A Mill Town Remembered," *Kannapolis Independent Tribune*, July 27, 2008, pp. 1–4; Closing quotation in Daniel, *Culture of Misfortune*, p. 280.

12. Widely considered a NASCAR legend, Earnhardt died in a last-lap crash at the 2001 Daytona 500. Audrey Beaver is quoted in Elizabeth Becker, "Textile Quotas to End Soon, Punishing Carolina Mill Towns," *New York Times*, November 2, 2004.

13. Robert Freeman interview with author on March 11, 1996, in Kannapolis, North Carolina.

14. Brad A. Hodges, "David Murdock Still Wheeling and Dealing," Salisbury (North Carolina) *Post*, February 6, 2000; "Timeline/History," *Where Do You Stand?: Stories from an American Mill* (Mighty Fine Films, 2004, produced and directed by Alexandra Lescaze), available at http://www.wheredoyoustand.info/timeline.html (accessed December 12, 2008); Raynor quoted in "Textile Workers Win Union," *Workers' World*, July 8, 1999, available at http://www.workers.org/ww/1999/unite0708.php (accessed December 12, 2008). Hard copies of both of these documents are in the author's possession. For a good summary of the historical significance of the 1999 union victory, see Daniel, *Culture of Misfortune*, pp. 280–81.

15. Jennifer Steinhauer, "Pillowtex to Acquire Fieldcrest for $400 Million," *New York Times*, September 12, 1997.

16. Marvin Lazaro, "Pillowtex Cuts Losses with More Closings," *Home Textiles Today*, May 21, 2001; Don Hogsett, "Pillowtex Done in by Aggressive Growth," *Home Textiles Today*, November 20, 2000 (quotation); "Changes at Pillowtex Could Have Widespread Impact," *Textile Web*, May 21, 2003, available at http://www.textileweb.com (accessed December 12, 2008, copy in author's possession).

17. Ken Elkins, "Michael Gannaway Can't Change Pillowtex Fortunes," *Charlotte Business Journal*, January 2, 2004.

18. Adam Bell and Gail Smith-Arrants, "Former Workers Pick Up Pieces," *Charlotte Observer*, July 27, 2008; Lauren Weber, "'Made in the USA' a Dying Phrase?" *Baltimore Sun*, January 31, 2005; "Plenty of Blame to Go around for Pillowtex," *Charlotte Business Journal*, August 29, 2003.

19. Scott Jenkins, "Kannapolis Nervous, Hopeful after Pillowtex Bankruptcy Filing," Salisbury (North Carolina) *Post*, November 19, 2000 (first three quotations); "Changes at Pillowtex Could Have Widespread Impact," *Textile Web*, May 21, 2003; Robert Neal interview with author on June 22, 2010, in Concord, North Carolina (closing quotation).

20. McNeely et al., "A Mill Town Remembered," p. 5 (Crawford quotation); "Tina" quoted on the *Kannapolis Independent-Tribune*'s "Pillowtex: Five Years Later" website at http://independenttribune.net/index.php/pillowtex/article/junior_bittle/ (accessed December 8, 2008, copy in author's possession).

21. Raynor quoted in Palmer, "No Future for Textiles in 'City of Looms.'" For a more detailed investigation of the union's efforts to find a buyer for the mills, see Myra Beatty, Douglas Longman, and Van Tran, "Community Response to the Pillowtex Textile Kannapolis Closing: The 'Rapid Response' Team as a Facilitative Device," April 2004, p. 7, University of North Carolina study available at www.unc.edu/depts/econ/PlantClosure/beatty_longman__tran.pdf (accessed December 8, 2008, copy in author's possession).

22. Paul Chesser, "Union Blocked Springs-Pillowtex Deal," *Carolina Journal*, September 15, 2003; Diana Furchtgott-Roth, "Labor Reconsidered: Pillowtex Tragedy," *The New York Sun*, August 31, 2007; U.S. Department of Labor, *The Past, Present and Future of Employment in the Textile and Apparel Industries: An Overview*, (Washington, DC: U.S. Government Printing Office, 2004), p. 73.

23. Beatty et al., "Community Response to the Pillowtex Textile Kannapolis Closing," p. 5; Barbara Hagenbaugh, "Lives Unraveled," *USA Today*, July 30, 2004.

24. U.S. Department of Labor, *The Past, Present and Future*, pp. 71–72; Sarah Nagem, "No More Mills: Changing Work Force Means Fewer Options for Dropouts," Salisbury (North Carolina) *Post*, December 14, 2008.

25. Ken Elkins, "Michael Gannaway Can't Change Pillowtex Fortunes," *Charlotte Business Journal*, January 2, 2004.

26. Paul Nowell, "N.C. Summit Focuses on Job Creation," *The State*, August 7, 2003, p. B7 (Freeman quotation).

27. Beatty et al., "Community Response to the Pillowtex Textile Kannapolis Closing," p. 5–6 (first two quotations on p. 6), p. 11; Barbara Hagenbaugh, "Lives Unraveled," *USA Today*, July 30, 2004 (Burton quotation); Brawley quoted in *American Jobs*.

28. Barbara Hagenbaugh, "Lives Unraveled," *USA Today*, July 30, 2004; U.S. Department of Labor, *The Past, Present and Future of Employment in the Textile and Apparel Industries*, pp. 11–12, 29–32 (Chao quotation on pp. 29–30, second quotation on p. 32).

29. Barbara Hagenbaugh, "Lives Unraveled," *USA Today*, July 30, 2004 (Geathers quotation); Lauren Weber, "'Made in the USA' a Dying Phrase?" *Baltimore Sun*, January 31, 2005 (Miller quotation); Closing quotation in Alexander Osang, "For Residents of Kannapolis, Unemployment Is as American as Apple Pie," *Spiegel*, October 1, 2005.

30. "The Human Cost of Cheaper Towels," *The Economist*, April 23, 2005, p. 30 (Burton quotation); H. Martin Lancaster, "When the Mill Closes: Worker Retraining in North Carolina's Community Colleges," n.d., available at the North Carolina Community College website at http://www.nccommunitycolleges.edu/External_Affairs/Presentations/millclosescover.htm (accessed December 11, 2008, copy in author's possession).

31. Testimony of Betty McGrath, Labor Market Information Division, Employment Security Commission of North Carolina, September 6, 2007, available at www.uscc.gov/hearings/2007hearings/transcripts/sept_6/betty_mcgrath.pdf (accessed December 8, 2008, copy in author's possession).

32. Lauren Weber, "'Made in the USA' a Dying Phrase?" *Baltimore Sun*, January 31, 2005 (Gambrell quotations); Elizabeth Becker, "Textile Quotas to End Soon, Punishing Carolina Mill Towns," *New York Times*, November 2, 2004 (Harrington quotation).

33. For detailed information on the rise of Wal-Mart, especially its labor relations policies, see Nelson Lichtenstein, *Wal-Mart: The Face of Twenty-First Century Capitalism* (New York: New Press, 2006); Moreton, *To Serve God and Wal-Mart*, pp. 67–72.

34. Tim Weiner, "Wal-Mart Invades, and Mexico Gladly Surrenders," *New York Times*, December 6, 2003; Hatley quotations in "Judy Hatley" profile, available on the *Kannapolis Independent-Tribune*'s "Pillowtex: Five Years Later" website at http://independenttribune.net/index.php/pillowtex/article/judy-hatley/ (accessed December 8, 2008, copy in author's possession).

35. Ruth Crisco interview with author on June 22, 2010, in Concord, North Carolina; Pat Treece quoted in *American Jobs*.

36. Minchin, *Hiring the Black Worker*, pp. 2–4; Hall et al., *Like a Family*, pp. 66–67.

37. C. A. Cannon and Don S. Holt to the Stockholders of Cannon Mills Company, April 14, 1969, White House Central Files (Subject Files: Human Rights–Equality–Employment), Richard M. Nixon Presidential Materials, National Archives and Records Administration, College Park, Maryland (first two quotations); Complaint, June 1, 1970, *Donald R. Hicks et al. v. Cannon Mills*, U.S. district court records held at the National Archives and Records Administration-Southeast Region, Morrow, Georgia (case number C-115-S-70).

38. Minchin, *Hiring the Black Worker*, pp. 61, 113, 133–34; Robert Neal interview with author on June 22, 2010, in Concord, North Carolina.

39. Griffith, *The Crisis of American Labor*, p. 47; Patterson quotation in "Textile Jobs in Decline," Transcript of *The Newshour with Jim Lehrer*, September 23, 2003, available at http://www.pbs.org/newshour/bb/economy/july-dec03/textile_9-23.html (accessed December 8, 2008).

40. Robert Neal interview with author on June 22, 2010, in Concord, North Carolina; Warren Ellis interview with author on June 22, 2010, in Concord, North Carolina; Ruth Crisco interview with author on June 22, 2010, in Concord, North Carolina.

41. Leon Fink, *The Maya of Morganton: Work and Community in the Nuevo New South* (Chapel Hill: University of North Carolina Press, 2003), p. 2; Minchin, *Fighting against the Odds*, pp. 168–71; Barbara Hagenbaugh, "Lives Unraveled," *USA Today*, July 30, 2004.

42. Alfred W. Stuart "Manufacturing," in *The North Carolina Atlas* at http://www.ncatlasrevisited.org/Manufacturing/mfgTitle.html (accessed December 11, 2008, copy in author's possession); Ruth Crisco interview with author on June 22, 2010, in Concord, North Carolina.

43. "The Human Cost of Cheaper Towels," *The Economist*, April 23, 2005, p. 30.

44. Ben McNeely, Josh Lanier, and Eric C. Deines, "A Mill Town Remembered," *Kannapolis Independent Tribune*, July 27, 2008, p. 4 (Anderson quotations); ESC study cited in Alfred W. Stuart, "Manufacturing," in http://www.ncatlasrevisited.org/Manufacturing/mfgTitle.html

(accessed December 11, 2008, copy in author's possession); Elizabeth Becker, "Textile Quotas to End Soon, Punishing Carolina Mill Towns," *New York Times*, November 2, 2004.

45. Harris Raynor interview with author on June 18, 2010, in Union City, Georgia; Beatty et al., "Community Response to the Pillowtex Textile Kannapolis Closing," pp. 5–10; Robert Pear, "Sluggish Start for Offer of Tax Credit for Insurance," *New York Times*, January 25, 2004, p. N16.

46. Ben McNeely, Josh Lanier, and Eric C. Deines, "A Mill Town Remembered," *Kannapolis Independent Tribune*, July 27, 2008, pp. 5, 7; Barbara Hagenbaugh, "Lives Unraveled," *USA Today*, July 30, 2004 (Neal quotations).

47. Barbara Hagenbaugh, "Lives Unraveled," *USA Today*, July 30, 2004 (Tokunboh quotations); Treece and Jacobs quoted in *American Jobs*.

48. "Bleedingheart," November 3, 2003, posted on http://www.democraticunderground.com/ (accessed December 9, 2008, hard copy in author's possession). A liberal site, the heavily used democratic underground contains several other reactions that are sympathetic to the Pillowtex workers.

49. Blog posted at http://medienkritik.typepad.com/blog/2005/10/kannapolis_piec.html (accessed December 11, 2008, hard copy in author's possession). A German site that is "dedicated to the documentation of anti-Americanism in the German media and the negative influence it has on Germans' perceptions of the United States," www.medienkritik.typepad.com contains other similar examples reacting to the Pillowtex closure. The original story that this blogger is reacting to is Alexander Osang, "For Residents of Kannapolis, Unemployment Is as American as Apple Pie," *Spiegel*, October 1, 2005.

50. Ben McNeely, Josh Lanier, and Eric C. Deines, "A Mill Town Remembered," *Kannapolis Independent Tribune*, July 27, 2008, p. 10. For an overview of Murdock's plans, see the official site of the North Carolina Research Campus at http://www.ncresearchcampus.net/the-plan.html (accessed January 21, 2009, copy in author's possession).

51. Gaddy quoted in Sharif Durhams, "Dropping Name That Made Kannapolis," *Charlotte Observer*, August 11, 2006; Ben McNeely, "Tumblin' Down: Pillowtex Smokestacks Toppled," *Kannapolis Independent-Tribune*, August 11, 2006. For more information on the demolition, see the items in the "Cannon Mills," folder (drawer item), Cannon Mills Papers.

52. First Murdock quotation in Susanne Deitzel, "Paying It Forward," *Greater Charlotte Biz*, November 2005, business publication available at http://www.greatercharlottebiz.com/article.asp?id=552&print=1 (accessed December 15, 2008); Simone Orendain, "Ribbon Cutting at the NCRC," October 21, 2008, local public radio story available at http://www.wfae.org/wfae/stat_search.cfm?id=4360&action=display (accessed December 15, 2008). Copies of both of these documents are in the author's possession.

53. Ken Elkins, "Research Ready to Start in Kannapolis," *Charlotte Business Journal*, December 21, 2007 (first quotation); Adam Bell, "New Chance for an Old Mill Town," *Charlotte Observer*, October 19, 2008 (second and third quotations).

54. Ben McNeely, "Economic Downturn Impacts Research Campus," *Kannapolis Independent Tribune*, February 7, 2009; Closing quotations in "The Vision" and "Planning and Progress," available from the North Carolina Research Campus website at http://www.ncresearchcampus.net/about-ncrc/vision.aspx and http://www.ncresearchcampus.net/about-ncrc/planning-construction.aspx (both accessed January 20, 2011, copies in author's possession). The tenant data is taken from "Companies on Campus," list available from the North Carolina Research Campus website at http://www.ncresearchcampus.net/businesses/company-profiles.aspx (accessed January 20, 2011, copy in author's possession). The closing data is taken from the North Carolina Research Campus website at http://www.ncresearchcampus.net/about-ncrc/ncrc-history.aspx (accessed April 2, 2012, copy in author's possession).

55. Bob Moser, "Mill Hill Populism," *The Nation*, April 24, 2008; Jim Tankersley, "North Carolina Transformation Has Winners, Losers," *The Seattle Times*, May 5, 2008; Closing slogan in "From Mill to Millions: N.C. Research Campus Transforms Kannapolis," *Rowan Magazine*, March/April 2008, available at http://www.rowanbusiness.com/marchapril2008.html (accessed December 9, 2008, copy in author's possession).

56. Adam Bell and Gail Smith-Arrants, "Former Workers Pick Up Pieces," *Charlotte Observer*, July 27, 2008 (Tucker quotation); "Pintobeans" quoted in reaction to Adam Bell, "New

Chance for an Old Mill Town," *Charlotte Observer*, October 19, 2008, available at http://www.charlotteobserver.com/business/story/263380.html (accessed December 9, 2008, copy in author's possession).

57. For more details of this study, see Robert Bowles, "Employment and Wage Outcomes for North Carolina's High-Tech Workers," *Monthly Labor Review* 127:5 (May 2004), pp. 31–39, data and quotation on p. 36; Harrison, *Rationalization, Restructuring, and Industrial Reorganization in Older Regions*, p. 89.

58. Alfred W. Stuart, "Manufacturing," at http://www.ncatlasrevisited.org/Manufacturing/mfgTitle.html (accessed December 11, 2008, copy in author's possession)

59. First quotation in untitled Ben McNeely Column, *Kannapolis Independent Tribune*, July 25, 2008 (supplied to author by Ben McNeely, copy in author's possession); Ben McNeely, Josh Lanier, and Eric C. Deines, "A Mill Town Remembered," *Kannapolis Independent Tribune*, July 27, 2008, p. 6 (third quotation), p. 8 (Crisco quotation), p. 9 (Overcash quotation).

60. Ruth Crisco interview with author on June 22, 2010, in Concord, North Carolina; Joeann Bullard interview with author on June 22, 2010, in Concord, North Carolina; Cook interview cited in Barbara Hagenbaugh, "Lives Unraveled," *USA Today*, July 30, 2004.

61. Ruth Crisco interview with author on June 22, 2010, in Concord, North Carolina; Sylvia Glover interview with author on June 22, 2010, in Concord, North Carolina.

62. Sylvia Glover interview with author on June 22, 2010, in Concord, North Carolina; Robert Neal interview with author on June 22, 2010, in Concord, North Carolina; "Stuffed with Thanks," *Southern Textile News*, November 24, 2003, p. 16.

63. Joeann Bullard interview with author on June 22, 2010, in Concord, North Carolina; Robert Neal interview with author on June 22, 2010, in Concord, North Carolina; Sylvia Glover interview with author on June 22, 2010, in Concord, North Carolina; Barbara Hagenbaugh, "Lives Unraveled," *USA Today*, July 30, 2004 (first Neal quotation).

64. Barbara Hagenbaugh, "Lives Unraveled," *USA Today*, July 30, 2004 (first quotation); J. Mac Holladay, "Kannapolis—Yesterday, Today and Tomorrow," *The Market Street Report*, Winter 2006 (Vol. 3), available through the Market Street Services economic consultants website at http://www.marketstreetservices.com/MSReport/winter2006/Article1.html (accessed December 22, 2008, copy in author's possession); Hugh Fisher, "Fieldcrest-Cannon Reunion Draws Hundreds," *Kannapolis Citizen*, May 28, 2008 (Bittle quotation).

# Epilogue

In the summer of 1996, the closure of Olympia Mills in Columbia, South Carolina, left workers devastated. The mill had operated for over a century, and it had played a central role in Columbia's history; the company had built the finest swimming pool in the city, and its boilers once generated enough extra electricity to power the streetcars downtown. "We ran Columbia," joked one former worker. Older workers, in particular, struggled to cope with the news that the mill was gone. "It's heartbreaking," commented veteran employee Brenda Sox. "I'll stay in there until they shut the doors." Some workers had toiled in the mill for over sixty years, and they still resided in Olympia, the old mill village next to the plant. When the mill finally closed, many of these senior workers were in tears.[1]

As the textile and apparel industry declined, the press carried thousands of stories detailing individual plant closures, and the reaction of the Columbia workers was representative.[2] Because of the industry's tendency to dominate local economies and offer decently paid jobs to people without formal qualifications, textile workers formed a deep sense of attachment to their jobs and their colleagues. Mill work, as one former employee put it, "instilled a sense of togetherness, fellowship, whatever you want to call it." Traditionally, workers started in the mills straight after high school and stayed there for the rest of their working lives. They consequently mourned the disappearance of these jobs, frequently comparing the experience to the loss of a family member.[3] In 2001, South Carolina mill owner George Diacou summarized broader trends particularly well: "Workers in cotton mills, double knits, finishing and garment manufacturing all held a great sense of pride. Their job was their life."[4]

This reaction was not confined to the South. In the 1980s, for example, a state-sponsored oral history project in Fall River, Massachusetts, conducted interviews with scores of retired mill workers, most of whom had lost their jobs in the industry's first wave of decline a generation or two earlier. Again and again, interviewees described poor working conditions and admitted that they were glad that their contemporary counterparts did not have to toil in such an environment. Many also doubted whether the younger generation could endure mill work, which was noisy and strenuous. At the same time, however, they repeatedly remembered the mills as being "like a family." As the *Boston Globe*'s Christina Robb noted, for interviewees the phrase summed up the "warm and unpretentious relationships they had with their coworkers."[5] In the 1990s, the same theme emerged from an oral history project carried out by the Lowell National Historical Park. According to Celia Thing, who spent twenty-one years in the city's mills, "If I had to be young again, I would go back to weaving, that's how much I liked it . . . the girls in there were very friendly . . . To me it was like going to a second home—second family."[6]

These reactions highlight how textile and apparel workers have been affected by deindustrialization just as much as their counterparts in industries that have received much more scholarly attention. Largely focused on the steel and auto industries in the Rust Belt, numerous case studies have demonstrated that workers in manufacturing industries identified heavily with their work. Most had been hired straight after high school, and they typically stayed on the job for many years, building close relationships with their colleagues in the process. Scholars such as Kathryn Marie Dudley, Steve Mellon, David Bensman, and Roberta Lynch have documented that workers were deeply affected by plant closures, with many left feeling shocked and betrayed. While warning of the dangers of romanticizing industrial jobs, Jefferson Cowie and Joseph Heathcott have summarized that any discussion of deindustrialization must start by recognizing the "despair and betrayal" that the process causes workers.[7]

There were, however, distinctive elements to the textile story. Because steel and automobile production was concentrated in certain cities, most books on deindustrialization have taken the form of community case studies. The story of the textile industry's decline, however, cannot be confined to particular communities or even a specific region. As John A. Salmond has shown in his national study of the General Textile Strike of 1934, the industry operated "from Maine to Alabama," and its demise consequently had wide-ranging ramifications. While a first wave of deindustrialization was concentrated in New England and the mid-Atlantic states, the industry's recent downfall has been centered in the South, a region more commonly associated with economic growth. As we have seen, the decline of the South's biggest industry has had broad-ranging social and political consequences, and this story deserves greater recognition. According to Roger

Milliken, ultimately the decline of the industry hurt workers "all over the country."[8]

The industry's size and geographical spread gave it significant political power, and it used it. "The textile industry," recalled former congressman Don Johnson, "has been a very powerful force in politics." Opponents claimed that the industry was the most protected of any in the nation, a testament to its effectiveness. Between the 1950s, when the first restrictions on Japanese textile imports were imposed, through to 2005, when the last textile and apparel quotas were lifted, the industry was able to slow the pace of its decline. As a result, arguably no other American industry experienced deindustrialization for as long. The textile bills of the 1980s were crucial, as they inspired a powerful grassroots campaign that undoubtedly saved jobs. As Congressman Ed Jenkins remembered, some of Reagan's aides privately acknowledged that the 1985 bill had assisted their efforts to renew the MFA. "The administration, even though they opposed me at every step of the way, privately some of their staff would say, 'Well, this will help us get a better agreement, with it.'"[9]

Because it fell short, the massive legislative fight to restrict imports was a turning point. Unable to link imports to the growth of the domestic market, the industry lost more and more jobs, and with them went lobbying power. In a changing economy, retailers and export-focused service industries gradually gained the upper hand, and the textile industry split as it tried to respond. While some companies embraced offshore production, others defended domestic manufacturing. Damaging divisions over NAFTA and CAFTA sealed the industry's fate. Although some companies struggled on, the bulk of the industry had gone for good. According to the *Southern Textile News*, the fight to impose extensive safeguards on Chinese imports as quotas were removed was the industry's "last stand." The *News* no longer exists, and neither does most of the industry that it represented. In 2009, moreover, the BLS projected that the textile and apparel industry would experience the "fastest declines" in employment of any American industry over the next decade.[10]

In other ways, too, the textile industry deserves to be at the heart of the literature on deindustrialization, a process that has been inextricably associated with the rise of international competition. Because of its low-wage and labor-intensive characteristics, the industry has become perhaps the ultimate global industry. In 1993, textile and clothing producers accounted for 9.3 percent of world exports of manufactures, a figure that increased in the years that followed. Contemporary America, moreover, is a land racked by deindustrialization and a gargantuan trade deficit to which the industry is a major contributor. The industry's decline was also inextricably linked to the rise of China, a key geopolitical development. In 2007, the Chinese textile sector was the largest industrial employer in that country and its primary earner of foreign exchange. Chinese textile and apparel exports were growing at a rate of 20 percent a year, and the Asian power had a textile trade surplus of $126 billion. If China does indeed replace the United States as the world's largest economy—as most experts predict it soon will—the textile and apparel industry will be partly responsible.[11]

Some popular works on globalization duly focused on the textile and apparel industry. They included Pietra Rivoli's *The Travels of a T-Shirt in the Global Economy* (2005), which used the example of the apparel industry to explore wider issues about trade and its costs. By following the production cycle of a single T-shirt, Rivoli illustrated how the clothing industry had become truly global. In another best-selling work, journalist Sara Bongiorni told her family that they would try to live for a year without buying Chinese-made products. They found it impossible to do so, partly because a "Chinese takeover of the world's textile industry" meant that staple clothing items were invariably "Made in China." Both authors concluded that while trade liberalization had created jobs in developing countries and benefited Western consumers, it had also displaced and exploited millions of workers.[12]

Throughout the 1980s and 1990s free-traders argued that any industry that needed protection did not deserve to exist, and they insisted that displaced textile workers could simply find jobs in other areas of the economy. Disputing this, the industry's supporters stressed workers' ties to the industry and the difficulties they faced in switching careers, problems that were also highlighted by independent studies. The material presented here, especially that derived from interviews, powerfully reinforces these conclusions. While some workers—primarily white-collar or supervisory employees with existing skills—were able to switch into new careers, for most the transition was extremely painful. Women and racial minorities, both of whom were concentrated in the industry, were disproportionately hurt. As the Kannapolis case study illustrates, older workers also had a particularly hard time. Many were loath to retool, and they also found that retail and service companies favored young staff, especially when they interacted with the public. As Harris Raynor recalled, this was a problem he had witnessed right across the industry: "If you're in retail, or if you're in the service industry, especially if you're dealing directly with the customers, you want young, attractive people. You go into the W Hotel and look at the waiters and the waitresses and they're all wearing black and they weigh 11 pounds, and my members didn't look like that. So it was a lot harder for people to get jobs, a lot harder for people to start over. They had houses, they had things to lose, and they lost them."[13]

With the onset of the global financial crisis, even supporters of globalization began to backtrack. While deindustrialization has been occurring for decades, the process has accelerated recently, and the collapse of the textile industry is a major part of this largely untold story. During the first seven years of George W. Bush's administration, for instance, 3.5 million manufacturing jobs disappeared, a figure that represented over 20 percent of such positions. As the job losses mounted—and as they affected many white-collar employees—even fervent free-traders began to shift their position. In August 2008, C. Fred Bergsten called for a "grand bargain" to address the costs of trade liberalization. Dubbed "one of Washington's high priests of free trade and globalization," Bergsten now wanted a "major expansion of governmental assistance to workers dislocated by trade." In a similar vein, Jagdish Bhagwati acknowledged that the developed world was going through a "very painful process of readjustment" that was much more disruptive than he had foreseen several years earlier, when *In Defense of Globalization* was published. "America," summarized economist Daniel Ikenson in 2008, "is witnessing a popular backlash against international trade."[14]

Economic issues were at the heart of the 2008 presidential election, in which Barack Obama won office by inspiring hopes that he could turn the situation around. During the campaign, Obama and other Democratic contenders repeatedly reached out to displaced manufacturing workers, especially textile workers. The son of a mill worker from Robbins, North Carolina, Senator John Edwards frequently toured struggling textile communities as he ran for the Democratic nomination in 2008, just as he had four years earlier. "People don't understand, it's not just a paycheck for you," Edwards told one crowd of displaced workers in Columbus, Georgia. "It has some effect on your self-respect and dignity. I hear that and I see it in your face, and I hear the same thing over and over and over across this country." In the Democratic primaries of 2008, both Obama and Hillary Clinton also appealed to laid-off factory workers. In April, Clinton visited Winston-Salem, North Carolina, and asserted that she would act to stem the loss of blue-collar jobs. "I want to have an emphasis on manufacturing again," she declared. "I believe you can't have a strong economy if you don't make anything anymore."[15]

A talented campaigner, Obama was keen not to be left behind. In August 2008, former Pillowtex worker Gloria Craven introduced the Illinois senator on his Raleigh "town hall" campaign stop. Craven told of the difficulties that the Pillowtex group were experiencing, especially as most had only ever worked in the mills. "We need someone who will not send our jobs overseas anymore," she declared. "We've been heading in the wrong direction. My hope is he'll (Obama) be the one to turn it all around." After the visit, Obama aired a TV ad that blamed John McCain for the loss of textile jobs. Titled "Mills," it featured a yarn company that had been forced to close seventeen plants after free trade deals allowed its customers to import cheaper yarn. McCain had supported these agreements. In the election, Obama's pledges to pursue "Fair Trade" attracted millions of disgruntled blue-collar voters, and the Democrats duly succeeded in winning North Carolina for the first time since 1976. Obama also won Virginia, where he met with laid-off textile workers and their families in Martinsville, a town with the state's highest unemployment rate.[16] Prior to the election, Obama also reached out to textile industry groups. "I am especially aware of the trade challenges faced by those working in our textile industries," he had written the NCTO in late October. "When safeguards on textile imports from China expired in 2004, imports surged and thousands of jobs were lost." If elected, Obama promised to carefully monitor Chinese imports and to support the Berry Amendment, which required that the Department of Defense and other federal agencies bought only American-made textiles. He also pledged his support for strict "yarn forward" rules, ensuring that countries with which the United States had special trade relationships did not become conduits for other nations' yarn.[17]

Once in office, Obama was able to deliver on some of these commitments. Passed by the House in February 2009, the administration's economic recovery package included a provision that required the Department of Homeland Security to purchase over one hundred thousand employee uniforms from American mills. Sponsoring the amendment was Representative Larry Kissell (D-NC), a former textile worker who related that forty-four mills had closed recently, including fourteen in his home state. "This is the right thing to do," he argued. The move built on the original Berry Amendment, which had first been applied to the Department of Defense's textile orders during World War II. Industry supporters were delighted. "Much thanks must also be extended to President Obama and U.S. Senate Majority leader Harry Reid," declared UNITE HERE president Bruce Raynor. "With the Kissell Amendment they delivered change all U.S. textile and apparel workers can believe in."[18]

While most of the industry continued to decline, some companies did buck wider trends. Taking advantage of the patriotic climate of the post-9/11 years, Wellstone Mills won the right to be the main supplier of the new U.S. Army combat uniform, as worn by troops in Iraq and Afghanistan. The lucrative order helped to secure the future of the company's six plants in South Carolina, Georgia, and Alabama. For other struggling firms, contracts with government agencies or pro-American organizations offered a vital lifeline. Alternatively, some mills continued to exist by specializing in niche products or by investing heavily in automation and technology. The high-tech field of medical textiles survived quite well, as did some other specialized and capital-intensive niches, although the ongoing development of the Chinese industry ensures that even these firms face an uncertain future.[19]

Occasionally, public outrage also saved a few jobs. In October 2010, there were widespread complaints when the owners of a family-run New Jersey firm that made uniforms for the Girl Scouts of America announced that they were in danger of losing their sole client. If the business went to China, around ninety workers in Passaic, a "once booming" city that epitomized the industry's demise, stood to lose their jobs. Following a "public uproar," on November 2 the Girl Scouts announced that the uniforms would be made domestically. The Girl Scouts had 2.4 million members in the United States alone, and they were behind the shift. "The idea almost made many people toss their cookies: Girl Scout uniforms made in China," summarized New Jersey*'s Star-Ledger*. The *Star-Ledger* also wondered, however, if consumers would buy American-made goods when they cost more. In numerous cases where there was little or no media attention, plants closed quietly and jobs went overseas. It is a trend that is unlikely to end.[20]

Deindustrialization remains a central issue in Obama's troubled America, where much of the fate of the forty-fourth president rests on his ability to heal the country's deep economic wounds. Manufacturers complain that many of their woes are caused by the devaluation of the Chinese currency, an issue that is crucial for the textile industry. The NCTO is a leading member of the China Currency Coalition, which has repeatedly lobbied the administration to act against "Chinese currency manipulation." Provoked by widespread concern about the ongoing loss of industrial jobs, in September 2010 Congress held hearings on China's currency. It then passed H.R. 2378, the Currency Reform and Fair Trade Act, by a vote of 348 to 79, although the Senate subsequently ran out of time to approve the bill. The measure was part of the Democrats' "Make It in America" initiative, which aimed to help domestic manufacturers and create jobs. In particular, the plan allowed the administration to impose antidumping duties on imports from countries with undervalued currencies. Following this, Obama pledged that he would take action against "unfair trade practices around the world," although Democratic losses in the 2010 midterm elections make it difficult for him to fulfill this commitment. Even if currency reform legislation is eventually passed, the scale of the trade deficit and the determination of the Chinese to protect their economic interests means that it is unlikely to be a panacea for America's embattled textile workers, who have watched their industry decline for decades.[21]

Right across the United States, the physical evidence of the demise of its first industry is everywhere. Old and neglected mills dominate the landscape of many New England towns, where authorities are still wrestling with the difficult task of finding new uses for them. Former workers often looked at the empty shells with sadness. In the early 1990s, for example, Regis Mannion stood in one of Lowell's vacant mills and reflected on his experiences of working in the industry for almost four decades. "After you spend thirty-eight years in a mill," he reflected, "it becomes like walking from your living room to your dining room. As you walk through the empty mills now, seeing everything empty, no sounds, no people walking around, it's very depressing to see its buildings empty." Overall, the industry's demise "was like seeing your own home fall apart and you couldn't do anything about it." While the authorities in Lowell were eventually able to find fresh uses for most mills, other New England mill towns have not been as successful.[22]

The South is now afflicted with the same problem. As the *Charlotte Observer* summarized in 2002, "Hundreds of empty mills are the most visible legacy of a textile industry that has closed 236 plants and shed nearly 75,000 jobs in the Carolinas in just the last five years." In growth-minded southern states, local officials were often embarrassed by the dilapidated factories, which dominated the landscapes of small towns. "These abandoned mills are a huge liability to our community," commented Richard Shirley, the mayor of Anderson, South Carolina, where five local mills stood empty. It was a sad end for an industry that had provided stable jobs to generations of local people.[23]

In the South, many of the old mills are still visible from Interstate 85, a vital economic route that runs through Gastonia, Spartanburg, and Anderson, as well as many other former mill towns. "Along the asphalt artery that binds the economy from Charlotte, N.C., through South Carolina and Georgia to Montgomery, Ala., it is the workers, many laid off by electronics and textile plants, who are begging," wrote *New York Times* journalist Peter T. Kilborn in 2001. Rather than working in the showcase business parks built along the highway, most dislocated textile workers held menial posts in the fast-food restaurants, retail stores, and motels that clustered around the exit ramps. The mills themselves stood empty and forgotten, surrounded by "padlocked gates and knee-high grass," as one press account put it. Those who had been involved in the industry could never forget it, however, and many were now participating in hastily organized efforts to preserve both the buildings and the memories of the people who had worked in them. In the North, similar efforts had been underway for some time. Former workers and their families knew that the industry—and the story of its decline—mattered. According to Lynn W. Rumley, the great-granddaughter of a Virginia textile worker and the executive director of North Carolina's Textile Heritage Center, "Without the textile industry and its people, there would be no 'New South.' These are hard-working people . . . who saved a region. [That] ought to be commemorated."[24]

## NOTES

1. Clark Surratt, "Mill Closing Marks End of Era for Neighborhood," *The State*, June 29, 1996, p. A1.

2. A search through the newspaper database www.newslibrary.com under "textile industry and closing," for example, yields over fourteen thousand stories, mainly from local papers in the southern states, and at least six hundred of these were highly relevant. The national press also contains many stories that track the process of deindustrialization in the textile industry. For good examples of national press coverage of the industry's decline and the devastating impact it has had on workers, particularly in the South, see John Holusha, "Squeezing the

Textile Workers; Trade and Technology Force a New Wave of Job Cuts," *New York Times*, February 21, 1996; Peter T. Kilborn, "Jobs Are Scarce in the Newest Economy," *New York Times*, October 9, 2001; Michael Janofsky, "For Bush, Loss of Jobs May Erode Support," *New York Times*, August 18, 2003; Edmund L. Andrews, "Textile Towns Appeal for Help, But Quotas May Not Suffice," *New York Times*, November 20, 2003.

3. Willie Drye, "In U.S. South, Textile Mills Gone but Not Forgotten," *National Geographic News*, October 19, 2004, available at http://news.nationalgeographic.com/news/pf/83884144.html (accessed November 12, 2008, hard copy in author's possession). The quotation is from Joel Jackson, who grew up in the mill town of Bemis, Tennessee.

4. George Diacou, "Textiles in Crisis," Spartanburg (South Carolina) *Herald-Journal*, November 4, 2001, p. A13.

5. Christina Robb, "Studying Work by Listening to Workers," *Boston Globe*, November 18, 1989, p. 9.

6. Interview with Celia Thing in *The Workers Remember* (VHS).

7. Dudley, *The End of the Line*, esp. pp. xi, xvi–xvii, 134; Bensman and Lynch, *Rusted Dreams*, esp. pp. 2–9; Mellon, *After the Smoke Clears,* esp. p. 7; Cowie and Heathcott, "Introduction: The Meanings of Deindustralization," in Cowie and Heathcott, eds., *Beyond the Ruins*, p. 1 (quotation); Bluestone and Harrison, *The Deindustrialization of America*, esp. pp. 11–12. For a broader context, see Sennett and Cobb, *The Hidden Injuries of Class*, esp. pp. 267–68.

8. Salmond, *The General Textile Strike of 1934* (quotation in subtitle); Roger Milliken to James A. Baker III, September 27, 1983, "Textiles (5)" folder, M. B. Oglesby files, Reagan Library.

9. Don Johnson interview with author on June 23, 2010, in Athens, Georgia; John A. Svahn to Ed Rollins, March 5, 1985, "Textiles: Textile Trade Paper for Ed Rollins 03/05/1985" folder, Michael A. Driggs files, Reagan Library; Ed Jenkins interview with author on June 25, 2010, in Jasper, Georgia.

10. "Chesnutt Comes Out Swinging," *Southern Textile News*, September 1, 2003, p. 12; Closing quotation in Rose A. Woods, "Industry Output and Employment Projections to 2018," *Monthly Labor Review* 132:11 (November 2009), p. 68.

11. John Singleton, *The World Textile Industry* (London and New York: Routledge, 1997), p. 1; "Witness Statement of Cass Johnson before the U.S. International Trade Commission," October 30, 2007, p. 2, available at http://www.ncto.org/newsroom/index07.asp (accessed August 20, 2009, copy in author's possession).

12. Rivoli, *The Travels of a T-Shirt in the Global Economy*, pp. xi, xiii; Sara Bongiorni, *A Year without 'Made in China': One Family's True Life Adventure in the Global Economy* (Hoboken, NJ: John Wiley, 2007), pp. 68–70, "takeover" quotation on p. 68. By September 2009, Bongiorni's book had already sold over 223,000 copies. See http://search.barnesandnoble.com/A-Year-Without-Made-In-China/Sara-Bongiorni/e/9780470379202 (accessed September 11, 2009).

13. Harris Raynor interview with author on June 18, 2010, in Union City, Georgia.

14. Tony Walker, "Give and Take of Globalisation," *Australian Financial Review*, August 21, 2008, p. 76; Ikenson quoted in Daniel Ikenson, "Democrats Would Rather Mislead Than Lead on Trade," *Pittsburgh Post-Gazette*, March 3, 2008, p. B7.

15. Rick Lyman, "Edwards Focuses His Efforts on 3 Promising Constituencies," *New York Times*, February 25, 2004; Bob Moser, "Mill Hill Populism," *The Nation*, April 24, 2008 (Clinton quotation).

16. First three quotations in "Former Textile Worker Gets Her Close Up," Raleigh (North Carolina) *News and Observer*, August 19, 2008, available at http://projects.newsobserver.com/tags/pillowtex (accessed January 21, 2011, copy in author's possession); Sean Mussenden, "Obama Blames McCain for Job Loss," Winston-Salem (North Carolina) *Journal*, October 9, 2008, p. A1; Mickey Powell and Ginny Wray, "Obama to Campaign Here," Martinsville (Virginia) *Bulletin*, August 17, 2008, available at http://www.martinsvillebulletin.com/article.cfm?ID=15143 (accessed December 22, 2008); "Economy Key during Obama's Virginia Trip," Roanoke (Virginia) *Times*, August 21, 2008.

17. Barack Obama to Cass Johnson, October 24, 2008, available at http://www.ncto.org/newsroom/index.asp (accessed August 20, 2009, copy in author's possession).

18. Brody Mullins and Elizabeth Williamson, "From Yachts to Textiles, Perks for Special Interests," *Wall Street Journal*, January 29, 2009 (Kissell quotation); Raynor quoted in "Cong. Larry Kissell (D-NC) Wins Passage of Legislation to Require U.S. Department of Homeland Security to Buy U.S.-Made Textiles and Clothing," NCTO et al. Press Release, February 13, 2009, available at http://www.ncto.org/newsroom/index.asp (accessed August 20, 2009, copy in author's possession).

19. "Defense Contract," *Southern Textile News*, January 3, 2005, p. 6; Karl Spilhaus interview with author on April 26, 2011, in Boston, Massachusetts.

20. First quotation in "Passaic Factory Fears China Will Get Girl Scout Work," CBS News website, October 29, 2010, available at http://newyork.cbslocal.com/2010/10/29/passaic-factory-fears-china-will-get-girl-scout-work/ (accessed November 28, 2010); "Public uproar" quotation in "Girl Scouts Uniforms to Keep Made in USA Label," AP, November 2, 2010, available at http://archive.chicagobreakingbusiness.com/2010/11/girl-scouts-to-keep-uniform-production-in-usa.html (accessed November 28, 2010); Closing quotation in "Girl Scout Uniforms: Made in the U.S.A." *New Jersey Star-Ledger*, November 3, 2010, available at http://blog.nj.com/njv_editorial_page/2010/11/girl_scout_uniforms_made_in_th.html (accessed November 28, 2010). Hard copies of all of these documents are in the author's possession.

21. Singleton, *The World Textile Industry*, p. 1; First quotation in "NCTO Calls on Administration to Accept 301 Petition on Chinese Currency Manipulation," NCTO Press Release, September 9, 2004, available at http://www.ncto.org/newsroom/index04.asp (accessed August 20, 2009, copy in author's possession); "This is the Moment We've Been Waiting For," *AAM Update*, September 16, 2010; "The House Passes Legislation to Stop China's Cheating," *AAM Update*, September 29, 2010; "Tackling China's Cheating in 2011," *AAM Update*, February 15, 2011; "Make It" quotation in "House Passes Bill to Crack Down on Chinese Currency Manipulation," September 29, 2010, available at http://blogs.abcnews.com/the note/2010/09/house-passes-bill-to-crack-down-chinese-currency-manipulation-.html (accessed December 14, 2010, copy in author's possession); *AAM Update*, January 14, 2011, and March 1, 2012 (Obama quotation). Copies of all cited *AAM Updates* are in the author's possession.

22. Regis Mannion interview in *The Workers Remember* (VHS).

23. Charles Lunan, "Empty Mills Burden Carolinas: Cavernous Brick Hulks Can Drain Remaining Vitality of Small Towns," *Charlotte Observer*, July 22, 2002, p. 1A.

24. Peter T. Kilborn, "Jobs Are Scarce in the Newest Economy," *New York Times*, October 9, 2001 (first quotation); Ken Moritsugu, "Where Looms Have Ceased Once Vital Textile Mills in Carolinas Are Dying a Slow Death," *Charlotte Observer*, September 17, 2001, p. 10D (second quotation); Donald W. Patterson, "History, Make Way for the Mills," Greensboro (North Carolina) *News and Record*, July 18, 2004, p. A1 (Rumley quotation).

# Bibliography

## MANUSCRIPTS


**Athens, Georgia**
Richard B. Russell Library for Political Research and Studies, University of Georgia
Harmony Grove Mills Papers (1898–1994)
Charles F. Hatcher Papers
Edgar L. Jenkins Papers
J. Roy Rowland Papers
Richard B. Russell Papers
Herman E. Talmadge Papers

**Atlanta, Georgia**
Jimmy Carter Presidential Library
American Textile Manufacturers Institute Name File
Stuart Eizenstat Files (Domestic Policy Staff)
White House Central Files

**Chattanooga, Tennessee**
Lupton Library, University of Tennessee at Chattanooga
Marilyn Lloyd Papers

**Clemson, South Carolina**
Strom Thurmond Institute, Clemson University
Carroll Campbell Papers
Strom Thurmond Papers

**College Park, Maryland**
National Archives and Records Administration
Richard M. Nixon Presidential Materials (White House Central Files)

**College Station, Texas**
George Bush Presidential Library
George H. W. Bush Vice Presidential Records
Nicholas E. Calio Files

Virginia Lampley Files
Daniel Sullivan and Jennifer Fitzgerald Files
John B. Taylor Files
White House Office of Records Management—Subject File TA004-13
(Textiles–Apparel–Leather Products–Trade)

**Columbia, South Carolina**
South Carolina Political Collections, University of South Carolina
Carroll A. Campbell Jr. Papers
Butler Derrick Papers
Ernest F. Hollings Papers
James R. Mann Papers

**Ithaca, New York**
Kheel Center for Labor-Management Documentation and Archives, School of Industrial and Labor Relations, Cornell University
Amalgamated Clothing and Textile Workers Union Papers
Amalgamated Clothing Workers of America Papers
International Ladies' Garment Workers' Union Papers
Union of Needletrades, Industrial, and Textile Employees Papers

**Kannapolis, North Carolina**
Hinson Local History Room, Cabarrus County Library
Cannon Mills Papers

**Lowell, Massachusetts**
Center for Lowell History, University of Massachusetts Lowell
Flather/Boott Mills Papers, 1836–1979
Human Services Corporation Papers
Paul E. Tsongas Congressional Papers
Paul E. Tsongas Presidential Campaign Papers
Osborne Library, American Textile History Museum
Crompton Company, West Warwick, Rhode Island: Records, 1817–1989 (MS1990.187.1)
Merrimack Manufacturing Company Business Records (MS1111.522)
National Association of Cotton Manufacturers/Northern Textile Association Papers, 1896–1970 (MSS 73/327).
Northern Textile Association Papers, 1890–1988 (MS2000.178.1)

**Madison, Wisconsin**
Wisconsin Historical Society
Textile Workers Union of America Papers (Mss. 396 and M78-173)

**Melbourne, Australia**
Borchardt Library, La Trobe University
Civil Rights during the Johnson Administration Papers (microfilmed from the Lyndon Baines Johnson Library, Austin, Texas)

**Morrow, Georgia**
National Archives and Records Administration, Southeast Region
*Donald R. Hicks et al. v. Cannon Mills*
Case No. C-115-S-70
United States District Court, Middle District of North Carolina, 1970

**Orono, Maine**
Raymond H. Fogler Library, University of Maine-Orono
William S. Cohen Papers

**Providence, Rhode Island**
Phillips Memorial Library, Providence College
John O. Pastore Papers

**Simi Valley, California**
Ronald Reagan Presidential Library
Roger Bolton Files
Geoffrey O. Carliner Files
Sherrie M. Cooksey Files (Office of the Counsel to the President)
Mary Dewhirst Files
Michael A. Driggs Files
Chuck Greener Files
Wendell W. Gunn Files
William B. Lacy Files
Susan Lauffer Files
Mari Maseng Files
Thomas G. Moore Files
Michael L. Mussa Files
M. B. Oglesby Files
Roger B. Porter Files
Richard Prendergast Files
White House Office of Legislative Affairs Records
White House Office of Political Affairs Records

## ORAL HISTORY INTERVIEWS

Brassil, Robert. Interview with Gray Fitzsimons, October 19, 2004, Lowell, Massachusetts, "Closing of the Merrimack Mills" series, Center for Lowell History, Lowell, Massachusetts (CLH).
Bullard, Joeann. Interview with author, June 22, 2010, Concord, North Carolina.
Chace, Malcolm. Interview with Mehmed Ali, December 21, 1998, Lowell, Massachusetts, "Ethnic Solidarity" series, CLH.
Chafe, Christopher. Interview with author, June 21, 2010 (telephone).
Chartrand, Valentine. Interview with Diane Novelli, October 8, 1994, Lowell, Massachusetts, "Mill Workers of Lowell" series, CLH.
Cooper, Robert. Interview with Mehmed Ali, September 12, 1998, Lowell, Massachusetts, "Ethnic Solidarity" series, CLH.
Crisco, Ruth. Interview with author, June 22, 2010, Concord, North Carolina.
Derrick, Butler. Interview with author, April 13, 2011, Easley, South Carolina.
Ellis, James. Interview with Mehmed Ali, July 30, 1999, Lowell, Massachusetts, "After the Last Generation 1" series, CLH.
Ellis, Warren. Interview with author, June 22, 2010, Concord, North Carolina.
Flather, Newell. Interview with author, April 27, 2011, Boston, Massachusetts.
Freeman, Robert. Interview with author, March 11, 1996, Kannapolis, North Carolina.
Glover, Sylvia. Interview with author, June 22, 2010, Concord, North Carolina.
Goodwin, John. Interview with Jim Beauchesne, October 8 1997, Chelmsford, Massachusetts, "Closing of the Merrimack Mills" series, CLH.
Howe, Richard P. Jr. Interview with author, April 28, 2011, Lowell, Massachusetts.
Howe, Richard P. Sr. Interview with author, April 28, 2011, Lowell, Massachusetts.
Jenkins, Ed. Interview with author, June 25, 2010, Jasper, Georgia.

Jenkins, Ed. Interview with Bob Short, July 7, 2008, "Reflections on Georgia Politics" series, interview-037, Richard B. Russell Library for Political Research and Studies, University of Georgia.
Johnson, Don. Interview with author, June 23, 2010, Athens, Georgia.
Kadir, John. Interview with Maryrose Lane, April 29, 1994, Lowell, Massachusetts, "Closing of the Merrimack Mills" series, CLH.
Lehner, Phil. Interview with Mehmed Ali, February 8, 1999, Lowell, Massaschusetts, "Ethnic Solidarity" series, CLH.
Loeung, Sovann-Thida. Interview with Mehmed Ali, January 22, 2006, Lowell, Massachusetts, "Khmer [Cambodians] II" series, CLH.
Maria, Frank. Interview with Jim Beauchesne, October 16, 1997, Warner, New Hampshire, "Closing of the Merrimack Mills" series, CLH.
Mattingly, Mack. Interview with author, June 13, 2010, St. Simons Island, Georgia.
Neal, Robert. Interview with author, June 22, 2010, Concord, North Carolina.
Paul, Scott. Interview with author, June 19, 2009, Washington, D.C.
Raynor, Harris. Interview with author, June 18, 2010, Union City, Georgia.
Ryan, Raymond. Interview with Jim Beauchesne, January 5, 1998, Dracut, Massachusetts, "Closing of the Merrimack Mills" series, CLH.
Sao, Narin. Interview with Suzette Jefferson, May 17, 1986, "Southeast Asians" series, CLH.
Sharpe, Ruth Ann. Interview with Maryrose Lane, April 14, 1994, Lowell, Massachusetts, "Closing of the Merrimack Mills" series, CLH.
Simon, Margaret. Interview with Jim Beauchesne, December 30, 1997, Nashua, New Hampshire, "Closing of the Merrimack Mills" series, CLH.
Smith, Robert Sidney. Interview with Joseph Mosnier, January 25, 1999, Southern Oral History Program Collection, interview I-0081, Wilson Library, University of North Carolina at Chapel Hill.
Spilhaus, Karl. Interview with author, April 26, 2011, Boston, Massachusetts.
Trumbull, David. Interview with author, April 26, 2011, Boston, Massachusetts.
Vergados, Louis. Interview with Mehmed Ali, August 15, 1997, Lowell, Massachusetts, "Ethnic Solidarity" series, CLH.
Weltman, David. Interview with Jim Beauchesne on October 22, 1997, in Boston, Massachusetts, "Closing of the Merrimack Mills" series, CLH.
Wyskoczka, William. Interview with Mehmed Ali, July 1, 1999, Lowell, Massachusetts, "After the Last Generation I" series, CLH.
Wood, Lloyd III. Interview with author, June 18, 2009, Washington, D.C.

## NEWSPAPERS AND JOURNALS

Akron (OH) *Beacon Journal*
Allentown (PA) *Morning Call*
Anderson (SC) *Independent-Mail*
*Atlanta Journal Constitution*
Augusta (GA) *Chronicle*
*Australian Financial Review*
*Baltimore Sun*
Baton Rouge (LA) *Advocate*
Baton Rouge (LA) *State Times*
*BBC Monitoring International Reports*
*Boston Globe*
*Boston Herald*
Brunswick (ME) *Times Record*
*Business Week*
*Carolina Journal*
Charleston (WV) *Daily Mail*
*Charlotte Observer*

*Chicago Tribune*
*Christian Science Monitor*
*Cleveland Plain Dealer*
Columbia (SC) *State*
Columbus (MS) *Commercial Dispatch*
*Dallas Morning News*
*Detroit Free Press*
Durham (NC) *Herald-Sun*
*Economist*
Erie (PA) *Times-News*
*Far Eastern Economic Review*
Fayetteville (NC) *Observer*
Fitchburg (MA) *Sentinel*
Forest City (NC) *Daily Courier*
Fort Payne (AL) *Times-Journal*
Gaffney (SC) *Ledger*
Greensboro (NC) *News and Record*
Greenville (SC) *News*
Harrisburg (PA) *Patriot-News*
Hendersonville (NC) *Times-News*
*Journal of Commerce*
Kannapolis (NC) *Citizen*
Kannapolis (NC) *Independent Tribune*
Kennebec (ME) *Journal*
Lebanon (NH) *Valley News*
*Los Angeles Times*
Lowell (MA) *Sun*
Martinsville (VA) *Bulletin*
*Miami Herald*
*Minneapolis Star Tribune*
*Nation*
*National Geographic*
*New Republic*
*Newsday*
*Newsweek*
*New York Sun*
*New York Times*
Norfolk (VA) *Virginian-Pilot*
*The Oak Ridger* (TN)
*Philadelphia Inquirer*
*Pittsburgh Post-Gazette*
Portland (ME) *Press Herald*
Quincy (MA) *Patriot Ledger*
Raleigh (NC) *News and Observer*
Richmond (VA) *News Leader*
Richmond (VA) *Times-Dispatch*
Riverside (CA) *Press-Enterprise*
Roanoke (VA) *Times*
Roanoke Rapids (NC) *Daily Herald*
*The Robesonian* (Lumberton, NC)
Rocky Mountain (CO) *News*
*Rowan Magazine* (NC)
Salisbury (NC) *Post*
*San Antonio Express-News*
*San Francisco Chronicle*
*San Francisco Examiner*

*San Jose Mercury News*
*Science Digest*
*Seattle Times*
Souderton (PA) *Independent*
Southbridge (MA) *News*
*South China Morning Post*
Spartanburg (SC) *Herald-Journal*
*Spiegel*
*Star-Ledger* (NJ)
Torrance (CA) *Daily Breeze*
Troy (NY) *Times Record*
*USA Today*
*U.S. News and World Report*
*Wall Street Journal*
*Washington Post*
*Washington Times*
Watertown (NY) *Daily Times*
Winston-Salem (NC) *Journal*
Woonsocket (RI) *Call and Reporter*
Worcester (MA) *Telegram and Gazette*
*Workers' World*
*Xinhua News Agency*

## TRADE AND UNION JOURNALS

*AFL–CIO News*
*Apparel Industry Magazine*
*The Business Journal of the Greater Triad Area*
*Cannon News*
*Charlotte Business Journal*
*Colorado Labor Advocate*
*Daily News Record*
*Fieldcrest Cannon Today*
*Greater Charlotte Biz*
*Home Textiles Today*
*Justice*
*Labor Unity*
*Liberty*
*Market Street Report*
*Paperworker*
*Southern Textile News*
*Textile Age*
*Textile Web*
*Textile World*
*Women's Wear Daily*

## GOVERNMENT DOCUMENTS

U.S. Congress, Senate, Committee on Interstate and Foreign Commerce. *Problems of the Domestic Textile Industry*, 85th Congress, 2nd Session, 1958.

U.S. Congress, House, Government Operations Committee. *Federal Enforcement of Textile and Apparel Import Quotas (Part 2)*, 99th Congress, 1st Session, 1985.

U.S. Congress, Office of Technology Assessment. *The U.S. Textile and Apparel Industry: A Revolution in Progress—Special Report*. Washington, DC: U.S. Government Printing Office, 1987.

U.S. Department of Labor. *The Past, Present and Future of Employment in the Textile and Apparel Industries: An Overview*. Washington DC: U.S. Government Printing Office, 2004.

## BOOKS, ARTICLES, AND DISSERTATIONS

Adams, Michael C. C. *The Best War Ever: America and World War II*. Baltimore and London: Johns Hopkins University Press, 1994.

Ali, Mehmed. "To Save a City: From Urban Renewal to Historic Preservation in Lowell, Massachusetts, 1920 to 1978." PhD dissertation, University of Connecticut, 2006.

Allegretto, Sylvia and Devon Lynch. "The Composition of the Unemployed and Long-Term Unemployed in Tough Labor Markets." *Monthly Labor Review* 133:10 (October 2010), pp. 3–18.

Anderson, Cynthia D., Michael D. Schulman, and Phillip J. Wood. "Globalization and Uncertainty: The Restructuring of Southern Textiles." *Social Problems* 48:4 (November 2001), pp. 478–98.

Arthur, Bill. "The Darlington Mills Case: Or 17 Years Before the Courts." *New South* 28:3 (1973), pp. 40–47.

Banister, Judith. "Manufacturing Earnings and Compensation in China." *Monthly Labor Review* 128:8 (August 2005), pp. 22–40.

Bartley, Numan V. *The New South, 1945–1980: The Story of the South's Modernization*. Baton Rouge: Louisiana State University Press, 1995.

Bensman, David, and Roberta Lynch. *Rusted Dreams: Hard Times in a Steel Community*. New York: McGraw Hill, 1987.

Bhagwati, Jagdish. *In Defense of Globalization*. New York: Oxford University Press, 2004.

Blewett, Mary H, ed. *Surviving Hard Times: The Working People of Lowell*. Lowell, MA: Lowell Museum, 1982.

———. *The Last Generation: Work and Life in the Textile Mills of Lowell, Massachusetts, 1910–1960*. Amherst: The University of Massachusetts Press, 1990.

Bluestone, Barry. "Foreword." In *Beyond the Ruins: The Meanings of Deindustrialization*, edited by Jefferson Cowie and Joseph Heathcott, pp. vii–xiii. Ithaca: ILR Press, 2003.

Bluestone, Barry, and Bennett Harrison. *The Deindustrialization of America: Plant Closings, Community Abandonment, and the Dismantling of Basic Industry*. New York: Basic Books, 1982.

Bongiorni, Sara. *A Year without "Made in China": One Family's True Life Adventure in the Global Economy*. Hoboken, NJ: John Wiley, 2007.

Boris, Eileen, and Nelson Lichtenstein, eds. *Major Problems in the History of American Workers*. Lexington, MA: D.C. Heath, 1991.

Bowles, Robert. "Employment and Wage Outcomes for North Carolina's High-Tech Workers." *Monthly Labor Review* 127:5 (May 2004), pp. 31–39.

Brattain, Michelle. *The Politics of Whiteness: Race, Workers, and Culture in the Modern South*. Princeton: Princeton University Press, 2001.

Brinkley, Alan. *American History: A Survey, Vol. II, since 1865, Eleventh Edition*. Boston: McGraw Hill, 2003.

Buss, Terry F., and F. Stevens Redburn. *Shutdown at Youngstown: Public Policy for Mass Unemployment*. Albany, NY: State University of New York Press, 1983.

Carlton, David L. *Mill and Town in South Carolina, 1880–1920*. Baton Rouge: Louisiana State University Press, 1982.

Chapman, S. D. *The Cotton Industry in the Industrial Revolution, Second Edition*. Basingstoke, UK: MacMillan, 1987.

Cobb, James C. *The South and America since World War II*. New York: Oxford University Press, 2011.

Cowie, Jefferson. *Capital Moves: RCA's Seventy-Year Quest for Cheap Labor*. Ithaca: Cornell University Press, 1999.

———. *Stayin' Alive: The 1970s and the Last Days of the Working Class*. New York: The New Press, 2010.

Cowie, Jefferson, and Joseph Heathcott, eds. *Beyond the Ruins: The Meanings of Deindustrialization*. Ithaca: ILR Press, 2003.

———. "Introduction: The Meanings of Deindustralization." In *Beyond the Ruins: The Meanings of Deindustrialization*, edited by Jefferson Cowie and Joseph Heathcott, pp. 1–15. Ithaca: ILR Press, 2003.

Cross, Malcolm A. *Dan River Runs Deep: An Informal History of a Major Textile Company, 1950–1981*. New York: The Total Book, 1982.

Cumbler, John T. *Working-Class Community in Industrial America: Work, Leisure, and Struggle in Two Industrial Cities, 1880–1930*. Westport, CT: Greenwood Press, 1979.

Dalzell, Robert F. Jr. *Enterprising Elite: The Boston Associates and the World They Made*. Cambridge, MA: Harvard University Press, 1987.

Dandaneau, Steven P. *A Town Abandoned: Flint, Michigan, Confronts Deindustrialization*. Albany, NY: State University of New York Press, 1996.

Daniel, Clete. *Culture of Misfortune: An Interpretive History of Textile Unionism in the United States*. Ithaca: ILR Press, 2001.

Devino, W. Stanley, Arnold H. Raphaelson, and James A. Storer. *A Study of Textile Mill Closings in Selected New England Communities*. Orono, ME: University of Maine Press, 1966.

Dicker, John. *The United States of Wal-Mart*. New York: Penguin, 2005.

Doherty, Maura. "Spindle City Blues: The Impact of the Maturing Industrial Economy on the City of Lowell, Massachusetts, 1947–1978." PhD dissertation, New York University, 1998.

Douglas, Sara U., and Michelle A. Morganosky. "Textile and Apparel Industry Support for the Crafted with Pride Campaign: A Systems Perspective." *Clothing and Textiles Research Journal* 9:1 (July 1990), pp. 37–44.

Downey, Lynn, Jill Novack Lynch, and Kathleen McDonough. *This Is a Pair of Levi's Jeans: The Official History of the Levi's Brand*. San Francisco: Levi Strauss and Company, 1995.

Dublin, Thomas. *Women at Work: The Transformation of Work and Community in Lowell, Massachusetts, 1826–1860*. New York: Columbia University Press, 1979.

———. *When the Mines Closed: Stories of Struggles in Hard Times*, with photographs by George Harvan. Ithaca: Cornell University Press, 1998.

Dudley, Kathryn Marie. *The End of the Line: Lost Jobs, New Lives in Postindustrial America*. Chicago: University of Chicago Press, 1994.

English, Beth. *A Common Thread: Labor, Politics, and Capital Mobility in the Textile Industry*. Athens: University of Georgia Press, 2006.

Eno, Arthur L., Jr., ed. *Cotton Was King: A History of Lowell, Massachusetts*. Somersworth, NH: New Hampshire Publishing Company, 1976.

Fairlie, Robert W., and Lori G. Kletzer. "Jobs Lost, Jobs Regained: An Analysis of Black/White Differences in Job Displacement in the 1980s." *Industrial Relations* 37:4 (October 1998), pp. 460–77.

Fink, Leon. *The Maya of Morganton: Work and Community in the Nuevo New South*. Chapel Hill: University of North Carolina Press, 2003.

Flamming, Douglas. *Creating the Modern South: Millhands and Managers in Dalton, Georgia, 1884–1984*. Chapel Hill: University of North Carolina Press, 1992.

Frank, Dana. *Buy American: The Untold Story of Economic Nationalism*. Boston: Beacon Press, 1999.

Freeth, Nick. *Made in America: From Levi's to Barbie to Google*. St. Paul: MBI Publishing Company, 2005.

Galbraith, John Kenneth. *The Affluent Society*. Boston: Houghton Mifflin, 1958.

Galenson, Alice. *The Migration of the Cotton Textile Industry from New England to the South, 1880–1930*. New York: Garland Publishing, 1985.

Gall, Lawrence D. "The Heritage Factor in Lowell's Revitalization." In *The Continuing Revolution: A History of Lowell, Massachusetts*, edited by Robert Weible, pp. 397–405. Lowell, MA: Lowell Historical Society, 1991.

Gaventa, John, and Barbara Ellen Smith. "The Deindustrialization of the Textile South: A Case Study." In *Hanging by a Thread: Social Change in Southern Textiles*, edited by Jeffrey Leiter, Michael D. Schulman, and Rhonda Zingraff, pp. 181–96. Ithaca: ILR Press, 1991.

Getman, Julius. *The Betrayal of Local 14: Paperworkers, Politics, and Permanent Replacements*. Ithaca: ILR Press, 1998.

Greyser, Stephen A., with the collaboration of Robert J. Kopp. *Cases in Advertising and Communications Management, Third Edition*. Englewood Cliffs, NJ: Prentice Hall, 1992.

Griffith, Barbara S. *The Crisis of American Labor: Operation Dixie and the Defeat of the CIO*. Philadelphia: Temple University Press, 1988.

Gross, Laurence F. *The Course of Industrial Decline: The Boott Cotton Mills of Lowell, Massachusetts, 1835–1955*. Baltimore and London: The Johns Hopkins University Press, 1993.

Haberland, Michelle. "Women's Work: The Apparel Industry in the United States South, 1937–1980." PhD dissertation, Tulane University, 2001.

Hall, Jacquelyn Dowd, James Leloudis, Robert Korstad, Mary Murphy, Lu Ann Jones, and Christopher B. Daly. *Like a Family: The Making of a Southern Cotton Mill World*. Chapel Hill: University of North Carolina Press, 1987.

Hareven, Tamara K., and Randolph Langenbach. *Amoskeag: Life and Work in an American Factory City*. New York: Pantheon Books, 1978.

Harrison, Bennett. *Rationalization, Restructuring, and Industrial Reorganization in Older Regions: The Economic Transformation of New England since World War II*. Cambridge, MA: Joint Center for Urban Studies of MIT and Harvard University, 1982.

Hartford, William F. *Working People of Holyoke: Class and Ethnicity in a Massachusetts Mill Town, 1850–1960*. New Brunswick: Rutgers University Press, 1990.

———. *Where Is Our Responsibility?: Unions and Economic Change in the New England Textile Industry, 1870–1960*. Amherst: University of Massachusetts Press, 1996.

Herz, Diane E. "Worker Displacement in a Period of Rapid Job Expansion." *Monthly Labor Review* 113:5 (May 1990), pp. 21–33.

High, Steven C. *Industrial Sunset: The Making of North America's Rust Belt, 1969–1984*. Toronto: University of Toronto Press, 2003.

Hodges, James A. *New Deal Labor Policy and the Southern Cotton Textile Industry, 1933–1941*. Knoxville: University of Tennessee Press, 1986.

———. "The Real Norma Rae." In *Southern Labor in Transition, 1940–1995*, edited by Robert H. Zieger, pp. 251–72. Knoxville: University of Tennessee Press, 1997.

Hoerr, John P. *And the Wolf Finally Came: The Decline of the American Steel Industry*. Pittsburgh: University of Pittsburgh Press, 1988.

Hollings, Ernest F., "Fritz" with Kirk Victor. *Making Government Work*. Columbia: University of South Carolina Press, 2008.

Honey, Michael K. *Going Down Jericho Road: The Memphis Strike, Martin Luther King's Last Campaign*. New York: W. W. Norton, 2007.

Horvath, Francis W. "The Pulse of Economic Change: Displaced Workers of 1981–85." *Monthly Labor Review* 110:6 (June 1987), pp. 3–12.

Irons, Janet. *Testing the New Deal: The General Textile Strike of 1934 in the American South*. Urbana: University of Illinois Press, 2000.

Kane, Nancy Frances. *Textiles in Transition: Technology, Wages, and Industry Relocation in the U.S. Textile Industry, 1880–1930*. Westport, CT: Greenwood Press, 1988.

Kennedy, David M., Lizabeth Cohen, and Thomas A. Bailey. *The American Pageant: A History of the Republic, Volume II, since 1865, Thirteenth Edition*. Boston: Houghton Mifflin, 2006.

Kerouac, Jack. *The Town and the City*. London: Quartet Books, 1973, originally published ca. 1950.

Kletzer, Lori G. *Job Loss from Imports: Measuring the Costs*. Washington DC: Peterson Institute for International Economics, 2001.

Koistinen, David. "The Causes of Deindustrialization: The Migration of the Cotton Textile Industry from New England to the South." *Enterprise and Society* 3 (September 2002), pp. 482–520.

Korstad, Robert R., and James L. Leloudis. *To Right These Wrongs: The North Carolina Fund and the Battle to End Poverty and Inequality in 1960s America*. Chapel Hill: University of North Carolina Press, 2010.

Kunz, Grace I., and Myrna B. Garner. *Going Global: The Textile and Apparel Industry, Third Edition*. New York: Fairchild Publications, 2007.

Lamphere, Louise. *From Working Daughters to Working Mothers: Immigrant Women in a New England Industrial Community*. Ithaca and London: Cornell University Press, 1987.

Leiter, Jeffrey, Michael D. Schulman, and Rhonda Zingraff, eds. *Hanging by a Thread: Social Change in Southern Textiles*. Ithaca: ILR Press, 1991.

Lett, Erin, and Judith Banister. "China's Manufacturing Employment and Compensation Costs: 2002–06." *Monthly Labor Review* 132:4 (April 2009), pp. 30–38.

Lichtenstein, Nelson. *Wal-Mart: The Face of Twenty-First Century Capitalism*. New York: New Press, 2006.

———. *The Retail Revolution: How Wal-Mart Created a Brave New World of Business*. New York: Metropolitan Books, 2009.

Linkon, Sherry Lee, and John Russo. *Steeltown USA: Work and Memory in Youngstown*. Lawrence, KS: University Press of Kansas, 2002.

Lynd, Staughton. *The Fight against Shutdowns: Youngstown's Steel Mill Closings*. San Pedro: Singlejack Books, 1982.

Meisenheimer, Joseph R., II. "The Services Industry in the 'Good' versus 'Bad' Jobs Debate." *Monthly Labor Review* 121:2 (February 1998), pp. 22–47.

Mellon, Steve. *After the Smoke Clears: Struggling to Get By in Rustbelt America*. Pittsburgh: University of Pittsburgh Press, 2002.

Miernyk, William H. *Inter-Industry Labor Mobility: The Case of the Displaced Textile Worker*. Boston: Bureau of Business and Economic Research, Northeastern University, 1955.

Milkman, Ruth. *Farewell to the Factory: Auto Workers in the Late Twentieth Century*. Berkeley: University of California Press, 1997.

Miller, Marc Scott. *The Irony of Victory: World War II and Lowell, Massachusetts*. Urbana: University of Illinois Press, 1988.

———. "Who Won the War?" In *The Continuing Revolution: A History of Lowell, Massachusetts*, edited by Robert Weible, pp. 301–21. Lowell, MA: Lowell Historical Society, 1991.

Minchin, Timothy J. *What Do We Need a Union For?: The TWUA in the South, 1945–1955*. Chapel Hill: University of North Carolina Press, 1997.

———. *Hiring the Black Worker: The Racial Integration of the Southern Textile Industry, 1960–1980*. Chapel Hill: University of North Carolina Press, 1999.

———. "Broken Spirits: Permanent Replacements and the Rumford Strike of 1986." *New England Quarterly* LXXIV:1 (March 2001), pp. 5–31.

———. *"Don't Sleep with Stevens!": The J. P. Stevens Campaign and the Struggle to Organize the South, 1963–80*. Gainesville: University Press of Florida, 2005.

———. *Fighting against the Odds: A History of Southern Labor since World War II*. Gainesville: University Press of Florida, 2005.

Minchin, Timothy J., and John A. Salmond. *After the Dream: Black and White Southerners since 1965*. Lexington: University Press of Kentucky, 2011.

Mittelhauser, Mark. "Employment Trends in Textiles and Apparel, 1973–2005." *Monthly Labor Review* 120:8 (August 1997), pp. 24–35.

Moody, Kim. *An Injury to All: The Decline of American Unionism*. New York: Verso, 1988.

Moreton, Bethany. *To Serve God and Wal-Mart: The Making of Christian Free Enterprise*. Cambridge, MA: Harvard University Press, 2009.

Murray, Lauren A. "Unraveling Employment Trends in Textiles and Apparel." *Monthly Labor Review* 118:8 (August 1995), pp. 62–72.

Myrdal, Gunnar, with the assistance of Richard Sterner and Arnold Rose. *An American Dilemma; The Negro in a White Nation, Vol. 1*. New York: McGraw Hill, 1964 edition.

Newby, I. A. *Plain Folk in the New South: Social Change and Cultural Persistence, 1880–1915*. Baton Rouge and London: Louisiana State University Press, 1989.

Ngai, Pun. *Made in China: Women Factory Workers in a Global Workplace*. Durham: Duke University Press, 2005.

Norton, Mary Beth, David M. Katzman, David W. Blight, Howard P. Chudacoff, Thomas G. Paterson, William M. Tuttle Jr., and Paul D. Escott. *A People and a Nation: A History of the United States, Sixth Edition*. Boston: Houghton Mifflin, 2001.

O'Donnell, Brian. "The Spindles Stop: Lowell, Massachusetts and Manchester, New Hampshire Respond to the Collapse of the New England Textile Industry." PhD dissertation, Massachusetts Institute of Technology, 1995.

Parker, Margaret Terrell. *Lowell: A Study of Industrial Development*. New York: The Macmillan Company, 1940.

Parrott, Charles, and Gretchen Sanders Joy. *Lowell Then and Now: Restoring the Legacy of a Mill City*. Lowell: Lowell Historic Preservation Commission, 1995.

Patterson, James T. *Restless Giant: The United States from Watergate to* Bush v. Gore. New York: Oxford University Press, 2005.

Reutter, Mark. *Sparrows Point: Making Steel—The Rise and Ruin of American Industrial Might*. New York: Summit Books, 1988.

Rivoli, Pietra. *The Travels of a T-Shirt in the Global Economy: An Economist Examines the Markets, Power, and Politics of World Trade, Second Edition*. Hoboken, NJ: John Wiley, 2009.

Rosen, Ellen Israel. *Making Sweatshops: The Globalization of the U.S. Apparel Industry*. Berkeley: University of California Press, 2002.

Russo, John, and Sherry Lee Linkon. "Collateral Damage: Deindustrialization and the Uses of Youngstown." In *Beyond the Ruins: The Meanings of Deindustrialization*, edited by Jefferson Cowie and Joseph Heathcott, pp. 201–18. Ithaca: ILR Press, 2003.

———. "The Social Costs of Deindustrialization." In *Manufacturing a Better Future for America,* edited by Richard McCormack, pp. 183–216. Washington DC: The Alliance for American Manufacturing, 2009.

Ryan, Loretta Anne. "Lowell in Transition: The Uses of History in Urban Change." PhD dissertation, Columbia University, 1987.

———. "The Remaking of Lowell and Its Histories." In *The Continuing Revolution: A History of Lowell, Massachusetts*, edited by Robert Weible, pp. 377–95. Lowell, MA: Lowell Historical Society, 1991.

Salmond, John A. *The General Textile Strike of 1934: From Maine to Alabama*. Columbia: University of Missouri Press, 2002.

Scranton, Philip. *Figured Tapestry: Production, Markets, and Power in Philadelphia Textiles, 1885–1941*. Cambridge: Cambridge University Press, 1989.

Sennett, Richard, and Jonathan Cobb. *The Hidden Injuries of Class*. New York: Knopf, 1972.

Serrin, William. *Homestead: The Glory and Tragedy of an American Steel Town*. New York: Vintage Books, 1993.

Shanahan, Mark Raymond. "Housing and the Urban Crisis: Selected Community Responses in Eastern Massachusetts." PhD dissertation, Case Western Reserve University, 1983.

Simmermaker, Roger. *How Americans Can Buy American: The Power of Consumer Patriotism, Third Edition*. Orlando: Consumer Patriotism Corporation, 2008.

Singleton, John. *The World Textile Industry*. London and New York: Routledge, 1997.

Smitka, Michael. "Introduction." In *The Textile Industry and the Rise of the Japanese Economy*, edited by Michael Smitka, pp. vii–xxi. New York: Garland, 1998.

Stanton, Cathy. *The Lowell Experiment: Public History in a Postindustrial City*. Amherst: University of Massachusetts Press, 2006.

Staudohar, Paul D., and Holly E. Brown, eds. *Deindustrialization and Plant Closure*. Lexington, MA: D.C. Heath, 1987.

Stein, Judith. *Pivotal Decade: How the United States Traded Factories for Finance in the Seventies*. New Haven: Yale University Press, 2010.

Talmadge, Herman E., with Mark Royden Winchell. *Talmadge: A Political Legacy, a Politician's Life*. Atlanta: Peachtree Publishers, 1987.

Terkel, Studs. *American Dreams, Lost and Found.* London et al.: Hodder and Stoughton, 1980.
Trimble, Vance H. *Sam Walton: The Inside Story of America's Richest Man.* New York: Dutton, 1990.
Tsongas, Paul. *The Road from Here: Liberalism and Realities in the 1980s.* New York: Alfred A. Knopf, 1981.
———. *Heading Home.* New York: Vintage Books, 1984.
Tyler, Gus. *Look for the Union Label: A History of the International Ladies' Garment Workers' Union.* Armonk, NY: M. E. Sharpe, 1995.
Vanderburg, Timothy Warren. "Cannon Mills: A Case Study in Southern Industrialization." PhD dissertation, Mississippi State University, 2001.
Ware, Caroline F. *The Early New England Cotton Manufacture: A Study in Industrial Beginnings.* Boston: Houghton Mifflin, 1931.
Weible, Robert, ed. *The Continuing Revolution: A History of Lowell, Massachusetts.* Lowell: Lowell Historical Society, 1991.
Williams, Juan. *Eyes on the Prize: America's Civil Rights Years, 1954–1965.* New York: Penguin, 1987.
Wolensky, Kenneth C., Nicole H. Wolensky, and Robert P. Wolensky. *Fighting for the Union Label: The Women's Garment Industry and the ILGWU in Pennsylvania.* University Park, PA: Pennsylvania State University Press, 2002.
Wolfbein, Seymour Louis. *The Decline of a Cotton Textile City: A Study of New Bedford.* New York: Columbia University Press, 1944.
Woloch, Nancy. *Women and the American Experience: A Concise History.* New York: McGraw Hill, 1996.
Woods, Rose A. "Industry Output and Employment Projections to 2018." *Monthly Labor Review* 132:11 (November 2009), pp. 52–81.
Zieger, Robert H., "Textile Workers and Historians." In *Organized Labor in the Twentieth-Century South*, edited by Robert H. Zieger, pp. 35–59. Knoxville: University of Tennessee Press, 1991.
———. *American Workers, American Unions, Second Edition.* Baltimore: The Johns Hopkins University Press, 1994.
———. "From Primordial Folk to Redundant Workers: Southern Textile Workers and Social Observers, 1920–1990." In *Southern Labor in Transition, 1940–1995*, edited by Robert H. Zieger, pp. 273–94. Knoxville: University of Tennessee Press, 1997.
Zieger, Robert H. and Gilbert J. Gall. *American Workers, American Unions, Third Edition.* Baltimore: The Johns Hopkins University Press, 2002.
Zingraff, Rhonda. "Facing Extinction?" In *Hanging by a Thread: Social Change in Southern Textiles*, edited by Jeffrey Leiter, Michael D. Schulman, and Rhonda Zingraff, pp. 199–216. Ithaca: ILR Press, 1991.

## DOCUMENTARIES AND TELEVISION SERIES

*American Jobs.* Spotts Films, 2004.
*John Ratzenberger's Made in America.* Travel Channel, 2007.
*Where Do You Stand?: Stories from an American Mill.* Mighty Fine Films, 2004.
*The Workers Remember.* Boott Cotton Mills Museum, 1994.

# Index

www.ingramcontent.com/pod-product-compliance
Ingram Content Group UK Ltd.
Pitfield, Milton Keynes, MK11 3LW, UK
UKHW041127071026
15587UKWH00009B/276

9 781442 220829